THE SPIRITUAL BRAIN

dressing those who think the thesis is false, or at least are willing to consider the possibility that it may be false."[10]

True or false, materialism was the dominant intellectual current of the twentieth century and provided the impetus for most major philosophical and political movements of the day. Indeed, many thinkers today see the primary purpose of science as providing evidence for materialist beliefs. They reject with hostility any scientific evidence that challenges such beliefs, as we will see in our discussion of the psi effect in Chapter Six. Every year, thousands of books are published, in dozens of disciplines, advancing materialist views.

Not this one. This book will show that Professor Dennett and the many neuroscientists who agree with him are mistaken. It will take you on a journey different from the one he has made. Not to the Galápagos Islands, but inside the brain. It will show you why he is mistaken. In the first place, the materialists' account of human beings does not bear up well under close examination. In the second place, there is good reason for believing that human beings have a spiritual nature, one that even survives death.

But first things first. Why should you embark on this journey unless you see the need for a nonmaterialist account of human nature? A new account is needed because the materialists' account is inadequate. It is failing in a number of areas. So let us begin by outlining some of the failures. Let's start with this question: What would you be left with if you accepted the materialists' explanation of *you*? Would you recognize yourself? If not, why not? What is missing?

Mind, Will, Self, and Soul

The brain and its satellite glands have now been probed to the point where no particular site remains that can reasonably be supposed to harbor a nonphysical mind.[11]
—*Sociobiologist Edward O. Wilson*

Why do people believe that there are dangerous implications of the idea that the mind is a product of the brain, that the brain is organized in part by the genome, and that the genome was shaped by natural selection?[12]
—*Cognitive scientist Steven Pinker*

What of the mind, the will, the self, the soul? Do they have a future in the new world of science?

Dennett is far from being the only materialist thinker who argues that there really is no *you* in you at all, that consciousness, soul, spirit, and free will are merely illusions bolstered by folklore. On the contrary, his view is in fact the standard assumption in current neuroscience. Dennett speaks for a number of neuroscientists when he says, "a brain was always going to do what it was caused to do by current, local, mechanical circumstances."[13] Your consciousness, your sense of yourself, is "like a benign 'user-illusion.'"[14] Anything resembling free will is unlikely or, at best, minimal and problematic.[15]

American culture critic Tom Wolfe put the matter succinctly in an elegant little essay he published in 1996, "Sorry, but Your Soul Just Died," which expounds the "neuroscientific view of life."[16] He wrote about the new imaging techniques that enable neuroscientists to see what is happening in your brain when you experience a thought or an emotion. The outcome, according to Wolfe, is:

> Since consciousness and thought are entirely physical products of your brain and nervous system—and since your brain arrived fully imprinted at birth—what makes you think you have free will? Where is it going to come from? What "ghost," what "mind," what "self," what "soul," what anything that will not be immediately grabbed by those scornful quotation marks, is going to bubble up your brain stem to give it to you? I have heard neuroscientists theorize that, given computers of sufficient power and sophistication, it would be possible to predict the course of any human being's life moment by moment, including the fact that the poor devil was about to shake his head over the very idea.[17]

Wolfe doubts that any sixteenth-century Calvinist believed so completely in predestination as these hot young scientists. The whole materialist creed that Wolfe outlines hangs off one little word, "Since"—"*Since* consciousness and thought are entirely physical products of your brain and nervous system ..." In other words, neuroscientists have *not* discovered that there is no you in you; they start their work with that assumption. Anything they find is interpreted on the basis of that view. The science does not require that. Rather, it is an obligation that materialists impose on themselves.

But what if scientific evidence points in a different direction? As we will see, it does. But before we get to the neuroscience, it may be worthwhile to look at some other reasons for thinking that the twentieth-century materialist consensus isn't true. Neuroscience is, after all, a rather new discipline, and it would be best to first establish that there are also good reasons for doubting materialism that arise from older disciplines.

What People Believe

If materialism is true, why don't most people believe it?

In April 1966, *Time* magazine announced that Americans were turning their backs on God. Selecting Good Friday (April 8) to spread the news, the cover story asked "Is God Dead?" implying that the answer is yes. Science was killing religion. Anything that could not be known by the methods of science, as interpreted at that time, was uninteresting or unreal.[18] From then on, the only valid philosophy or spirituality would be existential anguish. The *Time* editors were quite sure of this. And they could not have been more wrong.

A Beliefnet poll taken thirty-nine years later in 2005 asked 1,004 Americans about their religious beliefs—and found that 79 percent described themselves as "spiritual" and 64 percent as "religious." As *Newsweek* pointed out in its September 2005 cover story, "Spirituality in America": "Nobody would write such an article now, in an era of round-the-clock televangelism and official presidential displays of Christian piety."[19] *Newsweek*'s Jerry Adler comments:

> History records that the vanguard of angst-ridden intellectuals in *Time*, struggling to imagine God as a cloud of gas in the far reaches of the galaxy, never did sweep the nation. What was dying in 1966 was a well-meaning but arid theology born of rationalism: a wavering trumpet call for ethical behavior, a search for meaning in a letter to the editor in favor of civil rights. What would be born in its stead, in a cycle of renewal that has played itself out many times since the Temple of Solomon, was a passion for an immediate, transcendent experience of God.[20]

How did *Time* get it so wrong? Adler suggests that *Time*'s editors may have mistaken the values and lifestyles of midtown Manhattan for America in general. Also, *Time* focused on the problems of prestigious Protestant denominations and ignored the widespread Pentecostal revivals. Those revivals and similar phenomena such as the Jesus movement probably lured away more of those denominations' members than secularism did. Because *Time*'s editors in 1966 had the preconceived notion that religion was dying out, they apparently did not either notice these trends or grasp their significance.

There have been important changes in religion in America, to be sure. Possibly as a consequence of multiculturalism, the paths chosen today are much more diverse. Among mainstream Americans, hostility toward other faiths is much lower than a generation ago. But Americans, however they conceive God, are still "one nation, under God."

Atheism

Not many people have enough faith to be atheists. Worldwide, the proportion of atheists has declined in recent years. Although Europe is often thought of as highly secular compared to the United States, similar trends seem to be at work there. The numbers of true atheists in Europe, for example, has declined to the point where they are not numerous enough to be used in statistical research.[21] It is interesting to reflect that in 1960 half of the world's population was nominally atheist.[22] Nothing like that number could be so described today. In 2004, one of the world's best-known apologists for atheism, philosopher Antony Flew, announced that the apparent intelligent design of the universe and of life forms had convinced him that there really was some sort of deity.[23] Flew, it should be noted, did not join a religion, in the usual sense, but rather became a deist—that is, he came to believe in God based on external evidence, not personal experience.

The best-known portion of American society today in which atheism is widespread is elite scientists. For example, whereas 41 percent of American Ph.D. scientists believe in a God to whom one can pray, the picture changes drastically in elite academies such as the National Academy of Sciences (NAS). When polled by historians Edward Larson and Larry Witham in 1996, only 7 percent of members expressed personal belief in God and over 72 percent expressed personal disbelief. The remainder expressed doubt or agnosticism.[24]

This fact is not apparently very well known, even within that academy itself. In 1998, Bruce Alberts, then president of NAS, urged the teaching of Darwinian evolution in public schools, claiming that "there are many very outstanding members of this academy who are very religious people, people who believe in evolution, many of them biologists." Larson and Witham commented crisply: "Our survey suggests otherwise."

By contrast, most humans have never believed in atheism or materialism. Indeed, religion may well have been around as long as humans. Seventy thousand years ago, the Neanderthals, an extinct species of human, buried their dead with tools, apparently to be used in another world. Significantly, many Neanderthal dead were placed in a fetal position, suggesting that Neanderthals expected to be "born again" when they died.[25] British archaeologist Paul Pettitt reports:

> At the Sima de los Huesos ("Pit of the Bones") at Atapuerca in Spain, over 32 individuals of *Homo heidelbergensis* dating to over 200,000 years ago were found at the bottom of a deep shaft. It is possible that these bones ... all got there accidentally—but I doubt it. Caves and sinkholes are dark, mysterious places; they echo with the strange sounds of wind and water. In later periods they were regarded as gateways to the "otherworld." It seems far more likely that early Neanderthals perceived them in a similar way.[26]

Why don't most people believe in materialism? Early twentieth-century psychiatrists theorized that spirituality is driven by a desire for a father figure or an unconscious desire to avoid death. Those explanations were plausible attempts to explain spirituality, though, by their very nature, they were untestable. They also tended to be Eurocentric, assuming that developments in European Christianity or Judaism were representative of religion worldwide.[27] Unfortunately, the progress of science, far from shedding light, has led to a host of less plausible explanations today. Today's explanations have degenerated into notions that sometimes border on the frivolous, such as the supposed evolutionary fitness of religious people, theotoxins (poisonous chemicals in the brain), brain damage, memes, a God gene, or a God spot in the brain. We will look at many current proposed explanations and show why they are inadequate to the explanatory task. For now, note that all these contending explanations have one feature in common. Like the early twentieth-century psychiatrists' theories, they are attempts to explain *away* spirituality as something that does not in fact point to a spiritual reality.

Of course, if the materialists are right, spirituality must necessarily be an illusion. But as noted earlier, the materialists have simply assumed that they are right; they have not demonstrated it. They would have been wise to proceed with caution before writing off as an illusion the deepest beliefs that the majority of humankind have always had about *themselves*. We would not write off the horse's view of being a horse or the dog's view of being a dog. But materialist preconceptions require that we write off humans' view of being human. That in itself ought to make us suspicious.

One popular way of writing off spirituality is evolutionary psychology, an attempt to understand human behavior based on theories about the behavior that helped early hominids survive.

Evolutionary Psychology

Has our remote human past deluded us into doubting materialism?

In the later decades of the twentieth century, evolutionary psychology exploded as scientists from many disciplines attempted to tackle the fundamental questions about human nature and the human mind by beginning with a startlingly simple proposition: the higher-primate brain (that is, the human and ape brain)

> comprises many functional mechanisms, called psychological adaptations or evolved psychological mechanisms, that evolved by natural selection to benefit the survival and reproduction of the organism. These mechanisms are universal in the species, excepting those specific to sex or age.[28]

Papers proliferate, claiming that all human behavior, including altruism, economics, politics, sex, love, war, obesity, rape, and religion, is best understood in the light of the qualities that enabled our remote ancestors to survive. But who knows exactly why a given remote human ancestor survived? The farther back we go, the more significant these individual fates become. A widely accepted theory in genetics holds that a single woman, "mitochondrial Eve," who lived between 190,000 and 130,000 years ago, is the ancestor of every living human being. Was she especially fit? Especially lucky? Specially chosen? We just don't know.

Still less do we know how she thought, because she left nothing behind except mitochondria.

Some theorists argue that our inability to understand and accept this line of reasoning is itself a demonstration of its correctness. Richard Dawkins writes, "It is almost as if the human brain were specifically designed to misunderstand Darwinism, and to find it hard to believe."[29] But is evolutionary psychology a fruitful line of inquiry? We consider that in more detail in Chapter Seven, but for now let us address one key question: Can we find the answers to human nature in genetic programs from the deep reaches of our human or prehuman past?

> Friendship is unnecessary, like philosophy, like art.... It has no survival value; rather it is one of those things that give value to survival.
> —*C. S. Lewis,* The Four Loves

Some features of human behavior undoubtedly arose in the remote past. Consider, for example, jealousy. It is hardly unique to humans, or even to primates. Dogs and cats unambiguously demonstrate jealousy. But, for that very reason, discovering an origin for jealousy would be trivial. To truly explain human nature, evolutionary psychology aims to explain uniquely human behavior like altruism, the willingness of human beings to sacrifice themselves for others, sometimes even for strangers.

Altruism: Wrong Brain Wiring?

Altruism, or self-sacrifice for people other than one's own kin, is usually, though not always, related to spiritual beliefs; for example, Mother Teresa's image routinely appears in articles devoted to studying altruism. Altruism is easier to study directly than spirituality, precisely because it is a behavior that can be studied apart from a belief system. So how does evolutionary psychology account for altruism? As science writer Mark Buchanan explains in *New Scientist,* "In evolutionary terms it is a puzzle because any organism that helps others at its own expense stands at an evolutionary disadvantage. So if many people really are true altruists, as it seems, why haven't greedier, self-seeking competitors wiped them out?"[30]

Evolutionary psychology has not shrunk from the challenge of explaining altruism. Evolutionary biologist Robert Trivers, of Rutgers University, thinks he has an answer: evolution *is* wiping altruists out, but hasn't yet finished the job. "Our brains misfire when presented with a situation to which we have not evolved a response," he explains.[31] In other words, we should be selfish because evolution has wired us that way. And if we are not, our brains are wired wrong. Fair enough. If that is true, we should expect to see that altruists mainly cause trouble for themselves and others by their actions.

On Tuesday, August 2, 2005, during a torrential downpour, an Air France airbus carrying 309 people overshot a runway at Pearson International Airport in Toronto and subsequently burst into flames. The Canadian minister of transportation was informed that 200 people had died. The governor-general of Canada issued her heartfelt condolences to their grieving survivors. In fact, as the rain and smoke subsided, it emerged that no one had died (though 43 people had suffered minor injuries). Why was that? As it happens, the plane came to a halt near Highway 401, Ontario's main artery. Columnist Mark Steyn recounts:

> Eyewitness accounts vary: some people are said to have panicked, others to have stayed calm.... Passing motorists pulled off the road and hurried toward the burning jet to help any survivors. Of the eight emergency exits, two were deemed unsafe to use, and on a third and a fourth the slides didn't work. Nonetheless, in a chaotic situation, hundreds of strangers co-ordinated sufficiently to evacuate a small space through four exits in less than a couple of minutes before the Airbus was consumed by flames.[32]

Many evacuated passengers were later picked up on the shoulder of the 401 and driven by strangers to Air France's terminal.

So ... hundreds of unrelated people who would never see each other again cooperated to ensure that all got out in time? People offered rides to strangers from other parts of the world, even though some of them might well have been terrorists who were responsible for the grounding of the plane?

> Altruism is a necessary part of surviving in a group although there is the problem of the "free-loader." If "free-loader" genes were undetected then everyone would become a "free-loader" and social groups would disintegrate. Here the need for recognition and memory are important so that one can recognise and reward altruistic deeds (and punish "free-loaders"). Cost/benefit modules weigh up whether my altruistic deed will be rewarded

with altruistic deeds in return and whether by doing a good deed I will suffer in the short or long term.[33]

> —*From an online introduction to*
> *evolutionary psychology*

Your heart's desire is to give, so give in whatever way you are at peace about.[34]

> —*Trent Fenwick, who donated a kidney*
> *to a dying stranger*

Of course, one can always construct a plausible story set in prehistoric times to account for altruism as a self-seeking behavior, and many theorists have done so.[35] But surely it makes more sense to conclude that the Toronto strangers who took the risk of helping were not seeking any benefit, either for themselves or their descendants. Nor is evolution somehow bogged down in the process of wiping them out. Nor are their brains wired wrong. Nor are they secretly benefiting in some way relative to passing motorists who do not help. Evolutionary psychologists are simply looking in the wrong places to try to understand their behavior.

Indeed, if evolution were wiping altruists out, we should logically expect to see fewer altruists in the present day than in the past. But there is no evidence for that. Rather, religions such as Christianity, which directly promotes altruism, and Buddhism, which discourages selfishness and worldliness, have largely replaced the "cargo cults" of earlier historical times. This indirectly suggests that altruism has become more popular, not less.

Evolutionary Psychology as Science

Evolutionary psychology has come under fire from a number of quarters[36] on account of the lack of testability or falsifiability of any given hypothesis. Evolutionary biologist Jerry Coyne complains:

Evolutionary psychology suffers from the scientific equivalent of megalomania. Most of its adherents are convinced that virtually every human action or feeling, including depression, homosexuality, religion, and consciousness, was put directly into our brains by natural selection. In this view, evolution becomes the key—the only key—that can unlock our humanity.[37]

Evolutionary psychology, which we consider in more detail in Chapter Seven, fares poorly when it tries to explain religion or spirituality, a fact that was recognized nearly a century ago by Evelyn Underhill, a researcher of mysticism:

> Récéjac has well said that "From the moment in which man is no longer content to devise things useful for his existence under the exclusive action of the will-to-live, the principle of (physical) evolution has been violated." Nothing can be more certain than that man is not so content. He has been called by utilitarian philosophers a tool-making animal—the highest praise they knew how to bestow. More surely he is a vision-making animal; a creature of perverse and unpractical ideals, dominated by dreams no less than by appetites—dreams which can only be justified upon the theory that he moves towards some other goal than that of physical perfection or intellectual supremacy, is controlled by some higher and more vital reality than that of the determinists. We are driven to the conclusion that if the theory of evolution is to include or explain the facts of artistic and spiritual experience—and it cannot be accepted by any serious thinker if these great tracts of consciousness remain outside its range—it must be rebuilt on a mental rather than a physical basis.[38]

Ernst Fehr and Suzanne-Viola Renninger reach a less loftily expressed, but related, conclusion:

> In an age of enlightenment and secularization, scientists such as Charles Darwin shocked contemporaries when they questioned the special status of human beings and attempted to classify them on a continuum with all other species. Humans were stripped of all that was godlike. Today biology is restoring to them something of that former exalted position. Our species is apparently the only one with genetic makeup that promotes selflessness and true altruistic behavior.[39]

Lest there be any misunderstanding, it is *not* the purpose of this book to argue that evolution did not occur. There is a fossil record, after all. In spite of its many defects, the record shows that evolution occurred. Rather, the issue is whether human evolution is a fully naturalistic process that occurs without meaning, purpose, direction, or design in a fully materialist universe. This book offers evidence from neuroscience and other scientific disciplines that challenges that view.

THE
SPIRITUAL
BRAIN

A Neuroscientist's Case for the Existence of the Soul

MARIO BEAUREGARD

and

DENYSE O'LEARY

HarperOne
A Division of HarperCollinsPublishers

HarperOne

All art in this book is used by permission of the artist, Pierre-Alexandre Lévesque.

THE SPIRITUAL BRAIN: *A Neuroscientist's Case for the Existence of the Soul.* Copyright © 2007 by Mario Beauregard and Denyse O'Leary. All rights reserved. Printed in the United States of America. No part of this book may be used or reproduced in any manner whatsoever without written permission except in the case of brief quotations embodied in critical articles and reviews. For information address HarperCollins Publishers, 10 East 53rd Street, New York, NY 10022.

HarperCollins books may be purchased for educational, business, or sales promotional use. For information please write: Special Markets Department, HarperCollins Publishers, 10 East 53rd Street, New York, NY 10022.

HarperCollins Web site: http://www.harpercollins.com
HarperCollins®, ☛®, and HarperOne™
are trademarks of HarperCollins Publishers.

FIRST EDITION
Designed by Joseph Rutt

Library of Congress Cataloging-in-Publication Data
Beauregard, Mario.
The spiritual brain / Mario Beauregard and Denyse O'Leary. — 1st ed.
p. cm.
Includes bibliographical references and index.
ISBN: 978-0-06-085883-4
1. Psychology, Religious. 2. Brain—Religious aspects.
3. Theological anthropology. 4. Human beings. 5. Neurosciences.
6. Spirituality. I. O'Leary, Denyse. II. Title.
BL53.B363 2007
200.1'9—dc22 2007018398

07 08 09 10 11 RRD(H) 10 9 8 7 6 5 4 3 2 1

Contents

Acknowledgments

I am very grateful to my doctoral students Johanne Lévesque, Élisabeth Perreau-Linck, and Vincent Paquette, whose brain-imaging studies are presented in this book.

Also due acknowledgment are the Natural Sciences and Engineering Research Council of Canada (NSERC), the Metanexus Institute, and the John Templeton Foundation, without whose financial support the Carmelite studies could not have been conducted.

Susan Arellano, our literary agent, deserves our gratitude for her great efficiency.

Both of us wish to thank Eric Brandt, our editor at HarperOne, for his wise editorial suggestions, as well as production editor Laurie Dunne and copyeditor Ann Moru for their skill, patience, and understanding. We would also like to acknowledge the work of Pierre-Alexandre Lévesque on the visuals of the human brain.

Last, I want to thank my wife, Johanne, and my children, Audrey and Marc-Antoine, for their love and understanding.

Mario Beauregard

I wish to acknowledge my father, John Patrick O'Leary, who has maintained an interest in the central ideas of civilization all his life, encouraging me in this and all such projects, and my mother, Blanche O'Leary, who has never once complained about the difficulties of living with a writer while a book is in progress, and who has been an immense, incalculable help.

Denyse O'Leary

Introduction

When my doctoral student Vincent Paquette and I first began studying the spiritual experiences of Carmelite nuns at the Université de Montréal, we knew that our motives were quite likely to be misunderstood.

First, we had to convince the nuns that we were *not* trying to prove that their religious experiences did not actually occur, that they were delusions, or that a brain glitch explained them. Then we had to quiet both the hopes of professional atheists and the fears of clergy about the possibility that we were trying to reduce these experiences to some kind of "God switch" in the brain.

Many neuroscientists want to do just that. But Vincent and I belong to a minority—nonmaterialist neuroscientists. Most scientists today are materialists who believe that the physical world is the only reality. Absolutely everything else—including thought, feeling, mind, and will—can be explained in terms of matter and physical phenomena, leaving no room for the possibility that religious and spiritual experiences are anything but illusions. Materialists are like Charles Dickens's character Ebeneezer Scrooge who dismisses his experience of Marley's ghost as merely "an undigested bit of beef, a blot of mustard, a crumb of cheese, a fragment of an underdone potato."

Vincent and I, on the other hand, did not approach our research with any such materialist presumption. As we are not materialists, we did not doubt in principle that a contemplative might contact a reality outside herself during a mystical experience. In fact, I went into neuroscience in part because I knew experientially that such things can indeed happen.

Vincent and I simply wanted to know what the neural correlates—the activity of the neurons—during such an experience might be. Given the overwhelming dominance of materialism in neuroscience today, we count ourselves lucky that the nuns believed in our sincerity and agreed to help us and that the Templeton Foundation saw the value of funding our studies.

Of course, you may well ask, can neuroscience studies of contemplative nuns demonstrate that God exists? No, but they can—and did—demonstrate that the mystical state of consciousness really exists. In this state, the contemplative likely experiences aspects of reality that are not available in other states. These findings rule out various materialist theses that the contemplative is faking or confabulating the experience. Vincent and I also showed that mystical experiences are complex—a finding that challenges a vast variety of simplistic materialist explanations such as a "God gene," "God spot," or "God switch" in our brains.

Toronto-based journalist Denyse O'Leary and I have written this book to discuss the significance of these studies, and more generally, to provide a neuroscientific approach to understanding religious, spiritual, and mystical experiences. The discipline of neuroscience today is materialist. That is, it assumes that the mind is quite simply the physical workings of the brain. To see what this means, consider a simple sentence: "I made up my mind to buy a bike." One would not say, "I made up my *brain* to buy a bike." By contrast, one might say, "Bike helmets prevent brain damage," but not "Bike helmets prevent *mind* damage." But materialists think that the distinction you make between your mind as an immaterial entity and your brain as a bodily organ has no real basis. The mind is assumed to be a mere illusion generated by the workings of the brain. Some materialists even think you should not in fact *use* terminology that implies that your mind exists.

In this book, we intend to show you that your mind does exist, that it is not merely your brain. Your thoughts and feelings cannot be dismissed or explained away by firing synapses and physical phenomena alone. In a solely material world, "will power" or "mind over matter" are illusions, there is no such thing as purpose or meaning, there is no room for God. Yet many people have experience of these things, and we present evidence that these experiences are real.

In contrast, many materialists now argue that notions like meaning or purpose do not correspond to reality; they are merely adaptations for human survival. In other words, they have no existence beyond the evolution of circuits in our brains. As co-discoverer of the genetic code Francis Crick writes in *The Astonishing Hypothesis*, "Our highly developed brains, after all, were not evolved under the pressure of discovering scientific truths but only to enable us to be clever enough to survive and leave descendants." But are questions about our meaning or purpose merely survival mechanisms? If such an airy dismissal of the intellectual life of thousands of years sounds vaguely unconvincing, well, perhaps it should.

Suppose, for example, a healthy man donates a kidney for free to a dying stranger. The materialist may look for an analogy among moles, rats, or chimpanzees, as the best way to understand the donor's motives. He believes that the donor's mind can be *completely* explained by the hypothesis that his brain evolved slowly and painstakingly from the brains of creatures like these. Therefore, his mind is merely an illusion created by the workings of an overdeveloped brain, and his consciousness of his situation is actually *irrelevant* as an explanation of his actions.

This book argues that the fact that the human brain evolves does not show that the human mind can be dismissed in this way. Rather, the human brain can enable a human mind, whereas the mole brain cannot (with my apologies to the mole species). The brain, however, is not the mind; it is an organ suitable for connecting a mind to the rest of the universe. By analogy, Olympic swimming events require an Olympic class swimming pool. But the pool does not create the Olympic events; it makes them feasible at a given location.

From the materialist perspective, our human mind's consciousness and free will are problems to be explained away. To see what this means, consider Harvard cognitive scientist Steven Pinker's comments on consciousness in a recent piece in *Time* magazine entitled "The Mystery of Consciousness" (January 19, 2007). Addressing two key problems that scientists face, he writes,

> Although neither problem has been solved, neuroscientists agree on many features of both of them, and the feature they find least controversial is the one that many people outside the field find the most shocking. Francis Crick called it "the astonishing hypothesis"—the idea that our thoughts, sensations, joys and aches consist entirely of physiological activity in the tissues of the brain. Consciousness does not reside in an ethereal soul that uses the brain like a PDA [personal digital assistant]; consciousness is the activity of the brain.

Given that Pinker admits that neither problem concerning consciousness is either solved or anywhere close to being solved, how can he be so sure that consciousness is merely "the activity of the brain," implying that there is no soul?

One convenient aspect of Pinker's materialism is that any doubt can be labeled "unscientific" in principle. That preempts a discussion of materialism's plausibility. Certainly, materialism is a faith that many intellectuals would never think of questioning. But the strength of their conviction neither shows that it is a correct account of reality nor provides evidence in its favor. A good case can be made for the opposite view, as this book will demonstrate.

Yes, this book—departing from a general trend in books on neuroscience aimed at the general public—does question materialism. Much more than that, it presents evidence that materialism is not true. You will see for yourself that the evidence for materialism is not nearly so good as Steven Pinker would like you to believe. You can only retain your faith in materialism by assuming—on faith—that any contrary evidence you read about must be wrong.

For example, as we will show, a materialist readily believes—without any reliable evidence whatsoever—that great spiritual leaders suffer from temporal-lobe epilepsy rather than that they have spiritual experiences that inspire others as well as themselves. Where spirituality is concerned, this experiential data is an embarrassment to narrow materialism. That is because a system like materialism is severely damaged by any evidence against it. Consequently, data that defy materialism are simply ignored by many scientists. For instance, materialists have conducted a running war against psi research (research on knowledge or action at a distance, such as extrasensory perception, telepathy, precognition, or telekinesis) for decades, because *any* evidence of psi's validity, no matter how minor, is fatal to their ideological system. Recently, for example, self-professed skeptics have attacked atheist neuroscience grad student Sam Harris for having proposed, in his book entitled *The End of Faith* (2004), that psi research has validity. Harris is only following the evidence, as we shall see. But in doing so, he is clearly violating an important tenet of materialism: materialist ideology trumps evidence.

But other challenges to materialism exist. Materialists must believe that their minds are simply an illusion created by the workings of the brain and therefore that free will does not really exist and could have no influence in controlling any disorder. But nonmaterialist approaches have clearly demonstrated mental health benefits. The following are a few examples discussed in this book.

Jeffrey Schwartz, a nonmaterialist UCLA neuropsychiatrist, treats obsessive-compulsive disorder—a neuropsychiatric disease marked by distressing, intrusive, and unwanted thoughts—by getting patients to reprogram their brains. Their minds change their brains.

Similarly, some of my neuroscientist colleagues at the Université de Montréal and I have demonstrated, via brain imaging techniques, the following:

- Women and young girls can voluntarily control their level of response to sad thoughts, though young girls found it more difficult to do so.

- Men who view erotic films are quite able to control their responses to them, when asked to do so.

- People who suffer from phobias such as spider phobia can reorganize their brains so that they lose the fear.

Evidence of the mind's control over the brain is actually captured in these studies. There *is* such a thing as "mind over matter." We do have will power, consciousness, and emotions, and combined with a sense of purpose and meaning, we can effect change.

At one time, materialist explanations of religion and spirituality were at least worth considering. For example, Sigmund Freud argued that childhood memories of a father figure led religious people to believe in God. Freud's explanation failed because Christianity is the only major religion that emphasizes the fatherhood of God. But his idea, while wrong, was not ridiculous. Relationships with fathers, happy or otherwise, are complex human experiences, with some analogies to religion. Similarly, anthropologist J. G. Frazer thought that modern religions grew out of primal fertility cults and were only later spiritualized. Actually, the evidence points more clearly to spiritual experiences as the source of later religious beliefs and rituals. Still, Frazer's idea was far from trivial. It derived from a long and deep acquaintance with ancient belief systems.

But recently, materialistic explanations of religion and spirituality have gotten out of hand. Influenced by this materialistic prejudice, popular media jump at stories about the violence gene, the fat gene, the monogamy gene, the infidelity gene, and now, even a God gene! The argument goes like this: evolutionary psychologists attempt to explain human spirituality and belief in God by insisting that cave dwellers in the remote past who believed in a supernatural reality were more likely to pass on their genes than cave dwellers who didn't. Progress in genetics and neuroscience has encouraged some to look, quite seriously, for such a God gene, or else a God spot, module, factor, or switch in the human brain. By the time the amazing "God helmet" (a snowmobile helmet modified with solenoids that purportedly could stimulate subjects to experience God) in Sudbury, Canada, became a magnet for science journalists in the 1990s (the Decade of the Brain), materialism was just about passing beyond parody. Nonetheless, materialists continue to search for a God switch. Such comic diversions aside, there is no escaping the nonmaterialism of the human mind.

Essentially, there is no God switch. As the studies with the Carmelite nuns have demonstrated and this book will detail, spiritual experiences are complex experiences, like our experiences of human relationships. They leave signatures in many parts of the brain. That fact is consistent with (though it does not by itself demonstrate) the notion that the experiencer contacts a reality outside herself.

The fact is materialism is stalled. It neither has any useful hypotheses for the human mind or spiritual experiences nor comes close to developing any. Just beyond lies a great realm that cannot even be entered via materialism, let alone explored. But the good news is that, in the absence of materialism, there are hopeful signs that spirituality can indeed be entered and explored with modern neuroscience.

Nonmaterialist neuroscience is not compelled to reject, deny, explain away, or treat as problems all evidence that defies materialism. That is promising because current research is turning up a growing body of such evidence. Three examples addressed in this book are the psi effect, near death experiences (NDEs), and the placebo effect.

The psi effect, as seen in such phenomena as extrasensory perception and psychokinesis, is a low-level effect, to be sure, but efforts to disconfirm it have failed. NDEs have also become a more frequent subject of research in recent years, probably because the spread of advanced resuscitation techniques has created a much larger population that survives to recount them. As a result of the work of researchers such as Pim van Lommel, Sam Parnia, Peter Fenwick, and Bruce Greyson, we now have a growing base of information. The results do not support a materialist view of mind and consciousness, as advanced by Pinker, who writes in *Time* "when the physiological activity of the brain ceases, as far as anyone can tell the person's consciousness goes out of existence."

Most of us have not experienced unusual effects like psi or NDE, but we have all probably experienced the placebo effect: have you ever gone to your doctor to get a letter saying you can't go to work because you have a bad cold—and suddenly begun to feel better while sitting in the clinic, leafing through magazines? It's embarrassing, but easy to explain: your mind generates messages to begin the analgesic or healing processes when you accept that you have in fact started on a path to recovery. Materialist neuroscience has long regarded the placebo effect as a problem, but it is one of the best attested phenomena in medicine. But for nonmaterialist neuroscience, it is a normal effect that can be of great therapeutic value when properly used.

Materialism is apparently unable to answer key questions about the nature of being human and has little prospect of ever answering them intelligibly. It has also convinced millions of people that they should not seek to develop their spiritual nature because they have none.

Some think that the solution is to continue to uphold materialism a bit more raucously than before. Currently, key materialist spokespersons have launched a heavily publicized and somewhat puzzling "anti-God" crusade. Antitheistic works such as *Breaking the Spell: Religion as a Natural Phenomenon* (Daniel Dennett), *The God Delusion* (Richard Dawkins), *God: The Failed Hypothesis—How Science Shows that God Does Not Exist* (Victor J. Stenger), *God Is Not Great* (Christopher Hitchens), and *Letters to a Christian Nation* (Sam Harris) are accompanied by conferences such as the Science Network's "Beyond Belief" and campaigns such as the YouTube Blasphemy Challenge.

The remarkable thing is that there isn't a single new idea in anything they have to say. Eighteenth-century *philosophes* said it all long ago, to as much or little purpose. Granted, recent works have been spiced with the questionable assumptions of evolutionary psychology—the attempt to derive religion and spirituality from the practices that may have enabled a few of our Pleistocene ancestors to pass on their genes. But the Pleistocene ancestors are long gone, and not much can really be learned from a discipline that lacks a subject. There are also plenty of assurances about the illusory nature of mind, consciousness, and free will, and the uselessness or danger of spirituality.

A variety of experts of the mid-twentieth century had predicted that spirituality would slowly but surely disappear. Once supplied with abundant material goods, people would just stop thinking about God. But the experts were wrong. Spirituality today is more varied, but it is growing all over the world. Thus, its continuing vitality prompts speculations, fears, and some pretty wild guesses—but most of all, a compelling curiosity, a desire to investigate.

But how can we investigate spirituality scientifically? To start with, we can rediscover our nonmaterialist inheritance. It has always been there, just widely ignored. Famous neuroscientists such as Charles Sherrington, Wilder Penfield, and John Eccles, were not in fact reductive materialists, and they had good reasons for their position. Today, nonmaterialist neuroscience is thriving, despite the limitations imposed by widespread misunderstanding and, in a few cases, hostility. Readers are urged to approach all the questions and evidence presented in this book with an open mind. This is a time for exploration, not dogma.

Our book will establish three key ideas. The nonmaterialist approach to the human mind is a rich and vital tradition that accounts for the evidence much better than the currently stalled materialist one. Second, nonmaterialist approaches to the mind result in practical benefits and treatments, as well as promising approaches to phenomena that materialist accounts cannot even address. Lastly—and this may be the most important value for many readers—our book shows that when spiritual experiences transform lives, the most reasonable explanation and the one that best accounts for all the evidence, is that the people who have such experiences have actually contacted a reality outside themselves, a reality that has brought them closer to the real nature of the universe.

Mario Beauregard
Montreal, Canada
March 4, 2007

ONE

Toward a Spiritual Neuroscience

In June 2005, the historic World Summit on Evolution was held on the remote island of San Cristobal in the Galápagos Islands, off the coast of Ecuador. The unassuming location, Frigatebird Hill, was chosen because it was the very spot where Charles Darwin first docked in 1835 to probe the "mystery of mysteries"—the origin and nature of species, including (and perhaps especially) the human species.

These isolated Pacific islands lying on the equator later became a stopover for pirates, whalers, and sealers who drove the unique life forms that Darwin studied to the brink of extinction. But still later, under government protection in the twentieth century, the islands evolved into a sort of shrine to materialism—the belief that all life, including human life, is merely a product of the blind forces of nature.[1] In the materialist's view, our "minds"—soul, spirit, free will—are simply an illusion created by the electrical charges in the neurons of our brains. Nature is, as Oxford zoologist Richard Dawkins famously put it, a "blind watchmaker."[2]

The Galápagos meeting was quickly hailed as the Woodstock of Evolution. The scientists present, a "Who's Who of evolutionary theory,"[3] were well aware of their own importance and the significance of the proceedings. "We are simply stunned to be here," wrote one science journalist, recalling that the elite audience listened to the familiar tale of evolution "rapt, like children hearing the retelling of a favorite story."[4]

According to the favorite tale, human beings are merely "a bizarre tiny clade," in the words of one attendee.[5] And the mission of the next summit promises to tell that tale to the whole world.[6] However, to judge from the growing dissension around the teaching of evolution, the world has heard it already.

A Series of Mindless Events?

A key figure at the conference was American philosopher Daniel Dennett. Dennett, who bears a striking physical resemblance to Charles Darwin, is a world-famous philosopher of mind. He is the favorite philosopher of those who think that computers can simulate human mental processes. Curiously, for a philosopher of mind, he hopes to convince the world that there isn't really any such thing as a mind in the traditional sense. He is best known, perhaps, for saying that "Darwin's dangerous idea" is the best idea anyone ever had, because it firmly grounds life in materialism. As he understands it, human beings are "big, fancy robots" and, better still:

> If you have the right sort of process and you have enough time, you can create big fancy things, even things with minds, out of processes which are individually stupid, mindless, simple. Just a whole lot of little mindless events occurring over billions of years can create not just order, but design, not just design, but minds, eyes and brains.[7]

Dennett insists that there is no soul or spirit associated with the human brain, or any supernatural element, or life after death. Thus, his career focus has been to explain how "meaning, function and purpose can come to exist in a world that is intrinsically meaningless and functionless."[8] He came to the Galápagos to testify to that view.

Of course, many people are dismayed by ideas such as Dennett's and hope that they are false. Others welcome them as a means of freeing the human race from restraints imposed by traditional religions and philosophies. Let us progress, they say, toward a more humane system that both expects less of humans and blames them less for their failures—failures they can't help anyway, really.[9]

The question addressed in this book is not whether materialism is good news or bad news. Rather, the question is, does the evidence from neuroscience support it? As constitutional law professor Phillip Johnson, long a foe of materialism, which he terms "naturalism," writes: "If the blind watchmaker thesis is true, then naturalism deserves to rule, but I am ad-

Some well-traveled roads in the pursuit of understanding human nature in a purely materialist way are simply dead ends. The attempt to demonstrate that altruism or spirituality is really some sort of covert Darwinian survival mechanism is one of those dead ends. We can indeed draw some fact-based conclusions about the psychology of our remote ancestors—for example, we can conclude from early burial practices that they had some religious beliefs. But we have no real way of knowing whether those beliefs improved their chances of survival. Generally, spirituality is positively associated with health and happiness in society today, but we cannot assume, without evidence, that it has always been so. Was it really "fit" for the Neanderthals to bury useful objects with their dead? Or were they motivated by something that reached beyond Darwinian fitness?

But what about our nearest animal relatives, the chimpanzees and other large primates? Some scientists have spent their lives living with them and studying them in detail, hoping to shed light on the nature of the human.

Our Animal Nature

Does the answer to human nature lie in our animal nature? In our kinship with chimpanzees? With mammals in general? Should we go back beyond the specifically human past to experiences?

> Or, where old-eyed oxen chew
> Speculation with the cud,
> Read their pool of vision through,
> Back to hours when mind was mud[40]

So thought Victorian George Meredith, an enthusiast for materialism. Of course, it is easy for a gifted poet like Meredith, gazing into the huge, blank eyes of a contented ox, to imagine himself "back to hours when mind was mud." But it is easy for a gifted poet to imagine anything. How do we know which imaginations are true insights into the nature of reality?

Practically speaking, were there ever, could there ever have been, hours when all mind—whether inside our universe or beyond it—was mud? In other words, can mind merely evolve from nonmind without any help at all, as materialists insist? That question is at the heart of the conflict between materialism and all philosophies that ascribe meaning and purpose to the universe.

Focusing more narrowly on the human mind for the moment, two important research trends in recent decades have been to study ape behavior in the wild and to try to teach apes American sign language. Researchers in both areas hope to unlock the secrets of the human mind. The assumption, of course, is that the human being is simply "the third chim-

Can Humans and Chimpanzees Be Crossed?

Humans and chimpanzees are thought to have split off from a common ancestor about 5 to 7 million years ago, according to current evolutionary theory. Because chimps are the animal species closest to humans, many have speculated on the possibility of producing a hybrid, a "humanzee." According to documents unearthed from the former Soviet Union, Soviet dictator Joseph Stalin hoped to produce such half-man, half-ape super-warriors, announcing, "I want a new invincible human being, insensitive to pain, resistant and indifferent about the quality of food they eat."[41] The plan came to nothing, and the scientist in charge of it died in the vast Soviet prison system.

But more often the motive for producing a hybrid has been philosophical. British zoologist Richard Dawkins has enthused that if such a hybrid were born, "Politics would never be the same again, nor would theology, sociology, psychology or most branches of philosophy. The world that would be so shaken, by such an incidental event as a hybridisation, is a speciesist world indeed, dominated by the discontinuous mind."[42] By "discontinuous mind," Dawkins means the view that there are fundamental differences in quality between the human mind and the chimpanzee mind, a view with which he vehemently disagrees.

In any event, hybridization may be very difficult. Chimpanzees have forty-eight chromosomes and humans have only forty-six. The late paleontologist Stephen Jay Gould also explains:

The genetic differences between humans and chimps are minor, but they include at least ten large inversions and translocations. An inversion is, literally, the turning around of a chromosomal segment.

panzee," and that the human mind is merely a souped-up version of the chimpanzee mind. Two species of chimpanzee are currently recognized, the common chimpanzee (*Pan troglodytes*) and the smaller bonobo (*Pan paniscus*); if humans were classified with chimpanzees, we would be the third. According to one reckoning, we share about 98 percent of our DNA with chimpanzees, so surely, the reasoning goes, the 100 percent chimpanzees hold the secret.

There has even been a project to reclassify the chimpanzee in the genus *Homo*, along with modern humans and (extinct) Neanderthals.[43] More

> Each hybrid cell would have a set of chimp and a corresponding set of human chromosomes. Egg and sperm cells are made by a process called meiosis, or reduction division. In meiosis, each chromosome must pair (lie side by side) with its counterpart before cell division, so that corresponding genes can match up one to one: that is, each chimp chromosome must pair with its human counterpart. But if a piece of human chromosome is inverted relative to its counterpart in chimps, then gene-by-gene pairing cannot occur without elaborate looping and twisting that usually precludes successful cell division.[44]
>
> But, despite the technical difficulties, the idea refuses to die. Referencing a current theory that humans and chimps took some time to go their separate ways, University of Washington psychology professor David P. Barash recently hailed the day when "thanks to advances in reproductive technology, there will be hybrids, or some other mixed human-animal genetic composite, in our future." Echoing Dawkins, he reasons that a hybrid would erase the line between humans and other life forms, announcing, "It is a line that exists only in the minds of those who proclaim that the human species, unlike all others, possesses a spark of the divine and that we therefore stand outside nature."[45]
>
> Canadian science fiction writer Rob Sawyer, who focuses on key ethical issues in his work, has pointed out that—were it possible—it would hardly be ethical to reproduce even an extinct hominid in a lab, arguing, "If you brought back *Homo erectus*, he would be considered, by all the standards of our day, severely mentally retarded."[46] So, probably, would the humanzee, if its proponents were ever to succeed in producing it.

ambitious still, many authors have speculated on hybridizing a human and a chimpanzee, hoping that the resulting live birth would create social, moral, and legal confusion and thus help humans see that we are animals, after all, without a higher destiny.

The Great Apes

> Although a few years ago it would have seemed the most implausible science fiction, it does not appear to me out of the question that, after a few years in such a verbal chimpanzee community, there might emerge the memoirs of the natural history and mental life of a chimpanzee, published in English or Japanese (with perhaps an "as told to" after the byline).[47]
> —*Carl Sagan,* The Dragons of Eden

What can the great apes tell us about ourselves?

If we are really the 98 percent chimpanzee, then surely self, mind, will, soul, spirit, and spirituality are just human forms of a normal animal brain function. Maybe the 100 percent chimpanzee can indeed help us understand ourselves. But this approach to understanding the human mind has run aground. Here are some of the reasons:

The DNA evidence of similarity between humans and chimpanzees does not tell us what we need to know. Recall that only four nucleotides (A, C, G, T) write the entire genetic code, so a purely random assortment would report us as sharing 25 percent of our DNA with any known life form, whether or not it has a brain. Also, as evolutionary anthropologist Jonathan Marks reminds us, we share 40 percent of our DNA with fish, but no one suggests that fish are 40 percent of a human[48]—or for that matter that humans are 250 percent of a fish. Crude concepts like DNA sharing do not really provide much help in understanding the human mind because it is the differences we need to know about, not the similarities. In any event, current estimates of how much DNA humans and chimpanzees share range from 95 to over 99 percent, depending on the rules chosen by the researcher making the estimate.[49] So it is not even clear yet how much DNA we do share.

Apes are not really a mirror for human behavior or thinking. Primatologists study apes to provide an evolutionary explanation for human behavior, particularly violent behavior. As a result, they tend to focus on behavior that is common (or at least interesting) among humans even if it is rare among other primates. Robert Sussman, of Washington University, and Paul Garber, of the University of Illinois, pointed out recently, after a massive literature survey, that most apes are not even very *social,* let alone prone to violence. Gorillas spend only 3 percent of their time in social activities and chimpanzees only 25 percent. Comparisons between human and ape behavior are easily distorted by observer bias and cannot tell us much about ourselves.[50]

Chimpanzees and humans do not, in general, share close emotional bonds. If you want to live with a nonhuman who is emotionally close to humans, share your life with a dog, not a chimpanzee. Dogs have demonstrated in research studies a greater ability to understand human emotions than chimpanzees have—even though the human face is more similar to the chimpanzee face than it is to the canine face. As Colin Woodward notes in *The Chronicle of Higher Education:*

> Chimpanzees, our closest relatives, have been shown to follow a human's gaze, but they do very poorly in a classic experiment that requires them to extract clues by watching a person. In that test, a researcher hides food in one of several containers out of sight of the animal. Then the chimp is allowed to choose one container after the experimenter indicates the correct choice by various methods, such as staring, nodding, pointing, tapping, or placing a marker. Only with considerable training do chimps and other primates manage to score above chance.[51]

By 2001, experiments had shown that dogs were far better than chimpanzees at finding food using social cues provided by humans. So, greater genetic similarity does not mean greater community of mind between humans and chimpanzees.

The claims that apes have mental abilities similar to those of humans are questionable. Some researchers have devoted their careers to teaching simple deaf-language signs to apes, but, as Jonathan Marks notes:

> For all the interest generated by the sign-language experiments with apes, three things are clear. First they do have the capacity to manipulate a symbol system given to them by humans, and to communicate with it. Second, unfortunately, they have nothing to say. And third, they do not use any such system in the wild.[52]

Marks concludes: "Language is just not a chimpanzee thing. There is in fact very little overlap between chimpanzee and human communication."[53] Indeed, nonhuman primates probably lack the neural complexity to handle the abstract thought needed for a mind. Radiologist Andrew Newberg and his colleagues note:

> A rudimentary version of the parietal lobe is present in our close evolutionary relative, the chimpanzee. While chimps are smart enough to master simple mathematical concepts and develop non-verbal language skills, their brains appear to lack the neural complexity needed to formulate any significant kind of abstract thought, which is the type of thought that leads to the formation of cultures, art, mathematics, technology, and myths.[54]

One of the reasons that primatologists such as Jane Goodall have stressed the similarity between apes and humans is entirely praiseworthy: they want to provide protection for the natural habitats of endangered wild apes and to end inhumane treatment of captive apes in laboratories. But, as Marks has pointed out, apes need protection as apes, not as equivalent to humans. He notes, "Apes should be conserved and treated with compassion, but to blur the line between them and us is an unscientific rhetorical device."[55]

> It's refreshing to work with chimpanzees: They are the honest politicians we all long for. When the political philosopher Thomas Hobbes postulated an insuppressible power drive, he was right on target for both humans and apes. Observing how blatantly chimpanzees jockey for position, one will look in vain for ulterior motives and expedient promises.[56]
> —*Primatologist Frans B. M. De Waal*

> Genuine politics—even politics worthy of the name—the only politics I am willing to devote myself to—is simply a matter of serving those around us: serving the community and serving those who will come after us. Its deepest roots are moral because it is a responsibility expressed through action, to and for the whole.[57]
> — *Political prisoner and human-rights activist Vaclav Havel, later president of the Czech Republic*

So the chimpanzees cannot help us understand ourselves because the very thing that separates us from them *is* the human mind. How that mind arose and how it works is still a genuine puzzle. As science writer Elaine Morgan says:

> Considering the very close genetic relationship that has been established by comparison of biochemical properties of blood proteins, protein structure and DNA and immunological responses, the differences between a man and a chimpanzee are more astonishing than the resemblances.... Something must have happened to the ancestors of Homo sapiens which did not happen to the ancestors of gorillas and chimpanzees.[58]

So what can the chimpanzees and other great apes tell us? Not what we need to know, unfortunately. They can't answer for us the very questions they don't ask for themselves.

But perhaps the answer does not lie with life forms at all. If it is human *intelligence* we need to understand in order to comprehend the spiritual nature of humans, perhaps biology is merely a soupy mess that gets in the way of clean, mathematical binary code. Thus, many theorists have insisted that the answer really lies in artificial intelligence (AI), the intelligence of computers.

Artificial Intelligence

Supercomputers will achieve one human brain capacity by 2010, and personal computers will do so by about 2020.... By the 2030s, the nonbiological portion of our intelligence will predominate.[59]
    —*Ray Kurzweil,* The Age of Spiritual Machines

Do computers know? Can artificial intelligence reproduce mind or spirit?

In Douglas Adams's zany novel *Hitchhiker's Guide to the Galaxy,* Deep Thought, the second greatest computer of all time and space has been assigned the job of calculating the answer to the Ultimate Question of Life, the Universe, and Everything. The computer ponders for 7.5 million years and then announces the answer: "forty-two."

In response to general disappointment, Deep Thought replies, "The problem, to be quite honest with you, is that you've never actually known what the question is." Deep Thought then offers to design an even greater computer, called "Earth," which incorporates living beings. Earth will determine the question to which "forty-two" is the answer.

The question, when finally proposed, is:

WHAT DO YOU GET IF YOU MULTIPLY SIX BY NINE.
    "Six by nine. Forty-two."
    "That's it. That's all there is."[60]

Will advanced computers eventually do better than arithmetic-challenged "Earth," as Daniel Dennett hopes? Can they become "spiritual machines" that approximate the human mind, as artificial intelligence guru Ray Kurzweil has predicted? Will they be able to understand—or more probably eliminate—spirituality[61] as a concept?

> "Did you know," he said at last, "that it's possible to scan every neural net
> in a human brain and produce an exact duplicate of the subject's mind
> inside a computer? . . . What would you say if I told you that my brain had
> been scanned and duplicated?"[62]
> —*Robert J. Sawyer,* The Terminal Experiment

Philosopher of mind John Searle recounts that, in the closing decades of the twentieth century, many thinkers were utterly convinced that a computer that thinks like a human being was quite possible. After all, the human brain was thought to *be* a computer. He recalls:

> I cannot exaggerate the excitement that this idea generated, because it gave
> us at long last not just a solution to the philosophical problems that beset
> us, but it gave us a research program. We can study the mind, we can find
> out how the mind really works, by discovering which programs are imple-
> mented in the brain. An immensely appealing feature of this research pro-
> gram is that we do not actually have to know how the brain works as a
> physical system in order to do a complete and strict science of the mind. . . .
> We just happen, by a kind of evolutionary accident, to be implemented in
> neurons, but any sufficiently complex hardware would do as well as what
> we have in our skulls.[63]

So did Ray Kurzweil's "spiritual machine"[64] fulfill these hopes, as predicted?

Deeper and Deeper into the Blue ...

One long-standing artificial intelligence goal has been a computer big enough and cleverly programmed enough to beat any human at chess. Chess is a good game for a powerful computer because, like tic-tac-toe, it has strictly defined problems. Of course, chess is vastly more complicated. The thirty-two pieces and sixty-four squares provide a range of options that exceeds the estimated number of atoms in the universe.[65]

At first, progress was slow. In 1952 AI pioneer Alan Turing wrote the first computer chess program. Only in 1980 was the Fredkin Prize established: $100,000 would be awarded to the programmers of the first computer to beat a reigning world chess champion. For over a decade and a half, the programmers toiled at their craft without collecting the prize. In 1996 Russian grand master Garry Kasparov announced "Machines are stupid by nature," and proceeded to beat IBM's Deep Blue.

But, in 1997, Kasparov made headlines by losing to Deep Blue, and its three programmers shared the Fredkin Prize. According to many media sources, the age of the human was over and the age of the spiritual machine was about to begin.

> Machines are just passing over an important threshold: the threshold at which, to some extent at least, they give an unbiased human being the impression of intelligence. Because of a kind of human chauvinism or anthropocentrism, many humans are reluctant to admit this possibility. But I think it is inevitable.[66]
> —*Carl Sagan,* The Dragons of Eden

The commentators entirely missed the point that Deep Blue's programmers are just as human as Kasparov. So the question is not whether a machine can beat a human but whether a human who plays chess by writing a program fares better than a human who plays chess without writing a program. If the machine gives the impression of intelligence, as Carl Sagan has noted, that should be no surprise, for an intelligence created it. The lines that Shakespeare wrote for Hamlet give the impression of intelligence too, and for the same reason.

In any event, the age of the spiritual machine went by so fast that practically everyone missed it. In 2003, Kasparov tied the much more powerful Deep Junior and another program, X3dFritz.[67] This surprised many people because a powerful computer program is capable of considering many more strategies at once than a human being can. Generally, a chess-playing computer relies on its enormous parallel processing power to sort through a vast memory to evaluate millions of moves and choose the best one. Deep Junior powered through up to 3 million possible moves per second. Kasparov probably evaluated only two to three moves per second.

Well, that raises an obvious question: Why does Kasparov *ever* win? Shouldn't he always lose? The answer seems to be that what Kasparov is doing when he is thinking about his next play is different in kind from what Deep Junior is doing. Kasparov himself said, "Whatever [program-mers] Shay and Amir say about Junior's ability to run through millions of possible strategies, I, by contrast, might consider only a few strategies in any one game. But you can bet your life they will be the very best ones."[68] As philosopher and chess enthusiast Tim McGrew, of Western Michigan University, puts it: "Something is going on in the grand master's mind that is not only radically different ... but also inconceivably more efficient. It is a kind of computational miracle that humans can play chess at all."[69]

It also emerged, in the aftermath, that the grand masters are getting better at playing computers, even as the computers are becoming more powerful.[70] AI enthusiast Kenneth Silber complains:

> This is a disappointing state of affairs for enthusiasts of artificial intelli-gence. Chess, with its demands for calculation and memory, is an activity seemingly well-suited for computers. If computers are making only moder-ate progress in chess, what prospect is there for them to develop such capa-bilities as creativity, common sense and consciousness—let alone the superhuman intelligence that some experts predict?[71]

The answer may well be, no prospect at all. We will not find the answer in the soul of the new machine because the AI specialists misconceived the problem from the beginning. Computer chess doesn't help us understand human thinking because computers don't form or follow plans, nor do they have goals. They do not have overarching ideas, nor do they use anal-ogy or metaphor—and there is no way currently proposed to make them do so. What they do is perform calculations. The difficulty is that, as com-puter pioneer John Holland points out, "There are many artificial intelli-gence problems that cannot be solved by simply performing more calculations." As a result, he doesn't expect "conscious" computers any time soon.[72]

> I don't think there's anything unique about human intelligence. All the neurons in the brain that make up perceptions and emotions operate in a binary fashion.
> —*Software pioneer Bill Gates*

> The human mind is a computer made out of meat.
> —*Artificial intelligence guru Marvin Minsky*

Similarly, John Searle describes the early optimistic ideas about AI ("any sufficiently complex hardware would do as well as what we have in our skulls") as "hopelessly mistaken" and says that "nothing since the early days has changed my opinion."[73] As if to underscore Searle's comments, technomag *Red Herring* acknowledged in a 2005 overview article that AI ideas are useful in various business areas but "fall short of a grand ontological vision." Fair enough, but it was the grand ontological vision that drove AI in the first place.

Science is capable of astonishing achievements, *provided that* scientists understand clearly the nature of the system they are studying. The human brain is not a calculating machine, and a calculating machine cannot answer our questions about the meaning of life. Even science fiction writer Rob Sawyer's "calculating god"[74] could not answer our questions. Computers, however cleverly we build them, do not become spiritual machines, nor can they shed light on the spiritual nature of the human.

Humans' Spiritual Nature

Can humans have a spiritual nature in a universe without purpose or design?

As we have seen, the lines of inquiry that seek to ground human nature in a purely material reality have not succeeded. Evolutionary psychology, for example, fails at precisely the point where uniquely human behavior begins—with genuine altruism. Likewise, primate studies and AI research fail at the very points where we require answers.

However, the failure of current materialist explanations does not demonstrate that a nonmaterialist explanation is true. Indeed, if we seek to ground the nature of the human in a spiritual as well as a material reality, we face at the outset a serious, perhaps fatal, objection. Regarding the nature of the universe itself, twentieth-century British analytical philosopher Bertrand Russell famously concluded:

> Man is the product of causes which had no prevision of the end they were achieving; that his origin, his growth, his hopes and fears, his loves and his beliefs, are but the outcome of accidental collocations of atoms; that no fire, no heroism, no intensity of thought and feeling, can preserve an individual life beyond the grave; that all the labours of the ages, all the devotion, all the inspiration, all the noonday brightness of human genius, are destined to extinction in the vast death of the solar system, and that the whole temple of Man's achievement must inevitably be buried beneath the débris of a universe in ruins—all these things, if not quite beyond dispute, are yet so nearly certain, that no philosophy which rejects them can hope to stand.[75]

In that case, a spiritual nature for the human is impossible in principle. We must shun nonmaterialist explanations of human nature because they cannot possibly be right. An important consequence follows: even if materialist science does not offer satisfactory explanations now, we must stick with its unsatisfactory insights, in the hope that better ones will arrive someday.

Philosopher of science Karl Popper has called this line of thinking "promissory materialism."[76] In other words, if we adopt it, we are accepting a promissory note on the future of materialism. Promissory materialism has been immensely influential in the sciences because any doubt about materialism—no matter what the state of the *evidence*—can be labeled "unscientific" in principle.

Gathering Evidence Against Materialism

In the summer of 2005, Guillermo Gonzalez, a forty-one-year-old astronomer at Iowa State University, accidentally discovered the size of the debt of promissory materialism. As an assistant professor of physics and astronomy approaching tenure, he found out one day that 124 fellow faculty members (about 7 percent of the faculty) had signed a statement criticizing him on account of his alleged support for "intelligent design theory." (This theory proposes that, on the evidence, the present state of the universe is best interpreted as the product of intelligent causation or design, as well as of law and chance. It does not hold that all events are intelligently caused, but does not rule out intelligent causes in principle, where evidence warrants. One way of understanding this is that the universe is top down, not bottom up. Mind comes first and creates matter. Matter does not come first and create mind.[77])

What was Gonzalez's offense? He is a recognized expert in the obscure field of galactic habitability—the ability of a planet to support life as we know it.[78] He is also the lead author of a book, *The Privileged Planet: How Our Place in the Cosmos Is Designed for Discovery,*[79] in which he argues, based on his extensive research on various vantage points for astronomy in our solar system, that earth is remarkably convenient for astronomy—situated on the very plane of the ecliptic just off a spiral arm of our galaxy, with the result that humans can actually see deep into the galaxy.

> People who are into astronomy get into it very early. It's such a beautiful science. A lot of people have a deep sense of the infinite and the grandness of the universe....
>
> People have strong convictions that you can't bring God into science. But I don't bring God into science. I've looked out at nature and discovered this pattern, based on empirical evidence.... It obviously calls for a different explanation.[80]
>
> —*Astronomer Guillermo Gonzalez*

Gonzalez, a Christian, argues that this and similar findings mean that humans were meant to explore the universe. He is quick to stress that all his arguments are scientific—that is, evidence-based, testable, and falsifiable. But that does not pacify critics such as Jim Colbert, an associate professor of ecology, evolution, and organismal biology, who says, "We're not saying no one should believe in intelligent design. It's just that you can't accumulate evidence, so it's not science."[81]

What emerged clearly from the ensuing controversy was that neither the evidence of earth's position nor the quality of Gonzalez's research was an issue in dispute. The attempt to stop him from getting tenure was based, essentially, on promissory materialism.[82] Any research that uncovers the possibility of purpose, design, or meaning in the universe is perceived as a threat to science, because science is understood as an enterprise that upholds the view of the cosmos eloquently expressed by Russell. Gonzalez's sin was precisely that he *was* accumulating evidence against that view.

Although the fact that Gonzalez is a Christian predisposes him to think in this way, it is by no means necessary. Rob Sawyer has been keeping abreast of the larger (and growing) controversy, noting "I think there is a legitimate debate going on. It's not fringe stuff." Indeed, although Sawyer does not write from a religious perspective, he likes to rehearse the many examples of delicate fine-tuning of the universe (sometimes called anthropic coincidences)—for example, the fact that if the strength of gravity differed from its known strength by as much as one part in 1×10^{40}, stars like our sun could not exist, and therefore neither could a life-supporting planet like earth.[83] In this, he is joined by astrophysicist Paul Davies, who

Is Science a Search for Truth or for Support for Materialism?

Sometimes academic scientists are so convinced that providing support for materialism is the purpose of science that they end up violating conventional civil rights. This happened to Richard von Sternberg, a paleontologist who permitted a peer-reviewed article to be published in his journal, the Smithsonian's *Proceedings of the Biological Society of Washington*, an article suggesting that the explosion of complex life forms that occurred quite suddenly about 525 million years ago might best be explained by intelligent design. Almost all the existing large classifications of animals (phyla) emerged quite suddenly during a few million years, a mere sneeze of geological time. Sternberg was not himself a supporter of the intelligent design hypothesis, but he believed strongly in putting all the options on the table.

The mere suggestion of an origin that included intelligent causation set off a huge uproar, directed not at the author, geologist and intelligent design theorist Steve Meyer, but mainly at editor Sternberg. He was cross-examined about his political and religious beliefs by his employers, removed from his position, and denied access to collections of fossils he needed for his work as a paleontologist. Also, he recounted to the *Washington Post,* when the biological society made a statement disowning Meyer's article, he was counseled not to attend, because, in his words, "I was told that feelings were running so high they could not guarantee also espouses no particular religious position, but notes that "we can't avoid some anthropic component in our science, which is interesting, because after three hundred years we finally realize that we do matter."[84]

In the face of the evidence for fine-tuning, as set out by Gonzalez among many others, the only sturdy argument against purpose and design is the possibility that our universe is an accidental success amid a junk heap of failed universes.[85] However, we have no way of knowing that other universes exist or that they may have failed.[86]

Dimly, amid storms and uproars, people make their way to taking sides. Given what Tom Wolfe had to say about materialist neuroscience ten years ago ("the notion of a self ... is already slipping away, slipping away ... slipping away ..."),[87] it was quite a surprise to hear his thoughts in 2005 about Darwinism, the biological theory that underpins it: "Look

me that they could keep order."[88] He appealed to the Office of Special Counsel, a federal body that protects the civil rights of government employees, who found that he had had been subjected to retaliation and a misinformation campaign. A December 2006 Congressional report again vindicated Sternberg against many false allegations, accusing senior Smithsonian officials of having "harassed, discriminated against, and retaliated against" him.

It became apparent that Sternberg had violated not a written law but an unwritten one: Intelligent causation could not be considered, irrespective of either the state of the evidence or of whether or not scientists who were in any way associated with it had followed correct procedures in gathering and publishing evidence. Sternberg was supposed to have known better than to publish such a paper *even though* it had passed peer review.

Some argue that such unwritten rules actually hinder the very science they are supposed to protect. Mathematician and ID theorist William Dembski, for example, says, "Materialistic ideology has subverted the study of biological and cosmological origins so that the actual content of these sciences has become corrupted. The problem, therefore, is not merely that science is being used illegitimately to promote a materialistic worldview, but that this worldview is actively undermining scientific inquiry, leading to incorrect and unsupported conclusions about biological and cosmological origins."

at Darwin. My God, what a powerful theory. Incidentally, I give that one about 40 more years, and it will go down in flames."[89]

Of course, purpose and design in our universe or in life forms do not demonstrate that humans have a spiritual nature. They do, however, make the idea plausible enough to investigate. Put simply, if Russell is right, we cannot have a spiritual nature and should not attempt to look for one, any more than Gonzalez should look for evidence that earth's position may be meaningful. But if Gonzalez is right, we may indeed have a spiritual nature, and we can research the question, using the tools of science. The current evidence about the nature of the universe as a whole does not favor Russell's view of reality over Gonzalez's[90] and therefore should not be an impediment to considering the spiritual nature of humans.

The Limits of Materialism

But surely materialism could not be wrong? Great thinkers argue for it!

Materialism is wrong in its assessment of human nature because it is not in accord with the *evidence*. However, a couple of points are worth making about the limitations of materialism as a philosophical *assumption*.

Materialism is a *monistic philosophy*, that is, a philosophy that assumes that everything that exists is fundamentally of only one substance (e.g., matter). As Russell makes clear, it seeks to explain all of reality, from vast galaxy walls of the universe down to the subatomic quarks that underlie our own bodies, from the subtleties of the human mind down to the un-conscious mimicry of an orchid.[91] Two important consequences follow. First, in a monistic system, it is hard to know if we are wrong. Monists have nothing to compare their system with. As we have seen, one result is promissory materialism, in which problems with the assumptions of the system are simply deferred to future science; they do not result in a critical examination of the system itself.

Second, a monistic system like materialism can be destroyed by any evidence against it. That weakness is built into the system by its very nature; it cannot be attributed to harsh, unreasonable, or prejudiced critics. As a result, monistic systems tend to be hostile to investigations that provide evidence against the system's assumptions. Supporters of the system may seek to prevent such investigations. They may also seek to manipulate definitions so that such investigations are deemed to be outside science, irrespective of the evidence, as Guillermo Gonzalez discovered.

> I maintain that the human mystery is incredibly demeaned by reductionism, with its claim in promissory materialism to account eventually for all of the spiritual world in terms of patterns of neural activity. This belief must be classed as a superstition.... We are spiritual beings with souls in a spiritual world, as well as material beings with bodies and brains existing in a material world.[92]
> —*Neurologist and Nobel Prize winner*
> *Sir John Eccles*

Keeping these issues in view, we now turn to our key question: What evidence from neuroscience casts doubt on a materialist interpretation of the human mind and spirituality?

Support for the Spiritual Nature of Humans

So far, this book has only shown that materialist presuppositions, far from accounting for the nature of the human, restrict the areas we are permitted to research to certain well-worn, and by now mostly unproductive, areas such as speculations about prehistory, primate studies, and artificial intelligence. Does that mean that science itself, apart from the presuppositions of materialism, has nothing to contribute to the understanding of the spiritual nature of the human? Certainly not! The challenge for science is, rather, to develop hypotheses that take the observed facts seriously enough to go beyond the limitations of materialism.

Here is a key problem that must be addressed. Most of us, asked to give an account of ourselves, think that we have "minds," which we distinguish from our "brains." We consider that our minds generate the fundamental choice of action that the circuitry of our brains carries out. For example, a driver faced with an unexpected traffic jam may decide not to curse and hammer the horn, but simply to shrug and turn down a side street. We might describe the driver's thought process by saying, "Harry made up his *mind* not to get upset, but to just go home another way." We do not say, "Harry's brain circuitry caused him to take his hand off the horn and instead steer the car to the right, down a side street." We assume that Harry has free will, that he—or something in him—can really decide how he will act.[93]

As we have seen, a materialist neuroscience cannot account for a mind or for free will in this way. It assumes that Harry and any observers are the victims of an illusion of free will, because materialism has no model for how free will might actually work.

> The first dogma which I came to disbelieve was that of free will. It seemed to me that all notions of matter were determined by the laws of dynamics and could not therefore be influenced by human wills.
> —*Analytical philosopher Bertrand Russell (1872–1970)*

> Everything, including that which happens in our brains, depends on these and only on these: A set of fixed, deterministic laws. A purely random set of accidents.
> —*Artificial intelligence guru Marvin Minsky*

> All theory is against freedom of the will; all experience for it.
> —*English literary critic Samuel Johnson (1709–84)*

Do All Events Have a Material Cause?

Materialism requires all events to have a *material* cause, which means a cause governed by the physical forces of nature, as understood by classical physics. Inevitably, that means a "deterministic" cause. There is no way for an object to fail to act in accordance with those forces, any more than a billiard ball can fail to shoot off in whatever direction an impact sends it. Very well, let us assume for the present that all events are governed by the physical forces of nature. But do we have a correct *account* of those forces, especially as regards the forces that may be operating within our brains?

Most of us assume, simply because it seems reasonable, that at a fundamental level the material reality of our universe consists of little bits of matter. The Roman poet Lucretius explained reality like that in about 55 C.E.:

> All nature as it is in itself consists of two things—bodies and the vacant space in which the bodies are situated and through which they move in different directions.... Nothing exists that is distinct both from body and from vacuity.[94]

Isaac Newton, the brilliant seventeenth-century developer of the laws of gravity, was convinced of a similar idea:

> It seems probable to me that God in the Beginning formed Matter in solid, massy, hard, impenetrable, movable Particles, of such Sizes and Figures, and with such other Properties, and in such Proportion to space, as most conduced to the end for which he formed them; and as these primitive Particles being Solids, are incomparably harder than any porous Bodies compounded of them; even so very hard as never to wear or break in pieces; no ordinary Power being able to divide what God himself made one in the first Creation.[95]

As it happens, Lucretius and Newton were mistaken. The fundamental layers of physical reality are nothing like that at all. They are collections of force fields. In the early twentieth century, physicists showed that these force fields, the "quantum" level of our universe, do not necessarily obey the "laws of nature" with which we are familiar.

So what is this fundamental quantum level of our universe like? Electrons (the negative charges of atoms), for example, do not definitely exist in space and time. They are a cloud of probabilities; their existence at any given point is only potential. When they jump from one state of energy to

Can Newton's Laws Be Broken?

Why do Newton's laws work so well if he was wrong about the fundamental layers of physical reality? Newton's laws describe a middle level of reality, between the very small and the very large. At the very small, quantum, level, we must contend with fundamental quantum uncertainty. At the levels of organization that we normally observe, our bodies and other objects contain staggering numbers of packets of matter and energy. In that case, the approximations that Newton's laws describe can be relied on. Hence, if you drop this book, you can be sure it will fall to the floor. However, if we continue on to a very high level of organization in interstellar space, relativity theory takes over and dispenses with Newton's certainties again, though in different ways. For example, a triangle between stars might *not* add up to 180 degrees because space and time warp. What we must decide in each case is how much certainty we need and for what purpose.

another, they do not "pass through" the space in between. They simply reappear in a higher or lower state. One way to understand this is to picture a three-way bulb, a light bulb that emits 50, 100, or 150 watts, as the switch is turned, but nothing in between. There is *nothing* in between.[96] Even more strangely, if we measure these electrons, we make their existence at a given point real, at least for our purposes. So, in a sense, we are creating the thing we want to measure. There is a principle for this called the Heisenberg uncertainty (indeterminacy) principle. It says that subatomic particles do not occupy definite positions in space or time; we can find out where they are only as a series of probabilities about where they might be (we must decide what we want to know).

This area of physics, quantum physics, is the study of the behavior of matter and energy at the subatomic level of our universe. Briefly, the synapses, the spaces between the neurons of the brain, conduct signals using parts of atoms called ions. The ions function according to the rules of quantum physics, not of classical physics.

What difference does it make if quantum physics governs the brain? Well, one thing we can dispose of right away is determinism, the idea that everything in the universe has been or can be predetermined. The basic level of our universe is a cloud of probabilities, not of laws. In the human brain, this means that our brains are not driven to process a given decision; what we really experience is a "smear" of possibilities. But how do we decide between them?

> The indeterminacy principle is often discussed as if it represented the difficulty of accurately measuring the locations and trajectories of the particles. But the point is not that it is hard to find out just where, say, an electron is, but that the electron actually has no exact location. Depending on how it's measured, an electron can look specific as a pinpoint or vague as a cumulus cloud.[97]
> —*Timothy Ferris,* The Whole Shebang

> People had got used to the determinism of the last century, where the present determines the future completely, and they now have to get used to a different situation in which the present only gives one information of a statistical nature about the future. A good many people find this unpleasant.... I must say that I also do not like indeterminism. I have to accept it because it is certainly the best that we can do with our present

knowledge. One can always hope that there will be future developments which will lead to a drastically different theory.[98]
—*Quantum theorist Paul Dirac*

One quantum mechanics discovery that may help us understand how we decide is the quantum Zeno effect. Physicists have found that if they observe an unstable elementary particle continuously, it never decays— even though it would almost certainly decay if it were not observed. In quantum physics, it is not possible to separate the observer entirely from the thing observed. They are part of the same system. The physicists are, essentially, holding the unstable particle in a given state by the act of con- tinuing to measure it.[99] In the same way, experiments have shown that, because your brain is a quantum system, if you focus on a given idea, you hold its pattern of connecting neurons in place. The idea does not decay, as it would if it were ignored. But the action of holding an idea in place truly is a decision you make, in the same way that the physicists hold a particle in place by deciding to continue to observe it.[100]

Can the Adult Human Brain Change?

For many years, neuroscientists believed that the adult human brain was essentially finished. It did not and could not change, any more than a bil- liard ball could, and individual neurons did not regenerate. According to the classical view, in such a fixed system certain mental programs were simply run over and over. Individual decisions did not affect the function- ing of the system, but were rather a delusion created by the functioning of the system.

In recent years, however, neuroscientists have discovered that the adult brain is actually very plastic. As we will see, if neural circuits receive a great deal of traffic, they will grow. If they receive little traffic, they will remain the same or shrink. The amount of traffic our neural circuits re- ceive depends, for the most part, on what we choose to pay attention to. Not only can we make decisions by focusing on one idea rather than an- other, but we can change the patterns of neurons in our brains by doing so consistently. Again, that has been demonstrated by experiments[101] and is even used in psychiatric treatments for obsessive compulsive disorder.[102]

So what happens in our brains when we make a decision? According to the model created by H. Stapp and J. M. Schwartz, which is based on the Von Neumann interpretation of quantum physics, conscious effort causes a pattern of neural activity that becomes a template for action.[103] But the process is not mechanical or material. There are no little cogs and wheels in our brains. There is a series of possibilities; a decision causes a quantum collapse, in which one of them becomes a reality. The cause is the mental focus, in the same way that the cause of the quantum Zeno effect is the physicists' continued observation. It is a cause, but not a mechanical or material one. One truly profound change that quantum physics has made is to verify the existence of nonmechanical causes.[104] One of these is the activity of the human mind, which, as we will see, is not identical to the functions of the brain.

Where Is This Book Going?

An open-minded neuroscience can significantly contribute to a model of mind (that is not a delusion) and tell us some important facts about spiritual/mystical experiences. Along the way, this book will explain in detail why current materialist neuroscientific theories of mind and spiritual/ mystical experiences are mistaken.

A Model for Nonmechanical Causes

In the interpretation of quantum physics created by physicist John Von Neumann (1903–1957), a particle only probably exists in one position or another; these probable positions are said to be "superposed" on each other. Measurement causes a "quantum collapse," meaning that the experimenter has chosen a position for the particle, thus ruling out the other positions. The Stapp and Schwartz model posits that this is analogous to the way in which attending to (measuring) a thought holds it in place, collapsing the probabilities on one position. This targeted attention strategy, which is used to treat obsessive-compulsive disorders, provides a model for how free will might work in a quantum system. The model assumes the existence of a mind that chooses the subject of attention, just as the quantum collapse assumes the existence of an experimenter who chooses the point of measurement.

Chapters Two–Four present and critique popular theories about spiritual experience that support an atheistic worldview. Author Matthew Alper, for example, assumes that human beings are hardwired by evolution to believe in God. In *The "God" Part of the Brain,* Alper claims that human spirituality is not a rational deduction or intuition, but rather represents a genetically inherited trait of our species.

Chapter Two addresses this idea, showing why it is useless for discussing spiritual issues. Chapter Two also looks at the similar "God gene" argument proposed by molecular biologist Dean Hamer (chief of gene structure at the U.S. National Cancer Institute) in a recently published book, *The God Gene: How Faith Is Hardwired into Our Genes.* Hamer believes that humans, "a bunch of chemical reactions running around in a bag," are governed by their DNA. Like Alper, he claims that human spirituality is an adaptive trait (a trait that promotes survival and the ability to produce fertile offspring). We will see why it makes no scientific sense to speak of a "God gene."

Chapter Three examines the claim of Jeffrey Saver and John Rabin, of the UCLA–Reed Neurologic Research Center, and others that there is a "God module" in the brain. Such a module, they say, accounts for religious visions, feelings of ecstasy, and related phenomena. Some scientists have focused on epilepsy to research this idea. Vilayanur Ramachandran, director of the Center for Brain and Cognition at the University of California at San Diego, raised the stakes by suggesting that his 1997 study had discovered a "God spot (or module)" in the human brain that could underpin an evolutionary instinct to believe in religion. Popular media, the scientific community, and the academy have been attracted to this idea that religious belief was somehow "hardwired" into the human brain in such a module. My research shows that Ramachandran's findings simply indicate that the temporal lobes and the limbic system are involved in spiritual/mystical experiences. They do not mean that these areas create the experiences all by themselves. *The Spiritual Brain* demonstrates the role of a number of other regions in the brain.

Chapter Four reviews the work of Dr. Michael Persinger, a neuropsychologist at Laurentian University in Sudbury, Ontario, who has invented a helmet (called the Octopus or God Helmet) that allegedly induces spiritual/mystical experiences by electromagnetically stimulating the temporal lobes of those who wear it. The problem with this research is that, as was shown by the famous experiments conducted at the Montreal Neurological Institute by Wilder Penfield, it is not possible to consistently generate a specific type of experience by stimulating the human brain.

Chapter Five addresses a key question, "What is the mind?" The materialist view, which is a central dogma of current neuroscience, holds that the mind is a delusion created by the brain. Thus, for current neuroscience, the question does *not* turn on whether there is evidence that some individuals have had a given spiritual experience. By definition, according to current dogma, they *cannot* have had an experience that puts them in contact with a reality beyond themselves because there is no such reality. Therefore, their experience is an illusion created by the brain. But there is evidence that the mind and the brain are not identical, which means that an actual experience of a reality beyond themselves is a real possibility that we will investigate.

Chapter Six introduces studies showing that the mind acts on the brain as a nonmaterial cause. I also introduce a hypothesis for how the mind interacts with the brain. Some interesting new scientific studies conducted by Peter Fenwick, Sam Parnia, Bruce Greyson, and Pim van Lommel on near death experiences (NDE) provide additional support to this view. Also presented are some cases that were investigated by researcher Kenneth Ring, showing that people born blind can see during an NDE, and the case of Pam Reynolds, who was known to be clinically dead when her NDE occurred. Overall, the occurrence of NDEs during cardiac arrest raises questions about the possible relationship between the mind and the brain. Mind and consciousness appear to continue at a time when the brain is nonfunctional and clinical criteria of death have been reached. If this is the case, it is quite plausible that mystics are actually contacting something outside themselves when in a deep mystical state.

Chapters Seven–Nine discuss spiritual and mystical experiences generally. Chapter Seven discusses who has mystical experiences and what triggers them. Although most people do not have such experiences (which undermines a materialist evolutionary explanation for them), the experiences can be triggered in a variety of ways. Many popular and academic beliefs about mystics, in particular, will be examined. *The Spiritual Brain* will look at the work of Sir Alister Hardy, a distinguished zoologist who established the Religious Experience Research Unit (RERU) at Manchester College in Oxford in 1969. The aim of RERU was to collect and classify contemporary accounts of firsthand religious or transcendent experiences and to investigate the nature and function of these experiences. The findings of an eight-year survey of over three thousand firsthand accounts of mystical experience were later published as *The Spiritual Nature of Man.* The most frequent triggers were prayer, meditation, natural beauty, and participation in religious worship. Hardy's conclusions support the key role of prayer and contemplation in Christian mysticism.

Chapter Eight investigates how spiritual/mystical experiences affect those who have them. One of the significant features of spiritual/mystical experiences is that they generally change the life of the individual. That is, contemporary scientific psychological research examining the relationship between the self, personality, and spirituality indicates that spiritual/mystical experiences can result in profound life changes in goals, feelings, attitudes, and behaviors as well as improved health. In general, spiritual/mystical experiences have positive effects, but the examples of negative effects are interesting in their own right.

Chapter Nine introduces the research project I have conducted with my doctoral student Vincent Paquette. This project was conducted with Carmelite nuns using scientific tools to identify what happens in their brains when they recall and relive *unio mystica,* the mystical union with God (the ultimate goal of the contemplative techniques practiced by Christian mystics). We used two of the most powerful functional brain-imaging technologies available, functional magnetic resonance imaging (fMRI) and quantitative electroencephalography (QEEG). QEEG measures electrical patterns at the surface of the scalp that reflect brain-wave patterns. These can be statistically analyzed and translated into numbers, then expressed as a color map.

What the two neuroimaging studies demonstrate is that the experience of union with God is not solely associated with the temporal lobe. In other words, there is no God spot in the brain located in the temporal lobe. (This is one of the reasons that the electromagnetic stimulation of the temporal lobe with the "God helmet" does not work.) Rather, this experience is implemented via a spatially extended neural circuit encompassing brain regions involved in attention, body representation, visual imagery, emotion (physiological and subjective aspects), and self-consciousness. These findings are more consistent with an actual experience than with a delusion. Chapter Nine also discusses the few other studies carried out so far in the field of spiritual neuroscience, which significantly increase our knowledge and understanding of the neurobiology of spiritual/mystical experiences. The new knowledge gained in our research project sheds light on the circumstances under which spiritual/mystical experiences are most likely to occur.

Many people in present-day societies long to develop their spiritual side, but they wonder whether it really exists. They do not want to fool themselves, after all. By the time they have finished reading this book, they will see that their spiritual side does indeed exist. But like any faculty, it must be allowed to develop if they would like to see their lives transformed.

Chapter Ten addresses an important philosophical question: Did God create the brain or does the brain create God? On the one hand, spiritual/mystical experiences are significantly influenced by culture. For example, a Christian is unlikely to have a religious experience involving Brahman (Hinduism). Muslims and Jews are unlikely to have religious experiences that involve a triune God (in the Christian sense). However, on the other hand, some aspects of the mystical experience clearly transcend culture. A key characteristic is a state of knowledge, insight, awareness, revelation, and illumination beyond the grasp of the intellect. There is awareness of unity with the Absolute. Perhaps more significantly, people can change profoundly and irreversibly after these experiences. The change is generally interpreted as being for the better because the person becomes more loving and forgiving. This suggests, though it does not prove, that people who have spiritual/mystical experiences actually contact an objectively real force outside of themselves (God) and that the transformative power of spiritual/mystical experiences arises from an authentic encounter with ultimate reality (or God).

A Few Disclaimers

The external reality of God cannot be directly proven or disproven by studying what happens to people's brains when they have mystical experiences. Demonstrating that specific brain states are associated with spiritual/mystical experiences neither shows that such experiences are "nothing but" brain states nor proves that God exists. It shows only that it is reasonable to believe that mystics do contact a power outside themselves.

Consistent with this view, neuroscientific studies of faith experiences should not undermine faith. The fact that the human brain has a neurological substrate that enables it to experience a spiritual state can be construed as the gift of a divine creator or, if you prefer, as contact with the underlying nature or purpose of the universe. Materialist philosophers insist that such a substrate is meaningless and got there purely by chance. But, as pointed out earlier, materialism constrains them to think so. Nothing in the available scientific evidence requires that interpretation.

At the same time, no claim is made here that every activity pursued in the name of religion is good or equal. Consider the following well-known (and now deceased) figures:

Mother Teresa—founder of ministries to the poorest of the poor

Jim Jones—cult leader who led eight hundred followers to suicide

Baha'ullah—founder of a new religious sect encouraging interreligious peace

Mohammed Atta—9/11 suicide bomber

Mahatma Gandhi—founder of a nonviolent civil disobedience movement

David Koresh—killed in 1993, with seventy-five followers, in a standoff with the FBI

All these figures were motivated in some way by religion. Yet they did very different things, with very different outcomes. A positive case for specific religious beliefs must be made on its own merits and is not the purpose of this book.

Regarding classification, religious, spiritual, and mystical experiences cannot be separated in a completely systematic way. Some experiences fall squarely into one of these categories and do not overlap any of the others, but other experiences overlap two or all three.[105] For example, some individuals have had mystical experiences during the contemplation of nature or art. Should their experiences be called a spirituality or even a religion of nature or art? Some experiencers would accept the designation, but others would firmly resist it and insist that they have been misunderstood, perhaps even misrepresented. A visual demonstration of this problem might feature three circles whose centers all overlap.

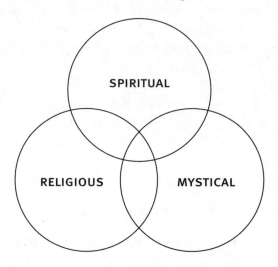

Therefore, it is wise to avoid controversies about terminology and instead focus on what can be learned from observing actual cases. The term RSMEs will often be used in this book to mean "religious, spiritual, and/ or mystical experiences."[106]

Neuroscience is a complex subject due to the nature of the human brain—the most complex living structure that we know. Maps of the brain, for example, are three-dimensional maps, not two-dimensional ones. However, technical terminology will be minimized wherever possible without distorting meaning. And now, onward!

Is There a God Program?

Spirituality comes from within. The kernel must be there from the start. It
must be part of their genes.[1]

—Behavioral geneticist Dean Hamer

In the summer of 2005, the London Zoo actually trumped the beach. The
zoo staged a hot-weather story that took the international media by storm.
For four days, August 26–29, in the wooded habitat on Bear Mountain,
three male and five female *Homo sapiens* were displayed. A label was af-
fixed to the display: "Warning: Humans in Their Natural Environment."
Zoo spokeswoman Polly Wills explained that the exhibit "teaches members of the public that the human is just another primate."[2]

The *sapiens* had not been acquired by the zoo in the usual way, however. Applicants responding to advertisements had to provide a persuasive
fifty-word pitch. A chemist, an aspiring actor, and a fitness enthusiast all
passed this test and found themselves installed in the display with "only
fig leaves to protect their modesty." Yes, their modesty. One patron professed disappointment that the *sapiens* turned out to be wearing swimsuits
beneath the cut-out, pinned-on paper fig leaves.

Another difference was that, after displaying their biceps and curves in
front of the holiday crowds (all the while protected from their grumpy
animal relatives by an electric fence), the *sapiens* departed each night—not
to a pile of bracken somewhere, but to their own flats. Curiously, one participant commented, "A lot of people think humans are above other ani-

mals. When they see humans as animals, here, it kind of reminds us that we're not that special."[3]

That is an interesting comment, given that the publicity stunt was only possible because precisely the opposite happens to be true. The cavorting cage dwellers willingly exhibited themselves to other humans for fun and possible career advancement. So why, precisely, are we supposed to take away the idea that humans are animals *in the same sense* as the voiceless creatures electrically fenced in the other enclosures, who cannot write a pitch, offer their thoughts to reporters, or (perhaps most poignantly) go "home" every night?

Yes, we are physically members of the animal kingdom and participate in all its risks and opportunities. But the participant's comment ("we're not that special") shows how entrenched philosophical materialism has become in our society. Faced with obvious differences between humans and the typical zoo denizens, many assume that they have actually seen similarities. It's not so surprising, really. Faced with a choice between what they see and what they hear, many people reduce cognitive dissonance by choosing to believe what they hear.

> Who are you going to believe, me or your own eyes?
> —*Chico Marx,* Duck Soup *(1933)*

This same materialist mind-set has dominated recent attempts to understand spirituality. Many researchers look for spirituality in a part of the brain or a gene, or perhaps in a hypothetical history or meme (a gene equivalent). In other words, they assume that humans are animals who have some kind of organ, gene, or programmed instinct for spirituality. For example, Matthew Alper argues, using Socratic logic, that there must be a specific part or circuit of the brain that governs religious ideas. Geneticist Dean Hamer thinks that he has found a gene or genes that code for spirituality. But what have they actually found?

The "God" Part of the Brain

> If the brain evolved by natural selection ... religious beliefs must have arisen by the same mechanism.[4]
> —*Edward O. Wilson,* On Human Nature

Wouldn't the fact that all human cultures, no matter how isolated, have believed in the existence of a spiritual realm suggest that such a perception must constitute an inherent characteristic of our species, that is, a genetically inherited trait?[5]

—*Matthew Alper,* The "God" Part of the Brain

Matthew Alper is a man with a mission, one that has inspired the admiration of eminent evolutionary biologist Edward O. Wilson[6] and sympathy among thousands of atheists. Like many thoughtful people, Alper is troubled by what he describes as "the problem of God."

Born and raised in New York City, he saw stints as a history teacher and a screenwriter. But he has also traveled the world to discover what lies behind the idea of God:

With all our knowledge, there still remains that one ever-elusive piece of the puzzle, that one mystery which looms tauntingly over all of the physical sciences, and that is the problem of God. This, more than anything, seems to be humankind's ultimate challenge, that one riddle which—should it ever be resolved—might possibly grant us that definitive picture for which we've so painstakingly been searching.[7]

In his quest, he tried both traditional and alternative religions and rejected them as logically flawed. He also tried mind-altering substances—with disastrous results. They triggered a severe clinical depression and anxiety disorder.[8]

After a medical regimen restored Alper to health, he concluded that his susceptibility to the effects of drugs showed that "human consciousness may be a strictly physical entity based in strictly physical processes." However, he realized that, whether his interpretation of consciousness is right or wrong, it would not solve his original problem, why people believe in God. So, armed with a history of science degree, Alper set out to look for a science that explains God. His book *The "God" Part of the Brain: A Scientific Interpretation of Human Spirituality and God* (2001) wrestles with the idea of God using concepts gleaned from evolutionary psychology. That is the branch of psychology which maintains that human brains, including any component that involves religion or spirituality, comprise adaptations or psychological mechanisms that have evolved by natural selection to benefit the survival and reproduction of the human organism.

In *The "God" Part of the Brain,* Alper argues that we are innately "hardwired" to perceive a spiritual reality and to believe in forces that transcend the limitations of our physical reality. In other words, God is not necessarily "out there," beyond and independent of us, but rather the product of an evolutionary adaptation within our human brain. He presents his case as follows:

Religion is so widespread that it must be a genetically inherited instinct. "If there is any behavior that has been universally exhibited among every human culture, that behavior must represent an inherent characteristic of the species, a genetically inherited instinct."[9]

Fear of death naturally selected an instinct for religious belief in early humans. "As generations of ... protohumans passed, those whose cerebral constitutions most effectively dealt with the anxiety resulting from their awareness of death were most apt to survive."[10]

Specific parts of the brain trigger religious belief as a survival mechanism. "The fact that all cultures have spoken of the healing properties of prayer leads me to believe that our species possesses a distinct set of prayer-responsive mechanisms that exist within our brains."[11]

As scientists continue to unravel and decipher the contents of the human genome, perhaps there will come a time when we will have knowledge of precisely which genes are responsible or those parts of the brain that give rise to religiosity and spiritual consciousness. In order to accommodate this new field, the sciences may have to look toward a whole new discipline—a new geno-theology—for its answers.[12]
          —*Matthew Alper,* The "God" Part of the Brain

Alper represents a broad strand in the current skein of thoughts on spirituality and neuroscience—the hope that neuroscience will provide support for an atheistic and materialist worldview. However, two problems dog Alper's thesis: (1) it begs the questions it attempts to answer; and (2) there is no real science behind it.

The Questions Begged

Having a normal human brain does not imply that you have religion. All it implies is that you can acquire it, which is very different.[13]
—*Pascal Boyer,* Religion Explained

Perhaps we can never really know the cultural assumptions of people who lived before thoughts were recorded in arts and literature. But we can be sure that some claims are immensely improbable, for example, the first two points in Alper's case above.

Religion is so widespread that it must be a genetically inherited instinct? The fact that a behavior is widely demonstrated across historical cultures does not show that it is genetically inherited. What human beings actually inherit is the *capacity* for abstract ideas like God, the future, ethics, free will, death, mathematics, and so forth. As we would expect, religious ideas normally correlate with regions of the brain that are well developed in humans. But the search for an inherited mechanism or process that governs specifically religious ideas (and not other ideas?) is misguided.

Meditation (or contemplation) correlates to specific brain regions, but that is because a specific mental/brain state is sought. On the other hand, general cultural ideas, beliefs, and practices connected with God or religion are too diffuse and idiosyncratic to be categorized as instincts in the way that Alper hopes. Buddha preaching the Fire Sermon, a widow lighting memorial candles, a charismatic Christian speaking in tongues, and a cargo cultist[14] awaiting Prince Philip may show very different mental/brain states. Yet all these activities can properly be classed as religion. What unites the activities—and separates them from the instinctive behavior of animals—is simply the human intelligence to conceive of and act on a general idea about reality, not any specific region or circuit in the brain.

Fear of death naturally selected an instinct for religious belief in early humans? Alper makes the curious assumption, widespread among atheists, that the origin of belief in God among our ancestors is a desire to survive death. But from what we know, most human cultures have simply *assumed* that humans survive death.[15] Some hope for heavens, some fear hells, and many anticipate living graveyards or endless rebirths in an unknown state. Indeed, in some religious systems an annihilation desperately sought by

the believer cannot be achieved until a high state of spiritual enlightenment has been reached, perhaps through many lives!

Far from fearing that souls will simply die, aboriginal cultures in historical times have assumed that the soul is easily detachable from the live
body, as anthropologist J. G. Frazer pointed out in *The Golden Bough*
(1890). Pleasing the spirits of ancestors has been a constant preoccupation
of many cultures for thousands of years. Shadows, reflections, photos, and
dreams have often been thought to be detached souls, traveling under their
own direction.[16] Animals and plants have been widely thought to have
souls of a sort too. Here is Frazer's account of a traditional hunter's view:

> [He] commonly conceives animals to be endowed with souls and intelli-
> gences like his own, and hence he naturally treats them with similar respect.
> Just as he attempts to appease the ghosts of the men he has slain, so he
> essays to propitiate the spirits of the animals he has killed.... In general it
> appears to be supposed that the evil effect of breaking such taboos is not so
> much that it weakens the hunter or fisher, as that, for some reason or other,
> it offends the animals, who in consequence will not suffer themselves to be
> caught.[17]

If the folk beliefs of traditional cultures in historical times are any
guide, our remote ancestors may never have considered that death means
annihilation. One might argue that Darwinian natural selection selects *for*
humans who avoid separation of their soul from their body. But we may
question whether the many time-consuming ascetic practices and taboos
that traditional cultures have imposed created any true selective advantage
for the believers.

> There is assigned to every animal a definite life term which cannot be
> curtailed by violent means. If it is killed before the expiration of the
> allotted time the death is only temporary and the body is immediately
> resurrected in its proper shape from the blood drops, and the animal
> continues its existence until the end of the predestined period, when the
> body is finally dissolved and the liberated spirit goes to join its kindred
> shades in the Darkening land.[18]
>
> —*Traditional Cherokee belief*

Alper assumes, for some reason, that all religion resembles the typical
Western type. Reviewer Michael Joseph Gross picks up on this problem:

Alper's evolutionary argument requires him to describe religion in universal terms but his ideas about religion are strictly Western, monotheistic and personal; and his representation of religious worldviews is exclusively dualistic.... This argument is a clay pigeon, and could be blown away from any number of angles. The word "Asia" should suffice.[19]

Indeed.

The Science Missing

What about the specific claim that there is a "God" part of the brain? If there is, finding it should be easy. Today, a neuroscientist can watch activity in specific parts of the brain of a subject, via functional magnetic resonance imaging (fMRI), as demonstrated in Chapter Nine.

Specific parts of the brain trigger religious belief as a survival mechanism? Complex cognitive and emotional processes have been shown to be mediated by neural networks comprising several brain regions, so it is very unlikely that there is a "God" part in the brain responsible for spiritual cognitions, sensations, and behaviors. Alper seems unfamiliar with neuroscience and never comes close to providing specific, detailed information. Instead, we read statements like this one:

> Rather than allowing ... fears to overwhelm and destroy us, perhaps nature selected those whose cognitive sensibilities compelled them to process their concept of death in an entirely new fashion. Perhaps after hundreds of generations of natural selection, a group of humans emerged who perceived infinity and eternity as an inextricable part of self-consciousness and self-identity. Perhaps a series of neurological connections emerged in our species that compelled us to perceive ourselves as spiritually eternal.[20]

Alper's claims are built on "perhapses," an unusual approach for a person who yearns for a strictly scientific basis[21] for understanding the complex of human religious, spiritual, or mystical behaviors. Hallmarks of a good theory in science are testability and falsifiability, and Alper's hypothesis does not pass these tests. It is unlikely to be correct in any event, because it does not address key relevant facts.

Alper is but one of many who have sought in evolutionary biology and neuroscience a materialist explanation for the spiritual nature of humans.

His book stays in print, and he lectures at various universities. And there is always a following.

But wait, what if someone actually *found* a gene that correlates with religiosity and religious experiences? Geneticist Dean Hamer claims to have done just that. We consider his work next.

God in Our Genes

In *The God Gene* I propose that spirituality has a biological mechanism akin to birdsong, albeit a far more complex and nuanced one.[22]
—*Behavioral geneticist Dean Hamer*

When tribes living in remote areas come up with a concept of God as readily as nations living shoulder to shoulder, it's a fairly strong indication that the idea is preloaded in the genome rather than picked up on the fly. If that's the case, it's an equally strong indication that there are very good reasons it's there.[23]
— *Jeffrey Kluger et al.,*
Time, *on Hamer's "God gene"*

If someone comes to you and says, "We've found the gene for X," you can stop them before they get to the end of the sentence.[24]
—*Medical geneticist John Burn*

Dean Hamer, chief of gene structure at the U.S. National Cancer Institute, thinks that he has indeed found God in our genes. He says that he has identified a gene that codes for the production of neurotransmitters that regulate our moods. *Time* magazine, quick to pick up on the significance of such a finding, reports "Our most profound feelings of spirituality, according to a literal reading of Hamer's work, may be due to little more than an occasional shot of intoxicating brain chemicals governed by our DNA."[25] *Time's* qualification "literal reading" seems superfluous because Hamer says, "I think we follow the basic law of nature, which is that we're a bunch of chemical reactions running around in a bag."[26]

When Dean Hamer was thirteen years old in 1966, a magazine left on the coffee table in the family den forged an indelible memory: "Although I must have seen hundreds of covers, I remember only one. It had no photograph or artwork, just a simple question printed in red ink on a black background, "*Is God Dead?*"[27] That was, of course, the Good Friday 1966 edition of *Time,* discussed in Chapter One. Looking back, Hamer sees that God is not dead—but is he simply a quirky gene?

Hamer started researching the question privately while looking at the relationship between smoking and addiction for the National Cancer Institute. In the standardized, 240-question Temperament and Character Inventory (TCI) personality test, administered to 1,000 volunteers, there is a measure for "self-transcendence." The measure, designed by psychiatrist Robert Cloninger, of Washington University, is thought to identify the ability to have spiritual experiences, which he describes as self-transcendence, a feeling of connectedness to a larger universe, or mysticism (in the TCI's terms, an openness to things not literally provable).

Hamer stresses that the TCI is not to be confused with typical descriptions of religious belief or practice. It is, in his words,

> independent of traditional religiousness. It is not based on belief in any particular God, frequency of prayer, or other orthodox religious doctrines or practices. Instead, it gets to the heart of spiritual belief: the nature of the universe and our place in it. Self-transcendent individuals tend to see everything, including themselves, as part of one great totality.... Non-self-transcendent people, on the other hand, tend to have a more self-centered viewpoint.[28]

It could mean a passion for the environment, social justice, or the pursuit of science. It does not include unconditional love and long-term positive changes in attitude and behavior, which, as Chapters Seven and Eight show, should be considered critical components of claims about spirituality or religion.

Hamer's Work

Would Hamer's work discredit the idea that there is a God? Not necessarily. As Hamer himself says, "My findings are agnostic on the existence of God. If there's a God, there's a God. Just knowing what brain chemicals are involved in acknowledging that is not going to change the fact."[29] Indeed, in the *Time* article, Buddhist studies professor Robert Thurman argued that the finding would bolster a popular Buddhist concept that we inherit a spirituality gene from our previous incarnation: "Smaller than an ordinary gene, it combines with two larger physical genes we inherit from our parents, and together they shape our physical and spiritual profile." As Thurman sees it, "The spiritual gene helps establish a general trust in the universe, a sense of openness and generosity."[30] But what evidence is there that any "spiritual gene" literally exists?

Hamer's Evidence

The basic idea behind Hamer's work is that self-transcendence is an adaptive trait (a trait that promotes survival and the ability to produce fertile offspring). As such, he sought it in a gene that we inherit because it is useful. He studied nine genes that promote the production of brain chemicals called monoamines—including serotonin, norepinephrine, and dopamine. These chemicals regulate mood as well as motivation. Monoamines are the chemicals that antidepressants attempt to control.

He argues that a variation in a gene known as VMAT2 (vesicular monoamine transporter) is the "God gene" responsible for coding this adaptive trait. According to his findings, VMAT2 (a C rather than an A at position 33050 of the human genome) seemed directly related to

---

A Question of Self-transcendence?

Researchers sometimes use checklists of traits or ask standard questions of their subjects so that they can compare their approaches to spirituality. The following are some traits commonly associated with spiritual experiences, and some questions that might appear on questionnaires. Self-transcendence:

    self-forgetfulness (gets lost in an experience)

    transpersonal identification (feels connected to larger universe)

    mysticism (openness to things not literally provable)

Some items on a self-transcendence scale (from *Beliefnet*):

Q1: When I'm doing something I like or am used to (like gardening or jogging), I often "zone out," getting lost in the moment and forgetting my concerns.

Q2: I often feel a strong spiritual or emotional connection with all the people around me.

Q3: There have been moments when I suddenly had a clear, deep feeling of oneness with all that exists.[31]

volunteer scores on the test for self-transcendence. Volunteers for whom the nucleic acid cytosine (C) was found in one specific place on the gene ranked higher. Others, for whom another nucleic acid called adenine (A) occupied the same place ranked lower. So, he argues, a single gene change relates directly to self-transcendence. (Incidentally, one thing Hamer did not find was any correlation between self-transcendence and anxiety,[32] which contradicts Alper's central thesis that religious beliefs arise from anxiety.)

Hamer bolsters his contention with twin studies that appear to show that identical twins are similar in religiosity. He argues:

> Children don't learn to be spiritual from their parents, teachers, priests, imams, ministers, or rabbis, nor from their culture or society. All of these influences are equally shared by identical and fraternal twins who are raised together, and yet the two types of twins are strikingly dissimilar in the extent to which they correlate for self-transcendence.... It must be part of their genes.[33]

Although it is certainly possible that some genetic traits predispose to RSMEs, current popular media quickly befriend any thesis that ascribes behavior to genes. The fat gene,[34] the infidelity gene,[35] and the gay gene (also sponsored by Hamer)[36] have all hit the front page in recent years. Social scientist Hilary Rose notes that in her native Britain, "biological determinist claims that bad behavior (usually about sex or violence) is genetically caused can be guaranteed generous and uncritical media attention, even by science journalists whose knowledge of contemporary genomics ought to have made them more alert to its problems."[37]

Indeed, repeated failure to replicate such findings means nothing in the face of a myth so powerful that it absolves us of the burden of responsibility for our lives.

Scientists on the God Gene

As the poet Keats ruefully noted, philosophy will clip an angel's wings. Popular media adore Hamer's thesis, but the science media have been decidedly less kind. Hamer soon found himself backing away from the position implied in his book's title and in the subsequent *Time* article.[38] He readily admits that even minor human traits involve hundreds or thousands of genes.

At one end of the spectrum, physicist and science writer Chet Raymo, who makes clear that he would *like* to believe Hamer's thesis, pronounces it "frail" and hopes others will defend it better.[39] Science writer Carl Zimmer suggests that VMAT2 is best titled "A Gene That Accounts for Less Than One Percent of the Variance Found in Scores on Psychological Questionnaires Designed to Measure a Factor Called Self-Transcendence, Which Can Signify Everything from Belonging to the Green Party to Believing in ESP, According to One Unpublished, Unreplicated Study."[40] At the far end of the negative spectrum, science writer John Horgan bluntly asks, "Given the track record of behavioral geneticists in general, and Dean Hamer in particular, why does anyone still take their claims seriously?"[41]

It should be noted that the reluctance of scientists to give Hamer's work much credit is *not* because of a global unwillingness to consider genetic determinist explanations. Quite the contrary, as sociologist Dorothy Nelkin notes:

> The language used by geneticists to describe the genes is permeated with biblical imagery. Geneticists call the genome the "Bible," the "Book of Man" and the "Holy Grail." They convey an image of this molecular structure as more than a powerful biological entity: it is also a mystical force that defines the natural and moral order. And they project an idea of genetic essentialism, suggesting that by deciphering and decoding the molecular text they will be able to reconstruct the essence of human beings, unlock the key to human nature. As geneticist Walter Gilbert put it, understanding our genetic composition is the ultimate answer to the commandment "know thyself." Gilbert introduces his lectures on gene sequencing by pulling a compact disk from his pocket and announcing to his audience, "This is you."[42]

Given the awe in which genes have been held, even by geneticists, genetic determinism of spirituality would surely be welcomed by scientists *if* it could be clearly and consistently confirmed by evidence. So mere prejudice is unlikely to have made scientists skeptical of Hamer's findings.

Sibling and Twin Studies

What about the sibling and twin studies? Aren't they, at least, pretty convincing? The trend was actually weak, not strong—less than 1 percent of the total variance.[43] So, assuming the VMAT2 claim holds up (and such claims almost never do), it does not mean much.

Apart from that, one problem with sibling and twin studies in a general area such as RSMEs is that we may be tempted to see sibs and twins as more similar than they actually are.[44] This will be especially likely, given the broad range of behavior that Hamer considers spiritual. For example, he points to two sisters he has met, Gloria and Louise.[45] Gloria has been a devout Christian and churchgoer all her life. Her sister, Louise, after struggling with substance abuse and bad relationships (resulting in four children) for twenty-five years, found God while participating in a twelve-step program. Hamer is struck by the sisters' similarity because they are now both believers. But if we are not *looking for* a sibling effect, we will hardly think their stories similar at all! The fact that both sisters would now say that they are religious may not even be particularly significant, considering that a majority of Americans consider themselves religious in Hamer's sense.[46]

Natalie Angier, reviewing Lawrence Wright's *Twins and What They Tell Us About Who We Are* (1998) for the *New York Times*, notes:

> The stories fed to a fascinated public are rife with tales of reunited twins, like the famous cases of James Lewis and James Springer, who had each married and divorced women named Linda and then remarried women named Betty.... What the public doesn't hear of are the many discrepancies between the twins. I know of two cases in which television producers tried to do documentaries about identical twins reared apart, but then found the twins so distinctive in personal style—one talky and outgoing, the other shy and insecure—that the shows collapsed of their own unpersuasiveness.[47]

Anthropologist Barbara J. King notes as well that siblings should not be assumed to have the same life experiences just because they grow up in the same household:

> One sister's younger years may coincide with a period of parental marital harmony while the other's may intersect with a prolonged divorce that stresses the whole family. Or perhaps one sister merely encounters a certain inspirational teacher or well-loved book that the other does not. Non-shared experiences like these heap contingency upon contingency as each girl develops. In the end, the two sisters may essentially grow up in divergent

emotional environments—and as a result make very different choices about the role of spirituality in their lives.[48]

Obviously, both similarities and differences that are not related to age, such as the influence of specific teachers and books, would affect identical twins as much as fraternal twins and sibs. They may similarly confound genetic interpretations of the ability to have spiritual experiences.

Minimal Evidence and Many Qualifications

In an interview, Hamer told *Beliefnet* that the God gene "refers to the fact that humans inherit a predisposition to be spiritual—to reach out and look for a higher being."[49] No one will likely dispute that in principle, but to what extent is such a predisposition simply an outcome of a human level of intelligence rather than linked to any specific genes? In the end, Hamer's thesis dies the death of minimal evidence aggravated by a thousand qualifications. Carl Zimmer has noted, "The time for writing pop-sci books about the discovery of a 'God gene' is *after* scientists publish their results in a peer-reviewed journal, *after* the results are independently replicated, and *after* any hypotheses about the adaptive value of the gene (or genes) have been tested."[50]

That time may never come. It is a mistake to look for a simple genetic basis for RSMEs. Our genes are the language of our physical lives, and therefore they are not powerless. They can certainly predispose a person to one personality type rather than another, and perhaps to some types of spiritual experiences more than others as a result. Over a century ago, William James, an early psychologist of religion whose work we discuss in detail in Chapter Seven, distinguished between "healthy-minded" and "morbid-minded" tendencies in spirituality. He did *not* mean these distinctions to be necessarily interpreted as "good" versus "bad," but rather that basic personality types can cause attraction to one broad form of spirituality rather than another. In other words, genes help provide the equipment for a sense of self-transcendence and may influence its direction, but they do not *create* the self-transcendence. Therefore, it makes no scientific sense to speak of a "God gene." To do so represents an extreme form of reductionist thinking.

As we will see, the mind-brain system is exceedingly complex. One must beware of the tendency to look for one single, simple explanation for any complex mental phenomena, let alone spirituality. As C. S. Lewis warned, "To 'see through' all things is the same as not to see."[51]

Actually, Hamer has only one foot in genetics anyway. The other is planted on the much softer turf of evolutionary psychology, which we discuss in detail in Chapter Seven. It is easy to see why evolutionary psychology provides an attraction here. If Hamer had indeed found a gene that systematically codes for transcendent spiritual experiences, he would not need to demonstrate that the gene benefited our ancestors, as he attempts to do. If a genetic effect were convincingly demonstrated, its origin would be a side issue at best. There is, for example, a simple genetic combination that results in blue eyes in some ethnic groups. Do blue eyes confer a benefit? Possibly they do in some cases,[52] but a clearly established inheritance pattern accounts for blue eyes. That makes the question of their prehistoric usefulness interesting but ultimately superfluous to an understanding of the origin of the trait. A genetic hypothesis regarding RSMEs must achieve that level of rigor to be scientifically tenable.

In the absence of a clear message from prehistory or genetics, evolutionary psychologists turn to theories based in functional neuroscience. Could there be, for example, a God module, that is, a visible feature or circuit of the brain that provokes the idea of God? Perhaps even a feature that provokes the idea of the divine specifically because it does not work properly?

THREE

Does the God Module Even Exist?

Even though it's common knowledge these days, it never ceases to amaze me that all the richness of our mental life—our religious sentiments and even what each of us regards as his own intimate private self—is simply the activity of these little specks of jelly in your head, in your brain. There is nothing else.[1]

—*Neuroscientist V. S. Ramachandran*

Science is wonderful at explaining what science is wonderful at explaining, but beyond that it tends to look for its car keys where the light is good.[2]

—*Jonah Goldberg,* Jewish World Review

In Mark Salzman's haunting novel *Lying Awake,* Sister St. John of the Cross faces a troubling decision. Decades earlier, she had traded an emotionally deprived childhood for the strict rule of silence, austerity, and prayer in a Carmelite convent near Los Angeles. Convent life offered order and peace, but nonetheless the years rolled on dry and unfulfilling. Then Sister John began to experience strange visions that she turned into beautiful writing, resulting in her popular book *Sparrow on a Roof.* The book helped pay the convent's expenses and even attracted another sister to the order. Indeed, dumpy Sister John became a spiritual "star" of sorts, showered with graces.

But with her visions came some serious headaches. Sister John welcomed them at first, thinking that she must suffer something for the love of God. But then the headaches got worse, and finally seizures ensued. She consulted a neurologist and learned the truth. She had temporal-lobe epilepsy (TLE), caused by a tiny tumor above her right ear. She was told that

> temporal-lobe epilepsy sometimes caused changes in behavior and thinking even when the patient was not having seizures. These changes included hypergraphia (voluminous writing), an intensification but also a narrowing of emotional response, and an obsessive interest in religion and philosophy.[3]

She was also informed that the apostle Paul *and* the foundress of her own religious order, Teresa of Avila, were "likely candidates" for temporal-lobe epilepsy.

The tumor could easily be removed, at which point the visions would cease. So were the visions never more than a disease? Sister John saw that her whole life could be viewed, from a materialist perspective, as a mere pathology, a sort of mental disease:

> The ideal of continual prayer: *hyperreligiosity.* The choice to live as a celibate: *hyposexuality.* Control of the will through control of the body, achieved through regular fasting: *anorexia.* Keeping a detailed spiritual journal: *hypergraphia.*[4]

Should she agree to the operation that would end the visions?

This chapter addresses the question of whether religious, spiritual, or mystical experiences result from brain disorders. For example, is epilepsy the correct explanation for spiritual experiences, as novelist Salzman suggests in his presentation of Sister John's dilemma?

Neurologists Jeffrey Saver and John Rabin at the UCLA–Reed Neurologic Research Center have argued that it might be. They think that epilepsy and RSMEs are closely allied and that the limbic system plays a pivotal role. Also, neuroscientist Vilayanur Ramachandran argues that temporal-lobe epilepsy may be a key trigger in RSMEs.

Are they right? Do brain disorders trigger a sort of God module or God circuit?

Before we get started, perhaps terminology should be clarified. For the purposes of this book, "religious" experiences are experiences that arise from following a religious tradition. Spirituality means any experience that is thought to bring the experiencer into contact with the divine (in other words, not just any experience that feels meaningful). Mysticism generally means pursuit of an altered state of consciousness that enables the mystic to become aware of cosmic realities that cannot be grasped during normal states of consciousness.

Divine Madness

Is epilepsy the *real* explanation for key spiritual experiences?

> Controversial new research suggests that whether we believe in a God may not just be a matter of free will. Scientists now believe there may be physical differences in the brains of ardent believers.[5]
> —*Liz Tucker,* BBC News, *on TLE research*

If newsmagazine articles are ever automated, a good test model would be the spate of reporting in recent years on epilepsy and spirituality.[6] Here's how to automate such an article:

1. Lead off by asking whether "our religious feelings" or "our most sacred thoughts" are "merely" a product of the workings of our brain. (Use the first-person plural for a personal touch.)

2. Define religion, spirituality, or mysticism so broadly as to include the volleyball team's fund-raising car wash, favorite music, or the capacity to wonder about the vagaries of life. Few readers can feel excluded, even if they would prefer to be.

3. Suggest that our brains may be "hardwired" for religion or God. (Speculation about early humans a million years ago comes in handy here, and who can prove you wrong?)

4. Emphasize that the findings, whatever they are, neither prove nor disprove that God exists. (Mustn't alienate religious readers. Their subscriptions are as good as anyone else's.)

5. Strew the article with qualifiers like "may," "might," or "possibly," or "Scientists now believe that so-and-so [a famous religious figure in the past] might have suffered from this type of epilepsy."[7] Paul the Apostle and Joan of Arc are good choices because both were visionaries and recognized martyrs. (The unsupported hypothesis can safely be disowned later if it is consistently hedged by qualifiers.)

6. Hint that little actual neuroscience underlies the proffered speculations, but do *not* contact neuroscientists who would critique the methods or results. (Do, however, encourage religious leaders to express angst or dismay, which appears to strengthen the case.)

Risky story strategy, you say? Not at all! Few readers or viewers know much about epilepsy or about the biographies of well-known religious figures. With any luck, most will not ask the fatal questions: How much of this is science and how much is speculation? And, how much of the speculation is fueled merely by materialist assumptions as opposed to scientific findings? Although it would be nice to say that the recipe above is a gross exaggeration, many stories about the relationship between spirituality and the brain do seem to be constructed in this way, perhaps only because not enough of the right questions have been asked.

Science purists are undoubtedly tempted to ask why media attention and spin matter much anyway. Isn't the science the only thing that matters? Actually, media accounts *do* matter because media interpret science to society. How a society understands scientific findings impacts its commitment to science. When media minimize, overblow, or otherwise distort the significance of neuroscientific findings, neuroscience as a discipline may feel the effect. But let us begin to understand the question by looking at the science.

The Temporal Lobe as the Source of RSMEs

In an influential 1997 paper, University of California neurologists Jeffrey Saver and John Rabin claimed that the limbic system of the brain—a system that lies within reach of the temporal lobes and functions as a medium for emotions—plays a pivotal role in RSMEs.[8] RSMEs, they argue, involve the loss of a sense of self as distinct from the environment and a tendency to see heightened significance in ordinary situations. And because nothing significant *is* actually happening when a person senses such an experience, the experience is difficult to describe in words.[9]

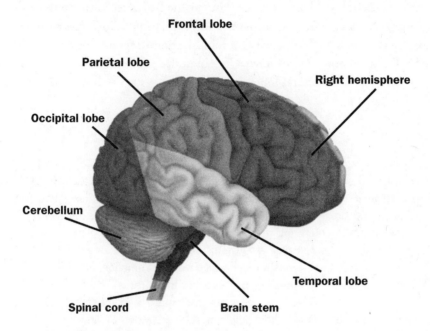

Sagittal view of the four cortical lobes (in the right hemisphere) and the cerebellum, brain stem, and spinal cord.

"The contents of the experience—the visual components, the sensory components—are just the same as everyone experiences all the time," neurologist Jeffrey Saver explained to *New Scientist* in 2001. "Instead, the temporolimbic system is stamping these moments as being intensely important to the individual, as being characterised by great joy and harmony. When the experience is reported to someone else, only the contents and the sense that it's different can be communicated. The visceral sensation can't."[10]

In their journal article, Saver and Rabin also discuss a distinctive type of religion-prone personality,[11] called a "temporal-lobe personality," that they associate with temporal-lobe epilepsy. This form of epilepsy can affect the limbic system. Saver and Rabin propose that many great religious figures of the past may have displayed symptoms of TLE.[12] Their hypothesis has been widely aired and embroidered by popular media. For example, a 2003 BBC program, "God on the Brain," featured two persons with temporal-lobe epilepsy, Rudi Affolter and Gwen Tighe, who experienced strong religious visions, explaining, "He is an atheist; she a Christian. He thought he had died; she thought she had given birth to Jesus."[13]

However, a careful look at Saver and Rabin's hypothesis reveals many weaknesses. First, a number of nonlimbic brain regions play a role in RSMEs, as Chapter Nine shows. So a hypothesis of RSMEs that focuses uniquely on the temporal lobes and the limbic system will necessarily be inadequate.

The Limbic System

The limbic system of the brain is associated with emotions and memories. Found in the middle of the brain, it forms a sort of border (*limbus*) around the brain stem, which governs basic functions like breathing. Above it is the cerebrum, the highly developed specifically human area. The limbic system is called a "system" because it includes a number of brain structures and areas through which we react emotionally. Emotions cannot, of course, be directly observed, but they are associated with activity in the limbic system, which neuroscientists can measure. Some neuroscientists examine the limbic system in order to find clues to RSMEs.

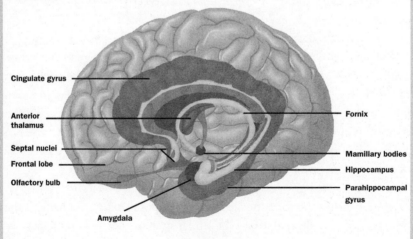

Medial sagittal view of the limbic system.

The mystical experience (as understood in the Christian sense[14]) can include a number of elements: the sense of having touched the ultimate ground of reality and the sense of the incommunicability of the experience, the sense of unity, the experience of timelessness and spacelessness, the sense of union with humankind, the universe, and God as well as feelings of positive affect, peace, joy, and love.[15] Such an experience is usually characterized by visual imagery and alterations of self-consciousness, emotional state, and body schema. As we will see in Chapter Nine, these alterations are associated with neural changes in many brain regions that normally support these functions. In other words, there is no special God module (or center) in the temporal lobes that produces RSMEs.

Second, we must ask whether "temporal-lobe personality" is as readily definable as Saver and Rabin suppose. If so, does it really play a major role in RSMEs? And last, what is the evidence that key religious figures really had TLE?

Key parts of the limbic system are:

The *hypothalamus,* below the thalamus, a sort of central thermostat that regulates body functions such as blood pressure and breathing and also governs the intensity of emotional behavior. The hypothalamus also controls the pituitary gland, the gland that regulates growth and metabolism.

The *amygdala,* located just behind the hypothalamus, which mediates emotions, especially those related to safety or well-being. It is sometimes called the *amygdalas* because it comprises two almond-shaped masses of neurons.

The *hippocampus* is a cerebral structure belonging to the limbic system and located inside the temporal lobe. The hippocampus, which resembles a seahorse, is involved in memory and spatial navigation.

The *fornix* and *parahippocampal gyrus,* connecting pathways of the limbic system.

The *cingulate gyrus,* a layer of neurons above the main connection between the brain's two hemispheres (the *corpus callosum*) that coordinates pleasant sights and smells with pleasant memories. The cingulate gyrus also participates in the emotional reaction to pain and in the regulation of emotion.

Temporal-Lobe Epilepsy (TLE)

The temporal lobes of the brain are located, one on each side of the head, just above the ears. TLE, a brief disturbance in normal brain electrical functions, is one of the commonest types of epilepsy, though there are no reliable statistics on how many people suffer from it.[16] TLE is not to be confused with the dramatic "tonic clonic seizures," sometimes known as "grand mal" seizures, that usually result in unconsciousness. However, about half of persons who experience TLE also have tonic clonic seizures.

Most often, TLE begins with simple partial seizures, involving voices, music, smells, tastes, forgotten memories, or unusually intense feelings.[17] These hallucinations, called auras, are brief—perhaps a smell such as lavender or rotten eggs. The brain state may then progress to a complex, partial seizure that classically results in lip smacking, rubbing the hands together, or other unconscious actions for about half a minute to two minutes. All these effects are called "partial" seizures because they affect only a part of the brain. (By contrast, a tonic clonic seizure affects the whole brain, which is why unconsciousness is the usual outcome.) TLE can result from a tumor, a head injury, or brain infection, but many cases are of unknown cause (idiopathic).

Treatment may include medication, surgery, diet, electrical stimulation of the vagus nerve, or biofeedback, but the most common treatment is medication. About half of children who have the disorder simply outgrow it, but repeated attacks of TLE in adults can lead to memory loss. Depression and anxiety are common side effects if TLE does not improve over time.[18]

Temporal-Lobe Personality

Is there a temporal-lobe personality that predisposes a person to temporal-lobe epilepsy (TLE)—and thus to religious experiences?

Early in the nineteenth century, the view originated that a certain type of religious intensity was associated with TLE, as described above. "Hyperreligiosity and intense philosophical and cosmological concerns" were said to be key features between epileptic episodes of this "putative syndrome,"[19] often called the Geschwind syndrome. The personality type was also characterized by "hypermoralism, deepened affects, circumstantiality, humorlessness, interpersonal viscosity [a tendency to cling to others in a way that may damage relationships], aggressive irritability, and hypergraphia."[20] Russian novelist Fyodor Dostoevsky is often cited as an excellent example of a temporal-lobe personality.[21]

However, despite the frequent citations in popular literature, subsequent research has not really borne much fruit. Some researchers have reported high religiosity scores among temporal-lobe patients, but others haven't.[22] The story gets even more complicated because University of Chicago neurologist John R. Hughes, who has investigated many claims about epilepsy in historical figures, notes that Vincent van Gogh, who definitely had a "temporal-lobe personality" that included religiosity, probably did *not* have TLE. Rather, van Gogh's losses of consciousness most likely stemmed from serious substance abuse.[23]

The putative Geschwind syndrome has not been recognized in standard diagnostic manuals. For example, the publicly accessible Pub Med database had this to say about the syndrome as of August 2006:

A characteristic personality syndrome consisting of circumstantiality (excessive verbal output, stickiness, hypergraphia), altered sexuality (usually hyposexuality), and intensified mental life (deepened cognitive and emotional responses) is present in some epilepsy patients. For identification, the term "Geschwind syndrome" has been suggested as a name for this group of behavioral phenomena. Support for, and criticism against, the existence of this syndrome as a specific personality disorder has produced more fire than substance, but the presence of an unsettled, ongoing controversy has been acknowledged. At present, the strongest support stems from the many clinicians who have described and attempted to manage seizure patients with these personality features. Carefully directed studies are needed to confirm or deny that the Geschwind syndrome represents a specific epilepsy/psychiatric disorder.[24]

In other words, there is a good question whether the syndrome actually exists. Most epileptologists today do not think that religiosity typically characterizes people with TLE.[25]

The picture that emerges is that TLE is often associated with obsessiveness. A small minority of patients may become obsessive about religion—as opposed to art, sports, sex, or politics, for example—but one cannot build a theory of religion on that alone.

Still, it is worth asking, is epilepsy associated in some way with vision or risk taking? After all, it has been regarded in the past as a sort of divine madness.

Famous People with "Epilepsy"

One is struck by the number of charismatic historical figures who are reported to have had epilepsy or, specifically, TLE. Pythagoras, Aristotle, Alexander the Great, Hannibal, Julius Caesar, Dante, Napoleon Bonaparte, Jonathan Swift, George Frederic Handel, Jean-Jacques Rousseau, Ludwig von Beethoven, Sir Walter Scott, Fyodor Dostoevsky, Vincent van Gogh, Lord Byron, Percy Bysshe Shelley, Edgar Allan Poe, Alfred Lord Tennyson, Charles Dickens, Lewis Carroll, Peter Tchaikovsky, and Truman Capote, to name only a few. Could there be some connection between epilepsy and vision or creativity in general? Patient literature often cites a number of historical figures who are said to have had epilepsy, undoubtedly to boost the self-esteem of the newly diagnosed patient.

Popular culture also accepts the mystique of epilepsy—to a degree that has invited concern. Sallie Baxendale, of the British National Society for Epilepsy, has complained that when epilepsy is shown in films,[26] "The dramatic potential of seizures is highly tempting to writers and directors with fertile imaginations." Men with epilepsy are "mad, bad and often dangerous," while women are "exotic, intriguing and vulnerable."

Epileptologist Hughes made detailed studies of the famous persons named above and concluded that, based on the available evidence of symptoms and family history, only Julius Caesar, Napoleon, and Dostoevsky definitely or probably had epilepsy.[27] Why were the others thought to have epilepsy when they likely didn't? For centuries, the term "epilepsy" was so comprehensive that it included all trancelike states. By contrast, an epileptic seizure—as understood today—is a sudden, temporary change in brain activity[28] that causes neurons to fire repeatedly, much faster than usual, until abnormal, automatic behavior or unconsciousness results.

Seizures can occur from a number of causes other than epilepsy. They can be caused by, for example, a sudden drop in blood pressure, low blood sugar, severe emotional stress, or withdrawal from drugs or alcohol.[29] These nonepileptic seizures may result in unconsciousness, but they are *not* directly caused by the abnormal firing of neurons that originates within the brain.

Hughes offers a variety of reasons[30] for mistaken modern diagnoses of famous individuals, including:

> *Simple mistake, repeated many times.* Historical records do not provide evidence that mathematician Pythagoras (582–500 B.C.E.), philosopher Aristotle (384–322 B.C.E.), or military commander Hannibal (247–183 B.C.E.) suffered any type of seizure disorder.

> *Losses of consciousness that are not seizures.* Michelangelo (1475–1564), for example, was apparently overcome by heat (heat syncope) while painting, not by epilepsy.

> *Socially aberrant behavior that does not include loss or alteration of consciousness.* In unpleasant social situations, Leonardo da Vinci (1452–1519) suffered from "spasms" that sound like panic attacks rather than epilepsy.

> *Alcohol/drug withdrawal seizures.* Some literary and artistic figures suffered seizures from drug withdrawal (Lewis Carroll, 1832–98) or alcohol withdrawal (Algernon Charles Swinburne, 1837–1909; Vincent van Gogh, 1853–90; Truman Capote, 1924–84; Richard Burton, 1925–84).

> *Psychogenic attacks.* These attacks, sometimes called "pseudoseizures," are triggered by specific psychological stress rather than spontaneous electrical discharges in the brain.[31] Lord Byron (1788–1824) and Gustav Flaubert (1821–80), both of whom experienced severe emotional stress, are suggested candidates.

Folk belief readily diagnoses epilepsy in famous visionary, creative, or charismatic persons who have any type of seizure[32] or sudden loss or alteration of consciousness[33] because epilepsy is stereotypically associated with (allegedly) mad visionaries or otherwise exotic people. Granted that folk belief is usually mistaken about historical figures, what about specifically religious ones? Might they not disproportionately suffer from epilepsy?

Religious Figures and Temporal-Lobe Epilepsy

What about specifically religious figures? Isn't it likely that most religious visions were the product of temporal-lobe epilepsy? In the current literature, researchers have suggested that many famous religious figures suffered from TLE. Saver and Rabin, for instance, suggested that the apostle Paul, Joan of Arc, Teresa of Avila, and Thérèse of Lisieux[34] might have had TLE. What does the evidence suggest?

Paul the Apostle (?–65 C.E.). Apart from the accounts in the New Testament, there is almost no historical data for the life of Paul (also called Saul[35]), who founded some of the earliest Christian churches. A Jew who was also a Roman citizen, Paul had studied under the great rabbi Gamaliel (Acts 22:3). But unlike his teacher he leaned toward fanaticism and actively persecuted the early Christian sect. He was on just such an errand when he had his "Damascus road" vision:

> Meanwhile, Saul was still breathing out murderous threats against the Lord's disciples. He went to the high priest and asked him for letters to the synagogues in Damascus, so that if he found any there who belonged to the Way, whether men or women, he might take them as prisoners to Jerusalem. As he neared Damascus on his journey, suddenly a light from heaven flashed around him. He fell to the ground and heard a voice say to him, "Saul, Saul, why do you persecute me?"
>
> "Who are you, Lord?" Saul asked.
>
> "I am Jesus, whom you are persecuting," he replied. "Now get up and go into the city, and you will be told what you must do."
>
> The men traveling with Saul stood there speechless; they heard the sound but did not see anyone.[36]

Paul spent the rest of his life founding and administering churches. A variety of materialist explanations have been offered for his vision.[37] One obvious suggestion is that heat prostration, aggravated by a sense of guilt over his extensive (and essentially volunteer) mission of persecution, had rendered him very suggestible.

But the specific claim that Paul had epilepsy stems from his mention of a mysterious "thorn in the flesh" (2 Cor. 12:7–9)[38] plus the fact that he undoubtedly had a mystical bent.[39] Saver and Rabin suggest that the thorn may be TLE.[40] But epilepsy is among the *least* likely explanations, given the word he used (*skolops,* "thorn"). Generally, a "thorn," in the language of the day, meant a source of irritation rather than a serious problem such as an illness.[41] More than two hundred interpretations[42] have been offered for the thorn, including homosexuality, bad eyesight, marsh fever, and poor public speaking skills. There is no independent evidence that Paul ever had any type of epilepsy.

Joan of Arc (1412–31). Joan was born near the end of the Hundred Years' War between France and England, which had devastated France. A pious peasant girl, she began to hear voices when she was thirteen, which she identified as the voices of saints and angels. They advised her to raise the English siege of Orleans and take the dauphin (crown prince) to the traditional place of coronation at Rheims to be crowned as king of France. Such a move would unite the French people around a workable government. Remarkably, by the time she was seventeen, Joan met these goals. However, she was later captured and sold to the English, who had her tried and burned at the stake as a heretic. Like Paul, Joan has been posthumously subjected to many diagnoses to account for her visions, including schizophrenia, bipolar disorder, tuberculosis, and of course TLE. The sheer variety of diagnoses should arouse suspicion.

There is much more documentation of Joan's life than of Paul's, if only because her captors were anxious to introduce evidence at her meticulously recorded trial to discredit her cause in the eyes of the French people. It emerged that Joan's complex, lucid visions often lasted for hours—which rules out epilepsy. Hughes notes:

> The possibility that Joan of Arc's voices and visions were epileptic phenomena has been considered, but clearly auditory and visual hallucinations are very uncommon in epilepsy. Epileptic phenomena are nearly always brief and primitive, like light flashes; the well-formed visions she described lasted hours, rather than just a minute or so. Thus the extremely pious and religious Joan of Arc likely experienced religious messages, rather than epileptic phenomena.[43]

Also, serious TLE, involving daily seizures, typically worsens over time,[44] but Joan showed no evidence of mental deterioration during her extremely demanding military life, lived almost entirely under watchful (and often hostile) eyes. Also, the military and political advice she attributed to her voices was generally sound, which undermines an explanation limited to disorder or disease.

Joan's voices can be interpreted in a materialist way. That is, she can be seen as a military genius in a culture that would refuse to recognize a peasant girl as such. Her culture did, however, offer the role model of the holy virgin who experiences visions and utters prophecies. In that case, she might experience her ideas as visions and utter them as prophecies. Catholic Christians would understandably discredit an explanation of this type. But at least it avoids the problem with most materialist explanations: the tendency to ascribe Joan's astounding career to a disease, when the *content* of her messages was in no way delusional. However, neuroscience cannot determine questions such as that, certainly not in the past tense. We *can* say, however, that the evidence does not suggest that Joan suffered a brain disorder.

Teresa of Avila (1515–82) and *Thérèse of Lisieux* (1873–97). The lives of Teresa of Avila and Thérèse of Lisieux are very well documented by themselves in their autobiographical writings as well as by others. Both women suffered many ailments, and Thérèse died young from tuberculosis, but there is no evidence that either suffered from temporal-lobe epilepsy.

Generally, the literature arguing for a link between TLE and RSMEs is not very convincing, for a number of reasons:

Well-documented intellectual[45] *or ecstatic auras*[46] *are extremely rare.* In fact, for neurological reasons, epileptic auras are almost always unpleasant,[47] and fear is the commonest emotion.[48]

Findings may be overinterpreted. Researchers' interest may be piqued by reported experiences of unreality of either the self or the external environment,[49] but these feelings may not be interpreted by the subject as RSMEs. Neurologist Orrin Devinsky admits that questionnaire responses from epileptics between seizures have "produced very mixed results,"[50] probably at least partly for that reason.

Too great reliance may be placed on old literature. Psychiatrist Kenneth Dewhurst and physician A. W. Beard (1970) note that "Conversion experiences ... are uncommon in the recent literature."[51] They then cite[52] six patients whose birth dates range between 1900 and 1921 who experienced religious (or, in one case, "de-religious") conversions following an epileptic attack, from a sample of sixty-nine.[53] Under the circumstances, it is hard to know how much of a role epilepsy specifically plays in these cases. Any serious health setback may result in a patient paying increased attention to religion, especially in a society where evangelical religion is part of the culture and religious counselors are readily available, often sponsored as chaplains by the medical institution.

The number of cited cases is often small. For example, Saver and Rabin cite a 1994 study of a family that exhibited a genetic tendency toward frontal dementia, in which three of twelve members showed "hyperreligious behavior."[54] It is not unusual in a large family group for a minority of members to be quite religious (often they have influenced each other in that direction).

RSMEs are relatively common in the population and do not require a medical explanation. As Saver and Rabin themselves note, religious-numinous experiences are common in both children and adults across different historical eras and across all cultures. In national surveys in the United States, Britain, and Australia, 20–49 percent of individuals report having personally had RSMEs, and this figure rises to more than 60 percent when in-depth interviews of randomly selected individuals are conducted.[55] Under the circumstances, there is no clear reason for invoking a rare or disputed syndrome to explain or shed light on such experiences.

Indeed, it is safe to say that (1) most people who have RSMEs are not epileptics; and (2) very few epileptics report RSMEs during seizures. If epilepsy really produced RSMEs, all or most epileptics would have them. Clearly, epilepsy simply does not play the role that Saver and Rabin have suggested.

As Devinsky has noted, "The genesis of intense religious experiences associated with neurological disorders remains poorly defined."[56] The most likely reason is that neurological disorders are not a particularly fruitful avenue for understanding intense religious experiences.

But what if neuroscientific evidence can *clearly* link certain epileptic brain states with religious convictions? Has neuroscientist Vilanayur Ramachandran found such evidence?

Epileptics and a "God Switch"

If we can selectively enhance religious sentiments, then that seems to imply there is neural circuitry whose activity is conducive to religious belief. It's not that we have some God module in our brains, but we may have specialised circuits for belief.

I find it ironic that this sense of enlightenment, this absolute conviction that Truth is revealed at last, should derive from limbic structures concerned with emotions rather than from the thinking, rational parts of the brain that take so much pride in their ability to discern truth and falsehood.[57]

— *Neuroscientist V. S. Ramachandran*

As we have seen, the hypothesis of a general connection between epilepsy (as understood today) and RSMEs is weak at best. However, we can't simply rule out the possibility that some epileptics may accidentally activate a "God circuit" during a seizure.

A specific model of neuroscience underlies that idea. Pioneer surgeons and neuroscientists such as Paul Pierre Broca (1824–80) and Carl Wernicke (1848–1905) first learned which brain area usually correlates with a spe-

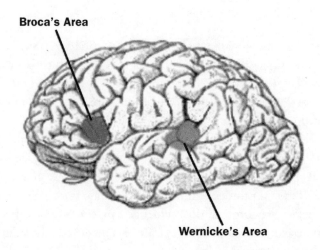

Sagittal representation of the brain displaying Broca's area and Wernicke's area, two key structures in the use of language.

cific ability by studying patients who had lost the use of that area through brain damage. For example, an inability to speak pointed to "Broca's area" of the brain and an inability to understand speech pointed to "Wernicke's area." In the last half century, some epileptics have had their brains surgically split or half removed to counteract uncontrollable seizures.[58] They, along with amputees who continue to feel pain in vanished limbs, have shed much light on the organization (and reorganization) of the human brain by volunteering for research.

Following this model—we understand health by observing pathology—V. S. Ramachandran has attempted to pinpoint a God circuit by looking at temporal-lobe epileptics who are thought to be obsessively religious.

> By the deficits, we may know the talents, by the exceptions, we may discern the rules, by studying pathology we may construct a model of health.[59]
> —*Neuropsychologist Laurence Miller*

> By studying neurological syndromes that have been largely ignored as curiosities or mere anomalies we can sometimes acquire novel insights into the functions of the normal brain—how the normal brain works.[60]
> —*Neuroscientist V. S. Ramachandran*

Can an Experiment Decide?

Ramachandran, director of the Center for Brain and Cognition at the University of California at San Diego, suggested in 1997 that he might indeed have uncovered a God circuit in the human brain that could underpin an evolutionary instinct for believing in religion. Media acclaim, of course, immediately followed. His team advanced expansive claims at the 1997 Society for Neuroscience meeting in New Orleans, including the following:

> There may be dedicated neural machinery in the temporal lobes concerned with religion.

> This may have evolved to impose order and stability on society.

> The results indicate that whether a person believes in a religion or even in God may depend on how enhanced is this part of the brain's electrical circuitry.[61]

More cautious than some of his admirers, Ramachandran has admitted that he is "skating on thin ice" with some of his ideas.[62]

One hypothesis that he had originally considered was that his hypothetical religious circuits are randomly strengthened by an epileptic attack, so that

> everything and anything acquires a deep significance, and when that happens, it starts resembling a religious experience. And if we can selectively enhance religious sentiments, then that seems to imply there is neural circuitry whose activity is conducive to religious belief.[63]

In other words, the random excess firing of neurons during the seizure causes the person to attribute mystical significance to everything.[64]

On the other hand, Ramachandran suggested another hypothesis to consider: "Could it be that human beings have actually evolved specialized neural circuitry for the sole purpose of mediating religious experience?"[65] He thought that the tendency to random excess firing might have evolved because religious experiences aided human survival.

He also thought of a way to decide between these two hypotheses:

> I contacted two of my colleagues who specialize in the diagnosis and treatment of epilepsy.... Given the highly controversial nature of the whole concept of "temporal lobe personality" (not everyone agrees that these personality traits are seen more frequently in epileptics), they were quite intrigued by my ideas. A few days later, they recruited two of their patients who manifested obvious "symptoms" of this syndrome—hypergraphia, spiritual leanings and an obsessive need to talk about their feelings and about religious and metaphysical topics.[66]

He then devised an experiment that involved the two TLE patients and a group of volunteers, of whom some were known to be highly religious and some were of unknown type or strength of belief. His team showed all participants a random sample of about forty words and images. Some words or images were ordinary, but others were chosen to provoke a reaction. Included were

> words for ordinary inanimate objects (a shoe, vase, table and the like), familiar faces (parents, siblings), unfamiliar faces, sexually arousing words and pictures (erotic magazine pinups), four-letter words involving sex, ex-

treme violence and horror (an alligator eating a person alive, a man setting himself afire) and religious words and icons (such as the word "God").[67]

How did Ramachandran know how the participants responded to the words they were shown? Electrodes attached to their hands measured the electrodermal response (EDR). In most people, areas of the hand are highly sensitive to emotions. There is a relationship between sympathetic nervous system activity (increased sympathetic activation) and emotional arousal, but that does not mean that the specific emotion can be identified. (The sympathetic nervous system is activated when stress or danger is perceived; the autonomic nervous system controls automatic activities such as heart rate and breathing.) Fear, anger, startle response, orienting response, and sexual feelings may produce similar EDRs.

Measured from the palm or fingertips, changes in the relative conductance of a small electrical current can be measured between electrodes. The change reflects sweat-gland activity and changes in the sympathetic nervous system as well as measurement variables—in Ramachandran's study, the variable was the intensity of the subject's emotional reaction to certain words. Conductance will increase if the activity of the sweat glands increases in response to sympathetic nervous stimulation.

In Ramachandran's study, the two religiously oriented temporal-lobe epileptics responded much more strongly to the religious words than to the ones about sex and violence. He therefore concluded that the first of the two hypotheses—that the person attributes mystical significance to anything and everything because of the random excess firing of neurons—had been ruled out. That first hypothesis couldn't be correct because the two TLE patients found only the religious words meaningful. If it had been correct, they should have found *all* the words that arouse strong emotions meaningful.

Ramachandran admits that, with only two TLE patients, it is impossible to draw conclusions. Indeed, he cautions:

> Not every temporal lobe epilepsy patient becomes religious. There are many parallel neural connections between the temporal cortex and the amygdala. Depending on which particular ones are involved, some patients may have their personalities skewed in other directions, becoming obsessed with writing, drawing, arguing philosophy, or, rarely, being preoccupied with sex.[68]

His study has not so far been published in a peer-reviewed journal; despite the publicity it received, it was never more than an abstract for a poster session at the 1997 Society for Neuroscience meeting.[69] But he argues that future studies may support his finding that we have specialized neural circuits for belief.[70]

Apart from lack of confirmation, there are several problems with Ramachandran's approach. The experience of union with God is not associated only with the temporal lobe; the experience is multidimensional. Brain regions implicated are related to awareness of the self, physiological and experiential aspects of emotions, and an alteration of the spatial sense of the self as well as of visual mental imagery.[71]

A more serious problem is that Ramachandran studied EDRs but did not measure *brain activity* while the two groups of subjects were exposed to the various categories of words. As a result, we do not know if the temporal lobe was activated while the epileptic subjects were seeing the religious words. In addition, passive viewing of words did not induce deep mystical states in the subjects with TLE. Based solely on his study, we cannot conclude that the temporal lobe mediates RSMEs.

Overall, two key limitations dog any study of RSMEs that focuses on pathology, such as those of Saver and Rabin, and Ramachandran. First, it may be difficult, as we have seen, to find a sufficient number of good, clear instances of a given pathology. Some proposed pathologies of interest, like "temporal-lobe personality" or the "Geschwind syndrome," are putative and controversial. And conclusions drawn from studies that depend on two individuals with a disputed pathology are risky, to say the least.

Second—and perhaps more important—the original reason for the pathology model was necessity, not excellence! It was the only way that the pioneer neuroscientists could begin mapping the enormous inner space of the brain. Today, neuroscientists can observe the actual workings of the healthy brain in detail. The pathology model may still provide useful information for certain purposes, but it should not remain the model of choice when we can image the brains of neurologically and psychologically *normal* experiencers of RSMEs, as my doctoral student Vincent Paquette and I have done at Université de Montréal (see Chapter Nine).

In conclusion, although the temporal lobes appear to be implicated in the perception of contacting a spiritual reality, as they are in many other types of perception, they are not a "God spot" or "God module."

The God Module

The wound over her ear had closed, but her heart gaped. Her doctor was right—life after epilepsy seemed dull.[72]
—*Mark Salzman,* Lying Awake

In Salzman's novel, *Lying Awake,* Sister John of the Cross decides to have the tumor that is causing her TLE removed, because continuing seizures would burden the other sisters in her religious community. Her visions promptly disappear, and with them her writing career.

As we have seen, the beautifully written novel presents a false dilemma.[73] Erik K. St. Louis, a physician who treats epilepsy, remarks in his review of the book that the temporal-lobe personality is "seen infrequently (if ever!) in clinical practice" and that "few actual patients are so similarly enamored of writing, religious zealotry, or, for that matter, their seizures themselves—most, when offered the opportunity, gladly part with them, when possible."[74] Yes, when possible. Sadly, in the nonfiction world, diseases do not come with ready-made spiritual insights that transform themselves into future best-sellers that can be dramatically sacrificed for the sake of the author's health.[75]

But what if a neuroscientist happened to stumble on a device—a helmet perhaps—that actually causes users to have RSMEs? We now come, in Chapter Four, to the amazing revelations of Michael Persinger and the God helmet.

FOUR

The Strange Case of the God Helmet

By inventing a piece of wired-up headgear that induces "religious" experiences in the people who put it on, Sudbury neurotheologist Michael Persinger has shaken the foundations of faith and science.[1]
—*Robert Hercz,* Saturday Night

Anyone who still doubts the brain's ability to generate religious experiences need only visit neuroscientist Michael Persinger at Laurentian University in the bleak nickel-mining town of Sudbury, Ontario. He claims almost anyone can meet God, just wearing his special helmet.[2]
—*Bob Holmes,* New Scientist

It would be in Mr. Dawkins' interests to experience religion for the first time under Mr. Persinger's helmet. After all, this would prove that mystical visions at last could be controlled by science and no longer were just at the mercy of a supernatural entity.[3]
—*Raj Persaud,* London Daily Telegraph

Could Britain's high priest of atheism, Richard Dawkins, find God merely by trying on a temporal-lobe helmet developed at a Canadian neuroscience lab? Dawkins had famously called religion a "virus of the mind" and "infantile regression."[4] In 2003, in what the BBC's *Horizon* program "God on the Brain" hyped as the ultimate test, the archatheist attempted to find God by donning Canadian neuroscientist Michael Persinger's famous "God helmet."

"Will Dr. Persinger succeed where the Pope, the Archbishop of Canterbury and the Dalai Lama have failed?" shrieked the blurbs. The program recorded Dawkins's forty-minute session in the God helmet, having his temporal lobes stimulated by weak magnetic fields. The odds for an RSME were said to be good. According to Persinger, 80 percent of the people who don his helmet have some kind of RSME. The transcript of "God on the Brain" reads:

> PROF. RICHARD DAWKINS (University of Oxford): If I were turned into a devout religious believer, my wife would threaten to leave me. I've always been curious to know what it would be like to have a mystical experience. I'm looking forward to the attempt this afternoon.
> . . .
> DAWKINS: I'm slightly dizzy.
> NARRATOR: Initially Dr. Persinger applied a field to the right-hand side of Richard Dawkins' head.
> DAWKINS: Quite strange.
> NARRATOR: Then to increase the chances of feeling a sensed presence, Dr. Persinger started to apply the magnetic field to both sides of the head.
> DAWKINS: Sort of a twitchiness in my breathing. I don't know what that is. My left leg is sort of moving, right leg is twitching.
> . . .
> NARRATOR: So after 40 minutes had Richard Dawkins been brought closer to god?[5]

Apparently not. He sensed nothing unusual and described himself as "very disappointed." He had really wanted to experience what religious people say they do. Persinger offered an explanation for Dawkins's insensitivity to the God helmet. He was "well below average" in temporal-lobe sensitivity to magnetic fields:

> We developed a questionnaire a few years ago called temporal-lobe sensitivity and what we found is a continuum of sensitivities from people who are not temporal-lobe sensitive to those who are very sensitive, and the experience end being the temporal-lobe epileptic. In the case of Dr. Dawkins his temporal-lobe sensitivity is much, much lower than most people we run, than the average person, much, much lower.[6]

And the *Horizon* narrator, undaunted by the atheist's intransigence, helpfully explained, "Despite the setback with Professor Dawkins, Dr. Persinger's research on over 1,000 human guinea pigs has gone further than any other to establish a clear link between spiritual or religious experience and the temporal lobes of the human brain."

So do RSMEs depend on temporal-lobe sensitivity to magnetism? Does lack of RSMEs depend on insensitivity? The question is important because, if RSMEs are caused by magnetism, they are irrelevant to any objective spiritual reality outside of ourselves. They will happen randomly to susceptible individuals in magnetic fields of the right direction and strength. According to Persinger, such magnetic fields explain not only RSMEs but also out-of-body experiences (OBEs) and reports of UFO abductions.

Many science journalists have seen Persinger's thesis, or other similar ones, as not only right but inevitable. CNN, BBC, Discovery Channel, popular science print media—all have touted the God helmet. There has been much talk of a new discipline of "neurotheology,"[7] which bridges the gap between science and religion, but mainly—it would seem—by demonstrating that there is nothing much to religion.

That is certainly Persinger's own view. Echoing Dawkins, Persinger has called religion "an artifact of the brain"[8] and "a cognitive virus."[9] Offering a simple explanation for RSMEs, he told *Time* magazine: "Anticipation of our own demise is the price we pay for a highly developed frontal lobe.... In many ways, [a God experience is] a brilliant adaptation. It's a built-in pacifier."[10]

He also thinks that his discovery of the true origin of religion and spirituality might promote world peace. As he explained in a 2002 paper, "Religious beliefs, in large part reinforced by personal experiences of sensed presences, are a persistent and powerful variable in large-scale killings of groups who endorse the belief in one kind of god by other groups who define themselves by a belief in a different god."[11]

> The experimental method is the most powerful tool that we have, that's how we find truth and non-truth.[12]
> —*Neuroscientist Michael Persinger*

Here, as before, the key question we must ask is not whether the God helmet threatens or offends religious people, but does it hold up as *science*?

Dr. Persinger's Remarkable Discovery

The reasons for religion's tenacity have become much easier to identify over the past five years, thanks to advances in several modern fields of study, including a new branch of science known as neurotheology. It seems that our brain structure predisposes us to spiritual belief.[13]
—*Patchen Barss,* Saturday Night

There are very few scientists who have the courage to pursue the essence of human existence.[14]
—*Neuroscientist Michael Persinger*

Astonishing things have happened in this chamber. One woman believed her dead mother had materialized beside her. Another felt a presence so powerful and benign that she wept when it faded.[15]
—*Robert Hercz,* Saturday Night

The God helmet started out as a very attractive idea. After all, many materialist neuroscientists had long hoped to account for RSMEs as bursts of excess electrical activity in the brain. Michael Persinger, an American-born neuroscientist based at Laurentian University in the mid-northern Ontario town of Sudbury in Canada, began research in the 1970s on this specific approach to RSMEs, which culminated in his God helmet project, begun in the early 1980s.[16]

Persinger was particularly interested in the concept of a "sensed presence"—the sense that someone is with us, a second self perhaps—when we are clearly alone.[17] He hypothesized that such experiences occur when the left hemisphere of the brain becomes aware of a sort of right-hemisphere "self."[18] In an early paper (1983), he called additional selves "temporal-lobe transients,"[19] later a "parasitic consciousness" (2002).

But what sort of experience evokes such a sensed presence? Persinger argued that magnetic fields of specific strengths might evoke this elusive presence by causing bursts of electrical activity in the temporal lobes. The sensed presence might in turn account for both traditional mystical experiences and modern accounts of alien abductions. As he told the BBC

Horizon audience, "When we look at correlational data there's an increase in seizures, temporal-lobe seizures and convulsions, when there's an increased global geomagnetic activity all over the earth."[20]

For the most part, an increase in magnetic-field activity is produced by solar flares, seismic activity, radio and microwave transmissions, electrical devices, and other external sources. But it can originate within the brain itself, which, as we have seen, has electrical components. Persinger proposed that these electrical microseizures within the temporal lobes generate a wide range of altered states, resulting in religious and mystical visions, out-of-body experiences, and even recollections of abduction by aliens.

He hoped that his "God helmet,"[21] which stimulates the temporal lobes with electromagnetic waves, would cause most subjects to experience a sensed presence. And that is precisely what he and his colleagues found in a series of studies conducted during the last two decades.

Persinger's Findings

In a study published in *Journal of Nervous and Mental Disorders* (2002), Persinger and Faye Healey reported that under double-blind conditions, they had exposed forty-eight right-handed university students (twenty-four men and twenty-four women) to weak (100 nT to 1 µT) complex, pulsed magnetic fields. The fields chosen were not much stronger than the ones that a computer monitor or a cell phone would generate. These fields were applied in one of three ways: primarily over the right temporoparietal region (the part of the brain located at the intersection of the temporal and parietal cortices), primarily over the left temporoparietal region, or equally across the temporoparietal region of both hemispheres of the brain (one treatment per group). They were applied for twenty minutes while subjects were wearing opaque goggles in a very quiet room. A fourth group was exposed to a sham field condition—that is, subjects were not exposed to a magnetic field, although all subjects were told that they might be.[22] Beforehand, the Hypnosis Induction Profile (Spiegel and Spiegel, 1978) was administered to subjects, to test for suggestibility.

Two-thirds of the subjects reported a sensed presence under the influence of the magnetic fields. But 33 percent of the control (sham-field) group reported a sensed presence too.[23] In other words, Persinger found that twice as many subjects reported a sensed presence under the influence of the magnetic field as those who reported one without a magnetic field.[24]

About half of these subjects stated that they felt "someone else" in the chamber. Another approximate half of the group described a sentient being who moved when they tried to "focus attention" upon the presence. About one-third of subjects attributed the presence to a deceased member of the family or to some cultural equivalent of a "spirit guide." In the study, those who had received more stimulation over the right hemisphere or both hemispheres reported more unusual phenomena than those who had received more stimulation over the left hemisphere.

Persinger concluded two things: that the experience of a sensed presence can be manipulated by experiment, and that such an experience "may be the fundamental source for phenomena attributed to visitations by gods, spirits, and other ephemeral phenomena."[25] The first conclusion is a research result that should be able to be replicated if it is valid. The second is, of course, an opinion.

So that was Persinger's actual finding, as published in the 2002 study in *Journal of Nervous and Mental Disorders*. How the popular science media dealt with his finding is quite another story. The popular science media of our culture have, as we have seen, accepted a role as promoters of materialist ideas about religion. Were they prepared to be appropriately critical of the ideas they chose to promote?

> It may seem sacrilegious and presumptuous to reduce God to a few ornery synapses, but modern neuroscience isn't shy about defining our most sacred notions—love, joy, altruism, pity—as nothing more than static from our impressively large cerebrums. Persinger goes one step further. His work practically constitutes a Grand Unified Theory of the Otherworldly: He believes cerebral fritzing is responsible for almost anything one might describe as paranormal—aliens, heavenly apparitions, past-life sensations, near-death experiences, awareness of the soul, you name it.[26]
> —*Jack Hitt*, Wired

Pop Science Tours Heaven and Hell

Reportedly, over a thousand people have tried on the God helmet.[27] This includes a number of science journalists and authors who have demonstrated their commitment to their discipline by making the pilgrimage to Sudbury, in ever tinier puddle jumpers, to take their personal turn under the helmet. Some have experienced surprising revelations.

British journalist Ian Cotton, who had visited Persinger's lab in order to find explanations for the growth of Pentecostal Christianity in recent decades, admitted, "The truth is, I was scared.... God knows what might be down at the bottom of *my* mind."[28] In the first session, Cotton recalled only his childhood home. In the second session, however:

> A little background sound was added, some vaguely New Age, Eastern temple bell sounds. Appropriately suggestible, my mind began a whole new mental tour, this time with a distinctly Eastern, Tibetan feel. It gradually increased in intensity and conviction, until suddenly, with a kind of booster rocket of realism, I was actually *in* a temple, *in* a line of solemn, Tibetan monks.

Cotton was sure that that he too was a Tibetan monk.[29]

Canadian journalist Robert Hercz, reporting for *Saturday Night*, was neither gladdened nor saddened by any such revelation; indeed, he was disappointed: "It's a brief, distorting, yet enjoyable sensation—but it's not the Meaning of Life." Dr. Persinger explained to Hercz that he was not a good subject for the experiment because he had come with expectations.[30]

Canadian science writer Jay Ingram was a bit luckier. In pursuit of a story on beliefs about extraterrestrial abductions, he hoped to "see" aliens. He recalls:

> Did I see aliens? Unfortunately not. I didn't even have the eerie feeling that someone was there in the chamber with me. My brain might not be prone to such vivid imagery. I did, however, see a series of tiny faces floating in front of me. They look like white Wedgwood china faces, all female, on a dark background, with the faces sometimes changing from one to another as I watched. They were entrancing, if somewhat fleeting.[31]

American journalist Jack Hitt saw girls too. But they were not so spectral:

> I'm not sure what it says about me that the neural sensation designed to prompt visions of God set loose my ancient feelings about girls. But then,

I'm not the first person to conflate God with late-night thoughts of getting laid.[32]

Some helmet wearers, however, have had truly remarkable experiences. British research psychologist Susan Blackmore, writing in *New Scientist*, recounted, among other things:

> Something seemed to get hold of my leg and pull it, distort it, and drag it up the wall. I felt as though I had been stretched half way up to the ceiling.
>
> Then came the emotions. Totally out of the blue, but intensely and vividly, I felt suddenly angry—not just mildly cross but that sort of determinedly clear-minded anger out of which you act—only there was nothing and no one to act on. After perhaps ten seconds it was gone but later was replaced by an equally sudden fit of fear. I was just suddenly terrified—of nothing in particular. Never in my life have I had such powerful sensations coupled with the total lack of anything to blame them on. I was almost looking around the little room to find who was doing it.[33]

Blackmore attributed her experiences to the magnetic-field changes.

The Wave of the Future?

In general, Persinger's electromagnetic wave helmet was treated by the popular science media as a dramatic and revolutionary discovery, as the journalists' comments show. Indeed, the helmet was a perfect science versus religion story; it was thought to deeply challenge religious people but provide only mild discomforts or none for materialists. For example, Jack Hitt wrote in *Wired:*

> To those of us who prefer a little mystery in our lives, it all sounds like a letdown. And as I settle in for my mind trip, I'm starting to get apprehensive. I'm a lapsed Episcopalian clinging to only a hazy sense of the divine, but I don't especially like the idea that whatever vestigial faith I have in the Almighty's existence might get clinically lobotomized by Persinger's demo. Do I really want God to be rendered as explicable and predictable as an endorphin rush after a 3-mile run?[34]

And from Canada's *Saturday Night:*

> The new discipline's [neurotheology's] findings are absolutely consistent, after all, with what science has been doing to religion for 500 years. No one should be shocked. Titillated, maybe, but not shocked.[35]

A third option—off the scale between titillation and shock—is caution. But in stories about the God helmet, caution flags such as the following were seldom, if ever, waved.

Few wondered why the discovery did not attract more attention from neuroscientists. The ability to bypass mental processes and act directly on the brain's neural circuits in order to plant specific types of ideas or trigger specific types of experiences should have been dramatic news in the professional science media. It wasn't. Why not?

The risk that psychological suggestion (the increased probability that we will experience an effect if our surroundings encourage us to anticipate it) *was the likeliest explanation was dismissed or discounted* with surprisingly little consideration of the actual setting[36] of Persinger's experiments. Sudbury is a town of about 160,000 people in a sparsely populated region of Ontario—Canada's second largest province. Persinger had attracted considerable international attention to Laurentian, the local university. How likely is it that students in his own psychology department, from which he recruited for his published experiment (2002), truly did not know what to expect from the "God helmet" in his "Heaven and Hell"[37] chamber? Some journalists, such as Jack Hitt, writing in *Wired,* appeared to sense the possibility, but it was never pursued:

> It may be that all preliminary talk about visions just set my rational left hemisphere into highly sceptical overdrive. Setting me up like that—you *will* experience the presence of God—might have been a mistake. When I bring this up later with Persinger, he tells me that the machine's effects differ among people, depending on their "lability"—Persinger jargon meaning sensitivity or vulnerability. And anyway, the clincher is, "Also, you were in a comfortable laboratory. You knew nothing could happen to you. What if the same intense experience occurred at 3 in the morning in a bedroom all by yourself?"[38]

The lack of consistency of the reported God-helmet experiences triggered no skepticism. For example, *New Scientist* explained:

> What people make of that presence depends on their own biases and beliefs. If a loved one has recently died, they may feel that person has returned to see them. Religious types often identify the presence as God.[39]

But that is just what we should expect if we are accounting for an experience triggered by psychological suggestion. The media of the experience are accounted for by the existing expectations, feelings, memories, and other mental resources of the individual.[40] But *if* the God helmet magnetically induces a neurological effect (as opposed to a psychological effect), should the subjects' experiences be all over the map? The brain is, after all, an organ. Genuine physical effects should result in diagnostic patterns, such as the simple, predictable, and short-lived hallucinations (auras) that precede a temporal-lobe seizure.

Persinger was routinely turned down for Natural Sciences and Engineering Research Council of Canada (NSERC) grants.[41] He was reported to finance most of his research in this area himself, through his work as a clinical psychologist. That does not, in principle, discredit his work, but it raises a question. In a highly secular country like Canada, the fact that Persinger's research might discomfit the religious is not a likely reason for NSERC's lack of interest. It is fair to ask whether Persinger's Canadian colleagues based their negative decisions on concerns that the popular science media have chosen to ignore.

> Research into consciousness is in its infancy, so what actually conjures the sentient presence is anyone's guess.[42]
> —*Robert Hercz,* Saturday Night

Neuroscientists who might offer a note of caution were rarely consulted for media articles. Temporal-lobe activity has been recorded during RSMEs (along with much other brain activity, as we see in Chapter Nine). But, given that Persinger's specific claim is that such experiences can reliably be *triggered* by electromagnetic waves directed at the temporal lobes, his claim must be supported in detail. When Dawkins failed to experience anything that he self-identified as significant, Persinger simply classed him as scoring low on temporal-lobe sensitivity. The difficulty with such an explanation is that Persinger himself developed the concept of temporal-lobe sensitivity. It is not independently validated.[43]

But the biggest single problem is this: *Persinger offers no imaging data*[44] *to support his claims about what is happening in subjects' brains;* rather, he relies on inference from the subjective reports of his subjects. Therefore, it is not possible to determine for certain that his targeted brain locations are in fact triggering (or failing to trigger) the experiences in the subjects or whether the magnetic stimulation is having its intended effect—or any effect at all. Given that neuroimaging techniques are now highly developed, it is interesting that so few of those who wrote about Persinger's work remarked on their absence.

> Dr. Persinger's work suggests that different shapes of field and whether they're applied over the left or right temporal lobe can make a difference to whether the subject experiences god or not.[45]
> —BBC's *"God on the Brain"*

Overall, media reports showed a certain tendency to defensiveness when any doubts did arise. For example, Jay Ingram, who saw the tiny white faces, wrote:

> Is Michael Persinger right that electrical events in the temporal lobes are responsible for the rash of reports of alien abductions? Not that you could demonstrate from my experience. But his hypothesis rings true for me, even though it must be admitted that there are gaps that must be filled in. . . . It's plausible, not proven.[46]

But, given that Ingram was researching a story on alien abductions, surely the *most* plausible explanation for his own vision was suggestion?

Similarly, Robert Hercz, of *Saturday Night,* said about Persinger, "If he's right, paradigms will shift and he'll be celebrated. But even if he's wrong, it's still science."[47] The possibility that Persinger's work might be science, but not *good* science or *up-to-date* science, was rarely considered. A story this good (for materialism) just *had* to be true.

The God Helmet and Popular Science

Jim lives in California and he's into extreme sport. But he's not testing his limits with gravity or exhaustion. His equipment consists of a darkened room, a blindfold, heavy-duty earplugs and eight magnetic coils, linked to a PC and attached to his head with a Velcro headband.

Next weekend the inventor of the Shakti headset, Todd Murphy, will be one of the speakers at the Religion, Art and the Brain festival in Winchester, along with Sufi dancers, the music of John Taverner, psychologists, neuroscientists and pharmacologists. The focus of their talks will be: "The evolution, experience and expression of the religious impulse—what triggers the brain to produce it and why?"

Rita Carter, a scientific advisor to the festival and author of a popular book on neuroscience entitled Mapping the Mind, has described an occasion when she became "at one" with the gas fire and then the whole room and finally the entire universe.[48]

—*Jerome Burnes,* The Times of London

Planting Ideas

Is it possible to plant ideas or memories using neuroscientific techniques? Many governments would find idea-control or memory-planting techniques very useful in dealing with dissident political factions. They would be happy to finance research in the area—if it were considered productive. Indeed, in the 1960s, the Pentagon apparently did fund neuroscientific experiments in this area.[49]

However, in 1978, E. Halgren and colleagues published a retrospective analysis of the mental effects of 3,495 electrical stimulations applied bilaterally to medial-temporal-lobe (MTL) sites in thirty-six human subjects. Halgren and colleagues found that most MTL stimulations (92 percent) failed to evoke any mental response, such as sensations, images, thoughts, emotional reactions, and so forth. These researchers also reported that mental alterations evoked by electrical stimulation of the MTL were highly variable, diverse, and idiosyncratic. These findings support the view that it is not possible to systematically induce a specific mental experience (e.g., RSMEs) by stimulating the temporal lobes, either electrically or magnetically.[50]

A technology for planting specific mental experiences may be impossible. One reason is that, as science journalist John Horgan pointed out in

The culture of popular science is one of unidirectional skepticism—that is, the skepticism runs only in one direction. It is skeptical of any idea that spirituality corresponds to something outside ourselves, but surprisingly gullible about any reductionist explanation for it. Not surprisingly, therefore, before any attempt at replication of Persinger's findings, the God helmet took on a life of its own. Pilgrim science journalists toiled up to Sudbury from distant lands to try it on. To some individuals, the story of the helmet seemed not only inevitable and true, but also ready for incorporation into popular culture and commercialization.

Persinger had foreseen that. He asked journalist Robert Hercz, "Can we use it to decrease the anxiety in an increasingly secular world?"[51] He continued:

> People are dying of cancer, who don't believe in God—we could use that stimulation to allow the feeling of wholeness, to allow the feeling of personal development. In the future, you may find a space in the average home, much like in the Eastern tradition, which is basically your God

a recent article in *Discover,* everyone programs his or her own brain differently. Even lab-rat brains differ from one maze to another and an individual rat brain differs from one maze location to another. University of Arizona neuroscience researcher Bruce McNaughton, a specialist in the area, doubts that there will ever be a dictionary for decoding human memories, "surely more complex, variable, and context sensitive than those of rats." As Horgan explains:

> At best, McNaughton suggests, one might construct a dictionary for a single person by monitoring the output of all her neurons for years while recording all her behavior and her self-described thoughts. Even then, the dictionary would be imperfect at best, and it would have to be constantly revised to account for the individual's ongoing experiences.[52]

Plus, he adds, "This dictionary would not work for anyone else." So movies like *Total Recall, The Matrix,* and *Eternal Sunshine of the Spotless Mind,* where memories are simply planted in people's minds, are exciting premises for science fiction but implausible in reality.

centre, where you sit down, "expose" yourself—it may not be a helmet by then—where you would be able to pursue your personal development. Do we have a technology here that will allow us to pursue the last greatest mystery, which is your own introspection?[53]

His colleague Todd Murphy began marketing a portable, consumer version of the helmet as a New Age device for creating instant spirituality. His neuromarketing goal, he hastened to say, was to "enhance spirituality, not to replace it."[54] Indeed, an entire neuromythology has begun to grow up around the God helmet. Murphy, for example, is exploring ways to marry Darwinian evolutionary theory with the Buddhist doctrine of reincarnation.[55]

> The first thing we need to do is accept the Darwinian theory of natural selection. If we do so, we are left with the conclusion that rebirth is an adaptation which contributed to our survival at some point in the history of our species. If this is so, then the specific mechanisms by which rebirth operates must be the same for everyone, because we all share a common evolutionary ancestry.[56]
>
> *—Todd Murphy, a collaborator*
> *of Michael Persinger*

Murphy now works independently from Persinger, and it is unclear whether his work can properly be classified as academic research at this point. "We don't have any formal studies going on," he told Brent Raynes of *Alternate Perceptions* magazine recently. "Rather people report their experiences and when they're interesting I forward them on to Dr. Persinger quite quickly."[57]

> Most institutions demand unqualified faith; but the institution of science makes skepticism a virtue.
>
> *—Robert K. Merton,* "Science and
> the Social Order"

One-Way Skepticism

Why does the skepticism run one way only? Many who tried on the God helmet pride themselves on their critical thinking. Indeed, some belong to and are honored by official skeptic societies.[58] Susan Blackmore, for example, is a Fellow of the Committee for the Scientific Investigation of Claims of the Paranormal (CSICOP) and was awarded the CSICOP Distinguished Skeptic Award in 1991. She is considered one of Britain's best-known media skeptics. But it is fair to ask what kind of "skeptic" would fail to recognize that the well-established psychology of suggestion easily explains the God-helmet effect, with no need to invoke electromagnetism?

Three factors may help provide an explanation. First, science journalism originated in a culture in which skepticism was aimed only in one direction. Sociologist Richard Flory notes that, beginning in the late nineteenth century, journalists began to see themselves as the natural successors to traditional religious or spiritual leaders. He writes, "Journalism was the ideal successor to religion because it alone could provide the appropriate guidance for both individuals and society."[59] Assuming that materialism is here to stay, many journalists assumed that their role was to promote materialism at the expense of traditional, spiritually oriented ideas of human nature. Journalism was thereafter to be modeled on science, with "objectivity" as a new standard. It would generally provide only trenchant criticism of the religious outlook that it replaced. As Flory notes:

> To the extent that religion was presented as having any positive role, it was in purely functional terms, in the sense that moral precepts from religion might be a source of strength for some individuals, but had no authority for modern society.[60]

The second factor is that an obvious tension in the new order of journalism became apparent fairly early. Objectivity, in the scientist's sense, is not a reasonable goal for the journalist. Responsible journalism (accurate, honest, courageous, empathetic, balanced, and free of conflict of interest) is certainly possible. But the journalist is a subject who writes about the activities of subjects for an audience of subjects. There is no place to stand, while covering a story, that eliminates subjectivity. So, in the new order, what would be the fate of objectivity?

Objectivity came to mean, among other things, hostility to a nonmaterialist approach to RSMEs. Thus, the science journalist's tradition was skeptical of everything *except* materialism. Of that, no skepticism is permitted. Acting as successors to a traditional spiritual perspective that they assume is *already* discredited (without wondering how or why), many journalists fully expect that a gene, drug, neural circuit, or even the God helmet is truly an explanation of RSMEs. Only the details need filling in, it seems.

Last, few science journalists know much about RSMEs. A century ago, Evelyn Underhill, a British Anglican, wrote *Mysticism,* a valuable guide to the thoughts and practices of Western mystics. A basic understanding of Western spirituality, such as could be acquired by reading such works, might prevent many misunderstandings, errors, and false trails. But, omi-

The Nature of Mystical Experiences

Traditional mystics do *not* seek an enlightenment that helps them in daily life or provides them with an unusual experience. They seek to understand ultimate reality in a way that goes beyond personal gain, pain, curiosity, individuality, or even otherworldly joy.[61]

Typically, mystical experience is unique and rare, so that it cannot be described easily in words or images. The ability to describe exactly and in detail what one has seen or experienced, as the God-helmet wearers mostly seem able to do, usually points to an experience that is not mystical.[62]

The mystic is motivated by love, not curiosity. "By love He may be gotten and holden, but by thought of understanding, never."[63] The mystic learns empathy for others, whether human or animal, and sympathy for their sufferings. Other outcomes should be suspect.

Contrary to Persinger's worry that mystical experiences may produce a tendency to religious violence, the mystic is unlikely to enlist in such a cause. Mysticism, as Underhill notes,

is in no way concerned with adding to, exploring, re-arranging, or improving anything in the visible universe. The mystic brushes aside that universe, even in its supernormal manifestations. Though he does not, as his enemies declare, neglect his duty to the many, his heart is always set upon the changeless One.[64]

Chapters Seven and Nine address mysticism in much more detail, but for now it is enough to say that most wearers of the God helmet were not on a mystical quest in this traditional sense.

nously, many journalists do not see any need to know about such things, even when researching a story about RSMEs.

Science thrives on replicated research, and eventually a Swedish neuroscience group did try to replicate Persinger's findings, using equipment borrowed from his own lab.

The God Helmet and the Double Blind

As far as Persinger knows, not a single researcher has been intrigued enough by his magnetic stimulation to start experimenting with it.... In science there is no credibility without replication.[65]
—*Robert Hercz,* Saturday Night

A group of Swedish researchers has now repeated the work, but they say their study involves one crucial difference.[66]
—*Roxanne Khamsi,* Nature News

An understated item in *Nature News* of December 2004 updated the story. A research team at Uppsala University in Sweden, headed by Pehr Granqvist, mirrored Persinger's experiment by testing eighty-nine undergraduate students, some of whom were exposed to the magnetic field and some of whom were not. Using Persinger's equipment, the Swedish researchers could not reproduce his key results. They attributed their findings to the fact that they "ensured that neither the participants nor the experimenters interacting with them had any idea who was being exposed to the magnetic fields, a 'double-blind' protocol."[67]

In a double-blind experiment neither the experimenter nor the subject can influence the results by knowing either (1) what the study is about or (2) whether the subject is a member of the experimental group (where significant things should happen) or the control group (an apparently identical situation where nothing significant should happen). Double blind is difficult to achieve in psychological experimentation on humans because humans are adept at picking up cues, often unconscious ones. When achieved, double blind is highly valued as a "gold standard" in research.

Granqvist's researchers made sure that their experiment was a double blind by using two experiment conductors for each trial. The first conductor, who was not told about the purpose of the study, interacted with the subjects. The second conductor switched magnetic fields off or on without advising either the first conductor or the subject. So if the subject had not already been advised that a religious experience was likely at Granqvist's laboratory, the study conductors were not in a position to provide that clue. The team consulted Persinger's collaborator Stanley Koren to ensure that conditions for replication were optimal.

Study participants included undergraduate theology students[68] as well as psychology students. Neither group was asked for prior information on spiritual or paranormal experiences, nor was any participant told that there was a sham-field (control) condition. Rather, participants were told only that the study investigated "the influence of complex, weak magnetic fields on experiences and feeling states." Personality characteristics that might predispose a person to report an unusual experience were used as predictors for which subjects would report one. These characteristics included absorption (the ability to become completely absorbed in an experience), signs of abnormal temporal-lobe activity, and a "New Age" lifestyle orientation.

Assessing its results, Granqvist's team did not find that magnetism had any discernable effect.[69] No evidence was found for a "sensed presence" effect of weak magnetic fields. The characteristic that significantly predicted the outcomes was personality. Of the three subjects who reported strong spiritual experiences, two were members of the control group. Of the twenty-two who reported "subtle" experiences, eleven were members of the control group. Those subjects who were rated as highly suggestible on the basis of a questionnaire filled out after they completed the study reported paranormal experiences whether the magnetic field was on or off while they were wearing the helmet. Granqvist and colleagues also noted that they had found it difficult to evaluate the reliability of Persinger's findings, "because no information on experimental randomization or blindness was provided," which left his results open to the possibility that psychological suggestion was the best explanation.[70]

Granqvist has charged publicly that Persinger's team's experiments were not really double-blind at all. He explained to *Nature News:*

> The individuals conducting the trials, who were often graduate students, knew what sort of results to expect, with the risk that that knowledge would be transmitted to experimental subjects by unconscious cues. Worse,

he says that the participants were frequently given an inkling of what was happening by being asked to fill in questionnaires designed to test their suggestibility to paranormal experiences before the trials were conducted.[71]

Persinger's team's subjects had completed "Personal Philosophy Inventories" developed by Persinger and Makarec (1993). The inventories, administered in class three months prior to the experiment, asked about "beliefs in conservative religious ideas (e.g., second coming of Christ) or beliefs in exotic ideas (e.g., aliens are responsible for UFO reports)."[72] Although Persinger's team did not know how individual subjects had answered the questions when the helmet tests were run, the subjects themselves must have known that these concepts interested the team.[73]

Also, after spending time under the helmet, Persinger's subjects also completed a scale called EXIT, again developed by Persinger himself. Granqvist comments that it is difficult to assess the results from such independently developed scales. In his view, Hood's mysticism scale and Tellagen's absorption scale (a measure of the ability to become absorbed in an experience, which his own team used) would be more appropriate because a number of researchers have found that these measures of subjective experience provide consistent results over time.[74]

The Granqvist team concluded flatly, "Any future replication, or extant findings cited in opposition to the present results, will also need to be based on a randomized, controlled, double-blind procedure to have credibility."[75] They offered no grand scheme for explaining RSMEs.

Persinger, as might be expected, disputed the Swedish findings. He insisted that some of his studies are double-blind, even though his study conductors may know his general area of interest, and that suggestibility is not a problem. He also argued that Granqvist and colleagues did not generate a "biologically effective signal," because they did not use the equipment properly or for a sufficient length of time.[76] Granqvist dismissed his objections, saying, "Persinger knew ahead of the experiments there would be two times of 15-minute exposures. He agreed to that time. His explanation comes now as a disappointment."[77]

There's only one way to resolve this of course: To have the two teams cooperate to perform a new set of experiments.[78]
            —*Jay Ingram,* Toronto Star

When I went to Persinger's lab and underwent his procedures I had the most extraordinary experiences I've ever had. I'll be surprised if it turns out to be a placebo effect.[79]

> — *Psychologist Susan Blackmore*

Insofar as prospective purchasers of such equipment are high on suggestibility, placing the helmet on their heads in a sensory deprivation context might have the anticipated effects, whether or not the cord is plugged in.[80]

> —*Neuroscientist Pehr Granqvist, on God helmets marketed to consumers*

The reaction of the popular science media, which controls so much of what the public hears about neuroscience, was most interesting. A palpable sense of disappointment hung over the coverage of the Granqvist team's findings—accompanied by a subtle hint that the Swedes must have made errors. The *Economist,* for example, suggested a third series of experiments.[81]

Jay Ingram, who also called for a third series, made the popular science agenda obvious by commenting, "Until then, the skeptics will be depressed, and those who believe there really are mysterious presences in our midst are celebrating."[82] In short, Ingram sees our choices as restricted to either radical materialism or an unsubstantiated belief in "mysterious presences." He ignores the possibility that normal human suggestibility accounts for the God-helmet effect, even though that is by far the most likely explanation, as Granqvist implies. Perhaps we don't always like to admit that we are more likely to experience an emotion or effect simply because we are led to believe that we will—but that is a well-established fact of human psychology. We certainly do not wish to acknowledge that we are more suggestible than others, especially if we pride ourselves on skepticism. But if our skepticism has only ever flowed in one direction, it is quite possible that we will be highly suggestible in that direction.

It's also possible that at least some individuals who tried on the God helmet had never "given themselves permission," so to speak, to experience a spiritual reality until then. For an avowed atheist, the helmet would feel safe because a materialist explanation was readily available. In any event, skepticism has fallen on hard times, indeed, if it must exclude such normal workings of human nature as suggestibility in order to account for the God-helmet effect.

A Path Out of the Wilderness

The Swedes' findings, or lack thereof, raise the spectre of bad science, in which the inability to reproduce an experiment calls neurotheology's methodology into question.[83]
—*Julia C. Keller,* Science and Theology News

The Brocken spectre "looked to every man like his first love."[84]
—*Scholar and author C. S. Lewis (1898–1963)*

The God helmet—has it come to this? A science journalist lamented recently, "If the traditional theory is wrong, scientists will be left struggling to explain how such thoughts and sensations are generated."[85] As it happens, Persinger's electromagnetic hypothesis wasn't exactly a "traditional theory"; it was merely a hot story for a decade or so. In any event, suggestibility easily accounts for the thoughts and sensations generated in his lab, so scientists will not be left struggling for long.

However, the journalist does have a point, even if it is not clearly expressed: materialist neuroscience does a very poor job of accounting for RSMEs. As we have seen, the search for God spots, modules, circuits, and helmets has been a complete waste of time. The hope that neuroscience would quickly identify some simple materialist explanation for the spiritual nature of the human has failed[86] and will continue to fail.

It is important to be quite clear about the implications of that failure. Materialism is a monistic philosophy. If the materialists are right and matter is all there is, then the best materialist theory about RSMEs must be true, even if its beliefs about human nature fly in the face of observation, even if cognitive dissonance is the only way to deal with its assumptions, and even if it is defended by the self-defeating argument that the human brain did not evolve in such a way as to understand that materialism is true. In other words, materialists are compelled to go on looking for God genes, helmets, spots, and modules indefinitely.

The plural of anecdote is not data.[87]
—*Researcher Frank Kotsonis*

You don't see the world as it is. You see it as you are.
—*Talmud*

But there is another way. We need not be materialists. Neuroscience needs a way to understand RSMEs, but it must begin by taking them seriously rather than trying to shuffle them away. What about the possibility, for example, that the human brain evolved so as to enable RSMEs *because they provide some insight into the real nature of the universe?*

A dogmatic faith in materialism requires us to reject such a proposition out of hand. But materialism is not providing useful answers, so we ought to look at the evidence again. Key questions must now be addressed in Chapters Five and Six. First, is a materialist theory of mind even tenable? If not, then it must be rejected even if we do not have another one. And second, what is the scientific basis for a nonmaterialist theory of mind?

FIVE

Are Mind and Brain Identical?

To study the brain is to study ourselves, but in a way that makes us both subject and object. It is as if we were trying to look both in and out of the window at the same time.[1]
—*Professor of religion Greg Peterson*

If one were to study the brain alone, while totally ignoring human behavior and subjective conscious states, one would never learn anything about consciousness or any other mental phenomena.[2]
—*Philosopher of mind B. Alan Wallace*

On July 17, 1990, U.S. president George H. W. Bush and the U.S. Congress jointly proclaimed the 1990s to be the Decade of the Brain. Sound policy reasons for public funding of brain research were duly cited. But it is clear from the proclamation that both Bush and his public very much wanted to know more about the brain for personal reasons. True, more precise knowledge helps us fight diseases and dependencies, but the knowledge is precious for its own sake. As Bush said at the time:

The human brain, a 3-pound mass of interwoven nerve cells that controls our activity, is one of the most magnificent—and mysterious—wonders of creation. The seat of human intelligence, interpreter of senses, and controller of movement, this incredible organ continues to intrigue scientists and laymen alike.[3]

The timing of the decade was good. After over a century of systematic brain research using a variety of methods, new techniques such as positron emission tomography (PET) and magnetic resonance imaging (MRI) were providing neuroscientists with a look into healthy, functioning human brains. They no longer needed to depend on animal studies or wait for the rare case of specific brain damage or unusual surgery.

Essentially, studies of how brain-damaged rats get food pellets can't help us understand human consciousness. Even studies of human beings who have suffered brain damage do not provide a clear picture of what a correctly functioning system—or a system that has successfully repaired itself or compensated for a problem—looks like. But all that was changing fast. Neuroscience was hot. TV host Larry King called the 1990s the decade of the brain. In 1998, William J. Bennett, who had been George H. W. Bush's drug czar, asked "Are neuroscientists the new Masters of the Universe?"[4]

Current Neuroscience

A typical brain contains 100 billion cells—almost as numerous as the stars in the Milky Way galaxy. And each cell is linked by synapses to as many as 100,000 others. The synapses between cells are awash in hormones and neurotransmitters that modulate the transmission of signals, and the synapses constantly form and dissolve, weaken and strengthen in response to new experiences.[5]

—*John Horgan,* Discover

Well, there were challenges too. As religion scholar Greg Peterson points out:

Asked to name the most exotic thing in the universe, most of us would mention either the very large (black holes and supernovas) or the very small (all those spooky little particles). But the most incredible structure in the entire universe may be what is sitting behind our eyeballs. Inside our heads is the most complex and sophisticated device in creation.[6]

Yes, indeed. Much was learned, much revised, and some key doctrines quietly forgotten. More than halfway through another decade, we can look back at surprising discoveries that help focus the key questions we are concerned with.

A central dogma of early neuroscience was that the neurons of the adult brain do not change. However, modern neuroscience now recognizes that the brain can reorganize (this reorganization is called "neuroplasticity") throughout life, not only in early childhood. Our brains rewire to create new connections, set out on new paths, and assume new roles.[7]

One outcome of the discovery of neuroplasticity was a reasonable explanation for the puzzling "phantom limb" syndrome. From the mid-nineteenth century onward, physicians have written—very cautiously, to be sure—about the fact that amputees sometimes feel pain in a limb that no longer exists. The conventional suspicion was that either the doctor misinterpreted the symptoms or the amputee was seeking attention. However, neuroscientist V. S. Ramachandran showed that neurons that once received input from a vanished hand could rewire themselves to report input from the face. If an amputee's brain has not changed its mental map of the body after the amputation, she will experience those feelings as if they came from her vanished hand.[8]

> Of all the organs of the body, the nervous system is unusual in that its total number of cells is fixed at birth. Any neurons that are destroyed are never replaced.... The possibility of restoring function is quite high in the young but gradually declines with age.[9]
> —*Neuroscientist Jean-Pierre Changeux*

> One of the fundamental findings of the last decade is the plasticity of the synapses—their ability to alter their strength in response to experience and the context of a situation. As this happens, the synapses are actually changing shape—getting fat, getting short, becoming concave or convex, forming mushroom shapes. We knew this happened in the developing brain, but we didn't know that as adult brains think and learn it happens dynamically too.[10]
> —*Neurobiologist Michael Friedlander*

Overall, the few traditional simplicities in neuroscience are vanishing. The brain turns out to be more like an ocean than a clockwork. For example, the long-standing assumption that the brain uses two specific areas for language (Broca's area for speech production and Wernicke's area for speech comprehension) gave way to the recognition of a series of connected areas that oversee a complex variety of tasks. Neuroscientists Antonio and Hanna Damasio, who found many of these connections, argue that similar connections may create our sense of the self.[11] But, in that case, are the sense of self and consciousness merely a buzz created by the activities of neurons? Or has materialist neuroscience essentially stalled, unable to progress further in the understanding of human consciousness because of the limitations of the materialist creed?

> Utterly contrary to common sense ... and to the evidence gathered from our own introspection, consciousness may be nothing more than an evanescent by-product of more mundane, wholly physical processes.[12]
> —*Michael D. Lemonick,* Time

> It is telling that the Decade of the Brain ... had that name rather than the Decade of the Mind. For it was in the brain rather than the mind that scientists and laypeople alike sought answers, probing the folds and crevasses of our gray matter for the roots of personality and temperament, mental illness and mood, sexual identity and even a predilection for fine food.[13]
> —*Jeffrey M. Schwartz and Sharon Begley,*
> The Mind and the Brain

Despite claims trumpeted in popular media, the new discoveries have *not* explained away basic concepts such as consciousness, the mind, the self, and free will.[14] Hypotheses that reduce the mind[15] to the functions of the brain or deny that the mind exists have remained just that—hypotheses. They are based not on convincing demonstrations of evidence, but on the promissory materialism that philosopher of science Karl Popper has warned about.

The Nature of Things: "Qualia"

There are good reasons for thinking that the evidence for materialism will actually never arrive. For example, there is the problem of *qualia*. Qualia (singular, *quale*) are how things appear to us individually—the experiential aspects of our mental lives that can be accessed through introspection. Every person is unique, so complete understanding of another person's consciousness is not likely possible in principle, as we saw in Chapter Four. Rather, when we communicate, we rely on general agreement on an overlapping range of meaning. For example, historian Amy Butler Greenfield has written a three-hundred-page book about one primary color,

A Perfect Red.[16] As "the color of desire," red is a quale if ever there was one. Reviewer Diane Ackerman notes:

> Anger us, and we see red. An unfaithful woman is branded with a scarlet letter. In red-light districts, people buy carnal pleasures. We like to celebrate red-letter days and roll out the red carpet, while trying to avoid red tape, red herrings and going into the red.[17]

Indeed, fashion houses rise and fall on the subtleties of shades of red. Yet, however "red" affects us individually, we agree communally to use the word for a range of meanings and connotations, not merely a range in the color spectrum.

Materialist neuroscience has a hard time with qualia because they are not easily reducible to a simple, nonconscious explanation. In *The Astonishing Hypothesis,* Francis Crick grumbles:

> It is certainly possible that there may be aspects of consciousness, such as qualia, that science will not be able to explain. We have learned to live with such limitations in the past (e.g., limitations of quantum mechanics) and we may have to live with them again.[18]

Ramachandran attempts to evade the problem of qualia at the close of his Reith Lectures (2003):

> The question is how does the flux of ions in little bits of jelly in my brain give rise to the redness of red, the flavour of marmite or mattar paneer, or wine. Matter and mind seem so utterly unlike each other. Well, one way out of this dilemma is to think of them really as two different ways of describing the world, each of which is complete in itself.[19]

He compares qualia to the fact that light is described as both particles and waves, depending on the context. This might be a useful approach as long as we are prepared to see mind as an objectively existing category that is "utterly unlike" matter, but Ramachandran's subsequent comments provide no ground for confidence that he himself is so prepared.

Philosopher of mind Daniel Dennett, on purely dogmatic materialist grounds, insists that "there are simply no qualia at all."[20] What Dennett means is that the eliminative materialism that he champions cannot easily account for qualia.

The Mind-Brain Problem

No satisfactory account of the mind is currently widely accepted. Here are a few of the many theories scientists and philosophers offer.

Epiphenomenalism

Mind does not move matter.[21]

—Neurologist C. J. Herrick

The mind exists, like a rainbow shimmering over the falls. Yes, it's there, but it doesn't affect anything. You know it's there because some experiences are unique to yourself, for example, whatever you personally associate with peanut butter. Merely a product of brain-body processes, the mind sometimes facilitates for itself the illusion that it affects those processes, much as if the rainbow thought it affected the falls in some way.

Eliminative Materialism

We now understand that the mind is not, as Descartes confusedly supposed, *in communication with* the brain in some miraculous way; it *is* the brain, or more specifically, a system or organization within the brain that has evolved in much the same way our immune system ... evolved.[22]

—Materialist philosopher Daniel Dennett

The mind-matter problem is resolved by denying that mental processes exist in their own right. "Consciousness" and "mind" (intentions, desires, beliefs, etc.) are prescientific concepts that belong to unsophisticated ideas of how the brain works, sometimes called "folk psychology." They can be reduced to whatever the neurons happen to be doing (neural events). "Consciousness" and "mind" as concepts will be eliminated by the progress of science, along with such ideas as "free will" and the "self." Current key exponents of this view include philosophers Paul and Patricia Churchland and Daniel Dennett.

Psychophysical Identity Theory

States and processes of the mind are identical to states and processes of the brain.[23]

— Stanford Plato Encyclopedia of Philosophy

We apprehend our own consciousness and mental processes in the first person, that is, in a subjective and experiential manner. Brain events, however, are measured in the third person, that is, from the outside in an objective manner. Brain events and mental processes are completely parallel, like the two sides of the same medal. This view is defended by neuroscientist Jean-Pierre Changeux. The underlying assumption is that the brain states create the mind states, not the other way around.

Mentalism

The whole world of inner experience (the world of the humanities) long rejected by 20th century scientific materialism ... becomes recognized and included within the domain of science.[24]
—Neuroscientist Roger Sperry

Mental processes and consciousness arise from brain activity (emergent), but they actually exist and make a difference (dynamic). Mental events (thoughts and feelings) can make things happen in the brain. Therefore, they are neither identical with nor reducible to neural events. But conscious experience cannot exist apart from the physical brain. Nobel Prize winner Roger Sperry is the main proponent of this view.

Substance Dualism

I think, therefore I am.
—Philosopher René Descartes (1596–1650)

Sometimes called Cartesian dualism after the French philosopher and mathematician Descartes, this position argues that there are two fundamental kinds of entirely separate substances: mind and matter.

Dualistic Interactionism

Since materialist solutions fail to account for our experienced uniqueness, we are constrained to attribute the uniqueness of the psyche or soul to a supernatural spiritual creation.[25]
—Neuroscientist John Eccles

Consciousness and other aspects of the mind, which can influence neural events, can occur independently of the brain, generally through aspects of quantum mechanics. This view is associated with neuroscientists John Eccles and Wilder Penfield as well as philosopher Karl Popper.

Why should the activity of a mass of neurons feel like anything? Why does pricking your finger feel like pain? Why does a red rose appear red? This has been dubbed the "hard problem" of consciousness.[26]
—*Helen Phillips,* New Scientist

The Nature of Consciousness

The puzzle that qualia present for materialist neuroscience is really an aspect of the puzzle of consciousness. How much does your consciousness—your awareness of yourself as a unified self—weigh? How many yards would your thoughts stretch if they were laid out end to end? In the seventeenth century, the French mathematician and philosopher René Descartes sought to protect the very existence of the human mind and consciousness from attack by the materialist philosophy growing up around him. That philosophy sought to reduce the universe to hard little balls that can be weighed and measured. He responded by declaring that mind is utterly different from matter (*substance dualism*).

Descartes' approach pleased many, but it created a practical problem. How can mind communicate with matter if the two substances are utterly different? How *does* the mind guide the brain to rule the body? Over the years, Descartes' substance dualism fell into disrepute because no material mechanism was found. After the apparent triumph of the hard little bits, the mind was ignored, marginalized, or even denied. After all, matter was what mattered! But philosophers of matter, much as they have tried, failed to explain away the fundamental puzzles and paradoxes of consciousness.

Science's biggest mystery is the nature of consciousness. It is not that we possess bad or imperfect theories of human awareness; we simply have no such theories at all. About all we know about consciousness is that it has something to do with the head, rather than the foot.[27]
—*Physicist Nick Herbert*

Nowhere in the laws of physics or in the laws of the derivative sciences, chemistry and biology, is there any reference to consciousness or mind.... This is not to affirm that consciousness does not emerge in the evolutionary process, but merely to state that its emergence is not reconcilable with the natural laws as at present understood.[28]
—*Neuroscientist John Eccles*

I think the biggest unanswered question is how the brain generates consciousness. It is the question I would most like to solve and the one I would tackle if I were starting out again.[29]
          —*Pharmacologist Susan Greenfield*

Conscious beings are both the observers and the observed.[30] The fact that objectivity is impossible in such a situation creates a difficulty, of course. But it is only the first of many difficulties. Consciousness cannot be directly observed. No single brain area is active when we are conscious and idle when we are not. Nor does a specific level of activity in neurons signify that we are conscious. Nor is there a chemistry in neurons that always indicates consciousness. As philosopher of mind B. Alan Wallace notes:

> Despite centuries of modern philosophical and scientific research into the nature of the mind, at present there is no technology that can detect the presence or absence of any kind of consciousness, for scientists do not even know what exactly is to be measured. Strictly speaking, *at present there is no scientific evidence even for the existence of consciousness!* All the direct evidence we have consists of nonscientific, first-person accounts of being conscious.[31]

The difficulty, Wallace goes on to note, is that mind and consciousness are not a *mechanism* of the brain in the way that, for example, cell division is a mechanism of cells and photosynthesis is a mechanism of plants. Although brains, minds, and consciousness are obviously interrelated, no material mechanism accounts for that relationship. Wallace continues:

> A genuine emergent property of the cells of the brain is the brain's semi-solid consistency, and that is something that objective, physical science can well comprehend ... but they do not understand how the brain produces any state of consciousness. *In other words, if mental phenomena are in fact nothing more than emergent properties and functions of the brain, their relation to the brain is fundamentally unlike every other emergent property and function found in nature.*[32]

For much of the twentieth century, the problem of consciousness was simply avoided. Starting before World War I, the reigning movement in psychology was behaviorism, which ruled out discussing mental events.

All behavior was to be explained in terms of stimulus and response, ignoring the question of consciousness. B. F. Skinner was the best-known mid-century behaviorist.

> It is in the nature of an experimental analysis of human behavior that it should strip away the functions previously assigned to autonomous man and transfer them one by one to the controlling environment.[33]
> —*B. F. Skinner,* Beyond Freedom and Dignity

Following the development of cognitive psychology in the 1950s, the computer was the favored model for human thinking. But the enthusiasm of the early AI proponents was dampened by the fact that consciousness is precisely what computer programs do *not* have. For example, if a software expert develops a program that beats a chess grand master who plays without a program, the program itself cannot know or care about the victory; only the human participants can. That is another small part of the "hard problem" of consciousness.

> The machines will convince us that they are conscious, that they have their own agenda worthy of our respect. We will come to believe that they are conscious much as we believe that of each other. More so than with our animal friends, we will empathize with their professed feelings and struggles because their minds will be based on the design of human thinking. They will embody human qualities and will claim to be human. And we'll believe them.[34]
> —*Ray Kurzweil,* The Age of Spiritual Machines

In a recent book on consciousness, Gerald Edelman and Giulio Tononi helpfully provide a list—which they emphasize is not exhaustive—of theories that account for the relationship between mind and brain, including Spinoza's dual-aspect theory, Malebranche's occasionalism, Leibniz's parallelism and doctrine of preestablished harmony, identity theory, central state theory, neutral monism, logical behaviorism, token physicalism, type physicalism, token epiphenomenalism, type epiphenomenalism, anomalous monism, emergent materialism, eliminative materialism, and functionalism (various types).[35] Clearly, no consensus has emerged.

> Studying consciousness presents us with a curious dilemma: Introspection alone is not scientifically satisfactory, and though people's reports about

their own consciousness are useful, they cannot reveal the workings of the brain underlying them. Yet, studies of the brain proper cannot, in themselves, convey what it is like to be conscious. These constraints suggest that one must take special approaches to bring consciousness into the house of science.[36]

—*Gerald M. Edelman and Giulio Tononi,*
A Universe of Consciousness

As we have seen, most theories of mind and consciousness are based on a materialism rooted in classical physics, which treats consciousness as an anomaly to be explained away. The materialist can be a wee bit hasty in this regard. For example, science journalist Michael Lemonick slickly explains the work of Francis Crick and Christof Koch on consciousness in *Time* (1995): "Consciousness is somehow a by-product of the simultaneous, high-frequency firing of neurons in different parts of the brain. It's the meshing of these frequencies that generates consciousness ... just as the tones from individual instruments produce the rich, complex and seamless sound of a symphony orchestra."[37] Well put, to be sure, but Crick himself admitted that his concept was highly speculative, not at all an assured result of modern neuroscience.

A frequent cop-out has been the announcement that Darwinian evolution has not equipped our brains to understand consciousness; another one is that the mind, consciousness, and self are just illusions.

Our highly developed brains, after all, were not evolved under the pressure of discovering scientific truths but only to enable us to be clever enough to survive and leave descendants.[38]

—*Francis Crick,* The Astonishing Hypothesis

And What of the Self?

"How does the three-pound gelatinous mass that we call the brain produce our identities?" asks Greg Peterson in *Christian Century*.[39] How indeed? Look at the figures. The average neuron, consisting of about 100,000 molecules, is about 80 percent water. The brain is home to about 100 billion such cells and thus about 10^{15} molecules. Each neuron gets 10,000 or so connections from other cells in the brain.

The Brain as a Complex Computer

The computational theory of mind has quietly entrenched itself in neuroscience.... No corner of the field is untouched by the idea that information processing is the fundamental activity of the brain.[40]

—Steven Pinker, *How the Mind Works*

Computers are general-purpose algorithm executors, and their apparent intelligent activity is simply an illusion suffered by those who do not fully appreciate the way in which algorithms capture and preserve not intelligence itself but the fruits of intelligence.[41]

—Software pioneer Mark Halpern

We must be wary of the "central executive" metaphor, which sees all of our humanity focused in the frontal lobes of the brain. Not only are we not walking frontal lobes, we are also not brains in a vat. Extreme reductionism—we can call it *brain anthropomorphization* or the celebrated "neuronal man"—merely misleads us. It makes such commonplace features of human behavior as emotional self-regulation and the placebo effect into problems (see Chapter 6), when no problem really exists.

We must keep in mind that the whole human person, not merely a part of a brain, thinks, feels, or believes. Indeed, the human person cannot be reduced to brain processes and events, and it is difficult to understand a whole human person without understanding the sociocultural context in which the person lives. Insightfully, social psychologist Albert Bandura has pointed out that mapping the activities of the neural circuits underlying Martin Luther King's "I Have a Dream" speech would reveal little about how it came to be created and nothing of its social power.[42]

The surgeon knows all the parts of the brain but he does not know his patient's dreams.[43]

—Richard Selzer, *Mortal Lessons*

The central-executive metaphor comes from a trend in neuroscience and cognitive psychology known as computationalism, which attempts to understand the human mind/brain as if it were a computer. Human behavior is assumed to be determined by the activity of unconscious subpersonal executive processors (modules) and their neural counterparts. These modules are thought to function somewhat like executable files in a computer program.

But how useful is this model? In an article reviewing the last half century in this field, software pioneer Mark Halpern notes that the celebrated Turing Test for machine intelligence (can you tell whether you are conversing with a human or a machine?) has simply not been met. For the most part, researchers attempt to argue for computer intelligence by changing the test or casting doubt on the idea of human intelligence.

He notes that, when challenged, they are "strong on indignation and weak in citing specific achievements." He also notes, significantly, that

> the AI champions, in their desperate struggle to salvage the idea that computers can or will think, are indeed in the grip of an ideology: they are, as they see it, defending rationality itself. If it is denied that computers can, even in principle, think, then a claim is being tacitly made that humans have some special property that science will never understand—a "soul" or some similarly mystical entity.[44]

The key defect of this "Turing Test" view is that human behavior does not really resemble computer programs at all. Consciousness is precisely what humans have and what computers, which are merely artifacts of human intelligence, do not have. Reading the literature produced by early computer enthusiasts, one gets the impression that they supposed that sheer computing power would somehow magically produce mind and consciousness, but they did not seem to understand the nature of consciousness well enough to see why that would not happen.

To make any sense of human behavior, we must confront mind and consciousness, which means confronting beliefs, goals, aspirations, desires, expectations, and intentions, none of which is relevant to the functioning of computers. Self-consciousness (consciousness of oneself as an immediate subject of experience), self-agency (experiencing oneself as the cause of an action), and self-regulatory capacities are all characteristics of human consciousness that are irrelevant to the workings of computers.

As conscious beings, we do not simply undergo experiences; we create them. A worm, bothered by light shining on its photosensitive spots, immediately seeks darkness. A human, faced with a similar unwelcome experience, may ask, "But must I flee? What if I don't? Can I learn from this?" No useful account of human nature ignores the significance of the fact that we humans ask such questions.

Within each neuron, the molecules are replaced approximately 10,000 times in an average life span. Yet humans have a continuous sense of self that is stable over time.

As consciousness researcher Dean Radin notes: "*All* of the material used to express that pattern has disappeared, and yet the pattern still exists. What holds the pattern, if not matter? This question is not easily answered by the assumptions of a mechanistic, purely materialist science."[45]

> What or where is the unified center of sentience that comes into and goes out of existence, that changes over time but remains the same entity, and that has a supreme moral worth?[46]
> —*Cognitive scientist Steven Pinker*

There are two widely accepted materialist approaches. One is to deny that the self or consciousness has any influence on events in the brain; it is merely an *epiphenomenon.* That is, in the absence of a material mechanism by which the mind might control the brain, the self exists, as a—possibly accidental—hologram of brain events. This view is not new; it was championed in the nineteenth century by Charles Darwin's colleague Thomas Huxley (1825–95). He famously said that consciousness was "as completely without any power of modifying that working [of the brain] as the steam whistle that accompanies the working of a locomotive engine is without influence upon its machinery."[47]

> "You," your joys and your sorrows, your memories and your ambitions, your sense of personal identity and free will, are in fact no more than the behavior of a vast assembly of nerve cells and their associated molecules. As Lewis Carroll's Alice might have phrased: "You're nothing but a pack of neurons."[48]
> —*Francis Crick,* The Astonishing Hypothesis

> If all this seems dehumanizing, you haven't seen anything yet.[49]
> —*Neuroscientist V. S. Ramachandran*

> Man no longer has need for "Spirit": it is enough for him to be Neuronal Man.[50]
> —*Jean-Pierre Changeux,* Neuronal Man

The other approach is to deny that consciousness or the self even exists. As Lemonick puts it:

> Despite our every instinct to the contrary, there is one thing that consciousness is not: some entity deep inside the brain that corresponds to the "self," some kernel of awareness that runs the show, as the "man behind the curtain" manipulated the illusion of a powerful magician in *The Wizard of Oz.* After more than a century of looking for it, brain researchers have long since concluded that there is no conceivable place for such a self to be located in the physical brain, and that it simply doesn't exist.[51]

According to this view—seriously argued by eliminative materialists— children are indoctrinated by prescientific cultures into a "folk psychology" that acts on them in such a way that they perceive a consciousness or self that does not exist.[52]

This explanation may sound bizarre, but it is important to recognize what lies behind it: materialism cannot account for mind, consciousness, or self. Because the promissory materialist "knows" that materialism must be true, mind, consciousness, or self simply cannot exist. The materialist denies human consciousness with a greater level of certainty than the American fundamentalist denies that evolution occurs because the materialist honestly believes that current science—which he understands as applied materialism—actually supports him.

A third option, of course, is to talk around the problem. On the concept of the self, Ramachandran argues:

> Our brains were essentially model-making machines. We need to construct useful, virtual reality simulations of the world that we can act on. Within the simulation, we need also to construct models of other people's minds because we're intensely social creatures, us primates. We need to do this so we can predict their behaviour. We are, after all, the Machiavellian primate.[53]

Of course, the obvious difficulty with Ramachandran's suggestion is that the process is actually the other way around. We are sure that *we* have a self and therefore we infer that other humans do. Without a self of our own, we could make no such inference about others. In the same vein, evolutionary psychologist David Livingstone Smith argues that self-deceit arose from the need to deceive others, because the most convincing way to do that is to deceive oneself.[54] Thus self-deceivers were supposedly selected through evolutionary psychology for Darwinian survival. As we have seen earlier, these types of hypotheses mainly show how difficult accounting for the self really is within a materialist framework.

What About Free Will?

Materialist neuroscience cannot accept free will, for a reason that is rooted in physics. In classical physics, only one state can exist at a time. Consider, for example, a woman who sometimes buys a newspaper on the way home from work. According to classical physics, she must proceed from one state to the next, governed by immutable laws. So if she buys the newspaper on a given day, it is because she *must*. Any notion that she "decided" to buy the paper is a user illusion—except that there is no actual user in this case. The dilemma about whether free will exists is the most important of the dilemmas concerned with consciousness.[55]

> We are descended from robots, and composed of robots, and all the intentionality we enjoy is derived from the more fundamental intentionality of these billions of crude intentional systems.[56]
> —*Daniel C. Dennett,* Kinds of Minds

> Supernatural contra-causal freedom really *isn't* necessary for anything we hold near and dear, whether it's personhood, morality, dignity, creativity, individuality, or a robust sense of human agency.[57]
> —*Tom Clark, Director, Center for Naturalism*

> Either we dispense with all morality as an unscientific superstition, or we find a way to reconcile causation (genetic or otherwise) with responsibility and free will.[58]
> —*Steven Pinker,* How the Mind Works

If there is no free will, what about ethics? Can we expect people to behave other than they must? Materialists sometimes teleport the ethical dilemma into a vague realm of nonscientific concepts that are immune to disproof. For example, cognitive scientist Steven Pinker writes:

> Like many philosophers, I believe that science and ethics are two self-contained systems played out among the same entities in the world, just as

poker and bridge are different games played with the same fifty-two-card deck. The science game treats people as material objects, and its rules are the physical processes that cause behaviour through natural selection and neurophysiology. The ethics game treats people as equivalent, sentient, rational, free-willed agents, and its rules are the calculus that assigns moral value to behavior through the behavior's inherent nature or its consequences.[59]

The difficulty with Pinker's approach is that, even though he knows that ethics is necessary for all human endeavors including science, he cannot ground it in an account of human nature that unites science and ethics. The question is not whether an "ethics game" can be developed whose rules treat people as "equivalent, sentient, rational, free-willed agents," but whether such an account is grounded in reality.

This question of free will is hardly an irrelevant squabble among philosophers of science. As philosopher George Grant observes, political and social theory in the Western world during the twentieth century leaned very much in the direction of freedom: "To modern political theory, man's essence is his freedom."[60] Whether or not one accepts that account of society, a presumed lack of free will greatly alters the character of any freedom that is asserted.

In a materialist view, freedom means simply that the determinist forces driving the neural circuits from within (genes, brain wiring, neurotransmitters) are not opposed by determinist forces driving them from without (social isolation, religious condemnation, laws). None of these forces is subject to rationality because rationality has no independent validity; it is merely one of the organizing illusions imposed by some neural networks on others.

In an unintentionally ironic open letter to the "atheist community," Tom Clark, director of the Massachusetts-based Center for Naturalism, advises that denying free will is not really an ethical problem because it "increases our powers of self-control, and encourages science-based, effective and progressive policies in areas such as criminal justice, social inequality, behavioral health, and the environment."[61] Self-control? Clark does not appear to recognize that, in a materialist account of the human, there is no self that controls and no self to control. As a result, his proposed "science-based, effective and progressive policies" are not offered by a self to other selves, but driven by an object at other objects.

An example of this problem is unintentionally provided by British evolutionary biologist Richard Dawkins. Arguing against the principle of retribution in the legal system, he writes:

> As scientists, we believe that human brains, though they may not work in the same way as man-made computers, are as surely governed by the laws of physics. When a computer malfunctions, we do not punish it. We track down the problem and fix it, usually by replacing a damaged component, either in hardware or software.[62]

Now, a good case can be made that retribution is an inadequate principle of justice, but notice that the scientific fixers of Dawkins's vision are "we" but the erring "fixee" is "it."

A key consequence follows. Those who charge that materialism (naturalism) results in evil policies miss the point. It is true that the most terrible regimes of the twentieth century, such as Nazism, Stalinism, and the Khmer Rouge, were materialist. But if the will is an illusion, the very idea of evil is evacuated. In the absence of good and evil, what fills the vacuum? Desires and dislikes. They drive the neural circuits unsupervised.

As C. S. Lewis warned, "When all that says, 'It is good' has been debunked, what says 'I want' remains."[63] In other words, government by materialists must mean government by entities that—on their own testimony—doubt moral responsibility.[64] We should hardly be surprised if such a government dehumanized its subjects, because it must deal with citizens as a farmer deals with livestock—humanely at best, and without assuming that they have moral understanding, free will, or a higher purpose than the one determined by the farmer. So even though Pinker's solution (treating science and ethics as separate "games") won't work, his concern about the consequences of the denial of free will is quite legitimate.

The Language of Mind, Consciousness, and Self

Having failed to explain away the mind, some materialists have turned to an interim strategy: banish terminology that refers to it. As Karl Popper explains:

We shall be talking less and less about experiences, perceptions, thoughts, beliefs, purposes and aims; and more and more about brain processes, about dispositions to behave, and about overt behavior. In this way mentalist language will go out of fashion and be used only in historical reports, or metaphorically, or ironically. When this stage has been reached, mentalism will be stone-dead, and the problem of mind in relation to the body will have solved itself.[65]

Recently, archaeologist Peter Watson complained in *New Scientist* that it isn't happening fast enough:

The social, psychological and cognitive sciences remain stuck with pre-scientific words and concepts. For many of us the word "soul" is as obsolete as "phlogiston," but scientists still use such imprecise words as "consciousness," "personality" and "ego," not to mention "mind."

Perhaps it is time that, in science at least, "imagination" and "introspection" are remodelled or, preferably, retired. Artists can have fun with them, but the serious business of the world has moved on.[66]

Watson provides no evidence that words such as "consciousness," "mind," and "imagination" create a problem for anyone other than the promissory materialist. Language is a group project, after all, and words that have truly lost meaning become obsolete by common consent, not banishment.

Biophysicist Harold J. Morowitz has drawn attention to a practical example of the promissory materialist's attempt to redefine language. The glossary of Carl Sagan's *The Dragons of Eden* does not offer the words *mind, consciousness, perception, awareness,* or *thought,* but does offer such neuroscience entries as *synapse, lobotomy, proteins,* and *electrodes.*[67] Readers can judge whether this approach promotes greater understanding.

The old habits of thought die hard. A man may, in religious terms, be an unbeliever but psychologically he may continue to think of himself in much the same way as a believer does, at least for everyday matters.[68]

—*Francis Crick,* The Astonishing Hypothesis

The Materialist Account

It is not really surprising that the materialist account of mind, self, and consciousness has stalled. There are at least six fundamental weaknesses that promissory materialism is powerless to address.

1. *Current materialist accounts aim to preserve materialism rather than account for the evidence.* Materialism has no workable science model for consciousness and no idea how to acquire one. Labeling consciousness as "folk psychology" is simply a dodge, as are efforts to rid the language of words that advertise the problem.

> As long as we refuse to admit into the debate the forever *private* awareness each person has of himself, his thoughts and feelings, his judgements and rationality, and as long as we insist on public and purely behavioral signs of these, radical materialism can remain in the debate.[69]
> —*John Eccles and Daniel N. Robinson,*
> The Wonder of Being Human

> This emergent feature of man has, in one form or another, been discussed by numerous anthropologists, psychologists, and biologists. It is part of the empirical data that cannot be shelved just to preserve reductionist purity. The discontinuity needs to be thoroughly studied and evaluated, but first it needs to be recognized. Primates are very different from other animals, and human beings are very different from other primates.[70]
> —*Biophysicist Harold J. Morowitz*

> The current belief that all mental processes are unconscious is so obviously contrary to experience that it can be regarded simply as a symptom of the metaphysical miasma induced by overexposure to scientific materialism.[71]
> —*B. Alan Wallace,* The Taboo of Subjectivity

2. *Materialism leads to major disconnects in thinking.* An excellent example of materialist disconnects is provided by Edelman and Tononi in *A Universe of Consciousness*. Explaining why they refuse to consider nonmaterialist approaches to consciousness, they write:

> Whatever the specialness of the human brain, there is no need to invoke spiritual forces to account for its functions. Darwinian principles of variation in populations and natural selection are sufficient, and the elements invoked by spiritualism are not required for our being conscious. Being

human in mind and brain appears clearly to be the result of an evolutionary process. The anthropological evidence emerging for the evolutionary origin of consciousness in humans further substantiates the notion that Darwin's is the most ideologically significant of all grand scientific theories.[72]

Let us look at each of the claims in this most interesting paragraph in order:

(1) The claim that "Darwinian principles" will solve the problem is merely a statement of faith—in this case, a faith at odds with historical experience.

(2) Edelman and Tononi do not say what they mean by "spiritualism," a term rarely if ever used by nonmaterialist neuroscientists in the context of their work. Thus they conveniently insulate themselves from arguing against a rigorous nonmaterialist hypothesis.[73]

(3) The fact that "Being human in mind and brain appear clearly to be the result of an evolutionary process" tells us nothing. The question is not whether evolution occurs, but what drives it and what exactly it has produced to date.

(4) Finally, whether "Darwin's is the most ideologically significant of all grand scientific theories" is irrelevant for the purposes of their discussion. Darwin's theory neither predicts consciousness nor describes it.

3. *Materialism leads to hypotheses that can never be tested.* In *The Creative Loop: How the Brain Makes a Mind,* Eric Harth raises one of the many difficulties that beset the materialist hope of determining exact brain states:

We would want to know in every millisecond (the time it takes a neuron to fire) which of the 100 billion or so neurons are active and which are not. If we denote activity by a "1" and inactivity by a "0," this would require a string of 100 billion zeros and ones every millisecond, or 100 trillion every second. To give a running account of the true neural state, I would have to produce in every second something like 110 million books, each containing a million symbols. This awesome record is to be compared with my mental states as they occur.[74]

That's bad enough, but it gets worse. As Harth acknowledges, every human mind and brain moves through life differently, changing as it goes, so the information obtained for his brain would not apply to anyone else's—or even to his *own* brain at a later time! Readers may recall that this point was raised in Chapter Four, but it bears repeating because it is so contrary to materialist hopes that it is often ignored in public discussions. One outcome, for example, is that Changeux's view that mind states and brain states are completely identical is untestable and lacks predictive value.

4. *Promissory materialism leads to the promotion of impractical projects in the indefinite future to avoid grappling with current issues.* Wrestling with the problem of qualia, Edelman and Tononi argue that one day we will create "conscious artifacts":

> Although the day when we shall be able to create such conscious artifacts is far off, we may have to make them—that is, use synthetic means—before we deeply understand the processes of thought itself. However far off the date of their construction, such artifacts shall be made.[75]

They admit, however, that "we will, even then, not directly know the actual phenomenal experience of that artifactual individual; the qualia we experience, each of us, artifact or person, rests in our own embodiment, our own phenotype"[76]—which amounts to admitting that the artifacts would not help much with understanding qualia.

5. *Taken seriously, materialism undermines our capacity to eventually understand the human mind and the human brain.* Steven Pinker, for example, muses: "Our brains were shaped for fitness, not for truth. Sometimes the truth is adaptive, but sometimes it is not."[77] How then do scientists and philosophers such as Pinker, Crick, and Dennett know that their ideas have escaped the necessity of evolution—and therefore have independent validity—but that their nonmaterialist opponents' ideas have not? Both sets of ideas can be found in the human population, and nonmaterialist ideas vastly predominate. Merely claiming that materialism is based on evidence will not do. Nonmaterialist ideas are based on evidence too. But materialist doctrines undermine our confidence in a capacity to assess evidence, so it is useless for materialists to claim that they have better evidence than nonmaterialists.

6. *Materialism is out of step with modern physics.* Classical physics conceives of the universe as independent bits of matter that interact according to mechanisms. The reason that consciousness is a problem for materialist neuroscience is that it does not appear to have a mechanism. Modern quantum physics conceives of the universe as superposed states. These states do not exist apart from each other, so their interaction is not governed by a mechanism. As B. Alan Wallace writes:

> As soon as one begins to understand subjective and objective, mental and physical phenomena as *relational* instead of *substantive,* the causal interactions between mind and matter become no more problematic than such interactions among mental phenomena and among physical phenomena. But the notion of a reified causal *mechanism* may no longer be useful in any of these domains.[78]

As a result, he notes, "the demand for a mechanistic explanation of causality has been long rejected in various fields of physics, including electromagnetism and quantum mechanics."[79]

The conflict between materialist biology and contemporary physics is becoming more obvious all the time. As Harold J. Morowitz has pointed out, biologists have been moving recently toward the hard-core materialism that characterized nineteenth-century physics, just as physicists have been forced by the weight of the evidence to move *away* from strictly mechanical models of the universe toward the view that the mind plays an integral role in all physical events. He comments, "It is as if the two disciplines were on fast-moving trains, going in opposite directions and not noticing what is happening across the tracks."[80] That raises a question: If physics fails to support biology, which discipline should rethink its position—physics or biology? On a practical note, can we reasonably expect much progress in neuroscience, given the problems, if we do not begin by reassessing the materialism that has characterized our hypotheses for decades?

There is a sound theoretical basis for a nonmaterialist approach to neuroscience, and— perhaps more pressing for many readers—there are valuable practical applications as well. We look at these areas in Chapter Six.

SIX

Toward a Nonmaterialist Science of Mind

My fundamental premise about the brain is that its workings—what we sometimes call "mind"—are a consequence of its anatomy and physiology and nothing more.[1]

—Astronomer and popular science writer
Carl Sagan

We regard promissory materialism as superstition without a rational foundation. The more we discover about the brain, the more clearly do we distinguish between the brain events and the mental phenomena, and the more wonderful do both the brain events and the mental phenomena become. Promissory materialism is simply a religious belief held by dogmatic materialists ... who often confuse their religion with their science.[2]

—John Eccles and Daniel N. Robinson,
The Wonder of Being Human

Can a nonmaterialist science of mind account for observed facts better than a materialist one? At this point, it is possible to sketch out some features of a nonmaterialist view of mind. Though no one current view answers all the questions, a nonmaterialist view can at least account for known features of human experience that, as we have seen, materialist views cannot account for and often deny.

For example, a nonmaterialist view can account for the neuroimaging studies that show human subjects in the very act of self-regulating their emotions by concentrating on them. It can account for the placebo effect (the sugar pill that cures, provided the patient is convinced that it is a potent remedy). A nonmaterialist view can also offer science-based explanations of puzzling phenomena that are currently shelved by materialist views. One of these is *psi,* the apparent ability of some humans to consistently score above chance in controlled studies of mental influences on events. Another is the claim, encountered surprisingly often among patients who have undergone trauma or major surgery, that they experienced a life-changing mystical awareness while unconscious.

If a nonmaterialist view is correct, then it should be useful in a practical field like medicine. Let's look at some evidence for its usefulness.

Nonmaterialist Neuroscience in Medicine

A brain was always going to do what it was caused to do by local mechanical disturbances.[3]

—*Materialist philosopher Daniel Dennett*

The time has come for science to confront the serious implications of the fact that directed, willed mental activity can clearly and systematically alter brain function.[4]

—*Psychiatrist Jeffrey M. Schwartz*

A nonmaterialist approach to the mind is not only philosophically defensible; it is critical to alleviating some psychiatric disorders. Obsessive-compulsive disorder and phobias, for example, may be more effectively alleviated if the mind recognizes and reorganizes destructive brain patterns. This is not to disparage the role of drugs, therapy, or other useful interventions, but ultimately the mind is the most effective agent of change for the brain.

Treating Obsessive-Compulsive Disorder

If, while driving, Dottie glimpsed a license plate containing either 5 or a 6, she felt compelled to pull over immediately and sit at the side of the road until a car with a "lucky" number in its license plate passed by.... If she made the slightest misstep, her son would go blind.[5]

> —*Description of a woman in the grip of an*
> *obsessive-compulsive disorder (OCD)*

Obsessive-compulsive disorder (OCD) is a neuropsychiatric disease marked by distressing, intrusive, and unwanted thoughts (obsessions) that trigger an urge to perform ritual behaviors (compulsions). This disorder should not be confused with the obsessiveness of the expert who bores acquaintances with the details of a beloved but minor field of expertise. OCD gives no joy and creates no value.

Worse, OCD sufferers know that their beliefs are mistaken and their activities are useless. They do not even experience them as a part of themselves. But they do not know how to stop them either. And sufferers won't get any peace from the panic button squealing in their brains unless they carry them out. Yet giving in to them makes them worse over time; the more they give in, the more persistent the beliefs and behaviors become. It is as if their brains have been hijacked. About one in fifty American adults suffers from some degree of OCD; severe cases imperil relationships and prevent employment. Obsessiveness sometimes runs in families but no single gene is likely responsible.

During most of the twentieth century, OCD was considered untreatable.[6] Freudian theory suggested that OCD originated in unconscious childhood sexual trauma, but that theory was untestable and unfruitful. Drugs were tried, but they had unpleasant side effects. Some health-care professionals tried behaviorist reconditioning. For example, compulsive hand washers were forced to touch toilet seats in public washrooms and then forbidden to wash their hands. Not surprisingly, many obsessive-compulsives preferred to suffer secretly rather than seek treatment. Even today, many are too embarrassed by their compulsions to ask for help.

My friend and colleague Jeffrey Schwartz, a nonmaterialist UCLA neuropsychiatrist, started working with OCD sufferers in the 1980s because he sensed that OCD was a clear case of an intact mind troubled by a malfunctioning brain. Schwartz began using positron emission tomography (PET, the use of emissions from decaying radioactive isotopes to image brain activity) to pinpoint where exactly OCD-afflicted brains go wrong.

He identified defective neural circuitry connecting the orbitofrontal cortex, cingulate gyrus, and basal ganglia, from which panic and compulsion are generated. When this "worry circuit" is working properly, people worry about genuine risks and feel the urge to reduce them. But, Schwartz found,

> when that modulation is faulty, as it is when OCD acts up, the error detector centered in the orbital frontal cortex and anterior cingulate can be overactivated and thus locked into a pattern of repetitive firing. This triggers an overpowering feeling that something is wrong, accompanied by compulsive attempts to somehow make it right.[7]

This line of research proved fruitful in explaining the disorder, but how could it be used to treat the disorder? Schwartz noted that the most recent (and thus most sophisticated) prefrontal parts of the human brain, in evolutionary terms, are almost entirely unaffected by OCD. That is why patients perceive the compulsions as alien. They *are* alien to the most characteristically human parts of the brain.[8] To the extent that the patients' reasoning power and sense of identity remain largely intact, they can actively cooperate with their therapy.

As a practitioner of Buddhist mindfulness meditation, Schwartz objected to behaviorist treatments that manipulate or force the patient, preferring to use in his own practice cognitive-behavioral treatments in which the patient is asked to voluntarily correct distorted views. However, he realized that his usual approach would not help OCD sufferers; they *already know* that their obsessions and compulsions are distorted. As he put it, "A patient basically knows that failing to count the cans in the pantry today won't really cause her mother to die a horrible death tonight. The problem is, she doesn't feel that way."[9] Schwartz needed to develop a treatment that gives the patient's mind a strategy for controlling and remapping the brain.

The key problem with OCD is that the more often the patient actually engages in a compulsive behavior, the more neurons are drawn into it, and the stronger the signals for the behavior become. Thus, although the signals appear to promise, "Do it one more time and then you will have some peace," that promise is false by its very nature. What was once a neural footpath slowly grows into a twelve-lane highway whose deafening traffic takes over the neural neighborhood. The challenge is to return it to the status of a footpath in the brain again. Neuroplasticity (the ability of neurons to shift their connections and responsibilities) makes that possible.

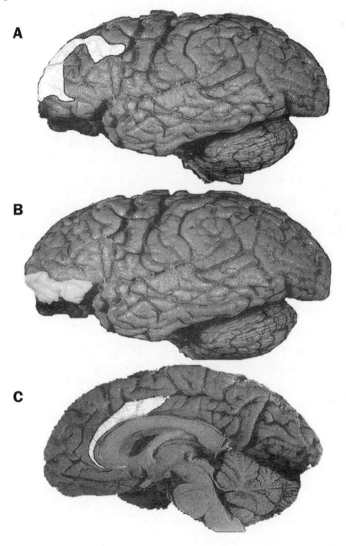

Three primary subdivisions of the prefrontal cortex: A. dorsolateral prefrontal cortex (DLPFC); B. lateral part of the orbitofrontal cortex (OFC); C. anterior cingulate cortex (ACC).

Schwartz sketched out a four-step program in which the patient is asked to Relabel, Reattribute, Reassign, and Revalue the OCD activities. For example, Dottie, the woman who feared 5 and 6, learned to say "It's not me: it's my OCD!" Schwartz notes, "Reattributing is particularly effective at directing the patient's attention away from demoralizing and stressful attempts to squash the bothersome OCD feeling by engaging in compulsive behaviors."[10] He was not simply getting patients to change their opinions, but rather to actually change their brains. He wanted them to substitute a useful neural circuit for a useless one,[11] for example, to substitute "go work in the garden" for "wash hands seven more times," until the neuronal traffic from the many different activities associated with gardening began to exceed the traffic from washing the hands. Over time, the hope was that the superhighway might slowly morph back into a dense but functional series of footpaths.

Schwartz's UCLA group performed PET scans on eighteen OCD patients with moderate to severe symptoms before and after they underwent individual and group four-step sessions. These patients were not treated with any type of drug. Twelve improved significantly during the ten-week study period. Their PET scans showed significantly diminished metabolic activity after the treatment in both the right and left caudate, with the right-side decrease particularly striking. There was also a significant decrease in the abnormally high, and pathological, correlations among activities in the caudate, the orbital frontal cortex, and the thalamus in the right hemisphere. In other words, these patients really had changed their brains.[12] As Schwartz notes:

> This was the first study ever to show that cognitive-behavior therapy—or, indeed, any psychiatric treatment that did not rely on drugs—has the power to change faulty brain chemistry in a well-identified brain circuit.... We had demonstrated such changes in patients who had, not to put too fine a point on it, changed the way they thought about their thoughts.[13]

Generally, Schwartz says, success with the four-step method depends on the patient doing two things: recognizing that faulty brain messages cause obsessive-compulsive behavior and realizing that these messages are not part of the self. In this therapy, the patient is entirely in control. Both the existence and the role of the mind as independent of the brain are accepted; indeed, that is the basis of the therapy's success.

Responsible Choices Are Possible

A victim of rape every minute somewhere in the world. Why? No one to blame but herself. She displayed her beauty to the entire world.[14]
> —*An Australian cleric sounding off on who is to blame for sexual assault*

There is no kernel of independent moral agency.... We are not, as philosopher Daniel Dennett puts it, "moral levitators" that rise above circumstances in our choices, including choices to rob, rape, or kill.[15]
> —*Tom W. Clark, Director, Center for Naturalism*

Folklore suggesting that sexually aroused men cannot exercise self-control lies at the heart of many traditional legal codes that assign the blame to the woman when a sexual assault occurs. Modern legal codes, espousing feminist principles, assume that men can indeed control themselves. Such a position is morally praiseworthy in principle, but it is easier to defend if it can be demonstrated to be factually correct. A few years ago, with my then doctoral student Johanne Lévesque, I decided to research the question using functional magnetic resonance imaging (fMRI).[16]

A magnetic resonance imaging unit is a huge cylindrical magnet that encloses a research volunteer or patient and creates a strong field. Inside the unit, radio waves affected by the field image the small, quick changes observed in the brain while a person is actually thinking, feeling, saying, or doing something (hence, it is called "functional"). Apart from its obvious value for research in neuroscience, fMRI is favored by brain surgeons preparing for an operation. Individual brains differ; in particular, a tumor or a stroke may cause normal functions to relocate to safer areas of the brain. Surgeons can minimize postoperative damage by pinpointing and avoiding an area that currently hosts a normal brain function.

We asked ten healthy young men, ranging in ages from twenty to forty-two (but predominantly in their mid-twenties) to watch four excerpts from emotionally neutral films (e.g., interviews, carpentry, etc.) and then four excerpts from erotic films. Each excerpt lasted 39 seconds, with 15 seconds in between for rest. The number and gender of the persons shown in both types of videos was the same in each case. The men were scanned in two different conditions, one in which they were asked to simply experience their reactions while watching the films through goggles, and one in which they were asked to down-regulate, or observe in a dispassionate, nonevaluative, and nonjudgmental manner, their reactions to the erotic films. In this second condition they saw similar but not identical films. At the end of the session, they were asked to complete a "strategy questionnaire" in which they described the strategies they employed when deliberately preventing themselves from being sexually aroused.

All of the men were sexually aroused by the erotic videos but they displayed little other emotion, according to the self-report scale. Significantly, they were all able to suppress their arousal when asked to do so. Sexual arousal was associated with the right amygdala and hypothalamus, among other areas, and suppression was associated with the right lateral prefrontal cortex and the right anterior cingulate cortex.

These results are consistent with findings indicating that the LPFC plays a role in top-down (metacognitive/executive) processes, that is, processes that can monitor and control the information processing necessary to produce voluntary action.[17]

The View from Neuroscience

The sexual arousal experienced in the research experiment in response to the erotic film excerpts was associated with activation in "limbic" and paralimbic structures, such as the right amygdala, right anterior temporal pole, and hypothalamus. These findings support the view that the amygdala plays a key role in the evaluation of the emotional significance of stimuli, that the hypothalamus is a pivotal brain structure implicated in the endocrine and autonomic expression of emotion, and that the anterior temporal pole is involved in imparting emotional color to subjective experience.[18] In addition, the suppression of the sexual arousal generated by viewing the erotic stimuli was associated with activation of the right lateral prefrontal cortex (LPFC; Brodmann area—BA—10) and right anterior cingulate cortex (ACC; BA 32).

The LPFC has been implicated in the selection and control of behavioral strategies and action, especially in the tendency to inhibit inherent responses. These results also concur with the view that the rostral-ventral subdivision of the ACC plays a key role in the regulation of the autonomic aspect of emotional responses, by virtue of its anatomic connections with brain regions implicated in the modulation of autonomic and endocrine functions, such as the amygdala and hypothalamus.

To sum up, the belief that men cannot really choose to reduce their arousal, whether based on ancient traditions or modern materialism, is simply mistaken. Penal codes that hold men accountable for sexual assault are based in neural reality, not simple-minded idealism.[19]

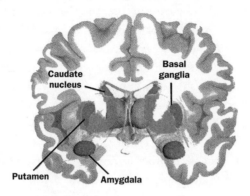

Coronal slice of the brain showing the amygdalae and a few cerebral structures belonging to the basal ganglia (caudate nucleus and putamen).

Depression: Taking Control of Sadness

Blue and white skies outside, blue and white pills inside. The sun is shining outside, so why do I feel so dark inside?[20]
—A person struggling with depression

Depressed people think they know themselves, but maybe they only know depression.[21]

—Psychiatrist Mark Epstein

How do we live and work effectively while dealing with the disappointments, losses, and bereavements of a normal life span? Some people seem able to control sadness so that it does not interfere with relationships or work, but others spiral into depression and anxiety. About 10 percent of the American population, for example, suffers at some point from clinical depression.

Depression is a serious and dangerous condition. Of people treated for depression in an outpatient setting, 2 percent subsequently die by suicide, as do 4 percent treated in an inpatient setting. Overall, according to National Institute of Mental Health (NIMH) studies, 6 percent die by suicide if they are hospitalized following a suicide attempt or serious suicidal thoughts.[22]

Can neuroscience help alleviate or prevent the suffering and loss by mapping what happens when people succeed in voluntarily suppressing sad thoughts without recourse to medication? The answer is important because the current generation of antidepressants often performs barely better than placebos, as we shall see. In other words, if a patient can effectively self-heal by learning, through focused therapy, how to recruit existing inner resources, antidepressants can be targeted to specific, focused needs.

With a few colleagues at the Université de Montréal,[23] Johanne Lévesque and I investigated the brain regions mediating the down-regulation of sad feelings in twenty psychologically healthy young women from the Montreal area.[24] These women were scanned while they watched excerpts from both emotionally neutral movies and sad movies. They were alone inside the scanner while they watched the films through goggles, so they could not have been influenced by any group sentiment regarding the sad film excerpts.

At first, the women watched four 48-second blocks of emotionally neutral film excerpts and then four blocks of sad film excerpts, with a 15 second break between each one. The emotionally neutral films, which featured various human activities (e.g., interviews, carpentry, etc.), were used to gauge the subject's brain state in the absence of an emotional reaction. However, the sad films featured the death of a beloved person. The excerpts were carefully matched as to the number and gender of persons portrayed.

At first, while watching the sad film excerpts, the subjects were asked to allow themselves to experience the sadness in a normal way. The second time around they watched four similar blocks of neutral excerpts followed by four sad excerpts. However, this time they were asked to down-regulate sadness by becoming a detached observer of the sad film excerpts and the sad response induced by these stimuli. Their brains were scanned during both conditions to see how they fared. All subjects reported indifference to the neutral films and sadness about the sad films, but all found that they could detach themselves from the sad films when they tried.[25]

It appears that, in principle, normal humans are not feeling robots, but are quite capable of adjusting their emotional reactions. This is true even of children, as Lévesque and colleagues discovered when they asked

The View from Neuroscience

In neurobiological terms, transient sadness was associated with significant loci of activation in the anterior temporal pole and the midbrain, bilaterally, as well as in the left amygdala, left insula, and right ventrolateral prefrontal cortex (VLPFC; BA 47). The midbrain is involved in the mediation of autonomic responses, such as skin conductance responses and body temperature changes. We therefore proposed that the midbrain activations noted during the sad condition likely reflected the autonomic responses accompanying subjects' sad feelings. We also posited that the insular activation measured in the sad condition was a neural correlate of the autonomic changes associated with the subjective experience of sadness, given the rich interconnection of the insula with regions involved in autonomic regulation. As for the VLPFC, increased VLPFC activity has been previously reported in association with sad thoughts or sadness in subjects with major depressive disorder. It thus appears that this brain region is associated with the processing of normal as well as pathological aspects of sadness.[26]

Interestingly, in the suppression condition, significant loci of activation were noted in the lateral prefrontal cortex (LPFC; BA 9) and the right orbitofrontal cortex (OFC; BA 11). The OFC activation during the emotional self-regulatory task is consistent with clinical neuropsychological studies indicating that this prefrontal region exerts an inhibitory control to protect goal-directed behavior from interference. Damage to the OFC leads to a frontal-lobe syndrome or pseudopsychopathic syndrome that is characterized by distractibility, impulsivity, emotional outbursts, shallowness, argumentativeness, verbal and physical aggressiveness, hypersexuality, hyperphagia, lack of concern for consequences of behavior, failure to observe social and moral rules, and risky decision-making behavior. Individuals with OFC lesions tend to be unpredictable, their humor is labile, and they often display inappropriate and childish humor. These individuals show abnormal autonomic responses to emotional elicitors, difficulty in experiencing emotion related to situations that would normally evoke emotion, and impaired understanding of the adverse consequences of detrimental social behaviors.[27]

fourteen eight- to ten-year-old girls[28] to watch the same neutral and sad films while inside the scanner. The children reported that they were able to keep their emotions in check during the second series, just as the adults had.

The difference between the parts of the brain that the children made use of and the parts that the adults made use of suggests that voluntary suppression of a primary emotion, such as sadness, requires more prefrontal work in children than in adults. It seems likely that conscious and voluntary self-regulation of emotion is more challenging (cognitively and affectively) in children than in adults because the maturation of the connections linking the prefrontal cortex and the limbic structures is not yet completed.

Learning to Live Without Fear

Arachnophobia: An abnormal and persistent fear of spiders. Sufferers from arachnophobia experience undue anxiety even though they realize the risk of encountering a spider and being harmed by it is small or nonexistent. They may avoid going barefoot and may be especially alert when taking showers or getting into and out of bed.
> —*MedicineNet medical dictionary*

Along came a spider
> And sat down beside her
> > And frightened Miss Muffet away.
> > > —*Traditional nursery rhyme*

Fear is never a good counsellor and victory over fear is the first spiritual duty of man.
> —*Philosopher Nicolas Berdyaev (1874–1948)*

The View from Neuroscience

In the children, significant loci of activation were found in the lateral prefrontal cortex (LPFC; BA 9–10), orbitofrontal cortex (OFC; BA 11), medial prefrontal cortex (MPFC; BA 10), and rostral anterior cingulate cortex (ACC; BA 24).

Over 11 percent of Americans suffer from unreasonable fears (phobias). Spider phobia (arachnophobia) is close to the top of the fear list. Most phobics are women, but 10 percent of British spiderphobes, for example, are men. Spider phobia can take over a life, resulting in bizarre behavior, career damage, and ruined relationships. Questions of where and how to live, work, vacation, or exercise may be dominated by an assumed need to avoid spiders. For example, phobics have been known to pour bleach between their kitchen appliances each night, put masking tape over tiny holes that they fear spiders might use, and inspect every inch of their bedrooms before sleeping. Many come to believe that spiders work in teams to watch them and follow them around. "I once ran outside completely naked," one woman confessed to Britain's *Daily Telegraph*. "I was about to have a shower and spotted two huge spiders on the wall. Luckily, it was sunny, so I hid in the garden until my husband came home."[29]

In Britain, about 1 million people are believed to suffer from spider phobia; indeed, it is the second most common British phobia, after public speaking. That would make spider phobia the most common *unreasonable* fear in Britain. Public speaking, after all, entails at least some genuine social and career risks, but British spiders are usually harmless.

Just why spider phobia is so common is unclear. Natural spider behavior may act as an unintentional trigger. Spiders sometimes lose their footing while walking upside down on ceilings, falling abruptly onto the heads or shoulders of people beneath them. They also have a disconcerting habit of lowering themselves by a strand of silk and hanging in midair or spinning a web right across a path and sitting motionless in the middle, perhaps accidentally creating the impression that they are stalking a human. Such an incident may trigger the beginning of a phobia in a susceptible child. Just as with OCD, a phobia is reinforced by the phobic behavior itself until it dominates the phobic's life. Movies like *Arachnophobia* (1990), in which a killer spider, armed with "eight legs, two fangs, and an attitude," moves in on a family, riff off existing fears.[30]

Generally, spider phobia can be cured. Cognitive behavior therapy (CBT) is especially effective. CBT consists of two parts. Phobics (1) gradually desensitize themselves to the presence of spiders and (2) learn natural facts about spiders that resolve fears. (For example, spiders do not work in teams, and they never stalk humans.) But reorganizing one's mind and brain around the nature of spiders raises a question of what is really happening. Is the phobic's brain simply being reprogrammed by outside forces, or is a mind that makes choices controlling and reorganizing its brain?

A few years ago (2003), Johanne Lévesque and Vincent Paquette, another doctoral student working in the lab at the Université de Montréal, helped twelve women, mostly in their late teens or twenties, get over spider phobia using CBT, all the while scanning their brains with fMRI to see what was happening physiologically.[31] They began by advertising in a Montreal newspaper for women who admitted that they dreaded spiders. After excluding from the study anyone who had a neurological or psychiatric disorder apart from the phobia, they administered standard questionnaires about phobias in general and spider phobias in particular to ensure that the subjects truly feared spiders. They also simulated part of the actual experiment, showing film excerpts of spiders to the phobic women inside a mock fMRI scanner, to make sure that they could tolerate enough contact with spiders and scanners to actually complete the study.

Meanwhile, thirteen psychologically healthy women of a similar age who claimed not to fear spiders were scanned while shown the same film excerpts. These women (controls) were used for comparison to the study group (spiderphobes) because the scans showed that they did not experience fear while viewing films of spiders.

During the experiment, the spiderphobes were scanned while they viewed film excerpts of living spiders and living butterflies. Butterflies are generally considered harmless, so the phobic's brain state while viewing butterflies can be compared with the same person's state while viewing spiders (nonfear vs. fear).

The therapy consisted of gradual exposure to spiders using guided mastery and education for the purpose of correcting mistaken beliefs about spiders. This approach was chosen because evidence shows that short intensive exposure sessions work best for specific phobias.[32] The phobics met for four weekly three-hour intensive group sessions (two six-member groups). The first week, they were asked to look at an exercise book containing fifty color pictures of spiders. The second week, they were gradually exposed to film excerpts of living spiders. They were also asked to continue to look at the printed pictures and watch the videotape at home between sessions. The third week, they were asked to stay in a room that also contained living spiders. Finally, during the fourth and last session, they were asked to touch a huge, live tarantula. And they all did.

These findings suggest that, without drugs, devices, rewards, or threats, the phobic subjects had gradually rewired their own brains over the four weeks, so that they no longer felt the fear that had limited their lives. They support the conclusions of previous PET studies showing that psychotherapy can lead to adaptive regional brain metabolic changes in patients suffering from major depression[33] and OCD.[34] They also indicate that the changes made at the mind level, through psychotherapy, can functionally "rewire" the brain. In other words, "change the mind and you change the brain."[35]

> All we are looking at is a piece of machinery, an analog chemical computer, that processes information from the environment.... You can look and look and you will not find any ghostly self inside, or any mind, or any soul.... The soul, that last refuge of values, is dead, because educated people no longer believe it exists.[36]
> —*Tom Wolfe,* "Sorry, but Your Soul Just Died"

It is interesting to revisit social chronicler Tom Wolfe's essay on neuroscience, "Sorry, but Your Soul Just Died," written halfway through the Decade of the Brain, after we have viewed evidence that the human mind can significantly influence the functioning of the brain. Wolfe's death announcement may have been a trifle premature, the worried reductionism a

The View from Neuroscience

Before CBT, exposure to the film excerpts of spiders produced significant activation of the right lateral prefrontal cortex (LPFC; BA 10), right parahippocampal cortex, and visual associative cortical areas (bilaterally) in phobic subjects. It was hypothesized that the LPFC activation reflected the use of metacognitive (pertaining to thinking about thinking) strategies aimed at self-regulating the fear triggered by the spider film excerpts, whereas the parahippocampal activation related to an automatic reactivation of the contextual fear memory that led to the development of avoidance behavior and the maintenance of spider phobia. At the conclusion of the treatment, all twelve spiderphobes showed a marked reduction in fear, and no significant activation was seen in the LPFC and the parahippocampal cortex. In other words, the pattern of activation in these subjects showed that they had become much more like the control group, who did not fear spiders.[37]

trifle greedy perhaps. Mind, consciousness, and self are not out of a job after all. In fact, as we shall now see via the placebo effect, mind, consciousness, and self play a key role in whether, how, and how soon we recover from illnesses.

Believing *Can* Make It So

Classical scientific assumptions simply do not account for how mind-body interactions, biofeedback, or the placebo effect works.[38]

—*Dean Radin,* The Conscious Universe

Health is thought to be a biological phenomenon. More psychosomatic elements are hard to deal with.[39]

—*Epidemiologist Robert Hahn,*
Center for Disease Control and Prevention

What a pity so many give undeserved credit to the drug, and not to their own efforts.[40]

—*Thomas J. Moore,* Boston Globe

In large measure, the history of medicine is the history of the placebo effect.[41]

— *Herbert Benson and Marg Stark,*
Timeless Medicine

By the 1990s, psychiatrists were skilled at treating depression with powerful antidepressants. In fact these pills were hailed as the ultimate weapon. Conventional wisdom discouraged wasting time on the mythical construct of the distressed mind; such rubbish was fit only for the soon to be extinct Freudians. Scientific medicine should focus on fixing the malfunctioning *brain*! As Tom Wolfe noted, "The demise of Freudianism can be summed up in a single word: lithium." Or Prozac, or Zoloft, or one of the many other conjured names.

Janis Schonfeld was a poster patient for this new generation of antidepressants. The forty-six-year-old interior designer, married with a daughter, was contemplating suicide when she found just enough hope to enroll in a drug study at UCLA. She put up with the greasy gel through which the EEG recorded her brain activity for forty-five minutes. But she couldn't wait to get started on those promising new pills. And the pills worked brilliantly. Yes, nausea was a tiresome side effect, but her competent and caring nurse had warned her about that. Much more important, her life got back on track. As *Mother Jones* magazine put it, Schonfeld seemed "yet another person who owed a nearly miraculous recovery to the new generation of antidepressants."[42]

On Schonfeld's last visit, one of the doctors took her and her nurse aside and told them both the truth: Schonfeld had been in the control group. She was taking a sugar pill—in the research lingo, a placebo. Her recovery, the doctor hastened to assure her, was entirely genuine. But the only drug she had received was an immaterial and immortal substance—hope. Schonfeld's main challenge, given that she lived in a materialist environment, was to accept the evidence of her own experience—that a recovery based on her inner resources is real—rather than the urgent cultural messages that only a brain-bending drug could really help her.

The placebo effect—the significant healing effect created by a sick person's belief and expectation that a powerful remedy has been applied when the improvement cannot have been the physical result of the remedy—must not be confused with natural healing processes. It depends specifically on the patient's *mental* belief and expectation that a specific remedy will work. For millennia, doctors have given placebos, knowing that they often help when all else fails. Since the 1970s, a proposed new drug's effectiveness is routinely tested in controlled studies against placebos, *not* because placebos are useless but precisely because they are so useful. Placebos usually help a percentage of patients enrolled in the control group of a study, perhaps 35 to 45 percent.[43] Thus, in recent decades, if a drug's effect is statistically significant, which means that it is at least 5 percent better than a placebo, it can be licensed for use.

In 2005, *New Scientist,* hardly known for its support of nonmaterialist neural theory, listed "13 Things That Don't Make Sense," and the placebo effect was number one on the list.[44] Of course, the placebo effect "doesn't make sense" if you assume that the mind either does not exist or is powerless.

The Neuroscience of the Placebo Effect

The sheer power of the placebo effect on depression was a remarkable discovery, but the effect also works for much less "subjective" conditions.

New Scientist, pondering the problem, cited one study in which the tremors of Parkinson's disease[45] were eased by a placebo (saline solution). Neural activity associated with tremors declined as the symptoms decreased, so the patients could not simply have been confabulating that they felt better. Believing that they had received a powerful medication had triggered the release of dopamine in their ailing brains.

Other studies of Parkinson's show similar results. Raül de la Fuente-Fernández and colleagues reported in 2001 that "our results suggest that in some patients, most of the benefit that is assumed to be obtained from an active drug might derive from a placebo effect." The researchers observed from PET scans that the placebo effect in Parkinson's patients was mediated through activation of the damaged nigrostriatal dopamine system.[46]

University of Michigan researchers recently demonstrated the placebo effect in young, healthy men. They injected saltwater into their volunteers' jaws and measured the impact of the resulting painful pressure via PET scans. Volunteers were told that they were receiving pain relief. They reported feeling better. The placebo treatment reduced the brain responses in a number of brain regions known to be implicated in the subjective experience of pain. No pain-relief drug was used in the study. The researchers commented (2004): "These findings provide strong refutation of the conjecture that placebo responses reflect nothing more than report bias."[47]

Similarly, Petrovic and colleagues showed by an fMRI study that placebo treatment could change neural activity in brain regions mediating perception of emotions, as it does in the brain regions supporting percep-

---

The View from Neuroscience

Recent functional magnetic resonance imaging (fMRI) experiments have found that placebo analgesia is related to decreased brain activity in pain-sensitive regions of the brain known as the thalamus, insula, and anterior cingulate cortex. Pain relief was also associated with increased activity in the prefrontal cortex (where thinking occurs) during anticipation of pain, suggesting that placebos act on pain-sensitive areas of the brain to alter the painful experience.[48]

—W. Grant Thompson, *The Placebo Effect and Health*

tion of pain. They asked a group of subjects to participate in a two-day study in which they watched three blocks of pictures. Subjects were lying down inside an fMRI scanner, wearing goggles. Some of the pictures were neutral and some unpleasant. After each block was presented, the subjects were asked to rate the pictures. The first block was presented on the first day, with no drugs. The second block was presented with a low dose of benzodiazepine (given intravenously), and the subjects did not find the unpleasant pictures so unpleasant. For the third block, the subjects were given a drug that acted the opposite of benzodiazepine (benzodiazepine receptor agonist), and they perceived the unpleasant pictures as unpleasant again. They were also informed that the entire treatment would be repeated on the second day, so they should have been aware of what to expect.

The next day, the subjects were told that they would be treated with the same drugs before seeing the unpleasant and neutral pictures. They were even told via a computer screen which one they were getting. They once again perceived the unpleasant pictures as much less unpleasant after they had received the benzodiazepine and as unpleasant again after they received the agonist. Only they hadn't. In both cases, they had received saltwater. So their views of the pictures were guided by what they thought the drugs would do to them.[49]

Sham Surgery

Perhaps even more remarkably, sham surgery works too. Sylvester Colligan of Beaumont, Texas, could barely walk before his 1994 knee operation. He was mobile and free of pain six years later. But, as he later learned, he was in the control group. Yes, he received three knee incisions, but he was just sewn up again afterward; no conventional arthroscopy had been done.[50] He would never have known that from his own body's responses. Similarly, a 2004 study compared thirty patients who received controversial embryonic stem-cell implants for Parkinson's disease to patients who received only a sham surgery. Those who thought they had received the stem cells reported better quality of life a year later than those who thought they had received the sham surgery, regardless of which surgery patients had actually received. And the ratings by medical personnel tended to concur with the patients' own views.[51]

In *Timeless Medicine,* Herbert Benson and Marg Stark list a number of conditions that are affected by patient beliefs. Most forms of pain are on the list, of course, but so are cold sores, duodenal ulcers, dizziness, and skin reaction to poisonous plants.[52]

Limitations

However, placebos are not a cure-all. They can't help every condition. Robert J. Temple found (2003) that placebos rarely help shrink cancerous tumors, though they do improve patients' pain control and appetite.[53] The placebo effect can also fail when the patient suffers a cognitive disorder. Fabrizio Benedetti, for example, found that Alzheimer's syndrome can rob a patient of the cognitive ability to expect a proven painkiller to work, and in that case it becomes less effective.[54]

How the Placebo Effect Works

Neuroimaging studies have now demonstrated that the placebo effect is real. It is not simply an artifact of medical record keeping or folklore. But when we try to understand how it works, we must look not only at the brain but also at the mind. The Mayo Clinic recently issued a press release that confirmed the importance of the effect and offered the following suggested explanations:

> Some patients respond well to frequent and intensive medical attention, whether or not a drug or treatment is potent.

> Some patients may train themselves to respond positively to a treatment, real or not.

> A patient who believes a treatment will work is more likely to experience the placebo effect than one who doubts it.

> A patient whose doctor is supportive and positive may benefit more from any treatment, active or placebo.

> Patients may feel better simply because they aim to please! They want to prove that they are good patients who value the time and attention that the medical staff has kindly provided them.[55]

No doubt these reasonable explanations cover most cases. One might also consider the "Hawthorne effect." Named after a study of worker performance done at a Chicago electric plant in the late 1920s and 1930s, this explanation suggests that people respond favorably because they have been enrolled in a study, apart from the usefulness of interventions.[56]

But none of these explanations accords with a materialist view, which holds that the mind does not exist or else it has no influence. Every one of them assumes that the mind is changing the brain and the body. For that matter, if we reverse any of them, we can account for the placebo effect's evil twin, the *nocebo* effect.

The Nocebo Effect

> Surgeons are wary of people who are convinced that they will die. There are examples of studies done on people undergoing surgery who almost want to die to re-contact a loved one. Close to 100 percent of people under those circumstances die.[57]
> —*Herbert Benson, Harvard Medical School*

Placebo means "I will please,"[58] and *nocebo* means "I will harm." The nocebo effect is the harmful health effect created by a sick person's belief and expectation that a powerful source of harm has been contacted or administered. Essentially, patients who are convinced that a medication is bad or useless will often exhibit symptoms that conform to that view. Consider the following:

> Volunteers for medical studies who have been warned about the side effects of the medication often develop those effects even though they are in the sugar-pill control group.

> Pills of a size or color that communicate the wrong "message" may work according to expectation, not pharmacology. Red and orange may stimulate but blue and green may depress, contradicting the chemically expected effect.[59] By contrast, a trusted brand name printed prominently on the side usually helps, even if the pill is only sugar.

> People who are convinced that they will get an illness are much more likely to get it.[60] For example, women in the massive Framingham study, begun in 1948, who believed that they were more likely than

others to develop heart disease, were indeed twice as likely to, even when they did not engage in the behaviors that promote heart disease.[61]

Of course, it should be noted that people who are convinced that they will get an illness may have good reason for thinking so. Family history is a powerful predictor of many diseases and may underlie the greater susceptibility. But, if the research findings noted above are generally correct, that expectation itself may function over time as a nocebo effect.

A controversial proposed example of the nocebo effect has been "voodoo death"—generally, heart failure after being cursed by a voodoo priest.[62] Some have argued that patronizing Western anthropologists have overplayed these incidents. However, it is worth noting that the criminal code of Canada, after denying that deaths supposedly caused by "the influence of the mind alone" are culpable homicide, nonetheless adds this rider: "This section does not apply where a person causes the death of a child or sick person by willfully frightening him" (sec. 228), which seems to recognize the nocebo effect of fear in a sick patient.

The nocebo effect has received increasing attention in recent years. For one thing, much noncompliance with treatment has been traced to it. The patient who doubts the value of a treatment may experience side effects that would not be observed if the treatment was believed to have value. Some sources of nocebo effects[63] include:

Media hype trumpeting a new treatment—followed by a scare about its possible downside.

Cold, impersonal health facilities run as if they are factories or businesses. These have long been recognized as a problem, but they are beginning to be considered seriously as an actual nocebo effect.

Conflict between scientific medicine and traditional or alternative treatments, so that patients are forced to choose. Subsequent conflict with caregivers or deception may provoke a nocebo effect.

A trickier problem is the possible nocebo effect of medical information provided specifically in order to avoid malpractice lawsuits. In principle, it is right and proper to give the patient all the relevant information. But a nocebo effect may be accidentally triggered if a patient interprets a long list of possible complications from a treatment as evidence that things are likely to go wrong.[64]

What the nocebo effect primarily demonstrates in reverse is the influence of the mind on the brain and therefore on the body.

Misconceptions About the Placebo Effect

The placebo effect is uninfluenced by intelligence or any test of susceptibility.[65]
—*W. Grant Thompson,*
The Placebo Effect and Health

The doctor who fails to have a placebo effect on his patients should become a pathologist.[66]
—*J. N. Blau, M.D.*

Some claim that the placebo effect is mythical, that it only applies to gullible people, or even that its use is unethical. What about that? Popular myths about placebos include the notions that they only work for about three months or that only certain personality types respond to them. There is no specific time limit on most placebo effects, nor is there any specific type of "placebo responder."[67]

But most of all, the placebo effect has been an embarrassment and a problem for drug studies. So there have been attempts to discredit it.[68] Danish researchers Asbjørn Hróbjartsson and Peter C. Götzsche recently did a metastudy of 114 studies that used placebos and found research flaws, such as that, in assessing the placebo effects, the authors relied heavily on quoting each other. Thus, they concluded that there was

little evidence in general that placebos had powerful clinical effects ... [and] ... compared with no treatment, placebo had no significant effect on binary outcomes, regardless of whether these outcomes were subjective or objective. For the trials with continuous outcomes, placebo had a beneficial effect, but the effect decreased with increasing sample size, indicating a possible bias related to the effects of small trials.[69]

No doubt some research methodology is flawed, but the placebo effect is one of the best-known facts of everyday clinical medicine and critical to assessing the usefulness of drugs. Like consciousness, it cannot simply be defined out of existence. In any event, the fact that neuroimaging data demonstrate the placebo effect obviates questions about its existence.

Science journalist Alun Anderson suggests: "Trust and belief are often seen as negative in science and the placebo effect is dismissed as a kind of 'fraud' because it relies on the belief of the patient. But the real wonder is that faith can work."[70] Anderson has identified a key issue. A materialist may well think that the placebo effect is a kind of fraud precisely because it implies that the mind can change the brain.

As a result, materialist accounts of the placebo effect are often incoherent. For example, it may be described as the way in which "the brain manipulates itself."[71] As we have seen, the placebo effect is actually triggered by the patient's mental state. In other words, it depends entirely on the patient's state of belief. An unconscious process initiated by the brain to manipulate itself (or any other part of the body) is a normal healing process, *not* the placebo effect. For example, had the Parkinson's patients' brains been able to manipulate and thus heal themselves, no treatment would have been required, whether by placebo, pharmaceuticals, sham surgery, or real surgery.

In one British study, 63 percent of two hundred doctors admitted to prescribing placebos.[72] Some ethicists have criticized the practice as unethical because the doctor is, in their view, deceiving the patient. But the accusation begs the question. Doctors are systematically taught to behave in a way that invokes the placebo effect (authoritative and reassuring language, framed medical degrees, trademark white coat and stethoscope, definite treatment plan). Indeed, Canadian journalist Martin O'Malley noted in *Doctors,* an in-depth portrait of working physicians:

> There are times when doctors have to be arrogant know-it-alls and even bluffers, for it would be distressing if they were to shrug "I dunno" to questions of which they were not absolutely certain. At all the best medical schools this "cloak of competence" is encouraged because it is known that supreme confidence alone often can work wondrous cures.[73]

If doctors didn't behave in a way that generates confidence, they would quickly evoke the nocebo effect. And nocebo ("I will harm") directly contradicts the Hippocratic Oath ("First, do no harm"). Physicians know, after all, that placebos regularly work; if they are not supervising a controlled study, they can prescribe one and allow their patients' expectations to do their work.[74]

The Placebo Effect and the Future of Medicine

> Neither the placebo nor the nocebo effect has been much studied—medical discomfort with such squishy phenomena aside, there's no money in it.[75]
>
> —*Susan McCarthy,* Salon

Ever since placebo-controlled studies began, an underlying economic issue has confounded the study of the placebo effect's true role in maintaining health. Hope cannot be trademarked. If a proposed drug "performs no better than placebo," that is bad news for the drug's developers *even if* 85 percent of the control group and 85 percent of the experimental group get better. The current view that mental states are powerless but drugs are powerful has hampered the proper study of the placebo effect.

Prescientific medicine depended largely on the placebo effect. The fact that it so often works helps us understand why many traditional peoples are reluctant to simply abandon prescientific medicine despite its questionable and often dangerous doctrines.[76] Unfortunately, prescientific practitioners often attribute their power to the *doctrines* they espouse when they should rather attribute it to the *effects* they have learned, by trial and error, to evoke. Scientific medical research is beginning to help resolve the dilemma by accepting the mind-based nature of the placebo effect. It can be studied as an authentic effect and its power can be targeted, perhaps increased, which is so much more productive than continuing to treat it simply as a nuisance.

A clear understanding of the placebo effect could also obviate some current controversies. For example, the ethical issues surrounding the use of embryonic stem cells in treating Parkinson's disease might be easier to resolve if placebo effects account for most of their assumed value. Similarly, controversial treatments in some parts of the world involve the body parts of endangered species. These treatments may owe most of their effect to the patient's belief in the efficacy of the exotic treatment. A clear demonstration of that fact can help conservation efforts.

As we have seen, many useful clinical applications flow from a nonmaterialist approach to neuroscience. When we treat the mind as capable of changing the brain, we can treat conditions that were once considered difficult or impossible to treat. But we also need a model for how the mind acts on the brain.

The Mind's Interaction with the Brain

If it is for mind that we are searching the brain, then we are supposing the brain to be much more than a telephone-exchange. We are supposing it to be a telephone-exchange along with subscribers as well.[77]
      —*Nobel Prize–winning neuroscientist*
      Charles Sherrington (1857–1952)

As we have seen, several lines of evidence demonstrate that mental phenomena can significantly alter brain activity. These lines include our fMRI studies about emotional self-regulation and the impact of CBT in spider phobia as well as the functional neuroimaging studies of the placebo effect. The results of this last set of studies clearly show that brain activity can be driven by the patient's mental belief and expectation in relation to a proposed medical treatment.

To interpret the results of these studies, we need a hypothesis that accounts for the relationship between mental activity and brain activity. The *psychoneural translation hypothesis* (PTH) is one such hypothesis. It posits that the mind (the psychological world, the first-person perspective) and the brain (which is part of the so-called "material" world, the third-person perspective) represent two epistemologically different domains that can interact because they are complementary aspects of the same transcendental reality.

The PTH recognizes that mental processes (e.g., volitions, goals, emotions, desires, beliefs) are neurally instantiated in the brain, but it argues that these mental processes cannot be reduced to and are not identical with neuroelectric and neurochemical processes. Indeed, mental processes—which cannot be localized in the brain—cannot be eliminated.

The reason that mental processes cannot be localized within the brain is that there is actually no way of capturing thoughts merely from studying the activity of neurons. This problem is similar to the problem of trying to determine the meaning of messages in an unknown language (thoughts) merely by examining its writing system (neurons). You would need a Rosetta Stone that compares the writing system of the unknown language to the writing system of a known language. But there is no such stone for the mind and the brain, and therefore no such comparison is possible.

As a result, the mentalistic terminology that describes these processes remains absolutely essential to a satisfactory account of the relationship between brain dynamics and human behavior. No one has ever seen a thought or a feeling, yet they exert a tremendous impact on our lives. Moreover, according to the PTH, conscious and unconscious mental processes are automatically translated into neural processes at the various levels of brain organization (biophysical, molecular, chemical, neural networks). In turn, the resulting neural processes are further translated into processes and events in other physiological systems, such as the immune or endocrine system.

Psychoneuroimmunology (PNI) is the scientific discipline that investigates the relationships between the mind, the brain, and the immune system. Neuroscientist Candace Pert calls the communication between the mind, the brain, and the other physiological systems the *psychosomatic network*. A correct understanding of the psychoneural translation mechanics can shed light on the way that mental processes affect the brain and body—for good or ill.

Metaphorically, we can say that *mentalese* (the language of the mind) is translated into *neuronese* (the language of the brain). For example, fearful thoughts increase the secretion of adrenaline, but happy thoughts increase the secretion of endorphins. This informational transduction mechanism represents a paramount achievement of evolution that allows mental processes to causally influence the functioning and plasticity of the brain. It is somewhat like writing our spoken words down in a symbol system that can be read by others at a distance.

One illustration of mind/brain translation is a neuroimaging study by our group[78] in which we measured changes in regional brain serotonin (5-HT) during self-induced states of sadness and happiness in professional actors. When people are asked to recall and relive an emotionally charged autobiographical event, they tend to activate the same brain areas as they would activate during an actual event.[79] One valuable outcome is that neuroscientists can study intense emotions through recollections.

A teleologically oriented (i.e., purposeful rather than random) biological evolution has enabled humans to consciously and voluntarily shape the functioning of our brains. As a result of this powerful capacity, we are not biological robots totally governed by "selfish" genes and neurons. One outcome is that we can intentionally create new social and cultural environments. Through us, evolution becomes conscious, that is, it is driven not simply by drives for survival and reproduction but more by complex sets of insights, goals, desires, and beliefs.

In my view, ethical achievements are the outcome of contact with a transcendental reality behind the universe and not simply the outcome of the multiplication of neurons in the prefrontal cortex of the human brain. It is unclear that, by themselves, the neurons would evolve any ethical system.

By virtue of the psychoneural translation mechanism, moral values associated with a given spiritual worldview can help us to govern our emotional impulses and behave in a genuinely altruistic fashion.[80] In such cases, moral conscience replaces innate programming as a regulator of behaviors. The capacity for rational and ethical behaviors in turn frees us from the primitive dictates of the mammalian brain. Such freedom is responsible for the fact that, even though the genome is the same across human societies, some cultures value and foster violence and aggression while other cultures perceive violence and aggression negatively and rarely

The View from Neuroscience

We measured serotonin (5-HT) synthesis capacity using the radiotracer 11C-alpha-methyl-tryptophan (11C-aMtrp) combined with PET. The reason we use tryptophan is that it will cross the blood-brain barrier, but serotonin will not. The subjects recalled autobiographical memories to induce sadness, happiness, and a neutral emotional state on three separate scan acquisitions. Results showed that the reported level of sadness was negatively correlated with 11C-aMtrp trapping increases in the left orbitofrontal cortex (OFC; BA 11) and the right anterior cingulate cortex (ACC; BA 25). By contrast, the reported level of happiness was positively correlated with 11C-aMtrp trapping increases in the right ACC (BA 32). In view of the PTH, these findings suggest that a specific emotional state that is voluntarily self-induced can rapidly be translated into a selective modification of brain regional 5-HT synthesis capacity.

employ them. Fortunately, many cultures have also begun to encourage people to move beyond a narrow sense of obligation to one's own kin or social group to an appreciation and compassion for all life, especially other humans because we can so easily identify with them.

But one question looms large when we consider the mind apart from the brain, a question that—as we have seen—was considered by Neanderthal man and by our earliest ancestors. What exactly happens at death? The brain dies. But does the mind die with it? Perhaps not. Let us look at that next.

Near-Death Experiences: The Light at the End of the Tunnel

Mainstream neuroscience ... insists that individual consciousness vanishes with the death of the body. However, given its ignorance of the origins and nature of consciousness and its inability to detect the presence or absence of consciousness in any organism, living or dead, neuroscience does not seem to be in a position to back up that conviction with empirical scientific evidence.[81]

—*B. Alan Wallace,* The Taboo of Subjectivity

Near-death experiences (NDE) occur with increasing frequency because of improved survival rates resulting from modern techniques of resuscitation. The content of NDE and the effects on patients seem similar worldwide, across all cultures and times.[82]

—*Cardiologist Pim van Lommel*

In 1991, thirty-five-year-old Atlanta-based singer and songwriter Pam Reynolds began to suffer dizziness, loss of speech, and difficulty moving. The news from her CAT scan could not have been worse. She had a giant basilar artery aneurysm (a grossly swollen blood vessel in the brain stem). If it burst, it would kill her. But attempting to drain and repair it might kill her too. Her doctor offered no chance of survival using conventional procedures. As she recalls:

I will never forget the terrible sadness that permeated the air as my husband drove to our attorney's office for the filing of my last will and testament. Somehow, we would have to tell our three small children that soon, Mommy would make the journey to heaven, leaving them with the few, short memories their tender years could afford them.[83]

But Reynolds's mother told her of a last, desperate measure that might offer hope. Neurosurgeon Robert Spetzler, at the Barrow Neurological Institute in Phoenix, Arizona, was a specialist and pioneer in a rare, dangerous, but sometimes necessary technique called hypothermic cardiac arrest, or "Operation Standstill." He would take her body down to a temperature so low that she was essentially dead, but then bring her back to a normal temperature before irreversible damage set in. At a low temperature, the swollen vessels that burst at the high temperatures needed to sustain human life become soft. Then they can be operated upon with less risk. Also, the cooled brain can survive longer without oxygen, though it obviously cannot function in that state.

So for all practical purposes, Reynolds would actually be dead during the surgery. But if she didn't agree to it, she would soon be dead anyway with no hope of return. So she consented. As the surgery began, her heart was stopped, and her EEG brain waves flattened into total silence. During a cardiac arrest, the brain's electrical activity disappears after 10 to 20 seconds. Her brain stem and cerebral hemispheres became unresponsive, and her temperature fell to 60 degrees Fahrenheit (as opposed to the usual 98.6 degrees).

When all of Reynolds's vital signs were stopped, the surgeon began to cut through her skull with a surgical saw. At that point, she reported that she felt herself "pop" outside her body and hover above the operating table. From her out-of-body position, she could see the doctors working on her lifeless body. She observed, "I thought the way they had my head shaved was very peculiar. I expected them to take all of the hair, but they did not."[84] She described, with considerable accuracy for a person who knew nothing of surgical practice, the Midas Rex bone saw used to open skulls. Reynolds also heard and reported later what was happening during the operation and what the nurses in the operating room had said. At a certain point, she became conscious of floating out of the operating room and traveling down a tunnel with a light. Deceased relatives and friends were waiting at the end of this tunnel, including her long-dead grandmother. She entered the presence of a brilliant, wonderfully warm and loving Light and sensed that her soul was part of God and that everything in existence was created from the Light (the breathing of God). This extraordinary experience ended when Reynolds's deceased uncle led her back to her body. She compared reentering her body to "plunging into a pool of ice" (perhaps not surprisingly, given that her body had been cooled to well below normal temperature).

Many near-death experiences (NDEs) have been reported, of varying degrees of credibility. Pam Reynolds's case is unique for two reasons. First, she had the experience at a time when she was fully instrumented under medical observation and known to be clinically dead. Clinical death is the state in which vital signs have ceased: the heart is in ventricular fibrillation, there is a total lack of electrical activity on the cortex of the brain (flat EEG), and brain-stem activity is abolished (loss of the corneal reflex, fixed and dilated pupils, and loss of the gag reflex). Second, she was able to recall verifiable facts about her surgery that she could not have known if she were not in some way conscious when these events were taking place.

Why is this story significant, other than as a tale of medical heroics? Pam Reynolds's case strongly suggests that: (1) mind, consciousness, and self can continue when the brain is no longer functional and clinical criteria of death have been reached; and (2) RSMEs can occur when the brain is not functioning. In other words, this case seriously challenges the materialist view that mind, consciousness, and self are simply by-products of electrochemical brain processes, and RSMEs are delusions created by a defective brain. Such a view is based on a metaphysical belief, not on scientifically demonstrated facts.

If Reynolds's case were the only one of its type, one might be wise to withhold any opinion. But she is by no means the only person whose account challenges materialist views of mind and consciousness. Dutch cardiologist Pim van Lommel reports a case in which a coronary-care nurse removed dentures from a cyanotic and comatose forty-four-year-old heart-attack victim and placed them in a drawer in the crash cart. The patient was revived by CPR, and a week later the nurse saw him again on the cardiac ward. She reports:

> The moment he sees me he says: "O, that nurse knows where my dentures are." I am very surprised. Then he elucidates: "You were there when I was brought into the hospital and you took my dentures out of my mouth and put them onto that cart, it had all these bottles on it and there was this sliding drawer underneath, and there you put my teeth." I was especially amazed because I remember this happening while the man was in deep coma and in the process of CPR.[85]

She noted that the patient recalled the details of the resuscitation room correctly.[86]

Systematic Study of NDEs

Life is full of anomalies,[87] and a couple of unusual cases do not challenge so widely accepted a paradigm in science as materialism. Thomas Kuhn famously pointed out, "To be accepted as a paradigm, a theory must seem better than its competitors, but it need not, and in fact never does, explain all the facts with which it can be confronted."[88] However, in this case, the matter is not quite that simple. Materialism is a complete, monistic doctrine, and therefore cases like these should not only be very rare; they should be impossible.

But NDEs are not even very rare.[89] When van Lommel was an intern in 1969, a patient described one. At the time, van Lommel did not pursue the information, but in the late 1980s, after reading another doctor's account of his own NDE, he began interviewing heart-attack survivors. Within two years, fifty patients had told him about an NDE.

Unfortunately, however, when he consulted the professional literature, all the research he could find was retrospective. That is to say, it reported on events of perhaps five to thirty-five years earlier. Apart from the inevitable risk that survivors may embroider or fantasize their accounts, there is often no way of determining that the experience occurred during clinical death. And clinical death is the critical element. Pam Reynolds was clinically dead when she apparently observed operating-room scenes and events.

In 1988, van Lommel started a prospective[90] study that interviewed 344 consecutive heart-attack survivors within a week of resuscitation. Recent heart-attack survivors are a favorite study group for NDEs because available medical records can confirm that after the arrest they were clinically dead. Their brains are anoxic, they are unconscious, and they will die from irreversible brain damage if not resuscitated within five to ten minutes. Only in recent decades have any significant number of people ever come back from the state of clinical death. Indeed, even the term *clinical death* is modern. At one time, there was just death.

Obviously, a person in a state of clinical death should not perceive anything. But sixty-two, or 18 percent, of the patients van Lommel interviewed reported some recollection from the time when they were clinically dead. The depth of their experiences varied, but a core group of 7 percent reported a very deep experience. In similar American and British studies, the rates were 10 percent (Greyson, 2003) and 6.3 percent (Parnia et al., 2001), respectively.

Van Lommel's NDE patients did not differ from his non-NDE control group in fear of death, foreknowledge of NDE, religion, education, medical condition, or treatment. Patients who had lost short-term memory as a result of lengthy CPR reported significantly fewer NDEs, but under the circumstances it is not possible to determine whether they in fact had fewer of them.

Types of NDEs

> All my life up till the present seemed to be placed before me in a kind of panoramic, three-dimensional review, and each event seemed to be accompanied by a consciousness of good or evil or with an insight into cause or effect. Not only did I perceive everything from my own viewpoint, but I also knew the thoughts of everyone involved in the event, as if I had their thoughts within me. This meant that I perceived not only what I had done or thought, but even in what way it had influenced others.[91]
>
> —*A heart-attack survivor's account of his NDE*

Van Lommel classified the experiences his patients reported by type:[92]

Out-of-body experience (OBE). This is an experience of floating outside one's own body, while retaining one's identity and a very clear consciousness. Most patients report looking down from above. As we have seen, in some cases, patients have reported information that was later verified.

Holographic life review. In the popular phrase, "I felt my whole life passing before my eyes." As van Lommel describes it:

> All that has been done and thought seems to be significant and stored. Insight is obtained about whether love was given or on the contrary withheld. Because one is connected with the memories, emotions and consciousness of another person, you experience the consequences of

your own thoughts, words and actions to that other person at the very moment in the past that they occurred.[93]

Encounter with deceased relatives or friends. Deceased persons are recognized by their remembered appearance, but communication appears to be through direct transfer of thoughts.[94]

Return to the body. Some patients learn, through wordless communication with a Being of Light or a deceased relative that they ought to return to life, especially if they have a task to fulfill. This choice, advice, or command is often carried out reluctantly.

Disappearance of fear of death. Almost every near-death experiencer (NDEr) loses the fear of death. This is partly because experiencers expect to survive death, but also because they experience love and acceptance rather than condemnation and uncertainty. The life review is not an external expression of divine wrath but a requirement that they experience the true outcomes of their choices. Generally, NDErs come from different religious backgrounds but have very similar experiences.

One curious phenomenon is that blind people sometimes report that they can see during an NDE. Forty-five-year-old Vicki Umipeg had been born blind, her optic nerve completely destroyed at birth when she was given too much oxygen in the incubator. Yet, apart from the fact that she could not distinguish color, Vicki's NDE unfolded as a sighted person's might.[95] Although that sounds surprising, it is worth noting that lifetime blind people often learn the world within their reach fairly accurately through touch rather than sight. They cannot detect color (as Vicki did not), background, or changes in the position of objects, but within those limits, their knowledge is accurate.[96]

Like van Lommel, American cardiologist Michael Sabom began to study NDEs among his patients in 1994. He was a bit worried about the best-seller status of books such as Raymond Moody's *Life After Life* (1975), which popularized the term "near-death experience" but did not read like scientifically grounded work. Sabom was anxious to put the study of NDEs on a professional footing. For example, he avoided interviewing survivors who had told their story to a mass audience or served as a subject in other research.

Over a period of two years, Sabom interviewed and surveyed 160 patients, mostly from his own clinical practice. He found that 47 had had NDEs as rated on the Greyson scale,[97] associated with a near-fatal physical crisis and unconsciousness.[98] Twenty-eight of the NDErs were women and 19 were men; they ranged in age from thirty-three through eighty-two and came from all walks of life. Fewer than half were traditional Christians, but all professed some belief in God. The non-NDE patients provided a baseline comparison.[99] Generally, Sabom's Atlanta-based patients reported NDE experiences similar to those of van Lommel's Dutch patients.

Negative NDEs

> I thought to myself that I could have been anything that I wanted to be. I had just destroyed it.[100]
>
> —*Attempted suicide survivor recounting a distressing NDE*

Only a minority of reported NDEs are distressing. Researchers Bruce Greyson and Nancy Bush took ten years to find fifty such cases.[101] Sabom eventually located two cases in his Atlanta study. One of them was an attempted suicide who vomited up the fatal dose during the NDE. A key finding is that when NDEs follow a suicide attempt, the patient typically abandons thoughts of suicide afterward. That's significant because many NDErs don't particularly want to be revived. Nonetheless, losing the fear of death seems to mean losing the fear of life as well.[102]

Some NDEs sound equivocal. For example, philosophical atheist A. J. Ayer (1910–89) describes an NDE he had in 1988:

> I was confronted by a red light, exceedingly bright, and also very painful even when I turned away from it. I was aware that this light was responsible for the government of the universe. Among its ministers were two creatures who had been put in charge of space. These ministers periodically inspected space and had recently carried out such an inspection. They had, however, failed to do their work properly, with the result that space, like a badly fitting jigsaw puzzle, was slightly out of joint.... I felt it was up to me to put things right.[103]

Ayer finally escaped the painful red light. He apparently remained an atheist until his death the following year, but he became, in the words of his wife, much nicer and more interested in other people.

Playwright William Cash, who staged a play based on Ayer's account at the Edinburgh Festival, received a somewhat different account of Ayer's reaction from his doctor at the time, Jeremy George. George recalls that Ayer told him, "I saw a Divine Being. I'm afraid I'm going to have to revise all my various books and opinions."[104] He did not do so, however. Toward the end, though, he admitted Jesuit philosopher Frederick Copleston—a former debating partner—as his closest friend. Even though Ayer's experience was equivocal, he exhibited greater compassion, a hallmark of NDE.

The Effects of NDEs

> In the latter part of the twentieth century, we have such a need to be unique, to be special, to be different. You know the thing that unifies so many of these people—they are so narcissistic. It's "Look at me. I saw God. I saw Jesus. I am different."[105]
>
> *—Professor Sherwin B. Nuland,*
> *Yale University Medical School*

> The purpose of life, most NDErs agree, is divine knowledge and love. Studies on the transformative effect of the NDE show that the cultural values of wealth, status, and material possessions become much less important, and the perennial religious values of love, caring for others, and acquiring knowledge about the divine ascend to greater importance.[106]
>
> *—Philosopher Neal Grossman*

Van Lommel and Sabom both found that NDErs like Ayer usually become more compassionate. But it is reasonable to ask, might most survivors of a close call with death put more emphasis on relationships, with or without an NDE? The NDErs get more public attention of course, especially if they tell their story to a wide audience on religious broadcasting networks.

Wanting more precise information, van Lommel followed up NDErs two years and then eight years later, matched with a control group who reported no NDEs. He found

> a significant difference between patients with and without an NDE. The process of transformation took several years to consolidate. Patients with an NDE did not show any fear of death, they strongly believed in an afterlife, and their insight in what is important in life had changed: love and compassion for oneself, for others, and for nature.... Furthermore, the long lasting transformational effects of an experience that lasts only a few minutes was a surprising and unexpected finding.[107]

Sabom also found that NDErs tended to put more emphasis on relationships. On the Life Changes Questionnaire,[108] NDErs typically showed an increase in faith, sense of meaning in life, capacity for love, and involvement with family that significantly exceeded those elements in post-op non-NDE patients.[109]

Materialist Science on NDEs

> If what you mean by "soul" is something immaterial and immortal, something that exists independently of the brain, then souls do not exist. This is old hat for most psychologists and philosophers, the stuff of introductory lectures.[110]
>
> *—Psychologist Paul Bloom,*
> *author of* Descartes' Baby

Generally, materialist science does not account convincingly for NDEs. Some proponents suggest that NDErs really are conscious in the usual sense. What if fragments of consciousness somehow linger in the brain or moments of lucid consciousness are lost, then regained, during CPR?

These hypotheses do not account for NDEs, because states of fragmentary, failing, or recovering consciousness produce confused memories, whereas NDE accounts are typically lucid. Some argue that the changes are simply the outcome of cerebral anoxia (loss of oxygen to the brain). But all 344 of van Lommel's patients were clinically dead. Thus, if that is the correct explanation, all or most of them should have reported NDEs, but only 18 percent did.

Some look for explanations from fleeting, fragmentary experiences induced by drugs, hypogravity, or electrical stimulation[111] in patients who are not unconscious or near death. But, as van Lommel notes, the induced non-NDE recollections

> consist of fragmented and random memories unlike the panoramic life-review that can occur in NDE. Further, transformational processes are rarely reported after induced experiences.[112]

The fact that an unusual mind state may occur as a result of drugs, stimulation, or hypogravity is not under dispute. However, NDEs occur when patients are in a state of clinical death, and they commonly result in significant life change. That's what requires explanation.

Some claim that NDErs merely embellish their memories of a medical crisis over time. But van Lommel's patients were interviewed within a few days of CPR, which is probably too soon for time to gild memories. Still, Canadian science journalist Jay Ingram notes that van Lommel's point of view is "repellent to many" and charges, "who's to say that some [NDEs] weren't falsely remembered in the days and weeks following the patients' hospitalization?"[113]

Who, indeed? Yes, patients might confabulate to get attention or please the doctors—except for one thing. The NDErs showed high rates of key attitude change years later (for example, loss of fear of death) relative to non-NDE patients. A more reasonable conclusion is that the NDErs experienced a lucid state that brought about actual changes—and that lucid state deserves further study.

Psychologist Susan Blackmore also tackles the NDE life changes, explaining:

> The limited evidence available suggests that this change is a function of simply facing up to death, not of having a near-death experience, but when NDErs behave altruistically, this helps spread their NDE memes—"I'm a nice person, I'm not so selfish now, believe me. I really did go to heaven." Wanting to agree with this honestly nice person helps spread the memes. And if the NDE survivor really does help you, you may take on the NDE memes as a way of returning the kindness. Thus, NDE memes spread, and among them is the idea that people who have had NDEs behave more altruistically.[114]

Blackmore's explanation doesn't explain anything. First, simply facing up to death does not induce NDE life changes. If so, almost all heart-attack survivors would change their lives, and research shows that they do not. As for the rest, she is simply arguing that the human mind is governed by "memes"—hypothetical units of thought that replicate themselves (see Chapter Seven), intellectual equivalents to Dawkins's "selfish genes." That is an entirely superfluous and untestable concept. By contrast, clinical death, verifiable accounts, and behavior change after NDE are all testable.

Neurologist Jeffrey Saver and physician John Rabin's treatment of the question illustrates the difficulties of the materialist position nicely.[115] Citing the NDEs of fallen Alpine mountaineers, they correctly identify key common factors: "Although some near-death experiences are distressing or hellish, most are serene and joyful and may produce profound and long-lasting changes in beliefs and values." To account for the experience, they suggest that "an underlying driving biologic mechanism appears likely." They argue that the NDE might be a survival mechanism, "endorphin-induced limbic system activity or a blockade of NDMA [N-methyl d-aspartate, an excitatory neurotransmitter in the mammalian nervous system] receptors for glutamate by 'putative' endogenous neuroprotective molecules, which might dampen glutamate excitotoxicity in hypoxic-ischemic settings."

But their suggestions do not explain what most needs explaining, that patients report information later verified and recount life-changing experiences from periods when they were known to be clinically dead. Perhaps sensing that they have not dealt with the main problem, Saver and Rabin proceed to invoke a by now familiar explanatory model, evolutionary psychology (we behave the way we do because that was how our ancestors survived):

> For prey trapped by a predator, passive immobilization, feigning death, may promote survival. More generally, the clarity of perception and insight associated with dissociation might allow individuals to identify and carry out previously unrecognized strategies to escape desperate, life-threatening circumstances.[116]

Feigning death? Frightened opossums do lapse into deep unconsciousness, and predators that despise carrion may toss them aside. It is also true that some humans have survived massacres by pretending to be dead. But near-death states cannot have been a survival strategy in the remote past because only high-tech interventions in recent decades have allowed a significant number of people to return from the near-death state to tell of their experiences. The NDEr, by contrast, is in an *unfeigned* state of verifiable clinical death, thus hardly in a position to invent clever survival strategies. Far from having a survival strategy, NDErs are often disappointed when they find themselves returned to life.

The NDE points to something beyond mere survival, which Saver and Rabin mistakenly assume to be the goal of all existence. Their suggestions primarily show that materialism so poorly accounts for NDEs that materialists cannot even address the basic substance of the NDE experience and thus begin to talk of something else—for example, how a primitive mammal, rendered unconscious by fright, is rejected as carrion. This is a frequent characteristic of materialist explanations of NDEs.

Religion and NDEs

> We must remember that Satan has the ability to appear as an "angel of light" and as a "servant of righteousness."... His goal, of course, is to lead people astray. He is happy to mimic a being of light if the end result is that he can lead people away from the true Christ of Scripture.[117]
> —*Ron Rhodes, Reasoning from the Scriptures Ministries, on the dangers of NDEs*

Materialists are not alone in their discomfort with NDEs. As philosopher Neal Grossman has pointed out, corroborated testimony from NDEs may not support the doctrines of some religious groups. Worse, it may support the doctrines of a competitive group. For example, if a religious group's identity and sense of mission are bound up with preaching a vengeful or inscrutable God, the group won't celebrate the general finding that

> there is judgment, to be sure, but the reports appear to be in agreement that all judgment comes from within the individual, not from the Being of Light. It seems, in fact, that all God is capable of giving us is unconditional love.[118]

On the other hand, some NDErs do experience anguish. That may contradict another group's claim that torment over past choices is impossible, even when it is self-inflicted. Thus, both groups may avoid or deny NDEs and continue to spar over doctrine, removed from the threat of evidence. Their concerns are likely unfounded for several reasons.

People interpret their NDEs using available language and concepts. As van Lommel notes, "The subjective nature and absence of a frame of reference for this experience lead to individual, cultural, and religious factors determining the vocabulary used to describe and interpret the experience."[119] How many known languages have a vocabulary for NDE? Languages are developed to interpret usual experiences, not unusual ones, and may simply fail at certain points. Not all knowledge bases are equally correct or useful for interpreting an experience and not everyone draws reasonable conclusions even from a correct and useful one. But the NDErs are not alone in their difficulty. Mystics frequently complain that language is not adequate to the task of describing mystical experiences, as we shall see in Chapter Seven.

NDErs' basic shifts in attitude are stable over time, compared with a control group. These changes must be accounted for. People do not change their lives toward a more spiritual orientation over fleeting illusions or trivialities.

NDErs generally confirm the basic values of the world's religions. As Grossman notes, NDErs tend to internalize the values of their religion, because they begin to see them not as speculations or dogma, but as verified facts. He comments, "A consequence of the life review is that it appears to be a great disadvantage to oneself to harm another person, either physically or psychologically, since whatever pain one inflicts on another is experienced as one's own in the life review."[120]

NDE Research and Medicine

> When they got me back, I felt a lot of guilt that I hadn't wanted to come back because I had felt so good. I worked with my doctor and my minister afterwards because it really bothered me a great deal that I wouldn't want to come back.... My son was two at the time and my daughter was five.[121]
> —*A patient describing mixed feelings after an NDE*

NDEs occur more often than medical personnel may realize. Most attitude and personality changes are positive, but some may pose a challenge. For example, many NDErs report mixed feelings about being revived. We don't know how many NDErs—unhappy with the prospect of survival—don't try hard and succumb in the early post-op period. Van Lommel, for example, discovered that significantly more patients who had a deep NDE died within thirty days of CPR than patients who did not have an NDE.[122] Health-care professionals who perceive that the patient has experienced death as attractive can better reorient the patient to everyday life. A practitioner can support the post-NDE patient without necessarily espousing the patient's position on the nature of the NDE.

NDEs in a Materialist Framework

Philosopher Grossman found that discussing NDEs with committed materialists is generally a waste of time. Reproducing a snatch of frustrating dialog, he recalls:

> Exasperated, I asked, "What will it take, short of having a near-death experience yourself, to convince you that it's real?"
>
> Very nonchalantly, without batting an eye, the response was: "Even if I were to have a near-death experience myself, I would conclude that I was hallucinating, rather than believe that my mind can exist independently of my brain."[123]

Grossman reflected later, "This was a momentous experience for me, because here was an educated, intelligent man telling me that he will not give up materialism, no matter what. Even the evidence of his own experience would not cause him to give up materialism."[124]

Materialists seem to think that NDEs cannot fit into a materialist framework, and they must be allowed to be the best judges of that. Nonetheless, there seems good reason to believe that mind, consciousness, and self can continue when the brain no longer functions and that therefore RSMEs can happen when the brain is clinically dead. But this implies something else—that mind can act in its own right. If so, can mind act on other minds or on objects?

Psi: The Effect That Wouldn't Be Discredited

These disturbing phenomena seem to deny all our usual scientific ideas. How we should like to discredit them! Unfortunately the statistical

evidence, at least for telepathy, is overwhelming. It is very difficult to rearrange one's ideas so as to fit these new facts in.[125]
—*Artificial intelligence pioneer A. M. Turing*

Turing took "cold comfort" in the idea that paranormal phenomena might be reconcilable in some way with well-established scientific theories. We differ with him. We suspect that if such phenomena as telepathy, precognition, and telekinesis turned out to exist (and turned out to have the remarkable properties typically claimed for them), the laws of physics would not be simply *amenable* to accommodate them; only a major revolution in our scientific world view could do them justice.[126]
—*Douglas R. Hofstadter and Daniel C. Dennett,*
The Mind's I

In the midst of all the nonsense and excessive silliness proclaimed in the name of psychic phenomena, the misinformed use of the term "parapsychology" by self-proclaimed "paranormal investigators," the perennial laughingstock of magicians and conjurers ... this is for real?
   The short answer is, Yes.[127]
—*Dean Radin,* The Conscious Universe

In 2004, *New Scientist* published a cover story, "Power of the Paranormal: Why It Won't Surrender to Science."[128] Readers expecting to hear of fraudulent mediums going high-tech would be disappointed. The stubborn problem turns out to be a small statistical effect from controlled laboratory studies, the *psi effect,* a general term for telepathic and psychokinetic phenomena. Humans, it turns out, can communicate with others without contacting them (*telepathy*) and move matter without touching it (*telekinesis*), such as influencing the diffraction pattern of a beam of light—consistently above statistical chance.

   As *New Scientist*'s John McCrone notes, "perhaps some statistical artefact will be unearthed to explain it."[129] Perhaps so, but this pattern has persisted for decades. McCrone goes on to complain: "In many ways, it is the skeptical community that is on the back foot, unable to explain away the results in terms of cheating, artefact or fluke. They are back to making suspicious noises about why believers get results."[130]

   As we have seen, the term "skeptical" has developed a rather restricted meaning. It no longer means "applying rigorous critical judgment" so much as "defending materialism." Skeptics, in this sense, are seldom skeptical of arguments in favor of materialism, even when they flub the evidence. But what *is* the evidence that makes McCrone and others nervous?

New Scientist was tacitly acknowledging an important shift in recent years in the treatment of psi effects. As nonmaterialist consciousness researcher Dean Radin notes, "There are disagreements over how to interpret the evidence, but the fact is that virtually all scientists who have studied the evidence, *including the hard-nosed skeptics,* now agree that something interesting is going on that merits serious scientific attention."[131] Interestingly, philosopher Sam Harris, hardly a sympathetic witness, admits this in *The End of Faith: Religion, Terror, and the Future of Reason* (2004), where he acknowledges "a body of data attesting to the reality of psychic phenomena, much of which has been ignored by mainstream science."[132] He concedes:

> The dictum that "extraordinary claims require extraordinary evidence" remains a reasonable guide in these areas, but this does not mean that the universe isn't far stranger than many of us suppose. It is important to realize that a healthy, scientific skepticism is compatible with a fundamental openness of mind.[133]

Harris has little to fear, for two reasons. A healthy scientific skepticism is *by definition* compatible with a fundamental openness of mind. In any event, parapsychology, the study of psi effects, is increasingly recognized as a legitimate scientific discipline.

The Parapsychological Association, an international scientific society, was elected an affiliate of the American Association for the Advancement of Science (AAAS) in 1969. Seminars on psi research have formed part of the regular programs of annual conferences of the American Association for the Advancement of Science, the American Psychological Association, and the American Statistical Association. Educated audiences at the United Nations, Harvard, and Bell Laboratories have invited lecturers on the state of psi research. Reports have been prepared by the Congressional Research Service, the Army Research Institute, the National Research Council, the Office of Technology Assessment, and the American Institutes for Research (this latter one commissioned by the CIA). All five of the reviews concluded that, based on experimental evidence, certain forms of psychic phenomena deserved serious scientific study.

But perhaps the most culturally significant change has been a new attitude toward psi effects in college textbooks, which generally teach orthodox and mainstream positions. In *Introduction to Psychology*, Richard L. Atkinson and three coauthors note in their 1990 preface:

> Readers should take note of a new section in Chapter 6 entitled "Psi Phenomena." We have discussed parapsychology in previous editions but have been very critical of the research and skeptical of the claims made in the field. And although we still have strong reservations about most of the research in parapsychology, we find the recent work on telepathy worthy of careful consideration.[134]

Despite the caveats, these comments signal a shift away from an approach in which psi effects were addressed mainly as an instance of the tendency of some individuals to believe things that are not true toward an approach that asks what the evidence reasonably suggests.

Celebrity Psychic Frauds

> "I get an older man here" is a question, a suggestion, and a guess by the "reader," who expects some reaction from the subject, and usually gets it. That reaction may just be a nod, the actual name of a person, or an identification (brother, husband, grandfather), but it is supplied BY THE SUBJECT, not by the reader.[135]
>
> —*Magician The Amazing Randi, explaining a standard trick*

Psi is a stable, *low-level* effect, typically a little too high to be chance. Thus a school bus driver who consistently scores higher than chance at telekinesis—however interesting he may be to researchers—will not win TV ratings wars. A celebrity psychic needs dramatic effects to stay in show business and may resort to crowd psychology or tricks to create the impression of astounding feats. Magician James Randi and others have become adept at identifying these manipulative techniques. But the techniques by which a celebrity psychic attracts and keeps an audience demonstrate nothing about psi in the laboratory. In science, it is the controlled studies that matter.

Actually, most magicians don't discount psychic phenomena merely on account of the media circus around celebrity psychics. The majority of magicians polled in two separate studies indicated that they believe that psi is a real effect.[136] What they don't do is claim that psi is the basis of their show business careers.

Another widespread misunderstanding is that psi should confer virtually magical powers or certify excellent character. In a recent press release on police use of psychics, a secular humanist group demanded to know, regarding recent cases of missing children:

> Where were [the psychics] when the parents and police were desperate for accurate information? If they can do what they claim, why aren't these psychic detectives actually out there saving people's lives instead of appearing on talk shows and promoting their books?[137]

Psi is *not* a form of magic. It is a low-level effect demonstrated in many laboratory studies—one that materialism does not account for. Whether celebrity psychics help the police or promote themselves irresponsibly is another matter.

Controlled Studies on the Psi Effect

> It is barely possible that a few of these paranormal claims might one day be verified by solid scientific data. But it would be foolish to accept any of them without adequate evidence.[138]
>   —*Carl Sagan,* The Demon-Haunted World

> Taking aspirin reduces the probability of a heart attack by a mere 0.8 percent compared with not taking aspirin (that's eight-tenths of one percentage point). This effect is about ten times smaller than the psi ganzfeld effect observed in the 1985 meta-analysis.[139]
>   —*Dean Radin,* The Conscious Universe

The existence of a psi effect is well verified. For telepathy, from 1974 through 1997, the results of about 2,550 ganzfeld (sensory deprivation) sessions were reported in at least forty publications by researchers worldwide, including studies that used computer-generated images (autoganzfeld) to avoid contamination by human interventions (the "greasy finger" effect). Generally, the studies show that people sometimes get small amounts of specific information from a distance that do not depend on the ordinary senses.[140] A meta-analysis (i.e., a technique of synthesizing research results by using various statistical methods to retrieve, select, and combine results from previous separate but related studies) of all ganzfeld telepathy studies up to 1997 revealed a probability of a million billion to one against chance.[141]

For psychokinesis, current research uses a random number generator (RNG), an electronic circuit that randomly flips an electronic "coin," while recording the results. In a typical modern experiment, random spikes of electronic noise or radioactive decay occurring several thousand times per second interrupt a crystal-controlled clock that is counting at a rate of 10 million cycles per second. The clock's state when interrupted will produce either 1 or 0. The experimental subject is asked to influence the RNG's output by "wishing" for 1's or 0's. A small but stable effect has been shown over sixty years of tossing dice and RNGs that is reliable irrespective of the subject or the experimenter and remains when independent or skeptical investigators participate.[142] A meta-analysis looking at 832 RNG studies conducted during the last decades showed odds against chance beyond a trillion to one.[143]

Then there's the curious case of the correlations of people who were separated. In a study published in *Neuroscience Letters* (2003), Jiří Wackermann and colleagues found that two human beings can coordinate their brain electrical states while separated from each other.[144] Interestingly, it didn't matter whether the subjects were emotionally close, and there was no one place in the brain where the effect was routinely most pronounced. The authors write, "We are facing a phenomenon which is neither easy to dismiss as a methodical failure or a technical artefact nor understood as to its nature. No biophysical mechanism is presently known that could be responsible for the observed correlations between EEGs of two separated subjects."

Overall, the more sophisticated the experiments become, the clearer the small but stable effect appears to be, and explaining it away becomes more and more difficult.

Materialism's Explanation of Psi

Despite the endless pronouncements and anecdotes in the popular press, and despite a steady trickle of serious research on such things, there is no significant or trustworthy evidence that such phenomena even exist. The wide gap between popular conviction on this matter, and the actual evidence, is something that itself calls for research. For there is not a single parapsychological effect that can be repeatedly or reliably produced in any laboratory suitably equipped to perform and control the experiment. Not one.[145]

—Materialist philosopher Paul Churchland

Science really can't talk about things like telepathy, belief, et cetera, in any kind of way. . . . All that we know about physical laws would say completely irrefutably that that doesn't happen, that's not the way things work.[146]

—Biologist and religious naturalist
Ursula Goodenough

Gradually by the 1990s, [skepticism] was shifting from controversies over whether the effect exists to how to explain it.... Skeptics who continue to repeat the same old assertions that parapsychology is a pseudoscience, or that there are no repeatable experiments, are uninformed not only about the state of parapsychology but also about the current state of skepticism![147]

—Dean Radin, The Conscious Universe

Generally, materialists respond to psi in four ways: flat denial, assertions that science cannot address psi, claims that it is a trivial effect, and proposing alternative hypotheses that remain untested. Paul Churchland, quoted above, might doubt that any laboratory that produces evidence of psi is "suitably equipped." Ursula Goodenough, also quoted above, doesn't explain how she knows, apart from evidence, that telepathy is not part of "the way things work." A useful discussion must move beyond that kind of thing.

Logical positivist philosopher A. J. Ayer advanced the "trivial effect" claim when he remarked in 1965 (by which time the pattern of psi effects was clear):

The only thing that is remarkable about the subject who is credited with extra-sensory perception is that he is consistently rather better at guessing cards than the ordinary run of people have shown themselves to be. The fact that he also does "better than chance" proves nothing in itself.[148]

That is an evasion. What "better than chance" demonstrates is that there is a psi effect, which is precisely what the psi researchers were attempting to determine. Although small, the effect is important because it shows that the current materialist account of the universe is not correct.

In science, small, persistent effects cannot be ignored. Sometimes they force a revision of major paradigms. For example, Lord Kelvin remarked in 1900 that there were just "two little dark clouds" on the horizon of Newtonian classical physics of the day, namely, Michelson and Morley's measurements of the velocity of light and the phenomenon of blackbody radiation. Kelvin was certain that these troubling little clouds would be blown away shortly.[149] Yet all of modern physics—relativity and quantum mechanics—derives from these two little dark clouds.

The fourth option, proposing alternative hypotheses but omitting to test them, is addressed by Dean Radin. The twofold outcome of that sort of "armchair quarterbacking," he notes, is that it discourages serious scientists, but encourages "believers" whose emotional commitments justify suspicion:

> If serious scientists are prevented from investigating claims of psi out of fear for their reputations, then who is left to conduct these investigations? Extreme skeptics? No, because the fact is that most extremists do not conduct research; they specialize in criticism. Extreme believers? No, because they are usually not interested in conducting rigorous scientific studies.[150]

Of course, we need not suppose that everyone is unhappy with this state of affairs. It retards the advance of psi to the forefront of evidence against materialism.

Psi Within a Science Framework

> Parapsychology is not a misguided search for bizarre mysteries, or a thinly veiled religious search for the soul. Instead, psi research is the study of an ancient and still completely unresolved question: Is the mind causal, or is it caused? Are we zombies with "nothing" inside, or are we self-motivated creatures free to exercise our wills?[151]
> —*Dean Radin,* The Conscious Universe

Psi must find its place within an evidence-based paradigm of physics, psychology, and neuroscience. However, working out and testing a hypothesis for psi faces some obstacles in a materialist environment.

Consider the fate of the placebo effect, for example. Although the effect is established beyond reasonable doubt in medicine, it is treated as either a mystery or a confounding nuisance. The reason is clear: in materialist science, a valid hypothesis of the placebo effect must explain away either its existence or its efficacy. So also with psi. An acceptable hypothesis examines the evidence in order to eliminate psi as a real effect. The study of psi should resemble exobiology (the study of extraterrestrial life forms), a study without a subject—except that one day exobiology may have a subject, but psi never.

Radin has suggested a relationship between psi and quantum entanglement that may generate testable hypotheses, though with some important qualifications. An adequate theory of psi, he says, will almost certainly not be quantum theory as it is presently understood.

> Instead, existing quantum theory will ultimately be seen as a special case of how *nonliving* matter behaves under certain circumstances. Living systems may require an altogether new theory. Quantum theory says nothing about higher-level concepts such as *meaning* and *purpose,* yet real-world "raw" psi phenomena seem to be intimately related to these concepts.[152]

In his view, science "slowly lost its mind" as a result of the separation of mind and matter that began about three centuries ago. The problem became serious in the early twentieth century with the feud between psychotherapy and behaviorism, the former unfalsifiable and the latter counterfactual.[153] Then dawned the era of "the mind as machine" in the 1950s. But computer models failed to answer important questions because computers are artifacts of minds and are not themselves conscious. Today, of course, we must choose between two falsified ideas, that mind and consciousness do not exist or that they exist but have no influence. New directions should be welcome at this point.

Radin suggests that parapsychology may point some new directions by forging links between psychology (which originated as a mind-oriented discipline) and neuroscience and cognitive science (which originated as matter-oriented disciplines). Parapsychology assumes that the scientific method can address the mind, provided that proposed hypotheses assume both the mind's existence and its efficacy.[154]

Psi and the End of Science

It is data which are the final arbiter of hypotheses.[155]
—*Harald Wallach and Stefan Schmidt,*
Journal of Consciousness Studies

Would the acceptance of psi lead to the end of science, as some fear? Psi effects in laboratory studies do not necessarily support sensational anecdotes or traditional beliefs as an accurate description of reality. Psi suggests only that the mind is less tightly bound in time and space than has been supposed, and that its effects are not limited within the confines of the brain and the body. It is compatible with well-established quantum effects, but science cannot go beyond that at present.[156]

Does psi show that miracles can happen? Claims about miracles (the direct actions of God in historical times) lie outside experimental science by definition because God cannot be deposed as a witness or compelled to serve as a subject in replicable research. Assuming, as most Americans do, that God exists, whether God gets involved now and then is a matter of opinion in which experimental science has no special expertise.

Some materialists, unfortunately, cheat by claiming that their theories disprove religious teachings about miraculous historical events. This creates unproductive conflict with religious leaders. To the extent that an event is explicitly identified as a divine intervention, science can say nothing one way or the other about its probability. For these reasons, among others, materialist doomsaying about the dangers of accepting the existence of psi can be discounted.

Some studies of the paranormal have tackled the question of faith healing (healing through spiritual power). Claims for faith healing are addressed in Chapter Eight, but in any event faith healing involves a different and much more complex assumption from the psi effect. In faith healing, *A* appeals for the healing of *B* to spiritual power source *C*. In other words, the process envisioned is triangular—it involves three parties. *A* is not even *attempting* to influence *B* directly. If faith healing is verified, it may work on principles different from those of psi.

Harald Wallach and Stefan Schmidt offer some useful suggestions for a next step in nonmaterialist scientific research in "Repairing Plato's Life Boat with Ockham's Razor" (2005). Occam's Razor is a sturdy scientific principle that, of two explanations, the simpler should be preferred. But razors, like all shearing tools, must be used with caution. Right now, we do not have a good theory of psi or a number of other nonmaterial phenomena that science is beginning to chart. Wallach and Schmidt offer a complementary principle, Plato's Lifeboat,[157] which permits us to rescue valid conflicting data for reevaluation later. We may put into Plato's Lifeboat phenomena for which there is at least some good evidence, even though we cannot yet assign them a place in the overall picture. About psi, they suggest:

> From the current state of our knowledge it is hard to establish ganzfeld telepathy as a fact. Nevertheless, there are too many studies with positive findings to negate the fact that at least sometimes this type of telepathy is possible. We think the data are challenging enough to place ganzfeld telepathy into Plato's life boat.[158]

They also suggest rescuing the efficacy of prayer and distant healing, direct mental interaction between living systems, interaction between intentionality and RNGs (microkinesis), precognition, telepathy, and macrokinesis (the "Pauli force").[159] There is enough evidence in each case to justify rescuing what we know and sorting it out later.

Is Psi a Supernatural Phenomenon?

To say that an event is "supernatural" is to say that it comes from above or outside nature. Theistic religions assume—as a starting point—that God is above nature (supernatural). So events caused by the direct, unmediated action of God are supernatural by definition.

However, as cosmologist Rocky Kolb, of the University of Chicago, noted recently, we don't understand 95 percent of nature (dark matter and dark energy).[160] Under the circumstances, it is a stretch to declare a phenomenon identified in a laboratory "supernatural" merely because it does not fit an established materialist paradigm.

Many materialists have argued that action at a distance is impossible; therefore psi must be supernatural. But, they say, the supernatural does not exist, and therefore psi does not exist. So the laboratory results must be wrong. Indeed, the driving force behind many attempts to discredit psi appears to be fear of the supernatural.

Practical Value of the Study of Psi

Some long-running, intractable controversies stem directly from materialist discomfort with psi effects. For example, the question of whether psychics ever assist the police in finding missing children is often subordinated in practice to a materialist agenda aimed at proving that psi effects never occur. Apparent failures of police psychics then bolster the materialists' *unrelated* claim that psi effects do not occur. Well-known psychics may then be tempted to counter the materialist agenda by inflating their successes. However, if psi is accepted as a stable, low-level effect—as the laboratory evidence appears to suggest—the question of whether, where, or when psi may assist the police can be resolved by ordinary decisions about how best to use resources.

An evidence-based account of psi might also help combat superstition. A Gallup poll reported in June 2005 that three-quarters of Americans hold some paranormal belief, little changed from similar results in 2001. There are no significant differences in beliefs by age, gender, education, or region,[161] though the percentages have apparently increased over the last quarter century.[162]

Perhaps, we should rather ask, what *is* the nature of nature? Can it include events that are not supernatural in the sense given above, but are also not easily accommodated by materialism?

Regarding psi, we can assume one of two things: (1) every single instance of psi is a direct interference in nature, presumably by a divine power from outside the universe; *or* (2) the universe permits more entanglement than the materialist paradigm does.

The second assumption creates many fewer problems than the first. We do not need to assume that every time a middle-aged bus driver beats the odds in a psi experiment, the universe has been invaded from the outside, let alone that, as unidirectional skeptics have often insisted, "science" is in danger or that "religion is invading science," or that "a new dark age" is upon us.

Research can determine the circumstances under which entanglement can occur above the quantum level, resulting in apparent action at a distance.

Some materialists retail baseless claims that psi effects have been discredited. People who attribute unusual experiences to psi react by simply disregarding science. As a result, they risk being victimized by superstitions for which there is actually *no* good evidence.[163] Nonmaterialist researchers have a clear advantage here because they have no hidden agenda to discredit all psi claims. They can thus help discriminate between assumptions about paranormal forces that are—and are *not*—supported by evidence.

Does Nonmaterialism Mean Antimaterialism?

> Materialist ontology draws no support from contemporary physics and is in fact contradicted by it.[164]
> —*Mario Beauregard*

> For scientifically minded people seeking a rational basis for the belief that truly ethical action is possible, James's epigram "Volitional effort is effort of attention" must replace *Cogito ergo sum* as the essential description of the way we experience ourselves and our inner lives. The mind creates the brain. We have the ability to bring will and thus attention to bear on a single nascent possibility struggling to be born in the brain, and thus to turn that possibility into actuality and action.[165]
> —*Jeffrey M. Schwartz and Sharon Begley,*
> The Mind and the Brain

The 2006 annual question from leading materialist think tank, the Edge, was "What is your dangerous idea?" One hundred and seventeen responses poured in, almost all from materialists of note. Reading them over, one is struck by how *un*dangerous the ideas actually are. The faculty lounge will only yawn at the idea that "we are nothing but a pack of neurons" (Ramachandran, quoting Crick), or that "there are no souls" (Bloom, Horgan, Provine), or that there is no free will (Dawkins, Metzinger, Shirky), or that the self is a zombie (Clark). No one will perk up on hearing that "the natural world is all there is" (Smith), that God is probably a fairy tale (Weinberg), or that "everything is pointless" (Blackmore). Not only are these ideas not dangerous in contemporary academe, they're not even surprising or interesting—or, at this point, particularly well supported.

Ironically, some of the top news stories of 2005 were controversies over ideas about science. For example, there was the intelligent design controversy. A scientist who wanted to say something genuinely dangerous could try saying that the universe or life forms show evidence of intelligent design.[166] Also, Harvard president Larry Summers ended up resigning over comments that differences in the gender makeup of science faculties reflect genuine differences between men and women, not merely bias. Neither the intelligent design advocates nor Summers waited long to be engulfed by fury.

If you want to say something dangerous, you must create risk where *you* live. Materialists' perception of their own ideas as "dangerous" in the contemporary climate is mere branding without substance. The real danger is that their ideas are slowly, systematically being disconfirmed. But that is *not* a danger they show the slightest sign of eagerness to address.

As we have seen, a scientifically coherent case can be made for a nonmaterial view of mind and consciousness. But nonmaterialism is not antimaterialism. That is, *nonmaterialist science can accommodate all phenomena that can be shown to be simply material in character. But it does not require that all phenomena be so shown—a crucial difference from materialist science.*

Nonmaterialist science avoids many unproductive projects, like trying to prove that all RSMEs are traceable to a wonky neural circuit, gene, or episode in evolutionary history, that consciousness and free will do not exist, that NDErs are mere fantasists, or that psi phenomena never occur. If a nonmaterialist view is correct, these dead ends will remain dead (despite brief flashes of glory in the pop science media), because *the researchers are on the wrong track.* As the evidence mounts, it must be addressed, not dismissed.

As we have seen, a nonmaterialist approach has practical applications as well as interesting research directions, particularly in medical science. It may:

bring formerly intractable mental disorders within the realm of treatment;

harness the power of the placebo effect, instead of treating it as an embarrassment;

enable health-care personnel to better understand the challenges faced by patients who have had NDEs; and

provide an evidence-based approach to psi effects.

In fact, through history, most human beings have simply acted as if nonmaterialism is true. Many have had RSMEs; some have become quite serious mystics. What are serious mystics like? What experiences have they reported? We look at that in Chapter Seven.

SEVEN

Who Has Mystical Experiences and What Triggers Them?

The study of the mystics, the keeping company however humbly with their minds, brings with it as music or poetry does—but in a far greater degree—a strange exhilaration, as if we were brought near to some mighty source of Being, were at last on the verge of the secret which all seek. The symbols displayed, the actual words employed, when we analyse them, are not enough to account for such effect. It is rather that these messages from the waking transcendental self of another, stir our own deeper selves in their sleep.[1]

—*Pioneer American psychologist William James*

Mysticism is among the most misused words in popular language. Over a century ago, American psychologist William James remarked that it had become an abusive epithet applied to "any opinion which we regard as vague and vast and sentimental, and without a base in either facts or logic."[2] Worse, said British mysticism researcher Evelyn Underhill, mysticism had been claimed as "an excuse for every kind of occultism, for dilute transcendentalism, vapid symbolism, religious or aesthetic sentimentality, and bad metaphysics. On the other hand, it has been freely employed as a term of contempt by those who have criticized these things."[3]

So what is mysticism really? Fortunately, in the last century or so, a number of scholars who were not mystics themselves have set out to study it seriously.

Mysticism as a Way of Knowing

One benefit of switching humanity to a correct perception of the world is the resulting joy of discovering the mental nature of the Universe. We have no idea what this mental nature implies, but—the great thing is—it is true.[4]

—*Physicist Richard Conn Henry*

W. T. Stace (1886–1967), a mid-twentieth-century scholar of mysticism, wondered whether some of the misunderstanding stems from an imagined identity between "misty" and "mysticism." The word "mysticism" actually derives from a Greek word (*muo*) meaning "conceal." Mist conceals because it limits vision. In that sense, there is nothing misty about mysticism.[5] Serious mystics seek access to levels of consciousness that are "concealed" from everyday life. Or, perhaps, not so much concealed as ignored. Levels of consciousness that do not help us get on in our careers or relationships tend to fall into disuse. If access to these levels could transform us, we would never know.

At any rate, to borrow a phrase from G. K. Chesterton, a thing so widely repudiated in such contradictory terms must have *some* merit. So then, what is mysticism, really? Stace explains:

> The most important, the central characteristic in which all fully developed mystical experiences agree, and which in the last analysis is definitive of them and serves to mark them off from other kinds of experiences, is that they involve the apprehension of an ultimate nonsensuous unity in all things, a oneness or a One to which neither the senses nor the reason can penetrate. In other words, it entirely transcends our sensory-intellectual consciousness.[6]

He also noted that mystical experience is not to be confused with telepathy or telekinesis (which, as we have seen, involve specific mind-matter interactions) and certainly not with a variety of claims about the "occult." Mystical experiences can be grouped into general categories; most fall into one of three general types: monistic mysticism, pantheistic mysticism, and theistic mysticism. Monistic mysticism is the mystical experience of sensing that the created universe revolves around a center from which everything issues. In pantheistic mysticism mystics sense that the entire external world is the ultimate power and that the experiencer is part of that power. In theistic mysticism one senses the presence of the highest power in the universe or a power from beyond the universe.

Mysticism and Science

As Dean Radin explains, mystics resemble scientists in several surprising ways:

> Science concentrates on outer, objective phenomena, and mysticism concentrates on inner, subjective phenomena. It is interesting that numerous scientists, scholars, and sages over the years have revealed deep, underlying similarities between the goals, practices and findings of science and mysticism. Some of the most famous scientists wrote in terms that are practically indistinguishable from the writings of mystics.[7]

Some scientists have described their own mystical experiences. Allan Smith, a thirty-eight-year-old medical researcher based in Oakland, California, was sitting at home alone one evening in 1976 when he experienced a state he describes as "Cosmic Consciousness":

> There was no separation between myself and the rest of the universe. In fact, to say that there was a universe, a self, or any "thing" would be misleading—it would be an equally correct description to say that there was "nothing" as to say that there was "everything." To say that subject merged with object might be almost adequate as a description of the entrance into Cosmic Consciousness, but during Cosmic Consciousness there was neither "subject" nor "object." All words or discursive thinking had stopped and there was no sense of an "observer" to comment or to categorize what was "happening." In fact, there were no discrete events to "happen"—just a timeless, unitary state of being.[8]

Now, from a scientific perspective, the proposition is quite simple. Either there are levels of consciousness that give us greater insight into our relationship to the reality underlying our universe or there aren't. If they exist, we can either reach them or we can't. If we do reach them, we either learn something or we don't. Mystics are akin to pioneer scientists, deep-sea divers, or astronauts, offering themselves as volunteers in the search and accepting the outcome. Underhill exclaims, "Over and over again the great mystics tell us, not how they speculated, but how they acted. Their favourite symbols are those of action: battle, search, and pilgrimage."[9]

Why access deep and unusual levels of consciousness? Mystics' explanations depend on their spiritual and other commitments, but there is a common thread. They believe that some fundamental facts about reality can never be correctly understood apart from observations made at this level. If mind is a fundamental character of the universe, as mystics believe, then the investigation must involve at least some experiments of mind—and the only mind mystics can volunteer is their own.

As Underhill explains in her landmark work, *Mysticism* (1911):

> Mysticism ... is not an opinion: it is not a philosophy. It has nothing in common with the pursuit of occult knowledge. On the one hand it is not merely the power of contemplating Eternity: on the other, it is not to be identified with any kind of religious queerness. It is the name of that organic process which involves the perfect consummation of the Love of God: the achievement here and now of the immortal heritage of man. Or, if you like it better—for this means exactly the same thing—it is the art of establishing his conscious relation with the Absolute.[10]

Mystics are motivated by love as well as by intellectual interest. But love is hardly a conflict of interest; it is a motive that mystics share with most pioneers. Few risk their very selves unless they love what they undertake—and are willing to accept whatever they find. Underhill warns:

> There is no sense in which it can be said that the desire of love is merely a part of the desire of perfect knowledge: for that strictly intellectual ambition includes no adoration, no self-spending, no reciprocity of feeling between Knower and Known. Mere knowledge, taken alone, is a matter of receiving, not of acting: of eyes, not wings: a dead alive business at the best.[11]

The Formal Study of Mysticism

> While consciousness lies in the no man's land between religion and science, claimed by both yet understood by neither, it may also hold a key to the apparent conflict between these two great human institutions.[12]
> —*B. Alan Wallace*, The Taboo of Subjectivity

Most writings on mysticism have been intended simply as guidance for mystics. However, in both the Eastern and Western traditions, formal study of contemplative and mystical consciousness dates back to at least the fourth century C.E.[13] It received broader attention in the nineteenth century with the advent of psychology as an academic discipline, in which three key researchers were William James, Evelyn Underhill, and W. T. Stace.

William James (1842–1910). James, who established the first psychology lab in the United States in 1875, influenced generations of thinkers worldwide through his efforts to understand consciousness and other mental phenomena, including spirituality. In *The Varieties of Religious Experience* (1902), he examined many RSMEs. He spotlighted the pathological aspects of the personalities of many experiencers, because he felt that "phenomena are best understood when placed within their series, studied in their germ and in their over-ripe decay, and compared with their exaggerated and degenerated kindred."[14] But, pragmatist though he was, he never succumbed to the temptation to suppose that the psychological sufferings of those who experienced RSMEs accounted for their experiences. James accepted the evidence that mystics do access a consciousness beyond themselves[15] and thus gave legitimacy to studies of spirituality, although his understanding of the mystics and their quest may have been hindered somewhat by his commitment to pragmatism as a school of philosophy.

Pragmatism is not to be confused with materialism. Materialism asserts that there is no nonmaterial reality. Pragmatism asks what the practical use (the "cash value") of an idea is. Mystics claim the value of mystical consciousness in its own right, for the same reasons as quantum physicists claim the value of quantum physics in its own right. Quantum physics had immense cash value, but that was hardly the motive of the original theorists. Pragmatism is not the best foundation for understanding any quest whose pioneers dismiss "practical" use.

Evelyn Underhill (1875–1941). Underhill, a Fellow of King's College, Oxford, was one of the first women in the British Anglican tradition to be given responsibility for spiritual direction. Perhaps that was because she was "unmatched by any of the professional teachers of her day" in theology, according to her *Times* obituary, even though she had no formal degrees. Her *Mysticism* (1911), a systematic study of the writings of serious mystics in the Western tradition, remains a classic and is an indispensable source for the point of view of Western mystics.[16]

Walter Terence Stace (1886–1967). Stace, a civil servant in India who later taught philosophy at Princeton, wrote two influential works, the scholarly *Mysticism and Philosophy* (1960) and *The Teachings of the Mystics* (1960), the latter intended for a popular audience. He reproduced writings on mystical philosophy from a variety of cultures and helped to rekindle scholarly interest. R. M. Hood (1975) followed up Stace's work by creating a mysticism *scale,* a measure that all teams of researchers studying a given question can use, thus enabling a comparison that might be impossible if they were all asking different questions.[17]

Despite the contributions of these and other scholars, the study of mysticism was largely neglected during the twentieth century, the heyday of

Identifying a Mystical Experience

According to pioneer psychologist William James (1902),[18] the chief characteristics of a mystical experience are:

1. *Ineffability:* "The subject of it immediately says that it defies expression."

2. *Noetic quality:* "Although so similar to states of feeling, mystical states seem to those who experience them to be also states of knowledge."

3. *Transiency:* "Mystical states cannot be sustained for long.... Often, when faded, their quality can but imperfectly be reproduced in memory." [This claim has been questioned.[19]]

4. *Passivity:* "When the characteristic sort of consciousness once has set in, the mystic feels as if his own will were in abeyance, and indeed sometimes as if he were grasped and held by a superior power."

However, Evelyn Underhill (1911)[20] posted a somewhat different list:

1. *True mysticism is active and practical,* not passive and theoretical. It is an organic life process, a something the whole self does, not something about which its intellect holds an opinion.

2. *Its aims are wholly transcendental and spiritual.* It is in no way concerned with adding to, exploring, rearranging, or improving anything in the visible universe.

Freudianism, behaviorism, and evolutionary psychology. The question was no longer, "What do mystics experience?" but "What's wrong with them, anyway? Can it be fixed? Or maybe it is okay because it is simply a means of spreading their genes!"

In general, since the Enlightenment, religion and RSMEs have been understood as primitive phenomena that will simply fade out with the advance of science and secularization. Émile Durkheim (1858–1917), a pioneer sociologist of religion, argued that the function of religion is to stabilize the social order. "Essentially, it is nothing other than a body of collective beliefs and practices endowed with a certain authority," he explained.[21] Rite and ritual became the focus of serious research because beliefs were thought to arise from the performance of the rituals that hold society together.[22] Sociology of religion, looking for hard data, concentrated on institutional religion, which is easy to study. It tended to ignore the effects of spirituality as such, which, the evidence suggested was much more significant.

---

3. This One is for the mystic not merely the Reality of all that is, but also *a living and personal Object of Love,* never an object of exploration.

4. *Living union with this One* is a definite state or form of enhanced life.

Philosopher W. T. Stace (1960)[23] distinguished between *extrovertive* and *introvertive* mystical experience:

Extrovertive: Nature, art, music, or mundane objects facilitate mystical consciousness. Suddenly, they are transfigured by awareness of the One.

Introvertive: The One is found "at the bottom of the self, at the bottom of human personality."

Generally, Stace regarded introvertive mysticism as much more important historically, because it escapes the limitations of the senses.

These lists are all useful, but for different purposes. James, who admitted that he was no mystic, describes mysticism in a more detached way than Underhill, who was personally sympathetic to the mystical temperament. Stace was primarily concerned to single out mystical consciousness from a variety of claims regarding unusual states of consciousness.

The resulting analyses accounted adequately for the role of established churches but would hardly explain the role of some Southern white American Christians in helping to end segregation in the United States in the 1960s, the four days of religious processions in the Philippines that brought down Marcos in 1986, or the ecumenical demonstrations that ended the Ceausescu regime in Romania in 1989.[24] Or even, for that matter, the conflict between Catholic investors and Dupont over environment issues in 2006. Such events spring from the "S" in RSMEs—spirituality. Often the spirituality originates in someone's mystical experience, the "M."

As sociologist of religion Peter Berger puts it, secularization theory held that "modernization necessarily leads to a decline of religion, both in society and in the minds of individuals."[25] Berger admits that his early work was based on this view, but now he thinks he was mistaken:

> Experiments with secularized religion have generally failed; religious movements with beliefs and practices dripping with reactionary supernaturalism (the kind utterly beyond the pale at self-respecting faculty parties) have widely succeeded.[26]

Generally, religion focused on spirituality has survived modernization, though it has inevitably become alienated from materialist science. An important reason is the prevalence of RSMEs. Materialist hypotheses, however they may be accepted in the academy, do not provide an adequate account for these experiences. For example, a recent paper in *Medical Hypotheses* (2005) argues that mystical experience in the mountains results from oxygen shortage and social isolation.[27] One wonders what the authors would make of mystical experiences in deserts, beside rivers, in cloisters, or on crowded trains.

Describing RSMEs

> In this ecstasy of mine God had neither form, color, odor, nor taste; moreover, that the feeling of his presence was accompanied with no determinate localization. It was rather as if my personality had been transformed by the presence of a *spiritual spirit*. But the more I seek words to express this intimate intercourse, the more I feel the impossibility of describing the thing by any of our usual images. At bottom the expression

most apt to render what I felt is this: God was present though invisible; he fell under no one of my senses, yet my consciousness perceived him.[28]
—Account of mystical experience given to psychologist William James (1902)

The cause of all things is neither soul nor intellect; nor has it imagination, opinion, or reason, or intelligence; nor is it reason or intelligence; nor is it spoken or thought.... It is neither science nor truth. It is not even royalty or winsome; not one; not unity; not divinity or goodness; nor even spirit as we know it....[29]
—Dionysus the Areopagite, first century C.E.

Mystics, famously, cannot find words to explain what they experience. Perhaps we should expect that. If everyone you know is color-blind, how will you explain red? No doubt you will say what red stands for—"dramatic," "love," "violent," "stop!" "sexy," "animal life," "dangerous," "tempting," "death," and such. Your hearers, of course, object that your explanation is both vague and contradictory. They hint that perhaps you only imagine that you see red. Psychologists can easily account for your behavior: you allow yourself feelings that you do not otherwise acknowledge, let alone express, by persuading yourself that you see this nonexistent color.

Naturally, you will soon become very frustrated. If only your hearers could just *see* red, even for a few moments, the apparent contradictions of your language would evaporate! They would clearly understand how a part of the color spectrum can evoke contradictory feelings, while remaining a specific property in its own right. Meanwhile, no verbal explanation suffices.

All sources agree that mystics face this problem to an acute degree when describing mystical consciousness. But as Underhill cautions, many mystics are articulate, and therefore quite happy to *try* to explain. Indeed, their explanations can become part of the problem:

All kinds of symbolic language come naturally to the articulate mystic, who is often a literary artist as well: so naturally, that he sometimes forgets to explain that his utterance is but symbolic—a desperate attempt to translate the truth of that world into the beauty of this.[30]

Rudolf Otto, author of *The Idea of the Holy* (1917), who followed Underhill and James in taking mystical experience seriously, suggested that mystics' word choices are best treated as ideograms rather than maps; indeed, taking mystics' words literally often results in useless theological controversy.[31]

Attempts at translation can lead to other misinterpretations as well. Freudians have detected perverted sexuality and clinicians have diagnosed insanity in mystics who were trying to describe their experiences in the language available. However, some useful terms have emerged from the mystics' descriptions. Three types of experience seem to be fairly general: contemplation, "dark night of the soul," and mystical union.

In contemplation, sometimes called meditation, recollection, or interior silence, consciousness is intentionally concentrated on one object or idea; distractions are simply noted and dismissed in the hope of encountering hidden levels of consciousness. The sixteenth-century Carmelite John of the Cross coined the term "dark night of the soul" to describe the sense of abandonment mystics sometimes feel when contemplation does not produce mystic consciousness; it is often associated with a residual unwillingness to give up a false sense of self. In mystical union (*unio mystica*) the mystic merges with God or the Absolute in love.

A related question, which we will look at shortly, is whether a common substrate links mystical experiences the world over. Or are such experiences so determined by language and culture that they cannot be understood apart from them? For example, do Christians and Buddhists have the same experiences but describe them differently—or are they having different experiences?

Some mystics have attempted to describe their experiences by negation. This *apophatic* tradition—explanation through denial—can be rhetorically effective, as in "No eye has seen, no ear has heard, no mind has conceived what God has prepared for those who love him."[32]

Misunderstanding has often resulted. Mystics do not seek to eliminate consciousness as such, but rather the everyday consciousness that generates high levels of mental noise, fatal to mystical experience. To access a buried level of consciousness, mystics must systematically negate or dismiss distracting thought patterns.[33] Thus, language difficulty stems from two separate sources: mystics negate readily understandable concepts, and yet cannot easily describe the mystical consciousness. James wisely cautions, "Their very denial of every adjective you may propose as applicable to the ultimate truth—He, the Self, the Atman, is to be described by No!

No! only, say the Upanishads—though it seems on the surface to be a no-function, is a denial made on behalf of a deeper yes."[34]

Similarly, mystics often describe their quest in apparently paradoxical ways. Zen Buddhism professes to aim, for example, at a state of mind that is beyond thought and "no-thought." However, as Jerome Gellman says, this should not be taken to mean a middle state between thinking and not thinking, which is logically impossible; rather, "often the intention is to point to a state of mind in which striving is absent, and labeling of mental activities ceases. The mind of 'no effort' strives neither for thought nor for no-thought."[35] Paradoxes apprise the hearer that mystical consciousness is different from the normal human thought stream.

What Do Mystics Experience?

All things I then forgot,
My cheek on Him Who for my coming came,
All ceased, and I was not,
Leaving my cares and shame
Among the lilies, and forgetting them.[36]
—*Carmelite mystic John of the Cross (1542–91)*

Mystical experiences are rare even for mystics. One reason is that the desire for such an experience poses a barrier. As Sister Diane of the Carmelite convent in Montreal explains: "You can't search for it. The harder you search, the longer you will wait."[37] Most mystics spend considerable time in prayer and contemplation; these practices reduce mental noise and pave the way for mystical consciousness, although they do not directly produce that consciousness.

In mystical traditions worldwide, some states of consciousness are familiar enough to be described, sometimes in a systematic way. Two are mystical union and abolition of self. In *mystical union* (Latin, *unio mystica*), generally the mystic senses unity with God or with the universe. Usually in the Christian tradition this is described in images such as "mystic marriage," or a drop of water absorbing the taste and color of the wine it falls into (Suso), or "iron within the fire and the fire within the iron" (van Ruysbroeck). The Jewish kabbalist Isaac of Acre spoke of absorption into God "as a jug of water into a running well." In Eastern traditions, the images more commonly reference emptiness, which is seen as ridding the mind of illusions.[38]

Abolition of self should not be confused with abolition of consciousness. As Underhill explains: "In this transcendent act of union, the mystic sometimes says that he is 'conscious of nothing.' But it is clear that this expression is figurative, for otherwise he would not have known that there had been an act of union: were his individuality abolished, it could not have been aware of its attainment of God." Rather, it means, abolition of "that hard separateness, that 'I, Me, Mine' which makes of man a finite isolated thing."[39] The mystic, who seeks a deeper consciousness, puts aside the artificially constructed selves that play out roles in everyday life. Or, as the Indian poet Tagore (1861–1941) puts it, "Nirvana is not the blowing out of the candle. It is the extinguishing of the flame because day is come."

The "Born Again" Experience

Many people in the Western Christian tradition have experienced the form of RSME that is known as a conversion or born-again experience, in which they first become aware of a spiritual dimension to their lives and choices. The experience, although often life-changing, usually does not involve mystical consciousness. As Stace puts it, these experiences have a "family resemblance" to mystical consciousness, but are not, strictly speaking, the same thing.[40]

Generally, the term "born again" refers to an intense conversion experience of the sort studied by William James and Alister Hardy. It is associated today with evangelistic crusades and charismatic renewals. According to Barna Research, in 1991 about 35 percent of Americans said they have had a "born again" experience. This percentage rose to 40 in 2005.[41] The Gallup organization has been asking a similar question for decades: "Would you describe yourself as a 'born-again' or evangelical Christian?" In 1976, 34 percent of respondents said yes, and in 1998 it was 47 percent. The average is about 39 percent.[42] The overall rise in percentages may relate to the growth of charismatic renewals and denominations over the last forty years.

The term "born again" itself ultimately derives from the New Testament ("No one can see the kingdom of God unless he is born again," John 3:3, NIV). Yet it was not widely used until the 1960s to describe a conversion experience and is still mainly used among Protestant rather than Catholic Christians. Catholics are more likely to think in terms of "becoming a Christian" (through baptism) or of "renewing one's baptismal faith." However, charismatic renewals among Catholics are just as likely to feature, and to emphasize, intense, life-changing experiences. Both the Protestant and Catholic varieties are spreading rapidly in Third World countries.

One reason that North Americans have been slow to embrace philosophical materialism is that many either have had or know someone who has had a born-again experience convincing them that the tenets of materialism are simply not true. Most of these people do not become mystics. The mystic has a more challenging quest: to find out what *is* true.

Misconceptions About Mysticism

> We can make no distinction between the man who eats little and sees heaven and the man who drinks much and sees snakes. Each is in an abnormal physical condition, and therefore has abnormal perceptions.[43]
> —*Analytical philosopher Bertrand Russell*
> *(1872–1970)*

As we have seen, popular accounts of mysticism sometimes convey misconceptions, such as that mystics generally hear voices and see visions and that science has provided a materialist explanation for them. Clearing away some of these misconceptions will help us understand mystics better.

Some Terms Associated with Conversion Experiences

charismatic: An expressive and uninhibited worship style, usually in a Catholic context.

evangelical: A style of religious belief that emphasizes, among other things, the need for a personal conversion experience.

pentecostal: An expressive and uninhibited worship style that may involve "speaking in tongues" (glossolalia) or similar phenomena.[44]

Mysticism is not, in principle, about hearing voices or seeing visions. Some famous religious figures like the apostle Paul experienced dramatic and life-changing visions. Some of these visionaries have been mystically inclined, as he apparently was, but others have not. Generally, serious mystics do not seek such manifestations, whether they are seen literally (corporeal visions) or seen with the mind's eye (interior visions), because they are not mystical consciousness *as such.* Pursuit of visions is viewed as a distraction from mystical consciousness.[45]

Incidentally, Freud did *not* "discover" that unconscious desires can fool people into believing that they see or hear things. Spiritual directors have known that all too well for centuries! Walter Hilton, writing in the early fifteenth century, advised the mystic who experiences any type of vision to "refuse it and assent not thereto."[46] John of the Cross later offered the same advice, explaining, "That which properly and generally comes from God is a purely spiritual communication."[47] Stace follows this up, noting that "a genuine mystical experience is nonsensuous. It is formless, shapeless, colorless, odorless, soundless."[48]

Mystics are not, as a rule, impractical idealists. Many mystics, such as the apostle Paul, Francis of Assisi, Catherine of Genoa (who directed a hospital), and Teresa of Avila, were capable administrators. Mystics spend considerable time in prayer and contemplation, but there is no inverse relationship between an ability to contemplate and an ability to act effectively.

Mystics commonly live ascetic lives to avoid distractions, not to punish themselves. Serious mystics, like serious athletes, must give up good things as well as bad things. Underhill explains that, through strict self-discipline, they seek freedom from "the results of environment and worldly education, from pride and prejudice, preferences and distaste."[49] In other words, they seek freedom from the normal contents of everyday consciousness. Historically, some mystics have had a self-punishing temperament—but so do many people who show no mystical tendencies.

In an old Buddhist tale, the itinerant master and his students commit to owning only the barest necessities. They carry their rice bowls in their hands while on the road. But some students insist on acquiring a bag for the bowls. The master says nothing, merely waiting for the students to see. Soon the bag develops a hole, and they must stop at a nearby town to repair it. Then one student suggests carrying a repair kit as well. An argument develops around the philosophy of the kit. Eventually, even the dullest student realizes that distractions multiply. None of the items is bad in itself, but all are distractions.

Science cannot explain away mystical consciousness. In the twentieth century, psychologists speculated about mystical consciousness, often attributing it to "the Unconscious," repressed sexuality, wish fulfillment, physical illnesses, or hysteria.[50] Some have even claimed that mystical consciousness stems from the social power that accomplished mystics acquire—that is, the mystic's sense of importance is thought to produce the altered state.[51]

This latter suggestion says more about materialism's difficulty in accounting for consciousness of any type than about mystical consciousness in particular. Few serious mystics seek such obviously fatal distractions as social power. The "social power" hypothesis also offers no explanation of how mystical consciousness is actually acquired. Jerome Gellman justly comments: "Naturalistic proposals of these kinds exaggerate the scope and influence of the cited factors, sometimes choosing to highlight the bizarre and eye-catching at the expense of the more common occurrences."[52] As in all scientific disciplines, the common occurrences are the proper focus of research.

For over a century, it was the fashion to assume that any speculations regarding mysticism were scientific if they were materialist and reductionist. In most cases, the reductionism was actually a fatal flaw. As Underhill says, distinguishing between mystical consciousness and hysteria (often thought by materialists to be equivalent):

Both mysticism and hysteria have to do with the domination of consciousness by one fixed and intense idea or intuition, which rules the life and is able to produce amazing physical and psychical results. In the hysteric patient this idea is often trivial or morbid but has become—thanks to the self's unstable mental condition—an obsession. In the mystic the dominant idea is a great one: so great in fact, that when it is received in its completeness by the human consciousness, almost of necessity it ousts all else. It is nothing less than the idea or perception of the transcendent reality and presence of God. Hence the mono-ideism of the mystic is rational, whilst that of the hysteric patient is invariably irrational.[53]

Apart from the work of pioneers like James, Underhill, and Stace, few attempts have been made to study mystics. Speculating on how to account for them was considered sufficient. In scientific terms, such speculations are not falsifiable; that is, there is no simple way to know if a given assertion is wrong, or falsified.

Another problem is that materialists often feel qualified to comment on mystical experience despite a lack of basic knowledge. For example, Edelman and Tononi write:

> It is a paradox that as conscious human beings, we cannot fully rid ourselves of higher-order consciousness, leaving only the ongoing event-driven rush of primary consciousness. That may, in fact, be the state toward which mystics aim their devotions.[54]

The primary consciousness Edelman and Tononi refer to—a continuous stream of transient and unmonitored mental events—is possibly experienced by dogs, but it is hardly the mystic's goal. The mystic attempts to experience the mind that underlies or embodies the universe. Edelman and Tononi appear confused by the fact that humans have difficulty achieving either a higher *or* a lower level of consciousness than the cerebral norm. But the two directions are not equivalent; they are opposite.

Oxford zoologist Alister Hardy (1896–1985) took a completely different and more fruitful approach. His fame as a scientist stemmed from developing a means of measuring the numbers of microscopic life forms in the ocean, but he also studied and collected examples of RSMEs for fifty years. Bucking the trend in biology to reduce RSMEs to some function or malfunction of the genes or neural circuits, he opened up a fruitful new area of research: Who has RSMEs? Are they the same across cultures, what causes them, and what are their outcomes?

Collecting Data on RSMEs

Belief can be explained in much the way that cancer can. I think the time has come to shed our taboo that says, "Oh, let's just tiptoe by this, we don't have to study this." People think they know a lot about religion. But they don't know.[55]

—Materialist philosopher Daniel Dennett

I always regarded the planning of my research as an exercise in human ecology, for, to me, one of the greatest contributions biology could make to mankind would be to work out an ecological outlook which took into account not only man's economic and nutritional needs but also his emotional and spiritual behaviour.[56]

—*Zoologist and pioneer spirituality researcher Alister Hardy*

Alister Hardy, despite being a mid-twentieth century zoologist, was no fan of reductionism. He insisted that animals must be studied as living wholes in their natural environment. They cannot be usefully reduced to physics and chemistry. He agreed with pioneer neuroscientists Charles Sherrington and John Eccles that the mind is distinct from the brain.

He was not aiming to demonstrate the truth of any specific religious doctrine, but fifty years of research had led him to conclude that "man was religious by nature" and that a craving for a spiritual philosophy that had its origins in human evolution was frustrated in the modern world. But he had a hard time finding scientific research on spirituality. In the mid-twentieth century, the research emphasis was on religion as an institution, although a few pioneers like Stace studied mysticism. Spirituality, apart from mystical consciousness, seemed to fall between the cracks.

Lack of information was not the problem. Religious groups gathered large numbers of accounts of spiritual experiences, to be sure, but always in support of an institution or a doctrine. These groups, although mostly honest, had no incentive to overcome the "file drawer" problem, infamous in scientific research: they intentionally solicited accounts that supported their views and avoided those that contradicted them. And, in a deeply ironic turnabout, for decades the "scientific" approach had been to concoct materialist theories based on little or no data. So the people who had the data could not look at it in an objective way, and the people who could do so preferred theory to data.

Not surprisingly for a zoologist, Hardy decided that the unavoidable first step was to go out into "the wilds," collect a large number of actual specimens, and then describe and classify them. Beginning in 1969, he asked, through a newspaper appeal and a pamphlet, for accounts of spiritual experiences from the British public at large. This approach displeased some social psychologists who thought he ought to have begun with a questionnaire. Hardy stood his ground, saying, "The specimens we are hunting are shy and delicate ones which we want to secure in as natural a condition as possible; we must at all costs avoid damaging or distorting them by trying to trap them within an artificial framework."[57] He and his colleagues studied the accounts they received carefully and followed up with a questionnaire—once they had had a chance to consider what they *should* ask.

At their newly opened Religious Experience Research Unit (RERU) at Manchester College in Oxford, Hardy's group received over four thousand firsthand accounts of "specific, deeply felt, transcendental experiences" that made the experiencers aware of a "benevolent non-physical power which appears to be partly or wholly beyond, and far greater than, the individual self":

> They do not necessarily call it a religious feeling, nor does it occur only to those who belong to an institutional religion or who indulge in corporate acts of worship. It often occurs to children, to atheists and agnostics, and it usually induces in the person concerned a conviction that the everyday world is not the whole of reality: that there is another dimension to life.
>
> Some people feel a personal devotional relationship with the power after their experience; some call it God, some do not. Some see it as an aspect of their wider self through which such an experience has come, whilst others see it as part of man's general consciousness.[58]

Hardy had begun his work with the hope that he could classify the accounts of experiences into a convenient taxonomy. But very few accounts featured only a single element. He and his colleagues later decided to group them into twelve general classifications for analysis.

Experiences Identified by Hardy

> I realize that the form of the vision and the words I heard were the result of my education and cultural background, but the voice, though closer than my own heartbeat, was entirely separate from me.[59]
> —*A woman hospitalized for depression recalling a comforting RSME*

Whilst I was looking towards the ruins of the Abbey I felt a great sense of peace as though I saw myself in the flow of history and knew where I fitted in to it … as though I were really in touch with Life in all its continuity and purpose.[60]

　　　　—A professor who tried but failed to "rationalize" his RSME

Going back on the bus that evening, I felt and was an entirely different person. I astonished myself by smiling at people, by making room for them instead of hating them for sitting next to me.[61]

　　　　—A person who experienced an attitude change following an RSME

Hardy and his colleagues identified a variety of "triggers," as they called them, for an RSME, everything from sacred places to sex or even an anesthetic. His decision to begin by asking for first-person accounts rather than by administering a questionnaire was vindicated because the less common triggers might not have been identified in advance. It also pointed up the wisdom of not relying only on the volunteers or information provided by religious groups associated with a specific approach.

The single most common trigger was depression or despair. Prayer or meditation was the second most common, but natural beauty was a close third, mentioned more often than religious worship.[62] Of course, these categories are not mutually exclusive. A subject may pray or contemplate nature while depressed. Some cultures use sensory and mental stimulation through drumming, singing, and dancing in shamanic trance states or the ingestion of psychedelics (entheogens) but, not surprisingly, these were rarely reported in the British accounts sent to Hardy. He also noted a marked absence of "superstition, wishful thinking, and contradictory theological theories" in the accounts he received.[63]

Many respondents experienced a sense of a numinous or transcendent presence. A few felt horror, guilt, or remorse. Some lost their fear of death as a result of their experience. Generally, the researchers found:

People experience the abstract power in a wide variety of ways. Some may describe their feelings in terms of trust, awe, joy, or bliss; exceptionally they may reach the heights of ecstasy. Others may have sensory impressions, see lights, hear voices, or have the feeling of being touched.[64]

RSMEs often brought a sense of purpose or new meaning to life and positive changes in attitudes, which we look at in more detail in Chapter Eight.

Who Has RSMEs?

Neither Hardy's group's pioneer research nor most subsequent findings have supported the *Washington Post* (1993) view that RSMEs correlate with being "poor, uneducated, and easy to command":[65]

Women were more than twice as likely to report RSMEs as men in the original 1969 study, but that was probably because the original data came from subjects who were asked to write a descriptive letter. Subse-

Mother Teresa

I know God will not give me anything I can't handle. I just wish that He didn't trust me so much.
—Mother Teresa, on her work with
the destitute

When the Albanian girl Agnes Bojaxhiu (1910–97) took up the religious life, she named herself after Carmelite mystic Thérèse of Lisieux, the "mystic of the ordinary." She explained that she would not presume to name herself after "the big Teresa," the great Carmelite mystic called Teresa of Avila.

This newly named Teresa served happily in a teaching order in India in the mid-twentieth century. But after four mystical experiences in 1946 and 1947, she went out onto the streets of one of the world's poorest cities and founded her own order, the India-based Missionaries of Charity, dedicated to serving the poorest of the poor. She was joined by some of her former students. One of their earliest projects was to collect destitute people who had been turned out of hospitals and take them to their newly founded Home for the Dying. She wanted these unfortunate people to be able to die within sight of a loving face, even if they could not be saved.

Mother Teresa herself never had another mystical experience after 1947, which caused her personal sadness. But her order's work has become known and valued worldwide.[66]

quent research by D. Hay and A. Morisy (1978) found that women were only somewhat more likely than men to recall an RSME when asked in an opinion poll.[67]

Older respondents were significantly more likely to report an RSME, according to Hay and Morisy, but, as Hay pointed out, that is a statistical effect. Older people have had more years in which to have such an experience.

Respondents in upper social classes and people with more education were more likely than others to report RSMEs, which, Hardy notes, undermines the hypothesis that RSMEs are a psychological mechanism for coping with social injustice.

Respondents who reported an RSME were "significantly more likely" to score well on a measure of psychological well-being than those who had not.

Andrew Greeley reported similar findings in America (1975) and other researchers have generally replicated these findings from Europe.[68]

Children's Religious Experiences

Fifteen percent of Hardy's respondents started their explanation with a reference to their childhood, though they had not been asked to do so.[69] Hardy's successor at RERU, Edward Robinson, later attempted to study childhood experience in more detail by asking these respondents for more information. Obviously, one difficulty with assessing such recollections is that memories alter over time. However, many claimed to have clear memories of numinous or spiritual experiences that are hard to discount. For example, referencing Freud's claim that childhood religious experiences arise from idealization of parents, one respondent stated:

> I do not think that my early idea of God was derived at all from what I saw in my parents. God was, so I was given to understand, the great Creator of all things, mysterious, wonderful, to be worshiped, obeyed and loved. He knew everything about everything. One could as well say that one got an idea of an elephant by looking at an ant.[70]

Interestingly, Hardy's respondents usually perceived religious instruction at school as negative. One factor may be that school-based religious instruction inevitably instills rational concepts, moral precepts, or catechism and seldom addresses spirituality, the element that had led the respondents to communicate with Hardy.

In the end, Hardy and his colleagues came to the same general conclusion as James, that "the visible world is part of a more spiritual universe from which it draws its chief significance," union with which is our true purpose.[71]

At the end of *The Spiritual Nature of Man* (1979), Hardy tackles the accusation that his prior commitments colored his thinking. He points out that he arrived at his conclusions for the same reason the pragmatist James did—because the evidence points clearly in that direction. Only a prior commitment to materialism, he suggests, would cause one to ignore such a large body of data. Indeed, when Hardy states his own views on prayer and God, he makes clear that he can live with materialist hypotheses where he thinks that the evidence sustains them.[72] But based on his accumulated findings, he concludes, "I believe we must revise the widely accepted outlook held by so many intellectuals today," and in support of his view he quotes Bronowski's *Science and Human Values* (1964):

> There is today almost no scientific theory which was held when, say, the Industrial Revolution began about 1760. Most often today's theories flatly contradict those of 1760; many contradict those of 1900. In cosmology, in quantum mechanics, in genetics, in the social sciences, who now holds the beliefs that seemed firm sixty years ago?

The basic outlines of Hardy's and his colleagues' findings of thirty-five years ago in Britain have been replicated in many settings since and garner increasing interest today. For example, in a 2005 *Newsweek*/Beliefnet poll, 57 percent of Americans surveyed said that spirituality was "very important" in their daily life.[73] But, we must ask, what about other cultures? What difference does culture make to RSMEs?

Mystical Experience the World Over

Almost any religious system which fosters unearthly love is potentially a nursery for mystics.[74]

—Evelyn Underhill, Mysticism

Whatever share of this world Thou dost bestow on me, bestow it on Thine enemies, and whatever share of the next world thou dost give me, give it to Thy friends. Thou are enough for me![75]

> —*Rabi'a of Basra,*
> *"Mystic Lover of Allah" (717–801)*

Not one or two, Subhuti, not one or two, but all the beings—men, women, animals, birds, trees, rocks. All the beings in the world. One should create such a determination that "I will lead all of them into nirvana."[76]

> —*Gautama Buddha (563–483 B.C.E.)*

RSMEs are a feature of human experience worldwide throughout history. They are not the result of any one culture or belief system.[77] However, all human experiences are interpreted in a context. In the Christian tradition, the Absolute is typically experienced as a Transcendent Personality, full of love and compassion, with whom one's personality becomes temporarily merged[78] and transformed into a similar, though finite, personality. In the Buddhist tradition, the Absolute is considered impersonal—and yet it cannot be experienced without compassion for all living things. For example, the Bodhisattva vow for Tibetan Buddhists who would attain mystic enlightenment is "May I attain Buddhahood for the benefit of all sentient beings." In sum, mystics' accounts of their experiences point in similar directions, but specific expressions depend on language and culture.

Perennial Philosophy and Mysticism

One school of thought, called *perennialism* or perennial philosophy, has attempted to identify common ground in mystical experiences. The term was coined by the mathematician Gottfried Leibniz (1646–1716), the coinventor of calculus. It was popularized by writer Aldous Huxley (1894–1963), best known for his prescient novel *Brave New World*, which warned against attempts to eliminate spiritual values from society.

Perennialists argue for an underlying reality that mystics actually perceive (as opposed to a delusion created by altered states of consciousness). Huxley thought that one reality underlies both matter and mind, but the nature of this one Reality is such that it cannot be directly or immediately apprehended except by those who have chosen to fulfill certain conditions, making themselves loving, pure in heart, and poor in spirit.[79]

Generally, perennialists argue:

The world of individual consciousness and matter is only a partial reality, which reflects an underlying divine ground.

The divine ground can be discovered by direct intuition, in which the knower and the known unite. (Assuming that a mind underlies the universe resolves the apparent paradox of the mystics' claim that they lose their selves in the mystical experience, yet remain aware of what is happening. A united consciousness is still a consciousness.)

Humans have both an exterior *(phenomenal)* self and a true self. Most of the time, we are aware only of our exterior "self," that is, the many ways we experience our environment or our own consciousness, often playing many roles at the same time. Uniting all these experiences is a true self, one that can reach the divine ground. It is usually quite difficult to find that self beneath many layers of exterior selves.

The chief value of existence is to identify with one's true self. Traditional religions give this state names such as eternal life, salvation, or enlightenment.

Perennialists believe that all humans possess the ability to discern spiritual truth, though it is often undeveloped. The insights from spiritual faculties are as much to be relied on as other senses.

Researcher W. T. Stace was a perennialist, and his distinction between extrovertive and introvertive mysticism[80] aimed in part to bridge cultural gaps in interpretation of mystical experiences. He also believed, more controversially, that theistic mystics are required by their culture to interpret experiences that are truly monistic or pantheistic in a way that does not challenge theism. As other scholars have pointed out, however, one can just as easily reverse the onus and say that pantheists and monists are required to interpret their experiences in a way that does not challenge *their* culture.[81]

The view opposite to perennialism is *constructivism,* which argues that culture and assumptions shape mystical experience to such a degree that

Buddhist and Christian mystics do not actually encounter the same reality. Some constructivists (hard constructivists) deny that a common substrate of mystical experience even exists. They argue that experience is entirely shaped by culture and assumptions. Such a claim is much more radical than asserting that the *language* in which the mystic explains the experience is shaped by culture and assumptions.[82]

To focus the argument between perennialists and constructivists, we might ask what sort of experience mystical consciousness is. Is it a specific experience like electric shock? Assume that there are two schools of thought on the pain created by a moderate shock. One argues that the pain is entirely the outcome of culture and assumptions, and the other argues that it is the outcome of real distress. The first, the "hard constructivist" school says that subjects' widely differing descriptions show that no one experience underlies the accounts. The second, the "perennialist" school says that a real experience does underlie the accounts, but different cultures and assumptions produce different descriptions. In some cultures, children are brought up to ignore pain as evidence of personal courage, but in others they are taught that self-expression connects them with others. Differing testimonies signal the need to consider culture when interpreting first-person accounts, but do not rule out the possibility that there is one universal experience underlying them.

All serious thinkers in this area are attempting to map a territory whose exploration has hardly begun. This book takes the perennialist position.

RSMEs and Evolutionary Psychology

Between two barbaric nations, the one that was the more superstitious of the two would generally be the more united, and therefore the more powerful.[83]

—*Eugenicist Francis Galton,*
on the origin of religion (1894)

The individual is prepared by the sacred rituals for supreme effort and self-sacrifice. Overwhelmed by shibboleths, special costumes, and the sacred dancing and music so accurately keyed to his emotive centers, he has a "religious experience."[84]

—*Sociobiologist Edward O. Wilson,*
on the origin of religion

Are RSMEs merely a quirk of a materialist evolution? For over a century, scientists have pondered RSMEs in relation to human evolution. Unfortunately, under materialist influence, the project became not so much exploring a way, but explaining away.

Evelyn Underhill noted at the turn of the twentieth century that mystical consciousness in particular was "a puzzling circumstance for deterministic philosophers, who can only escape from the dilemma here presented to them by calling these things illusions, and dignifying their own more manageable illusions with the title of facts."[85] She framed the conflict between the mystic and the materialist succinctly:

> That there is an extreme point at which man's nature touches the Absolute: that his ground, or substance, his true being, is penetrated by the Divine Life which constitutes the underlying reality of things; this is the basis on which the whole mystic claim of possible union with God must rest.[86]

Underhill's contemporary William James saw that "evolution" was itself becoming a new religion and a rival to Christianity.[87] James disliked the new religion, not because he doubted evolution, but because speculations about animal or early hominid sensations seemed a poor substitute for studying the depths of contemporary human consciousness. He warned, "A bill of fare with one real raisin on it instead of the word 'raisin,' with one real egg instead of the word 'egg,' might be an inadequate meal, but it would at least be a commencement of reality."[88]

Meanwhile, the rise of logical positivism in the 1920s reinforced *scientism,* the view that only the methods of natural sciences such as physics and chemistry provide real knowledge. Relativity and quantum mechanics had hardly begun to shape thinking at that time, so, practically speaking, "natural science" meant nineteenth-century materialism. Scientism is the ultimate origin of the current project to account for RSMEs through the new discipline of evolutionary psychology, by attempting to demonstrate that RSMEs can be understood as outcomes of an unguided evolution.[89]

As always in this area, the stakes are high. If RSMEs have an obvious materialist explanation, the mystics' claims are irrelevant. At first blush, however, evolutionary psychology is not a promising hypothesis. Evolution depends on leaving fertile descendants, but mystics and spiritual adepts commonly vow celibacy or, at a minimum, do not view worldly success as the goal of life. But a number of alternative evolutionary psychology hypotheses have been put forward in recent years to address this difficulty: RSMEs were accidental by-products of useful mental states, a "strategy" by which genes get copied, or even an unspecified neural copying program (a meme). All these ideas have been advanced in the name of science, under the banner of evolutionary psychology.

Evolutionary Psychology's Explanation of Human Behavior

> What then are we to make of the purposes and goals obviously chosen by human beings? They are, in Darwinian interpretation, processes evolved as adaptive devices by an otherwise purposeless natural selection.[90]
> —*Sociobiologist Edward O. Wilson*

> Science now reveals that love is addictive, trust is gratifying and cooperation feels good. Evolution produced this reward system because it increased the survival of members of our social primate species.[91]
> —*Michael Shermer,* Scientific American

Evolutionary psychology proposes that human brains comprise adaptations, or evolved psychological mechanisms. These adaptations evolved by natural selection to benefit the survival and reproduction of the organism. RSMEs are, according to evolutionary psychology, one of these mechanisms.

Now, this claim involves several assumptions: (1) that each individual's brain contains a number of separate but similar inherited modules that handle specific types of functions, (2) that these modules are adapted to the hunter-gatherer way of life of our Pleistocene ancestors, and that (3) a universal human nature results, one that is credulous regarding RSMEs. In other words, people experience RSMEs because RSMEs help us survive and leave fertile offspring. The RSMEs do not arise from any deeper reality behind the universe nor do they provide any true insights—or if they do, it is an accidental outcome.

Philosopher of science David J. Buller was an evolutionary psychology enthusiast. "When I first started reading it, it just all seemed intuitively right to me," he told *Scientific American* in 2005.[92] Indeed, his experience was widely shared. Since the 1970s, evolutionary psychologists have claimed to explain not only RSMEs, but altruism, crime, economics, emotions, group loyalty, infidelity, laughter, law, literature, love, marketing, music, number sense, obesity, patriotism, sexual orientation, violence, voting conservative, war, and why the United States does not go to war against Canada as well as why children dislike vegetables—and this is only a partial list.[93] Evolutionary psychology is the theoretical background of *neurotheology*, which "analyzes the biological basis of spirituality" and "deals with the neurological and evolutionary basis for subjective experiences traditionally categorized as spiritual."[94]

The pop science media love evolutionary psychology, as we noticed in Chapter Two. Of course they do! In a world obsessed with celebrity gossip, how could a neglected science section resist a Valentine's Day story on "infidelity genes"? As a result, evolutionary psychology in general has received popular attention out of all proportion to its theoretical rigor. That is especially problematic for a nonexperimental discipline based on the interpretation of prehistory, where so much is simply nontestable and nonfalsifiable.[95]

We simply do not know what early humans thought about many of the relevant questions because they left so few artifacts. We know that some buried their dead in a fetal position, with grave goods, or in awe-inspiring places, which implies that they expected the dead to be born again. The cave paintings at Lascaux[96] (15,000 B.C.E.) and the Willendorf Venus[97] (25,000 B.C.E.) point to the great antiquity of shamanism and fertility cults. But beyond that, we have mostly speculation—often well informed by original ideas—but still speculation.

Despite the best efforts of researchers such as Dean Hamer, there is no clear link between religion and specific genes. So in the absence of evidence from the genome, evolutionary psychologists generally choose between one of two arguments. Either our hunter-gatherer ancestors were more likely to survive if they had religious beliefs, or they had the capacity to produce such beliefs as a by-product of other abilities. These two different arguments take us in different directions.

RSMEs as Adaptations for Survival

> Why does our craving for God persist? It may be that we need it for something. It may be that we don't need it, and it is left over from something that we used to be. There are lots of biological possibilities.[98]
> —*Materialist philosopher Daniel Dennett*

Fitting RSMEs into evolutionary psychology requires leaning very heavily on the "R" in RSMEs, the religion part. It is true that religions usually organize society and thus aid survival. Indeed, a religion, however it started, tends to share the cultural characteristics of its era. For example, hunter-gatherers were initiated into totem clans. Tibetan Buddhists have a lama who is thought to reincarnate previous lamas. American Christian denominations that originated in dramatic tent revivals nonetheless have presidents and bulky administrations. Social anthropologists have done much fruitful work in identifying the ways in which religious institutions organize societies.

But there is a serious weakness to this approach to explaining RSMEs. To study mysticism or spirituality as if it derives from religion is to reverse the usual course of events.[99] The religion is a later development, typically beginning in a mystical insight or spiritually significant event. That original RSME is usually irrelevant to survival; the religion that grows out of it will probably flourish if it aids survival and die out if it does not. But the fate of the religion doesn't tell us much about the origin of the RSME.

Explanations that argue for an assumed survival value of RSMEs also tend to confound mysticism and magic. Traditional shamans necessarily practice both, but the quests are separate: the mystic seeks enlightenment; the magician seeks power.

Having decided that religion is best understood in terms of its usefulness in our hunter-gatherer past, the evolutionary psychologist asks, is it adaptive or nonadaptive in historical times (times for which we have written records)? Different theorists give different answers.

Hardwired for the Wrong Worldview

> Religious belief itself is an adaptation that has evolved because we're hardwired to form tribalistic religions.[100]
> —*Sociobiologist Edward O. Wilson*

Edward O. Wilson argues in *Sociobiology* (1980) that religion is adaptive, because it promotes social organization, which in turn promotes survival.

The problem, as he explains in *Consilience* (1998), is:

> The essence of humanity's spiritual dilemma is that we evolved genetically to accept one truth and discovered another. Is there a way to erase the dilemma, to solve the contradictions between the transcendentalist and empiricist world views? No, unfortunately, there is not.[101]

Why not? "The central idea of the consilience world view is that all tangible phenomena, from the birth of stars to the workings of social institutions, are based on material processes that are ultimately reducible, however long and tortuous the sequences, to the laws of physics."[102] Or, as he explained to Steve Paulson of *Salon* in 2006, "Knowledge of the world ultimately comes down to chemistry, biology and—above all—physics; people are just extremely complicated machines."[103] Wilson also suggested to Paulson the need for a "spiritual atheism," but he complained, citing Camille Paglia, that three thousand years of Yahweh beats one generation of Foucault.

Now, physicists are not nearly as ready to endorse materialism in physics as biologists are. But in any event, we must ask why humanity would evolve or be "hardwired" to accept a worldview that is incorrect. For reasons that we have looked at earlier (see Chapter Five), it is not clear how exactly humans can be hardwired to accept any worldview. But if so, why one that contradicts reality? If Foucault dies out in a generation but Yahweh endures forever, is the best explanation that human brains are "hardwired" wrong? Or should we look for another?

To see where adaptationism can lead, consider, for example, the views of Casper Soeling and Eckert Voland, who explain in *Neuroendocrinology Letters* (2002) that they understand mysticism as follows:

> Intuitive ontologies are the basis for mystical experiences. Usually they serve to classify reality into animate and inanimate objects, animals or plants, for example. For a variety of psychological reasons, supernatural experiences result from a mixture of different ontological categories.... We feel it appears to be justified to attribute to religiosity the evolutionary status of an adaptation.[104]

As if mystics have been much concerned to distinguish between animals and plants ...

Factual Versus Practical Reasoning

> Adaptation is the gold standard against which rationality must be judged, along with all other forms of thought.[105]
>
>   —*Biologist and anthropologist David Sloan Wilson*

David Sloan Wilson, a biologist and anthropologist, has come up with a slightly different approach. He does not argue that humans are somehow hardwired to accept a wrong view of reality. His argument is more sophisticated. In *Darwin's Cathedral* (2002), he distinguishes between two types of reason, factual (based on literal correspondence) and practical (based on behavioral adaptedness).

Religious beliefs, Wilson tells us, are not factually reasonable, but they are practically reasonable. That is, they help us get on in life. Therefore, it is not unreasonable to believe them. Indeed, he says, "An atheist historian who understood the real life of Jesus but whose own life was a mess as a result of his beliefs would be factually attached to and practically detached from reality."[106] But the distinction we are asked to make between factual and practical realism comes at a high price: rationality is not as valuable as we thought. "Rationality," D. S. Wilson insists, "is not the gold standard against which all other forms of thought are to be judged."[107]

But where does that leave science? Wilson defends science as follows: "Science is unique in only one respect: its explicit commitment to factual realism. Virtually every other human unifying system includes factual realism as an important and even essential element but subordinates it to practical realism when necessary." He doubts that the values of factual realism are adequate to support a unifying system, but believes that the values of practical realism can.[108]

Now the actual history of science barely supports D. S. Wilson's contention that in science factual realism triumphs above all else. Eventually, truth prevails in science, but everything else seems to prevail first, sometimes for decades or centuries. As Thomas Kuhn notes:

> The state of Ptolemaic astronomy was a scandal before Copernicus' announcement. Galileo's contributions to the study of motion depended closely upon difficulties discovered in Aristotle's theory by scholastic critics. Newton's new theory of light and color originated in the discovery that

none of the existing pre-paradigm theories would account for the length of the spectrum, and the wave theory that replaced Newton's was announced in the midst of growing concern about anomalies in the relation of diffraction and polarization effects to Newton's theory. Thermodynamics was born from the collision of two existing nineteenth-century physical theories, and quantum mechanics from a variety of difficulties surrounding black-body radiation, specific heats, and the photoelectric effect. Furthermore, in all these cases except that of Newton ... one can appropriately describe the fields affected by it as in a state of growing crisis.[109]

Science is not very different in this respect from government or religion. Often change occurs only when stoutly defended systems are collapsing from their own unworkability. But what D. S. Wilson means by "science" appears to be materialism, which he treats as factual realism. Since he has defined his terms that way, there is no arguing the case with him.

But the main difficulty with his thesis is that mystics who found religions *are* in fact seeking factual realism. That is precisely their purpose. Based on their experiences, they tend to describe ultimate reality as *supra*rational, not as *sub*rational. Where the materialist sees the universe as bottom up (mud to mind or monad to man), they see it as top down (Mind to mind/matter). They do not abandon reason, but they find that conventional argument falls short of conveying mystical consciousness, much they might wish otherwise. As we have seen in Chapter Six, materialists have no conclusive evidence that they are right and mystics are wrong.

If indeed religion is more adaptive than irreligion, the most likely explanation is this: the mystics are right. Materialism is false, but *most nonmaterialist systems contain at least some elements that are true.* As we might expect, some contain many more true elements than others. If this is correct, we should expect people who have RSMEs to generally be well adapted to life, and—as we explore in Chapter Eight—we usually do see that.

However, the main problem with D. S. Wilson's position is the one that Leon Wieseltier observed while reviewing materialist philosopher Daniel Dennett's *Breaking the Spell* (2006). It is self-defeating: "You cannot disprove a belief unless you disprove its content. If you believe that you can disprove it any other way, by describing its origins or by describing its consequences, then you do not believe in reason." He adds:

If reason is a product of natural selection, then how much confidence can we have in a rational argument for natural selection? The power of reason is owed to the independence of reason, and to nothing else. (In this respect, rationalism is closer to mysticism than it is to materialism.) Evolutionary biology cannot invoke the power of reason even as it destroys it.[110]

D. S. Wilson attempts to avoid this problem, as we have seen above, by declaring that science is somehow above the fray in its support for factual realism. But that will not work because actual science has a great deal of difficulty with factual realism when it disconfirms paradigms, and under those circumstances, science behaves in much the same way as other human institutions. And to the extent that D. S. Wilson means by "science" the philosophy of materialism, it hardly helps his case to announce that rationality is not a gold standard.

But we must also consider the second approach of evolutionary psychology: RSMEs are not adaptive at all, but merely accidental free riders on useful systems. In that case, they could appear to be associated with good physical or mental health or genuine insights into the nature of reality, even though they make no sense in a purely material universe and do not really contribute to the benefits they are associated with.

Spirituality as an Accidental By-product

Religious concepts ... realize the miracle of being exactly what people will transmit simply because other variants were created and forgotten or abandoned all along. The magic that seems to produce such perfect concepts for human minds is merely the effect of repeated selective events.[111]
—*Pascal Boyer,* Religion Explained

Anthropologist Pascal Boyer, who studies concepts of agency and personhood, has refreshingly little use for the usual tropes and truisms of evolutionary psychology. In his ambitiously titled book *Religion Explained* (2001), he discounts simple-minded genetic determinism: "Having a normal human brain does not imply that you have religion. All it implies is that you can acquire it, which is very different."[112]

Dismissing the endless evolutionary psychology storytelling about supposed events in the Pleistocene era—why cave dwellers who got religion were more likely to survive than those who didn't, and thus they passed it on in their genes—he offers a more thoughtful and sophisticated argument. He argues that only certain types of religious concepts are likely to be acquired or passed on, and these concepts are consistent with normal reasoning, whether factual or practical (in D. S. Wilson's sense). For example, a religion that teaches that God exists on every day except Tuesday will win few adherents.

Thus, he argues, religious ideas are mere parasites on the normal ways that we judge everyday events. Spiritual beliefs are "a by-product of standard cognitive architecture." Some systems he thinks relevant are

> a set of intuitive ontological expectations, a propensity to direct attention to what is counterintuitive, a tendency to recall it if it is inferentially rich, a system for detecting and over detecting agency, a set of social mind systems that make the notion of well-informed agents particularly relevant, a set of moral intuitions that seem to have no clear justification.[113]

Now, Boyer's thesis is not only a reductive explanation of RSMEs; it serves an agenda. In an article in *Skeptical Inquirer*,[114] he offers a handy table of reductive or negative explanations for religious beliefs. For example, he suggests, instead of telling people that "Religion allays anxiety" (therefore it is a false hope), one should rather point out that religion generates as much anxiety as it allays (therefore it is a false fear).

And how do we know that both the hope and the fear are false? Because, as he explains to his not always skeptical readers, we now know, among other things, that "our minds are only billions of neurons firing in ordered ways." That, of course, amounts to saying that the mind is the same thing as the brain. Boyer does not really argue that case; he assumes it is true.

But the main problem with Boyer's approach is that it is irrelevant. No one doubts that RSMEs are usually mediated through standard cognitive architecture (see Chapter Nine). But that hardly "explains" them, because, as we have seen, the mind is not the same thing as the brain. His work depends largely on studies of equatorial African witchcraft beliefs and of other byways such as the views of contemporary small children. Thus, experiences that are usually considered religious or spiritual—for example, conversion[115]—do not really figure in the explanation. But these are precisely the types of experiences for which explanations are usually sought.

So where are we now? Efforts to locate RSMEs in genes (adaptedness) or brains (by-product of cognitive architecture) don't work. Suppose, however, we take a more expansive approach to the gene? Unlike Dean Hamer, we will not seek an individual gene, but will simply attribute certain characteristics to genes in general.

"Selfish Genes" and Spirituality

> *We* were constructed to serve the interests of our genes, not the reverse....
> The reason we exist is because it once served their ends to create us.[116]
> —*Keith E. Stanovich,* The Robot's Rebellion

> "What Jones really wants" is what his ancestors were selected for wanting in the old days back on the savannah. The trouble is, of course, that Jones wants no such thing—not consciously or unconsciously either.[117]
> —*Philosopher Jerry Fodor*

In 1976, Richard Dawkins livened up the discussion with his book *The Selfish Gene*. He was convinced that evolution occurs because genes succeed in getting passed on; they, not we, are the true immortals. Although Dawkins has always denied attributing motive or determinism to genes in an anthropomorphic way, his language is often ambiguous. And cognitive scientist Steven Pinker recently defended Dawkins's ambiguity in an essay in honor of *The Selfish Gene*'s thirtieth anniversary. Ridiculing philosopher Mary Midgley for protesting that "genes cannot be selfish or unselfish, any more than atoms can be jealous, elephants abstract or biscuits teleological,"[118] he writes:

> If information-processing gives us a good explanation for the states of knowing and wanting that are embodied in the hunk of matter called a human brain, there is no principled reason to avoid attributing states of knowing and wanting to other hunks of matter.[119]

So the problem, it turns out, is not that Dawkins attributes motive to genes but that we humans attribute it too easily to our own consciousness, which is reducible to "information processing." Neither Pinker nor Dawkins makes clear just how we can ground our freedom from the selfish gene in that case; neither seems to believe in free will.[120]

These problems aside, the selfish gene was a hugely attractive concept. Attributing agency to genes separates agency from motive. A "selfish gene" explanation need only propose a way in which a behavior might spread genes. For example, women who think that God wants them to be celibate may really be helping their brothers and sisters raise more children, thus spreading their own shared genes (according to the key neo-Darwinian theory of inclusive fitness). There is no way to disprove such a claim because the religious celibate's unfeigned disinterest in spreading her genes is completely irrelevant. Her genes, not she herself, are the alleged actors in the piece. In this respect, selfish-gene theory was a great advance over Freudianism. The Freudian typically insisted that the religious celibate had unconscious sexual motives. Perhaps so, but most religious celibates have strong conscious motives as well, and it was never clear why unconscious motives should be assumed to rule. Eliminating human motive altogether greatly simplifies matters for the reductive materialist.

But, of course, many found the selfish gene simplistic, unfalsifiable, and—this is the big problem—unrepresentative of what we actually know of human nature. As philosopher Jerry Fodor writes:

> Over the years, people keep proposing theories that go: "what everybody really wants is just ..." (fill in the blank). Versions fashionable in their times have included: money, power, sex, death, freedom, happiness, Mother, the Good, pleasure, success, status, salvation, immortality, self-realization, reinforcement, penises (in the case of women), larger penises (in the case of men), and so on. The track record of such theories has not been good; in retrospect they often look foolish or vulgar or both. Maybe it will turn out differently for "what everybody really wants is to maximize his relative contribution to the gene pool." But I don't know any reason to think that it will, and I sure wouldn't advise you to bet the farm.[121]

Of course, in fairness, Dawkins is not saying that everybody wants to spread their genes, but that everybody's genes want to be spread. On the other hand, he insists, genes don't really have purposes. He also concedes that humans can have purposes unrelated to reproduction. But that raises the question, what *is* the conceptual use of the selfish gene? What does it predict, rather than postdict? As Fodor notes:

The scientific world-view does not entail that writing *The Tempest* was a reproductive strategy; that's the sort of silliness that gives it a bad name. First blush, there seem to be all sorts of things that we like, and like to do, for no reason in particular, not for any reason that we have, or that our genes have; or that the Easter Bunny has, either. Perhaps we're just that kind of creature.[122]

Indeed, as Australian philosopher David Stove has pointed out, we *are* that kind of creature. Humans have not systematically aimed to spread their genes:

> Religion is not at all the only thing in human life which has a marked tendency to repress or extinguish reproduction, and even to mortify the sexual impulse itself. Intense and prolonged thought, in the few people who are capable of it, has the same tendency. So does high artistic creativity. In fact either of these things is, in general, far *more* strongly and uniformly unfavorable to reproduction than religion in general is.[123]

One might add that mere affluence, unconnected with any special talent, usually leads to a fall in birthrates as well. But Dawkins had another card up his sleeve in case the selfish gene proved recessive. In the same book, he introduced the gene's psychic correlate, the *meme,* which actually looked far more promising as a reductive account of RSMEs.

RSMEs as "Memes"

> The survival value of the god meme in the meme pool results from its great psychological appeal. It provides a superficially plausible answer to deep and troubling questions about existence. It suggests that injustices in this world may be rectified in the next. The "everlasting arms" hold out a cushion against our own inadequacies which, like a doctor's placebo, is none the less effective for being imaginary.[124]
>
> —*Richard Dawkins,* The Selfish Gene

> We might think we humans designed all those computers and phone links for our own pleasure, but from the meme's-eye-view we are just their copying machines, and they are using us to design a vast planet-wide system for their own propagation.[125]
>
> —*Susan Blackmore,* Times Higher
> Education Supplement

The general idea of memes has been a seductive one; people want to believe it.[126]

—*Philosopher William L. Benzon*

Can RSMEs be understood as "memes," which mindlessly copy themselves? It is unclear just what memes are. As Susan Blackmore explains, "Memes are stories, songs, habits, skills, inventions and ways of doing things that we copy from person to person by imitation. Human nature can be explained by evolutionary theory, but only when we consider evolving memes as well as genes."[127] Now that last sentence is a surprising admission from a stalwart evolutionary psychologist. If the meme cannot be validated, evolutionary psychology cannot explain human nature.

The meme is best described as a theoretical unit of self-replicating information, the partner of the theoretical selfish gene. Indeed, as Blackmore explains, "we are part of a vast evolutionary process in which memes are the evolving replicator and we are the meme machines."[128] Memes function like genes—unless they are "viral memes," like religions, in which case they function like viruses.

As a reductive approach to RSMEs, the meme is of vastly greater use than the selfish gene. Genes, however else we may wish to think of them, are strings of nucleotides in living cells that replicate the information that is essential for continuing life processes in daughter cells. The awkward dance around the question of whether genes, as such, can have independent purposes does not derive from observation of actual genes. It derives from materialist theories of evolution and of mind. In any event, as we have seen, RSMEs are not consistently useful in spreading genes. So the meme concept is analogous to the *idea* of genes and, when needed, to the *idea* of viruses,[129] or even phenotypes,[130] but is not constrained by the mundane functions or actions of any of these verified entities. As Dawkins explains:

> Once the genes have provided their survival machines with brains that are capable of rapid imitation, the memes will automatically take over. We do not even have to posit a genetic advantage in imitation, though that would certainly help. All that is necessary is that the brain should be capable of imitation: memes will then evolve that exploit the capacity to the full.[131]

Well, brains can imitate. And, in Blackmore's view, this explains "our incurably religious nature, our unusual forms of cooperation and altruism, our use of language, and our ability to defy our genes with birth control and genetic engineering."[132] RSMEs, in her view, depend not merely on memes but on entire memeplexes:

> When we look at religions from a meme's eye view we can understand why they have been so successful. These religious memes did not set out with an intention to succeed. They were just behaviours, ideas and stories that were copied from one person to another in the long history of human attempts to understand the world. They were successful because they happened to come together into mutually supportive gangs that included all the right tricks to keep them safely stored in millions of brains, books and buildings, and repeatedly passed on to more.[133]

Like almost everyone who shares her views, Blackmore exempts science from the roster of deceitful meme gangs. She is sure that what she does is science. And what she likes best about science is that it is testable. Religious theories, by contrast, can thrive "in spite of being untrue, ugly, or cruel."[134] Well, are memes or memeplexes testable? Could we know if they were not a correct explanation?

To the extent that Blackmore's ideas depend mainly on Dawkins's ideas, theologian Alister McGrath thinks not. In *Dawkins' God: Genes, Memes, and the Meaning of Life* (2005), he observes, "If all ideas are memes or the effects of memes, Dawkins is left in the decidedly uncomfortable position of having to accept that his own ideas must also be recognized as the effects of memes." Dawkins has argued strenuously against that position, saying, "Scientific ideas, like all memes, are subject to a kind of natural selection, and this might look superficially virus-like. But the selective forces that scrutinize scientific ideas are not arbitrary or capricious. They are exacting, well-honed rules, and they do not favor pointless self-serving behavior."[135]

McGrath, however, does not let Dawkins off so easily, charging:

> This represents a case of special pleading, in which Dawkins makes an unsuccessful attempt to evade the trap of self-referentiality. Anyone familiar with intellectual history will spot the pattern immediately. Everyone's dogma is wrong except mine. My ideas are exempt from the general patterns I identify for other ideas, which allows me to explain them away, leaving my own to dominate the field.[136]

All that would be mere water under the bridge if anyone could demonstrate that the meme truly exists, in the way that the gene has been demonstrated to truly exist. Gregor Mendel's nineteenth-century work demonstrated that the gene must exist; it was the only reasonable explanation for the predictable regularities of controlled experiments in plant breeding. Later researchers such as James Watson and Francis Crick showed how the genome is organized. By contrast, the mere word "meme" has assumed a life of its own in popular culture. It originally identified a fad, a trend, or a tendency of thought to which one considers oneself superior, but now appears to be fading into a general synonym for an idea.[137]

But language aside, in what sense does a meme exist? Is it a downmarket Platonic idea? No, because that is just the sort of concept that Dawkins and Blackmore would reject. Thus we must look for memes in the brain. Neurobiologist Juan Delius has pictured his conjecture of a meme as "a constellation of activated neuronal synapses." But as McGrath notes, a picture is not evidence that memes exist:

> I've seen countless pictures of God in many visits to art galleries. And that verifies the concept? Or makes it scientifically plausible? Delius' proposal that a meme will have a single locatable and observable structure is purely conjectural, and has yet to be subjected to rigorous empirical investigation. It's one thing to speculate about what something might look like; the real question is whether it is there at all.[138]

Practically speaking, one serious difficulty with the meme having any locatable or observable structure is that everyone's brain receives and processes information in a different way. For example, when Jiří Wackermann and colleagues found (2003) that two separated human beings can coordinate their brain states, no one place in the recipients' brains routinely received the effect.[139] Thus, there is no apparent staging area for memes.

Was the meme never more than an analogy? If so, McGrath warns, "There is a massive gap between analogy and identity—and, as the history of science illustrates only too painfully, most false trails in science are about analogies which were mistakenly assumed to be identities."[140]

Sympathetic critics, as well as hostile ones, have also begun to question the meme. Biological anthropologist Robert Aunger, author of *The Electric Meme* (2002), also edited the anthology *Darwinizing Culture*

(2001),[141] which asks whether memetics is even a discipline. He lists a number of problems: no obvious correlation with brain states, no high-fidelity replication, no independence, and no clear way to trace origins, given that a number of people may get the same idea at once. He summarizes, "Even this brief foray into attempts at defining memes suggests there is disarray at a fundamental level in the subject."[142]

Susan Blackmore discounts such criticism, arguing:

> Robert Aunger challenged us to provide an existence proof for memes, or to come up with supported, unique predictions from meme theory. I suggest that no existence proof is required because memes are defined as information that is copied from person to person. So, as long as you admit that imitation occurs, they must exist.[143]

In that case, memes are not mental genes or viruses after all, but the mere fact of imitation. For those not convinced that this explanation gives the meme independent legitimacy, she goes on to argue that the large human brain was designed by evolution for the benefit of both genes and memes.[144] Under the circumstances, that is like saying that earth was designed for the benefit of both humans and leprechauns.

Actually, Dawkins has backed off memes somewhat, a fact that Daniel Dennett has noticed. Dennett suggests that Dawkins had to backtrack because sociobiology (evolutionary psychology's predecessor) is currently unpopular, but McGrath offers, "I think it rests more on growing realization of the massive evidential underdetermination of the thesis."[145]

The Memes for Memes and Assorted Other Exotics

> Viruses of the mind, and the whole science of memetics, represent a major paradigm shift in the science of the mind.[146]
> —*Richard Brodie,* Virus of the Mind

> Memetics is surely a very immature science at present, if a science at all.[147]
> —*Robert Aunger,* Darwinizing Culture

Actually, in a materialist culture, the meme needed only to be introduced; it did not need to be demonstrated. For example, Robert Aunger toyed with the idea of a new discipline of "neuromimetics" in *The Electric Meme* (2002). As philosopher William L. Benzon noted, the neuroscientific literature does not address memes, so it is irrelevant to Aunger's enterprise. But no matter, the idea was too good to pass up.[148] Similarly, Joseph Giovannoli's *The Biology of Belief* (2000) would persuade us of the existence of psychogenes,[149] beliefs with the properties of genes. And Howard Bloom, in *The Lucifer Principle* (1997), argues that "memes are ideas, snatches of nothingness that leap from mind to mind" that somehow morph into a force that makes society "very hungry"—hungry for trouble, apparently.[150]

Microsoft Word developer Richard Brodie offers a classic example of the genre in *Virus of the Mind* (1996). Brodie's book, billed as the first popular work on memes, is part pop science and part self-help. In the general confusion, originating with Dawkins himself, about whether a meme resembles a gene (in which case, you cannot avoid it) or a virus (in which case you can and should), Brodie's "long-awaited scientific theory unifying biology, psychology, and cognitive science" leans toward the viral view.[151] He assures us that "people who understand memetics will have an increasing advantage in life, especially in preventing themselves from being manipulated or taken advantage of."[152]

Of course, Brodie knows what to make of RSMEs—they are "some of the most powerful mind viruses in the universe." Not to worry though:

> You can consciously program yourself with memes that help you with whatever you're up to in life. That's one of the main strategy-memes in the memetics paradigm. It goes against that strategy to believe religious dogma without having consciously chosen it as empowering to your own life. It's also counter to the memetics paradigm to believe religious memes or any memes are True, rather than half-truth useful in a given context.[153]

Brodie's "religious memes" divide so easily into those that empower and those that don't. "That's it! That's all there is to it!" he exclaims. "None of the religions is the True one; they're all variations on a theme—or a meme. But let's take a closer look at what memes make for a successful religion."[154]

What, one wonders, would John of the Cross or Buddha's disciple Subhuti make of a "successful religion." One thinks of William James's century-old excoriation of his country's national disease—the squalid "bitch goddess," success. James was a pragmatist, but he knew of places where pragmatism wisely fears to tread.

However, what if evolutionary psychology makes testable predictions? That might provide evidence for its claims about RSMEs—not necessarily conclusive evidence if other approaches predicted the same outcomes with equal success, but at least some evidence.

Evolutionary Psychology and Modern Society

Evolutionary psychologists have offered some testable insights into present-day social problems, for example, the widely recorded claim that stepfathers are more likely to abuse children than natural fathers. As Sharon Begley explains in a *Wall Street Journal* profile of science philosopher David Buller:

> A Stone Age man who focused his care and support on his biological children, rather than kids his mate had from an earlier liaison would do better by evolution's scorecard (how many descendants he left) than a man who cared for his stepchildren. With this mindset, a stepfather is far more likely to abuse his stepchildren. One textbook asserts that kids living with a parent and a stepparent are some 40 times as likely to be abused as those living with biological parents.[155]

Data of this type might help establish evolutionary psychology as a viable discipline—if they held up. But when Buller examined the evidence, he found that stepfathers were far more often *blamed* for abuse than natural fathers—in life as in fairy tales—but they were not more likely to actually abuse children.[156]

Another evolutionary psychology prediction, that men prefer fertile young women who can spread their genes, did not pan out either. In fact, men (like women) prefer mates in the same general age group as themselves. The statistics are skewed because most men who are still *seeking* mates are young.[157] As Buller told *Scientific American:*

> What I thought needed to be brought out for a more general readership were some of the methodological problems involved in these very highly publicized discoveries that evolutionary psychologists claim to have made, things that get covered in the *New York Times* on pretty much a weekly basis. I wanted people to know that there are grounds for skepticism.[158]

Buller, as we have seen, was initially a supporter, but started to question the grand claims of evolutionary psychology and ended by calling it a "Flintstones" theory of human nature—satisfactory as long as we do not take it seriously.

Not Testable in the Past Tense

Generally, evolutionary psychologists have defended their theories of RSMEs on the grounds that any hypothesis based on Darwinian evolution theory must have more merit than a hypothesis that discounts its importance. But, as David Stove points out, Darwinian evolution has demonstrably *not* been true for human beings for any time period for which we have specific information.[159] The main reason is that passing on genes, which is fundamental to Darwinian evolution, is not a simple, predictable drive in humans, as it is in, say, geese. It is true, as we shall see in Chapter Eight, that people who have RSMEs generally enjoy good physical and mental health, but Darwinian theory, whose driving force is natural selection, depends on producing viable offspring, which is a different matter from experiencing a personal benefit.

To see the difficulty, assume there are two approaches to rearing offspring among geese. Because both populations of geese mate according to reliable instincts, we can study the outcome and determine which approach produces more viable offspring. But we have no similar way of knowing how many surviving offspring our recent human ancestors would have had if they exercised no voluntary control over procreation. Thus the population studies that might shed light on whether people who have RSMEs are better or worse adapted—in a purely Darwinian sense—cannot even be done. That is the main reason the claims of evolutionary psychology are hard to test.

In addition, almost all known civilizations—usually acting under the guidance of spiritual visionaries—have intentionally banished Darwinian evolution by eliminating the "struggle for survival" to the greatest extent possible. That makes it even harder to compare Darwinian fitness between populations of recent ancestors.

Relevance to RSMEs

As the reigning paradigm in evolutionary psychology has produced
questionable results, the evolutionary study of human psychology is still in
need of a guiding paradigm.[160]

—*David Buller,* Trends in Cognitive Science

Is evolutionary psychology even relevant to RSMEs? A key difficulty with
evolutionary psychology theories is that spirituality, like pure mathematics, is not useful—either accidentally or otherwise—in the Darwinian
sense. The fact that pure mathematics may eventually lead to applied
mathematics or that religious communities may eventually evolve into
safer places to live is irrelevant, because Darwinian evolution *explicitly*
rules out awareness of future goals. RSMEs are a genuinely new characteristic of humans that is irrelevant to the algorithms of natural selection.

Indeed, the problem with evolutionary psychology is not evolution; it
is materialism. Yes, evolution occurs, but—in the perennialist view—the
evolution of human consciousness toward an awareness of the universe as
a great thought rather than a great machine happened because the universe is actually more like a great thought than a great machine. The evidence points pretty clearly in that direction.

It is fair to ask, at this point, how much evidence we must be prepared
to jettison in order to protect twentieth-century materialism. Some evolutionary psychologists are prepared to jettison the very idea that rationality
and coherence correspond to a real feature of the universe. The German
philosopher and theologian Rudolf Otto had a better idea.

A Better Way to Understand RSMEs

The best atheists agree with the best defenders of faith on one crucial
point: that the choice to believe or disbelieve is existentially the most
important choice of all. It shapes one's whole understanding of human life
and purpose, because it is a choice that each of us must make for him or
herself.[161]

—*Adam Kirsch,* New York Sun

The truth of religion lies less in what is revealed in its doctrines than in
what is concealed in its mysteries. Religions do not reveal their meaning

directly because they cannot do so; their meaning has to be earned by worship and prayer, and by a life of quiet obedience. Nevertheless truths that are hidden are still truths; and maybe we can be guided by them only if they are hidden, just as we are guided by the sun only if we do not look at it.[162]

—*Roger Scruton,* The Spectator

Rudolf Otto (1869–1937) thought a good deal about evolution and spirituality during World War I. His principle work, *The Idea of the Holy*,[163] offers a useful approach to the study of RSMEs. He coined the term "numinous" to signify the type of experience—roughly equivalent to a deep RSME—that underlies the development of religious and spiritual traditions. He insisted that "there is no religion in which it does not live as the innermost core, and without it no religion would be worthy of the name," and that

> all ostensible explanations of the origin of religion in terms of animism or magic or folk psychology are doomed from the outset to wander astray and miss the real goal of their inquiry, unless they recognize this fact of our nature—primary, unique, underivable from anything else—to be the basic factor and the basic impulse underlying the entire process of religious evolution.[164]

By a numinous experience, Otto meant the sense of a presence much greater than oneself, something Wholly Other, which creates awe. Awe, of course, is not the same thing as fear; it is not driven by practical concerns. Fearing a bear attack in the wilderness and feeling awe while watching a Spirit Bear on a distant mountainside are quite different experiences.[165] All efforts to explain RSMEs in terms of self-interest or the drives of the "merely natural" man fail, Otto predicted, because the merely natural man does not even understand them:

> On the contrary, *so far as he understands it,* he tends to find it highly tedious and uninteresting, sometimes downright distasteful and repugnant to his nature, as he would, for instance, find the beatific vision of God in our own doctrine of salvation, or the *henōsis* of "God all in all" among the mystics. "So far as he understands," be it noted; but then he does not understand it in the least.[166]

Because humans are mythmakers by nature, we hold on to a numinous experience by objectifying or rationalizing it in myths, cults, and dogma. Prehistoric beliefs about spirits, in Otto's view, are an early effort to rationalize the numinous.[167] But all such attempts attest to the fact that the numinous experience itself has *already* evaporated.[168] Close analyses of the aftereffects are interesting and sometimes instructive, but, as noted earlier, they do not capture the primary effect.

Otto warned perceptively against the modernist tendency to rationalize the essential core of RSMEs as a means of producing moral virtue or concern for social justice. These are normal outcomes of such experiences, to be sure, but they are neither their origin nor their goal. He was also prescient in seeing that if the numinous is denied for a long time in a given tradition, it can burst forth with bizarre effects.[169] The Toronto Airport Blessing (a sudden charismatic Christian revival near the Toronto airport that impacted thousands of people worldwide in 1994), which featured controversial, bizarre effects alongside the normal "changed life" outcomes, is a modern-day example.[170]

Otto was not arguing that "all religions are equally valid" or that "all religions teach the same thing." His point is, rather, that all religions originate in a numinous experience. What adherents think, say, or do afterward is a different matter. Otto's approach to RSMEs was eclipsed by the drift toward materialism in the study of RSMEs in the latter half of the twentieth century, but it experienced a revival in the 1990s with the rise of an evidence-based approach to RSMEs.

But let us turn now from the study of the nature of RSMEs to the study of their effects. If spirituality is natural to us as conscious beings, looking beyond ourselves *is*—other things being equal—the best way for us to live. In that case, we might reasonably expect it to coincide with good mental and physical health. In Chapter Eight, we look at the evidence from research into spirituality and health.

EIGHT

Do Religious, Spiritual, or Mystical Experiences Change Lives?

So just what is the experimental evidence that God is bad for you? Dawkins presumes that it is publicly accepted within the scientific community that religion debilitates people, reducing their potential for survival and health. Yet recent empirical research points to a generally positive interaction of religion and health. That there are pathological types of religious belief and behavior is well known; yet this in no way invalidates the generally positive estimation of religion's impact on mental health to emerge from evidence-based studies.[1]
—*Theologian Alister McGrath*

To great fanfare, Daniel Dennett, director of the Center for Cognitive Studies at Tufts University, published *Breaking the Spell: Religion as a Natural Phenomenon* (2006). His airing of evolutionary psychology and memes was greeted by the usual puff pieces[2] and denunciations. But there was a curious difference from what might have happened a decade ago. Of course, he was scolded on the right. For example, books editor Adam Kirsch challenged him in the *New York Sun*:

At the heart of organized religion, whether one accepts or rejects it, is the truth that metaphysical experience is part of human life. Any adequate account of religion must start from this phenomenological fact. Because Mr.

Dennett ignores it, treating religion instead as at best a pastime for dim-wits, at worst a holding cell for fanatics, he never really encounters the thing he believes he is writing about.[3]

But, in a surprising turn of events, Dennett's effort also attracted criticism from a source that should have been an ally. He was scolded on the left as well. Leon Wieseltier, literary editor of *The New Republic,* dismissed his opus as "evo-psychobabble": "In the end, his repudiation of religion is a repudiation of philosophy.... What this shallow and self-congratulatory book establishes most conclusively is that there are many spells that need to be broken."[4]

Similarly, British champion of materialism Richard Dawkins produced a two-part TV special in 2006 on Britain's Channel 4 about religion, *The Root of All Evil?* Dawkins professed astonishment that religion is gaining ground in the twenty-first century and attributed it to the fact that parents and teachers apprise children of their own beliefs about ultimate reality.

Again, in a similar turnabout, Dawkins was assailed on the left as well as the right. One might have expected Roger Scruton to chide Dawkins in the *Spectator,* observing that

> the leap of faith itself—this placing of our life at God's service—is a leap over reason's edge. This does not make it irrational, any more than falling in love is irrational. On the contrary, it is the heart's submission to an ideal, and a bid for the love, peace and forgiveness that Dawkins too is seeking, since he, like the rest of us, was made in just that way.[5]

But Madeleine Bunting, of the left-wing *Guardian,* was much less charitable than Scruton. Scorning Dawkins's TV effort as an "intellectually lazy polemic not worthy of a great scientist," she notes:

> There's an underlying anxiety that atheist humanism has failed. Over the 20th century, atheist political regimes racked up an appalling (and un-matched) record for violence. Atheist humanism hasn't generated a compelling popular narrative and ethic of what it is to be human and our place in the cosmos; where religion has retreated, the gap has been filled with consumerism, football, Strictly Come Dancing and a mindless absorption in passing desires.[6]

Why so much questioning, discomfort, and distaste for materialism? Have long-suppressed questions begun to surface at last? In an ambivalent 2003 review of a previous Dennett book, *Freedom Evolves,* psychologist David P. Barash writes:

> I suspect that we all—even the most hard-headed materialist—live with an unspoken hypocrisy: even as we assume determinism in our intellectual pursuits and professional lives, we actually experience our subjective lives as though free will reigns supreme. In our heart of hearts, we *know* that in most ways that really count (and many that don't), we have plenty of free will, and so do those around us. Inconsistent? Yes, indeed. But like the denial of death, it is a useful inconsistency, and perhaps even one that is essential.[7]

At this point, to quote Wieseltier, ancient rabbis might ask, "Have your ears heard what your mouth has spoken?" The resolution of Barash's dilemma is that materialism is mistaken. What we know in our heart of hearts is actually true. Free will—whether denied or affirmed—is real.

Indeed, the problem with the materialist project all along is that, although materialism demands to be seen as the only truth, many undeniable facts of human experience make sense only if we assume that materialism is *not* true. One of them, which has only recently begun to receive the attention it deserves, is the fact that people who develop their spirituality generally enjoy better physical and mental health.

The Connection Between Spirituality and Health

Drawing on recent, speculative work by evolutionary theorists, Mr. Dennett sketches a picture of how religion might have arisen as a naturally selected adaptation to the early human environment. Perhaps, he suggests, credulous Homo sapiens had a higher survival rate because they were more susceptible to the placebo effect, and thus more likely to be "cured" of diseases by the ministrations of a shaman.[8]
—*Adam Kirsch,* New York Sun

Following this bouncing ball of belief as we have throughout history, it has taken just over 150 years for humanity to come full circle—to abandon and then redeem the beliefs that aided the survival of men and women from the very start.[9]
—*Herbert Benson and Marg Stark,*
Timeless Medicine

As we have seen, in a materialist environment, science offers two basic approaches to spirituality. One approach sees it as an accidental by-product of human brain development, so any relationship between spirituality and health is accidental. Indeed, many scientists have assumed an inverse relationship without good evidence—or any evidence at all. The other approach sees spirituality as good for humans because it promotes evolutionary fitness. But that view is problematic because, as we have seen, specifically evolutionary fitness[10] is not necessarily either a goal or an outcome of spirituality. The problem has been that materialism lacks an underlying theory that accommodates but does not distort the evidence for the spiritual nature of humans and its outcome in physical or mental health.

Dr. Herbert Benson, who spent his career working in Harvard Medical School's teaching hospitals, is one of a handful of medical investigators who established the scientific field recognized today as mind/body medicine. Associate professor of medicine at Harvard Medical School, he founded Harvard's Mind/Body Medical Institute at Boston's Deaconess Hospital. Observing how patients got better—or didn't—he became convinced that

> our bodies are wired to benefit from exercising not only our muscles but our rich inner, human core—our beliefs, values, thoughts, and feelings. I was reluctant to explore these factors because philosophers and scientists have, through the ages, considered them intangible and unmeasurable, making any study of them "unscientific." But I wanted to try, because, again and again, my patients' progress and recoveries often seemed to hinge upon their spirit and will to live. And I could not shake the sense I had that the human mind—and the beliefs we so often associate with the human soul—had physical manifestations.[11]

He zeroed in on the placebo effect, which we looked at in Chapter Six. He prefers to call it "remembered wellness," or the propensity of the body to turn a mental belief into a physical instruction. After reviewing the scientific literature available in the 1970s, he concluded that this effect is much more powerful for many conditions than the conventional estimate of 30 percent, originally given by Henry K. Beecher in a 1955 study and used as a benchmark today. He reviewed many cases where the placebo effect was closer to 70 to 90 percent of the total treatment effect.[12]

One finding that intrigued Benson was that treatments for conditions such as angina or bronchial asthma often worked well *as long as* the patient and the physician believed in them, even though the treatment itself was later discarded after systematic investigation as medically useless. Indeed, in the case of angina, the treatments declined in value when physicians stopped believing in them. No doubt the physician's uncertainty was either subtly or bluntly conveyed to the patient.[13] Indeed, in one study published in *Lancet* (1990), men who did not take their placebos regularly were more likely to die than men who did.[14]

Benson does not dismiss pharmacy or surgery, nor does he embrace nonscientific medicine, whose successes he ascribes largely to the "remembered wellness" (placebo) effect. On the contrary, his image of optimal medicine is a three-legged stool, which aims for stability by adding to pharmacy and surgery a third science-based tool—an intentional and efficient use of the placebo effect. The placebo effect is often used unwittingly and inefficiently in health-care practice. Sometimes it is unintentionally reversed, producing the deadly nocebo effect, as Benson was to discover himself.

Early in the twentieth century, medicine came down firmly against the idea that the mind influenced the body and sought to trace illness to single, specific sources. Indeed, by the 1930s, the *Index Medicus* contained not a single reference to the effect of mental states on physiology.[15] However, in the 1940s, "psychosomatic medicine" was introduced to foster better understanding and management of the relationship between mind and body in health. But the tendency to treat the body as a machine and the mind as an irrelevance prevented much advance in this area. In *Timeless Medicine* (1996), Benson illustrates how deeply this mechanistic approach affected medicine. A woman who suffered recurrent temporary bouts of numbness and weakness in several body parts was at first dismissed as merely imagining her symptoms. However, a new doctor conducted extensive tests and diagnosed multiple sclerosis, an incurable neurological disease that was disabling her and would eventually kill her. Her response? "Oh, I'm so relieved, I thought it was all in my head."[16]

Indeed, by the 1960s, materialism was so pervasive in medicine that Benson had a hard time persuading his colleagues that mental stress could contribute to high blood pressure. Mentors warned that he was risking his career when he began to study the physiology of meditation in an effort to understand how the mind influences the body.[17] Meanwhile, doctors told early researchers into the placebo effect that their colleagues were three times more likely to employ that effect than they themselves were.

The doctors were not attempting to deceive anyone; most likely, they failed to recognize their own use of the placebo effect, even though they noticed when other doctors did it. As we saw in Chapter Six, the placebo effect is part of the normal practice of clinical medicine. But it is not a practice that doctors would have found easy to discuss. The medical system, after all, offered little reward for working effectively with a patient's mental states. A doctor who reported, "Mr. Y accepted my advice to meditate when he feels overwhelmed by job stress; as a result, his ulcer attacks have diminished in severity, and he can reduce his medications," might be accused of practicing "unscientific" medicine or even of "dragging in religion." The fact that the doctor's approach had worked would be irrelevant in an environment focused on the prescription of drugs, treatments, or surgery.

Clearly, much progress has been made in recent decades in understanding the mind's real influence on the body. In 2000, the National Institutes of Health held a conference on the subject. Although the scientific study of mental states still creates anxiety in some,[18] mental influences on high blood pressure, for example, are no longer controversial.[19] Indeed, a recent study found that loneliness[20] significantly increases the risk of high blood pressure, especially in seniors. Richard Suzman, director of the Behavioral and Social Research Program at the National Institute on Aging (NIA), expressed surprise over "the magnitude of the relationship between loneliness and hypertension in this well-controlled cross-sectional study."[21]

To better understand twentieth-century medicine's discomfort with any mental influences at all, never mind RSMEs, we must recognize that nineteenth- and twentieth-century medicine had triumphed in many areas while simply ignoring mental states. Antiseptics, treated water, vaccinations, antibiotics, incubators, intravenous drips, and defibrillators greatly reduced death tolls without addressing or even according any importance to them. Inevitably, many researchers conflated ignoring mental states with improving treatment outcomes. But that was a mistake. All trends peak, and it began to be clear that many illnesses resist effective treatment when mental states are ignored. One thinks, for example, of the recent deflation of claims for many once-heralded antidepressants.[22]

Benson encouraged his patients to repeat a phrase to themselves to help them relax and thus avoid disrupting normal healing processes. He was intrigued by the fact that 80 percent chose prayers, whether they were Jewish, Christian, Buddhist, or Hindu.[23] Yet, when Robert Orr and George Isaac studied 1,066 papers in seven major American primary-care journals in 1992, only 12 (1.1 percent) addressed RSMEs.[24] Similarly, David Larson found that of 2,348 empirical studies published in four major psychiatry journals, only 2.5 percent contained a relevant measure.[25] Despite that, considerable evidence was building that RSMEs were associated with better physical and mental health.

The Effect of Spirituality on Health

[RSMEs are] ... a regression, an escape, a projection upon the world of a primitive infantile state.[26]
　　　　　—Group for the Advancement of Psychiatry report on RSMEs

What is perhaps most surprising about these negative opinions of religion's effect on mental health is the startling absence of empirical evidence to support these views. Indeed, the same scientists who were trained to accept or reject a hypothesis based on hard data seem to rely solely on their own opinions and biases when assessing the effect of religion on health.[27]
　　　　　—Spirituality and health researcher David Larson

Treatment approaches devoid of spiritual sensitivity may provide an alien values framework.... A majority of the population probably prefers an orientation to counseling and psychotherapy that is sympathetic, or at least sensitive, to a spiritual perspective.[28]
　　　　　—Psychologist Allen Bergin

In addition to effects such as the placebo effect—that is, the power of mental states favorable to healing *as such*—there is considerable evidence that RSMEs in particular are associated with good physical and mental health. Edward B. Larson (1947–2002), an epidemiologist and psychiatrist, approached this question at a slightly different angle from Benson. Just as Benson was puzzled by the medical literature's avoidance of the sheer size of the placebo effect, Larson, a devout Christian, was puzzled by its avoidance of and hostility to RSMEs.

One problem stemmed from the way in which research was conducted. Patient histories that ask for a religious affiliation, for example, cannot distinguish "intrinsic" from "extrinsic" faith. Pioneer sociologist of religion Gordon Allport defined intrinsic faith as internalized experience; extrinsic faith expresses group membership. The distinction is important where health is concerned, because health benefits come mainly from intrinsic faith, the sort associated with RSMEs.[29] In addition, sophisticated instruments for measuring attitudes were rarely used in the research on RSMEs, and study samples were often unrepresentative of the general population.[30]

But Larson found that there was also considerable bias. The *Diagnostic and Statistical Manual of Mental Disorders* (DSM-III) used many case examples that characterized religious patients as "psychotic, delusional, incoherent, illogical, and hallucinating," suggesting a general psychopathology[31] that misrepresented clinical experience.[32] When that edition of the manual was in use, only 3 of 125 medical schools in the United States provided any instruction on the relationship between health and RSMEs—in a nation where roughly a third of the population claims to have had an RSME. Despite his sudden, untimely death in 2002, Larson played a key role in helping to revise the DSM-III. And, thanks in part to his work with the Templeton Foundation, nearly two-thirds of medical schools offer course work relevant to RSMEs today.[33]

Meanwhile, in the 1980s, together with Jeff Levin and Harold Koenig, Larson pioneered an evidence-based approach to the relationship between health and RSMEs. Whereas many research reviews provide an overview of those articles a reviewer wishes to highlight, he developed a "systematic review" method that avoids selection bias by looking at every quantitative article published during a given number of years in a single journal. This method provides a comprehensive survey of findings that is both objective and replicable.[34] In *The Faith Factor: An Annotated Bibliography of Clinical Research on Spiritual Subjects,* Larson, Dale Matthews, and Constance Barry conducted a detailed review of 158 medical studies on the effects of religion on health, 77 percent of which demonstrated a positive clinical effect.[35] Thus, it is not surprising that Benson's patients generally chose prayers for their meditations; they probably knew of personal or anecdotal evidence of their value.

Similarly, a prospective study of nearly four thousand seniors (aged 64–101) who were not disabled but lived in a residence during 1986–92 found that private religious activities such as meditation, prayer, and Bible study were associated with greater survival rates. The researchers concluded that "older adults who participate in private religious activity before the onset of ADL [activities of daily living] impairment appear to have a survival advantage over those who do not."[36]

But seniors' beliefs are not always so positive. Some beliefs are nocebos that adversely affect health. One study found that ill elderly patients were more likely to die if they had a conflicted relationship with their religious beliefs. The researchers studied 595 patients of fifty-five or over at Duke University Medical Center and Durham VA Medical Center. They achieved a complete follow-up on 444 patients, including 176 who had died. Those patients who strongly agreed with statements like "wondered whether God had abandoned me; felt punished by God for my lack of devotion; wondered what I did for God to punish me; questioned God's love for me; wondered whether my church had abandoned me; decided the Devil made this happen; and questioned the power of God" were significantly more likely to die (19–28 percent greater mortality during the two-year period after discharge from hospital). The authors concluded: "Certain forms of religiousness may increase the risk of death. Elderly ill men and women who experience a religious struggle with their illness appear to be at increased risk of death, even after controlling for baseline health, mental health status, and demographic factors."[37]

Clearly, it makes a difference whether beliefs create hope or despair. But does it make a difference what God one prays to? Dale Matthews, a physician associate of Larson, notes: "While science has demonstrated that being devout provides more health benefits than not being devout, we haven't shown that being a devout Christian will make you healthier than being a devout Buddhist."[38] This does not, of course, mean that theology is irrelevant; it suggests rather that the *health effect* of RSMEs derives less from beliefs about causes than from resulting mental states.

The research results do not, of course, substantiate notions that "the mind heals all" or "faith surely heals," let alone that medical interventions are superfluous. They demonstrate only that both mental states and choices in mental attention are important in maintaining and restoring wellness—a role that has begun to receive long overdue attention.

In fact, in recent years, the discussion has become much more focused. That is, the question, "Does spirituality make any difference?" is giving way to "*Under what circumstances* does spirituality make a difference?" Some interesting recent research includes:

Evidence that patients often want their doctors to know about their spiritual beliefs and take them into account. In a 2004 study involving 921 adults attending family-practice clinics, 83 percent wanted doctors to ask about their spiritual beliefs "in at least some circumstances" in order to increase physician-patient understanding. Life-threatening illnesses (77 percent), serious medical conditions (74 percent), and loss of loved ones (70 percent) were the top-rated scenarios, as might be expected. The patients interviewed hoped that, as a result, doctors could "encourage realistic hope (67 percent), give medical advice (66 percent), and change medical treatment (62 percent)."[39] Patients also report, however, that such discussions rarely take place. Doctors report that they avoid the topic for a number of reasons: concern about doing harm, invasion of privacy, lack of expertise, and the difficulty of determining which patients want to talk. However, the cited difficulties crop up in any sensitive discussion (about sex or domestic abuse, for example); perhaps the key question should be, what are the potential costs of *not* having the discussion?

Evidence that doctors themselves are more likely to have spiritual beliefs than academic or research scientists. In a recent survey of over 1,100 American physicians, 55 percent agreed with the statement, "My religious beliefs influence my practice of medicine." Family physicians and pediatricians were the most religious and psychiatrists the least.[40] This finding raises an interesting point: if over half of physicians say that their religious beliefs influence their practice of medicine, patients might want to know what the doctor does believe, just as they might want the doctor to know what *they* believe.

Further evidence that some specific religious attitudes/practices reduce post-operative stress, but that others increase it. Researchers interviewed 202 people scheduled for open-heart surgery, before and after the surgery, at the University of Michigan Medical Center between 1999 and 2002. Prayer to a "dependable higher power" was associated with less distress after surgery, but subjective religiosity, accompanied by doubt about whether the higher power was benevolent, was not.[41]

As the influence of the mind on health becomes more widely accepted, researchers continue to refine the topic, because the answers to current questions are leading, inevitably, to further questions. One question we have not yet addressed is intercessory prayer (praying for someone else to be healed). How effective is that? For that matter, can we even determine how effective it is?

Can Prayer for Others Help?

A study of more than 1,800 patients who underwent heart bypass surgery has failed to show that prayers specially organized for their recovery had any impact, researchers said on Thursday. In fact, the study found some of the patients who knew they were being prayed for did worse than others who were only told they might be prayed for—though those who did the study said they could not explain why.[42]
—*Michael Conlon,* Reuters

If a religious person offers to pray for you next time you fall ill, you may wish politely to ask them not to bother. The largest scientific study into the health effects of prayer seems to suggest it may make matters worse.[43]
—*Oliver Burkeman,* The Guardian

Outcome researchers must be vigilant in asking the question of whether a well-intentioned, loving, heartfelt healing prayer might inadvertently harm or kill vulnerable patients in certain circumstances.[44]
—*M. Krucoff et al.,* American Heart Journal

I think that prayer absolutely does work and that God answers prayer and that we can continue to pray for our loved ones.[45]
—*Faith and health researcher Harold Koenig*

Early in 2006, the *American Heart Journal* reported the outcome of the Study of the Therapeutic Effects of Intercessory Prayer (STEP), a large "blue ribbon" study of the effects of prayer for the healing of others (intercessory prayer), mainly funded by the Templeton Foundation and headed by Herbert Benson.[46] Four previous studies that merited attention had split evenly about whether intercessory prayer affected outcomes, so the challenge was to tease out prayer's actual effect.

Some studies had already provided evidence that intercessory prayer makes a difference. For example, William Harris and colleagues found that "supplementary, remote, blinded, intercessory prayer produced a measurable improvement in the medical outcomes of critically ill patients" (1999).[47] In their study, the first names of patients admitted to the coronary-care unit were given to a prayer group of Christian intercessors from a variety of backgrounds, who prayed for them every day for four weeks. These patients did not know that they were prayed for, and the intercessors had never met them. The patients for whom the researchers had recruited prayer stayed as long as others in the coronary-care unit, but they had fewer adverse outcomes. However, Dale Matthews and colleagues (2000) found a significant effect from distant intercessory prayer in elderly women with rheumatoid arthritis *only* if the patient was prayed over by the intercessor in person at the hospital.[48] In that case, it would be difficult to disentangle the specific effect of intercessory prayer from the placebo effect or an RSME effect (the patient's own spirituality).

In their study, hailed as the largest and best designed ever, Benson and his colleagues were not examining God, miracles, faith healing, or prayer for loved ones. Nothing they discovered would be evidence for or against any of these concepts. They wanted to study a much more specific variable: Does a patient's knowledge that he or she is receiving prayer affect the surgical outcome? Thus, they divided 1,802 heart patients awaiting coronary-artery bypass graft (CABG) surgery at six American medical centers into three groups, as follows:

Group 1 patients were told that they might or might not receive intercessory prayer, but in fact did.

Group 2 patients were told that they might or might not receive intercessory prayer, but in fact did not.

Group 3 patients were told that they would receive intercessory prayer, and in fact did.

The groups chosen by the researchers to do the intercessory prayer were serious about their task. Two were Roman Catholic religious congregations and one was a Protestant prayer community. The groups prayed one to four times a day for fourteen days, beginning just prior to the surgery, for "a successful surgery with a quick, healthy recovery and no complications."[49] However, the members of these groups never met anyone that they prayed for. They were told only the first name and the first initial of the last name.

The results? After thirty days, all three groups experienced similar mortality, and the complication rate was statistically insignificant between the first two groups. By far the highest percentage of postsurgery complications (59 percent as opposed to 51 percent and 52 percent) was recorded among the patients who *knew* they were being prayed for by the researchers' prayer group:

> Intercessory prayer itself had no effect on complication-free recovery from CABG, but certainty of receiving intercessory prayer was associated with a higher incidence of complications.[50]

As the *American Heart Journal* editors summarized, "The assumption imbedded in the analysis plan was that blinded prayer would be effective and unblinded prayer even more effective, with expected complication rates of 50 percent in the standard care group, 40 percent in the blinded prayer group, and 30 percent in the unblinded prayer group—exactly the opposite of what was actually observed."[51]

Can we now simply dismiss intercessory prayer? Not at all, because the key finding was a *statistically significant* negative effect among the patients who knew that they were prayed for by the prayer groups organized by the researchers.

So we must ask, along with the *Heart Journal* editors, what happened here? The placebo effect and the RSME effect are both accepted and powerful and should have produced some signal, given that two-thirds of patients stated that they strongly believe in spiritual healing. And it did—a negative signal, a nocebo effect. But why? Skeptics of intercessory prayer (a minority in this study) view such prayer as powerless rather than as harmful.

The flummoxed researchers suggested that the outcome "may have been a chance finding," thus prompting a stringent rebuke from the *Heart Journal*'s editors:

> Culturally, "harm" resulting from prayer is generally ascribed to overtly "negative" prayer, such as hateful prayer, voodoo, spells, or other black

magic. Positively intended intercessory prayer is considered a priori to be only capable of doing good, if it does anything at all. But this cultural dichotomy is medically problematic and ethically unacceptable in the setting of a clinical trial performing structured experimentation on human subjects.[52]

In other words, a remedy of interest to science must be traced to forces that could potentially do harm as well as good. A placebo effect, reversed, becomes a nocebo effect precisely because it is a powerful effect. As the *Journal* editors say, "In the history of medicine there has never been a healing remedy that was actually effective without having potential side effects or toxicities."[53]

The editors suggest some possible nocebo effects. Patients who were certain they were prayed for by the researchers' prayer groups were also asked to *hide* that fact from their own bedside staff. Also, "Approaching a patient to participate in a prayer study before a procedure could inadvertently alarm a patient, 'You mean I'm so sick that I might need prayer?'"[54] This is especially likely in an environment where, as we have seen, doctors and patients are generally reluctant to discuss spirituality.

It's not hard to see why the editors criticized the study design. They concluded that a higher rate of complications may suggest that the study design itself, rather than chance, was at fault. Recall that, in the Harris study (1999), which showed a favorable prayer effect, the patients had *not* been told that the researchers had recruited intercessors, so increased anxiety was unlikely (and apparently did not occur).

If Benson and his colleagues were disappointed by the outcome of their study, they could at least be gratified that the issues they raise are now taken seriously, not merely dismissed—a significant positive change from earlier decades. But the study of intercessory prayer is difficult in principle. Prayer for oneself should often work because the placebo effect and the RSME effect follow observed patterns, some of which we have explored in this book: specifically, a focus of attention on positive mental states that conform to the real nature of the universe can produce changes in the brain and body that overrule other, less positive, ones.

By contrast, prayer for the healing of others requires *at a minimum* action at a distance. Action at a distance assumes that person *A* attempts to directly influence the health of person *B* through prayer (presumably by, at least, influencing *B*'s mental state). There is some evidence for action at a distance, as we have seen, but it is a lower-level effect, less well understood and thus more controversial. However, there is another difficulty. Prayers for healing in most traditions actually triangulate: *A* appeals for the healing of *B* through spiritual power source *C*. In any triangulation, the number of possible complications rises dramatically, and teasing them out requires a very sophisticated research design.

New Questions Raised by Current Research

Some questions raised by researchers in the aftermath of STEP include:

Basically, how do we define a prayer? Are all forms or traditions of prayer equally effective? Does it matter whether the people who pray are virtuous, according to their religious tradition? Does it matter when, where, or how long they pray? Does it matter whether the intercessor knows or cares about the person prayed for? Does it matter how many people pray for a given outcome? How can intercessory prayer be separated from the placebo effect in an ethically designed study?[55] A scientific evaluation of intercessory prayer may need to begin by developing ways of answering these questions.

How can we rule out prayer that might interfere with the study? Approximately 95 percent of STEP patients, including the group not prayed for by the researchers' recruited prayer groups, believed that friends, relatives, and fellow believers prayed for them. In a nation in which the vast majority assumes that some religious order underlies the universe, any research design for intercessory prayer must address the effects of this "wild" prayer. It must also assume that many patients pray for their own health (43 percent of Americans, according to a 2004 survey[56]).

Should more mundane issues be established first? Harold Koenig, a colleague and friend of the late Edward B. Larson, has suggested that researchers begin more simply with questions like, "Do patients who have a chaplain visit before surgery do better after surgery?" or "If a doctor takes a spiritual history of patients along with their medical history and supports their religious beliefs, will it make difference in medical outcomes?"[57]

Should we assume that the patient thinks that survival is the best outcome in all cases? The *American Heart Journal* editors who criticized the STEP study design pointed out that many traditional prayers for the sick ask for an easy death, if that is the best outcome.[58] Heart-surgery patients are usually mid- to late-life adults who might anticipate considerable suffering if they do survive, which complicates the question of prayer outcomes in the field of cardiac surgery—currently the most popular field for prayer study. If, for example, the chosen field had been circumcision of healthy male infants, this question would not likely arise.

How can prayer studies accommodate ethical requirements for both informed consent and avoidance of undue anxiety? Harris and colleagues simply did not tell patients about the extra intercessors and obtained a good result. Some STEP patients were informed, but told to conceal the fact (presumably to prevent any change in caregivers' behavior or judgment), but these patients experienced a statistically worse outcome. Protocols for prayer studies must find a way to recruit patients in a transparent way without invoking a nocebo effect.

It must be emphasized that the STEP study did *not* show that prayer by loved ones was irrelevant or harmful because, as we have seen, the researchers' prayer teams did not know the patients they were praying for. In any event, there are grounds for believing that the study design itself introduced a nocebo effect that loved ones' prayers would not likely create.

Some, of course, argue that prayer should not be studied at all, because it "represents bad science, poor medical care, and it trivializes religion,"[59] or it amounts to prying into God's business or trying to control God, or science is not equipped to explore these issues. However, there is no easy way to tell, apart from actual research, what might trivialize religion, what business belongs exclusively to God, or what science is equipped to explore.

The field has come a long way in the last couple of decades. In 1990 Gary P. Posner felt free to begin a critique[60] of a 1988 study[61] that showed positive effects from intercessory prayer by announcing: "The day of publication of the July 1988 issue of the *Southern Medical Journal* must have been one Hell of a busy news day, literally." Posner's critique raises legitimate conventional issues about research design. But his underlying assumption is that intercessory prayer must be ineffective in principle, and therefore issues in research design are simply barriers to research. That is a far cry from the position taken by the *American Heart Journal* editors in 2006, who did not at all dispute the effects traced to spirituality, but did insist that prayer advocates address the outcomes of their own research design.

Many people would benefit from knowing whether or how intercessory prayer affects situations that greatly concern them. Perhaps current research should focus on specific questions such as the ones suggested by Koenig above in an attempt to design studies that measure effects more accurately and less intrusively. But given the comparative complexity of intercessory prayer, the next big challenge is developing study designs that are sufficiently sophisticated to measure the effects.

Do RSMEs Change Lives?

In 1966 I was one day alone in the house when quite suddenly I became aware of my own attitude to life. I realized that I was wrapped up in deep self-pity, that my thoughts were all for myself and my own sorrows, that I had not thought of others. I thought how others in the world suffered too. I was rather shocked at my selfish attitude and was filled with compassion for others; then, as if without thinking, I knelt down in the room and made a vow to God that from then on for the rest of my life I would love and serve mankind.[62]

—*Account of spiritual experiences given to biologist Alister Hardy*

Compassion actually has a spiritual source and is something more than the mixed human passion of love and sorrow. Another term for compassion is mercy, and true mercy is actually a divine attribute.[63]

—*Unsigned editorial,* Christian Science Monitor

Do RSMEs tell us something about the real nature of our universe? If so, they tell us that the universe is essentially meaningful and purposeful, not meaningless and purposeless. We are not animals in competition with each other for survival, but rather spiritual beings connected to the source of our spiritual nature. Insights derived from RSMEs should result in empathy, the ability to "feel with" other spiritual or sentient beings. Many historical examples record such a growth in empathy, leading to major life changes. Generally, a basic character type is not changed; rather the experiencer's priorities are changed. But are such changes true only of mystics and otherwise especially spiritual persons?

Evidence for Changed Lives

It should be of selective advantage for young children to be self-centered and relatively disinclined to perform altruistic acts based on personal principle.[64]
—*Sociobiologist Edward O. Wilson*

One of the earliest emotions that even tiny babies display is, admirably enough, empathy. In fact, concern for others may be hard-wired into babies' brains. Plop a newborn down next to another crying infant, and chances are, both babies will soon be wailing away.[65]
—*Pat Wingert and Martha Brant,* Newsweek

In 2003, Hope Stout, a twelve-year-old North Carolina girl, was fighting bone cancer (osteosarcoma). Officials from the Make-a-Wish Foundation came to ask her, amid family, flowers, and cards, to make a last wish, to take her mind off her terminal illness. Would she perhaps like to attend a teen fashion show? Have lunch with a movie idol? Visit a resort?

She asked, "How many children are waiting for wishes to be granted?" On learning that the agency was aware of 155 in her part of North Carolina, she declared, "Then my wish is to raise money to grant all of their wishes." Hope herself never made it to the extravaganza that was organized to raise the money, because she died a few days beforehand. But in an interview taped before her death she explained, "I just saw that God had given me a whole lot, and I had already been to Disney World and stuff. But I figured a lot of other kids hadn't."[66]

Generally, empathy is a natural development in human beings and a sense of God's presence leads to an increase in empathy, even in children. Indeed, *Guardian* columnist Roy Hattersley, who describes himself as an atheist, insists that atheism inhibits empathy. Reflecting on the aftermath of Hurricane Katrina, he begins, "Faith does breed charity: We atheists have to accept that most believers are better human beings." He continues:

The Salvation Army has been given a special status as provider-in-chief of American disaster relief. But its work is being augmented by all sorts of other groups. Almost all of them have a religious origin and character. Notable by their absence are teams from rationalist societies, free thinkers' clubs and atheists' associations.[67]

Alister Hardy's research found that the main consequences of a self-reported RSME were a sense of purpose or new meaning to life and changes toward more personally meaningful religious belief accompanied by a more compassionate attitude toward others.[68] The specific content of the belief may not have been as important as Hattersley supposes. In one case, the respondent appeared outwardly to have abandoned religion (which she described as "churchianity"), but Hardy notes, "She has moved from one form which was meaningless to her to another which provided her with a deep sense of spiritual reality."[69] If we recall Allport's distinction between extrinsic religion (group membership) and intrinsic religion (personal spiritual experience), one might say that RSME experiencers tend to focus on the latter. If they retain rather than change a current religious identity, they reinterpret it in the light of personal experience.

Generally, people who claim to be "religious" (and therefore may have had an RSME) are significantly more likely to donate time or money—irrespective of their actual income—to charitable causes, both religious and nonreligious.[70] But some have argued that RSMEs do not make enough difference. Ron Sider, an American evangelical social justice activist, argues that practical materialism has won out in the lives of most who claim to believe that materialism is not true. Sider is anything but a skeptic or cynic. Indeed, he told *Christianity Today,* "The stats just break my heart. They make me weep."[71] He notes that although religious people in the United States give more than others, their giving has declined for some decades, even though their incomes have increased.

In 2005, paleontologist Gregory S. Paul[72] offered a survey of data from eighteen countries, arguing that religious belief contributes to a high level of social disorders, including murder, suicide, and sexually transmitted diseases (STDs). He received widespread publicity, as might be expected, with headlines such as "Societies Worse Off 'When They Have God on Their Side.'"[73]

One aspect of Paul's work that did *not* receive nearly as much publicity was the fact that he made a point of not using standard sociological tools such as regression and multivariate analyses. That makes his results idiosyncratic and not comparable with the vast range of data that points in the opposite direction. Pollster George H. Gallup, Jr., asked pointedly:

> Can he identify a single other study published in a major scientific journal comparing results across countries that did not employ multivariate analysis to control for differences among nations? No, because multivariate analysis is required for cross-national comparisons of this sort.[74]

Essentially, social scientists use agreed-upon statistical methods to ensure that comparisons between populations capture key relevant information. For example, a nation in which the average age is eighteen might be expected to feature a much higher rate of gang warfare than one in which the average age is forty. Beliefs, of course, play a key role, but when assessing that role, we must ask, who is even *tempted* to join the local street gang? According to Gallup:

> A mountain of survey data from the Gallup and other survey organizations shows that when educational background and other variables are held constant, persons who are "highly spiritually committed" are far less likely to engage in antisocial behavior than those less committed. They have lower rates of crime, excessive alcohol use, and drug addiction than other groups.[75]

Generally, he noted, the research shows that the more spiritually committed a person is, the more he or she will spend time, energy, and money helping others.

One barrier to understanding the effects of RSMEs has been misconceptions. For example, there is a widespread belief among academics (who are much less likely to be religious believers than the general public) that most evangelical Christian Americans—most of whom claim to have had an RSME—are hard-core members of the Christian Right. Actually, as Chip Berlet points out in *The Public Eye Magazine,* only 14 percent of the American electorate self-identifies as Christian Right, even though 33 percent or more, depending on the poll, considers itself "born again." Nearly half of those who self-identified as members of the "religious right" did not even vote in the 2000 election. Black evangelicals who do vote overwhelmingly choose liberal candidates.[76] The key distinctive of people who describe themselves as evangelical, charismatic, or born again is actually irrelevant to politics: it is the belief that a personal spiritual experience is essential for a meaningful life.[77]

If we want truth for anything other than itself, we do not want truth. Thus, as Harald Wallach and K. Helmut Reich caution, a purely utilitarian approach to spirituality is actually impossible:

> Spirituality cannot be forced to produce willed results. Being a way toward a better knowledge of oneself, toward cosmic embedding, toward a healthier life, and toward community and solidarity, it requires humbleness, patience, persistence, and personal engagement to lead to positive results whenever they arrive. This does not mean that one cannot or should not make conscious efforts toward developing one's spirituality, only that such an enterprise has its own "laws," which are quite different from, say, training for proficiency in computer use.[78]

Thus, certain desirable social outcomes can reasonably be anticipated from RSMEs, but that is not the reason they occur, nor can they be produced for such purposes.

Spirituality and Withdrawal from Life

> The greatest challenge of the day is: how to bring about a revolution of the heart, a revolution that has to start with each one of us?[79]
> —*Catholic social activist Dorothy Day*
> *(1897–1980)*

> Be the change that you want to see in the world.[80]
> —*Indian sage Mohandas Gandhi (1869–1948)*

Some argue that RSMEs are a retreat from the demands of real life. It was fashionable in the last century to contrast spirituality with realism or even with concern for social justice. Of course, the historical record runs opposite, both past and present. Many social activists and reformers, from Gandhi through to Dorothy Day, have been motivated by RSMEs, which is not surprising when we consider that people who work for justice face serious risks and must have strong reasons for persisting.

There is also a popular misconception that true mystics segregate them-selves from the world because they have lost interest in its problems. Not so; the mystic wants to stop thinking, speaking, and acting out of layers of false consciousness, that is, to stop being one of the world's *problems* and start being the desired *change,* as Gandhi put it. The mystic believes that no other approach will really work in the long run. But when mystics are sure that they are acting from a true instinct, they often become quite active indeed.

Underhill, for example, urges her readers to consider the public minis-try of the mystic Catherine of Siena (1347–80), who played a key role in reforming the papacy, no mean feat for a medieval woman of humble origin who died at the age of thirty-three. She also exhorts:

> Remember the humbler but not less beautiful and significant achievement of her Genoese namesake [Catherine of Genoa[81]]: the strenuous lives of St. Francis of Assisi, St. Ignatius, St. Teresa, outwardly cumbered with much serving, observant of an infinitude of tiresome details, composing rules, set-ting up foundations, neglecting no aspect of their business which could conduce to its practical success, yet "altogether dwelling in God in restful fruition." Are not all these supreme examples of the state in which the self, at last fully conscious, knowing Reality because she is wholly real, pays her debt?[82]

However, it is true that mystics tend to understand social action some-what differently from many others. They are wary of ideology because they typically view it as a false consciousness. Thomas Merton (1915–68), a Trap-pist monk who was both a mystic and an interfaith ecumenist, counseled a young friend who was in danger of burning out in a struggle for peace:

> It is so easy to get engrossed with ideas and slogans and myths that in the end one is left holding the bag, empty with no trace of meaning left in it. And then the temptation is to yell louder than ever in order to make the meaning be there again by magic.

Merton counseled his friend to approach his mission in a different way:

> Gradually you struggle less and less for an idea and more and more for spe-cific people. The range tends to narrow down, but it gets much more real. In the end, it is the reality of personal relationships that saves everything.[83]

Of course, if mystics are right about the nature of the universe, that is precisely what we should expect to find. The transpersonal does not reduce merely to the abstract, and the personal does not reduce merely to the material. We cannot escape or disprove ourselves, and so we must live with ourselves, come what may.

Is godlessness moving from one end of the campus to the other?[84]
—*David Glenn,* Chronicle of Higher Education

In 2005 Elaine Howard Ecklund and Christopher P. Scheitle presented preliminary results from an ongoing study of the religious beliefs of 1,646 scholars at the 2005 annual meeting of the Association for the Sociology of Religion. Their key finding may shed some light on a question we have been pursuing: Why do scientists cling to materialism in the face of mounting contrary evidence, often accepting questionable explanations for phenomena such as consciousness or psi?

In 1969, a Carnegie Commission on Higher Education study had found that natural scientists were much more likely than social scientists to self-identify as religious. However, over the decades, the pattern has apparently reversed itself. Fully 55.4 percent of the natural scientists (physics, chemistry, biology) surveyed self-identified as atheists or agnostics, but only 47.5 percent of the social scientists (sociology, economics, political science, and psychology) did so. Biologists were the least religious at 63.4 percent.[85]

Interestingly, economists were the least irreligious at 45.1 percent. A related trend may be the fact that economists have recently begun to take demonstrated human nature more seriously. Craig Lambert writes in *Harvard Magazine:* "Economic Man has one fatal flaw: he does not exist. When we turn to actual human beings, we find, instead of robot-like logic, all manner of irrational, self-sabotaging, and even altruistic behavior."[86]

Many detractors of RSMEs come, as we have seen, from the ranks of biology. It is interesting to reflect that pioneer students of RSMEs William James (psychologist) and Alister Hardy (zoologist) were firmly grounded in the natural sciences and made great advances in the study of RSMEs for precisely that reason. James, for example, grasped the importance of identifying a wide range of examples, not only the approved, classic ones;

Religion and Violence

Can RSMEs propel believers toward hatred and self-destruction?

Recent world events such as suicide bombings and beheadings prompt the claim that "religion leads to violence." The reality is more complex. When immature people experience a strong passion—lust, greed, envy—they can easily be incited to violence. A religious context for such passions does not, by itself, change such people. Personal change comes only through contact with an authentic spiritual reality. Otherwise, immature believers may merely cite religion as a justification.

Recently, Canadian political scientist Salim Mansur traveled the border area between Algeria and Tunisia, where sixteen hundred years ago the great Christian thinker Augustine (354–430) served as bishop. Mansur, a Muslim who studies comparative culture, was carrying a copy of Augustine's *Confessions* (an autobiography that focuses on the state of the soul). He wanted to understand better the growth of religiously inspired violence in the Middle East and North Africa. Mansur also carried with him the writings of Arab historian and philosopher Ibn Khaldun (1332–1406), who was born a millennium later in the same region as Augustine.

Studying Augustine and Ibn Khaldun together, Mansur concluded that their writings "shed greater light on terrorism causes than any recent writings of experts in the subject." Both of these ancient thinkers focused on what Augustine called the "interior disposition"—for example, the likelihood that a frustrated person will resort to violence. "A man awakened to his inner reality could do no evil—for instance, be a terrorist—since, filled with goodness, there would be no evil in him," Mansur argues. Speaking of some of his coreligionists, he adds:

> Muslim terrorists have closed shut their "interior disposition." For them, belief is reduced to outward rituals of conformity, in pursuit of power over other men, rather than an awakening to the infinity inside of them, filled with God in whose image they have been made. Hence they do evil for they are insufficient in goodness, despite their insistence on calling upon God according their faith tradition.[87]

Religion divorced from the desire for personal spiritual transformation becomes a great theater of the passions, and a highly dangerous one at that.

Hardy insisted on finding examples undisturbed in their natural environment. And both came away convinced that RSME experiencers do confront real facts about the cosmos.

But in recent decades, when natural sciences have fallen captive to radical materialism, naturalistic approaches to RSMEs have mainly amounted not to hard data but to questionable concepts such as purely theoretical brain structures or circuits, questionable syndromes such as temporal-lobe personality, selfish genes, and gangs of memes. A key task for neuroscience today is to use the power of the natural sciences effectively, while circumventing these unproductive ideologies. One promising approach is to study RSMEs under conditions in which neuroscience can capture information. We shall turn to that in Chapter Nine.

NINE

The Carmelite Studies:
A New Direction?

Neuroscience more than other disciplines is the science at the interface between modern philosophy and science. No opportunity should be given to anybody to use neuroscience for supporting transcendent views of the world.[1]

—Neuroscientist Zvani Rossetti,
opposing the Dalai Lama's lecture

This research is a first pass on a new topic, and you just can't do perfect science the first time through. You get curious about something and you mess around. That's what science is in the beginning, you mess around.[2]

—Neurobiologist Robert Wyman,
supporting the Dalai Lama's lecture

My confidence in venturing into science lies in my basic belief that as in science, so in Buddhism, understanding the nature of reality is pursued by means of critical investigation.[3]

—The Dalai Lama,
The Universe in a Single Atom

In its spring 2005 newsletter, the Society for Neuroscience notified members of a new feature attraction at the upcoming 2005 annual meeting in Washington, D.C. The Dalai Lama had agreed to be the first-ever speaker in an annual lecture series, "Dialogues Between Neuroscience and Society."

The Dalai Lama encourages the scientific study of consciousness, which is no surprise considering that Buddhists have pursued this topic for about two and a half millennia.[4] The current lama has always been interested in science; he enjoyed friendships with such luminaries as philosopher of science Karl Popper and physicists Carl von Weizsäcker and David Bohm. He has eagerly embraced the new neuroscientific research tools. He also helped establish and serves as honorary chairman of the Mind and Life Institute, which sponsors both neuroscientific research and in-depth dialogues between Buddhism and science. He has even encouraged his monks to serve as research subjects. On the face of it, the seventy-year-old lama seemed an ideal choice to set the pace for a series of lectures on neuroscience and society.

Political protest might have been anticipated. The Dalai Lama, who won the Nobel Peace Prize in 1989, is not only the leader of Tibetan Buddhism, but a revered figurehead of the Tibetan movement for independence from China. (He fled Chinese troops in 1959 and has lived in India ever since.) But the society's president, Carol Barnes, was assailed by a protest campaign that went well beyond politics.

Some neuroscientists urged the society to cancel the lecture, dismissing the neuroscientific study of Buddhist meditation as "little more than mumbo-jumbo."[5] A petition was organized, announcing:

> It is ironic for neuroscientists to provide a forum for and, with it, implicit endorsement of a religious leader whose legitimacy relies on reincarnation, a doctrine against the very foundation of neuroscience. The present Dalai Lama explicitly claims the separation of mind and body, which is essential to the recognition of the Dalai Lama as both a religious and a political leader.[6]

Now, that was a revealing statement, to say the least. Neuroscience has no evidence to offer on the Tibetan Buddhist doctrine of reincarnation, any more than it has evidence to offer on the Christian doctrine of incarnation. A scientific discipline can offer evidence on the subjects it can actually research. The neural states associated with mystical consciousness, for example, can be researched; hence the growing interest in the area. And the question of the relationship between the mind and the brain is, to put it mildly, hardly settled.

In any event, the controversy soon reached mainstream science media. The eminent science journal *Nature* weighed in on the Dalai Lama's side, observing that he was invited because he "has tried for many years to encourage empirical research into the claims he makes for the value of meditation." The journal suggested that the protesters be patient and raise their concerns at the postlecture forum.[7]

To its credit, the Society for Neuroscience did not back down. The Dalai Lama gave his scheduled address. Indeed, he stressed:

> I am speaking of what I call "secular ethics" that embrace the key ethical principles, such as compassion, tolerance, a sense of caring, consideration of others and the responsible use of knowledge and power—principles that transcend the barriers between religious believers and nonbelievers, and followers of this religion or that religion.[8]

In the end, we are left asking, what's so frightening about meditation anyway? Why can't science-based questions about meditation be answered in the normal way, using conventional scientific tools? The Dalai Lama's offer of collaboration is an excellent research opportunity. A population of monks or contemplatives willing to permit neuroscientists to study their meditative states is *not* easy to find and retain! It is hardly surprising, on the face of it, that the society would wish to recognize the lama's support.

Critics of research into meditation often raise legitimate issues, but one senses a distinct underlying discomfort that the area is studied at all. For example, neuroscientist Richard Davidson, who helped arrange the Dalai Lama's talk, coauthored recently published research that suggests that the neural networks of trained meditators are better coordinated than those of untrained persons. That finding, published in a prestigious journal, correlates with the meditators' subjective reports of heightened awareness.[9] However, the protesters claimed that Davidson's team's research is flawed because meditating monks were compared with much younger university students:

> The monks being studied were 12 to 45 years older than the students, and age could have accounted for some of the differences. The students, as beginners, may have been anxious or simply not skilled enough to find a meditative state in the time allotted, which would alter their brain wave patterns. And there was no way to know if the monks were adept at generating high gamma wave activity before they ever started meditating.[10]

Now, that's a fair question—and a researchable one too. Do age or chance variations in gamma waves rather than skill make the difference? Current anecdotal evidence suggests that time spent in meditation or prayer, rather than chronological age or chance, is the key factor—but older meditators have obviously had more time to practice as well. However, University of Florida neuroscientist Jianguo Gu, who signed the petition against the Dalai Lama, responded to the issues by threatening to cancel his own presentation.[11] Other protesting neuroscientists threatened to boycott the meeting.

The protesters' stated concern was to avoid "entanglement with religion or politics." Yet by ignoring the research opportunities and focusing instead on implicitly or explicitly denouncing the Tibetan Buddhist doctrine of reincarnation, they were creating precisely the problem of entanglement with religion that they claim to deplore.[12] Their disagreement in principle is at least one point of agreement between themselves and, for example, Pope Benedict XVI, who denies that reincarnation occurs. But they have no information that would justify their involvement *as neuroscientists* in such matters.

> Reincarnation ... is part of the history of human origin. It is proof of the mindstream's capacity to retain knowledge of physical and mental activities. It is related to the theory of interdependent origination and to the law of cause and effect.[13]
> —*The Dalai Lama,*
> *preface to* The Case for Reincarnation

> There is no reincarnation after death.[14]
> —*Catechism of the Catholic Church,*
> *supervised by Pope Benedict XVI*

> To argue that the Dalai Lama's views on reincarnation are "against the very foundation of modern neuroscience" is simply not true and shows a profound lack of understanding of where and what those foundations are.[15]
> —*Cellular neurobiologist John H. Hannigan*

We can legitimately ask, is something more going on here? Were neuroscientific tools supposed to prove that the mind does not exist? In that case, the source of anxiety becomes apparent: the study of meditative or mystical consciousness may threaten the comfort many take in materialism. What if we can image the brain, neuron by neuron, and *still* not demonstrate that materialism is true?

The fact that the protesters were unable to co-opt neuroscience on behalf of materialism may signal a slow but sure change. Protests or no, research goes on. Contemplative Christian nuns, for example, have also been willing to assist neuroscience. And this brings us to the Franciscan nuns who cooperated with the studies done by Andrew Newberg, Eugene D'Aquili, and others.

Brain Activity During Prayer

> After years of research … our understanding of various key brain structures and the way information is channeled along neural pathways led us to hypothesize that the brain possesses a neurological mechanism for self-transcendence.
>
> The mind remembers mystical experience with the same degree of clarity and sense of reality that it bestows upon memories of "real" past events. The same cannot be said of hallucinations, delusions, or dreams. We believe this sense of realness strongly suggests that the accounts of the mystics are not indications of minds in disarray, but are the proper, predictable neurological result of a stable, coherent mind willing itself toward a higher spiritual plane.[16]
>
> —*Andrew Newberg et al.,*
> Why God Won't Go Away

A few years ago, Andrew Newberg, a University of Pennsylvania radiologist, undertook a research program to outline the neural underpinnings of various meditative and contemplative states. Inspired by the fact that a colleague is a serious Buddhist meditator, he and some colleagues have scanned eight Buddhist meditators[17] and three Franciscan nuns[18] using single photon emission computed tomography (SPECT), a technique for mapping blood flow and metabolism after the injection of radioactive substances. The scope of the present book does not permit a wide-ranging assessment of all types of contemplative states, so we will consider only the study of the Franciscan nuns.

The nuns were scanned while they performed a "centering prayer" to open themselves to the presence of God. Subjectively, they reported a "loss of the usual sense of space." The neuroscientific data correlated with their self-report.

This pilot study showed that meditative and contemplative states can be studied using neuroimaging techniques, a fact not readily granted in some quarters. As Newberg and colleagues have recognized, the main difficulty is that their sample was very small (only three). Moreover, the researchers did not attempt to analyze and quantify in a rigorous and systematic manner the nuns' subjective experiences during their "centering prayer." That is, they did not interview the nuns using standard measures such as Hood's Mysticism Scale (1975). In other words, Newberg and colleagues could not determine whether focusing attention on a phrase from a prayer over a period of time really led the nuns to feel the presence of God. So Newberg team's work, although interesting, has limited value in determining whether the Franciscan nuns did effectively contact a spiritual reality outside themselves.[19]

Another problem with that study is the poor spatial and temporal resolution of the neuroimaging technique used. Indeed, the blurred images produced by SPECT can lead to substantial errors in the measurement of regional brain activity. Given this, it is likely that loci of activation (or deactivation) were not detected in various regions of the brain. Today, fMRI (which has an excellent anatomical resolution and a much better temporal resolution than SPECT or PET) is the tool of choice for studying the neural correlates of perceptual, cognitive, and affective functions. This is why we decided to use this brain-imaging technique to identify the brain regions involved in mystical states and experiences.

The View from Neuroscience

The analysis of the SPECT data revealed a significant increase in regional cerebral blood flow (rCBF) in the prefrontal cortex, inferior parietal lobes, and inferior frontal lobes. In addition, there was a significant positive correlation between the change in rCBF in the right prefrontal cortex and that in the right thalamus. The change in rCBF in the prefrontal cortices showed a strong inverse correlation with that in the ipsilateral superior parietal lobe.

Newberg's Approach and Materialism

Newberg and his late colleague Eugene D'Aquili part company with strict materialists in favor of the hypothesis that there may indeed be a state of "Absolute Unitary Being" (AUB) that lacks awareness of space and time, which mystics contact. Indeed, they simply dismiss the "pathology" model of RSMEs that we looked at in Chapter Three:

> We do not believe that genuine mystical experiences can be explained away as the results of epileptic hallucinations or, for that matter, as the product of other spontaneous hallucinatory states triggered by drugs, illness, physical exhaustion, emotional stress, or sensory deprivation. Hallucinations, no matter what their source, are simply not capable of providing the mind with an experience as convincing as that of mystical spirituality.[20]

As a result of their studies, Newberg and D'Aquili concluded: "At the heart of our theory is a neurological model that provides a link between mystical experience and observable brain function. In simplest terms, the brain seems to have the built-in ability to transcend the perception of an individual self. We have theorized that this talent for self-transcendence lies at the root of the religious urge."[21] Their approach is consistent with the one advanced in this book, which led to the brain-imaging studies of the Carmelite nuns.

Brain-Imaging Studies of Contemplative Nuns

Sister Diane compares her love for God to the way two people love each other. When they fall in love, they feel a physical rush. They blush. They feel tingly. That, she says, is the kind of love young nuns feel for God when they experience *unio mystica.* But over time, the love deepens and matures. It isn't as thrilling, she says. It becomes more of a day-to-day relationship.[22]

— *Sister Diane on* unio mystica

To be a mystic is simply to participate here and now in that real and eternal life; in the fullest, deepest sense which is possible … as a free and conscious agent.[23]

— *Mysticism researcher Evelyn Underhill*

One question that has intrigued some neuroscientists over the years is whether specific brain states are associated with mystical contemplation. Remember, we cannot determine what a person is actually thinking— brain states are much too complex for that. We can, however, determine what type of brain activity is generated and where.

My doctoral student Vincent Paquette and I particularly wanted to study mystical union (*unio mystica*), a state in which one feels completely united with God, which is the ultimate goal of the contemplative Christian mystic. Typically, a very intense mystical experience occurs only once or twice in a lifetime of contemplation.[24] It can also include a number of other elements, such as the sense of having touched the ultimate ground of reality, the sense of the incommunicability of the experience, the sense of unity, the experience of timelessness and spacelessness, and the sense of union with humankind and the universe as well as feelings of positive affect, peace, joy, and unconditional love.[25] It results in a profound transformation of life, which includes compassion, unconditional love, and long-term positive changes in attitude and behavior.[26] What images of the brain could we capture during such a period? Specifically, we wanted to use functional magnetic resonance imaging (fMRI) and quantitative electroencephalography (QEEG) to learn more about brain activity during a mystical experience.[27] fMRI produces images of brain changes by means of radio waves within a strong magnetic field (see Chapter Six), and QEEG measures electrical patterns at the surface of the scalp that reflect brain-wave patterns, which can then be statistically analyzed and translated into a color map.

We were in a good position to undertake such a study for two reasons. We work at the Centre de recherche de l'Institut universitaire de gériatrie de Montréal (CRIUGM) and the Centre de Recherche en Neuropsychologie et Cognition (CERNEC) at the Université de Montréal.[28] As a result, we had access to powerful neuroimaging techniques, which we could supplement with personal interviews with our subjects. Most important, we were able to secure the cooperation of Carmelite nuns in Quebec, religious women who spend a great deal of time in contemplation and prayer. That latter point is tricky because a contemplative would not typically be willing to serve in a possibly controversial research project that does not flow directly from her vocation.

Looking for Mystics in Modern-day Montreal

God only comes to those who ask him to come; and he cannot refuse to come to those who implore him long, often, and ardently.[29]
—*Philosopher and mystic Simone Weil*

Carmelite nuns live a life of silent prayer. When they aren't praying, they cook, garden, bake hosts (Communion wafers), and sew, wash, and mend habits. They produce crafts to support themselves. They talk to each other only during two twenty-minute recreation periods, after lunch and supper. If a Carmelite has something pressing to say in the evening, she writes a note. Carmelites generally have had a fruitful experience with mysticism over their nine-century history. For example, the fifteen nuns in our study had collectively spent about 210,000 hours in prayer. So if prayer and contemplation can lead to mystical consciousness, these women should certainly demonstrate it.

Of course, securing the nuns' cooperation was not easy. We had to reassure them that we were not researching this area simply to "prove" that mystical consciousness does not occur. We were able to tell them truthfully that we were not materialists and were not trying to debunk the mystical experiences that had led them to become nuns. We did not doubt, in principle, that the contemplative may at times contact a reality outside herself or that such a contact can change the direction of her life in a positive way. What we specifically wanted to know was whether neuroimaging techniques can identify neural correlates for such experiences, and the nuns were among the few people who might be able to help us. Fortunately, Cardinal Archbishop Jean-Claude Turcotte of Montreal agreed to write a letter to the nuns, advising them that there was no religious objection to working with us if they chose to do so.

Even so, we did face some difficulties. As we have seen, contemplatives such as the Carmelites do not usually leave the convent or involve themselves in scientific research. So, before submitting a letter asking for funds from the John Templeton Foundation, I called the Carmelite convent in Montreal and spoke with the prioress, Sister Diane. After stumbling through an explanation of my proposed study, I endured a long silence at the other end of the line. But in the end, Sister Diane did not say no. She simply said that she would need to talk to her nuns about my proposal.

A few days later, when I called back, she told me that some of the nuns would participate if Templeton agreed to fund the project. Templeton notified me in March 2003 that funds were available, so all I had to do was make sure that the nuns were still interested. In the end, fifteen Carmelite nuns aged twenty-three to sixty-four (their mean age was about fifty) from convents around Quebec agreed to take part in the study. All said they had experienced an intense mystical union at least once.

Objections to the Study

> Dr. Beauregard does not, in fact, believe there is a neurological "God centre." Rather, his preliminary data implicate a network of brain regions in the Unio Mystica, including those associated with emotion processing and the spatial representation of self. But that leads to another criticism, which he may find harder to rebut. This is that he is not really measuring a mystical experience at all—merely an intense emotional one. This is because the nuns are, so to speak, faking it.[30]
>
> —"Mystical Union," The Economist

> If their experiences are of any substance, they will never forget them; and, if they are of a kind that can be forgotten, there is no point in writing them down.[31]
>
> —Teresa of Avila,
> on recording spiritual experiences

Objections to our research project soon surfaced. Of course, there were the anticipated objections from materialists, of the sort that led to the controversy over the Dalai Lama's lecture at the 2005 neuroscience convention. Many of our colleagues do not think that spirituality should be studied scientifically, and they have not been slow to make their views known. Materialists who hold decision-making positions have been known to refuse permission for research in this area.[32] However, we have been fortunate in securing funding for our work.

We sometimes heard objections from the religious side as well. For example, Rev. Raymond Lawrence, Jr., of New York's Presbyterian Hospital, complained in Science and Theology News that our work "has nothing to do with the truth of religion," adding, "At the end of the day, you only have an experience. It doesn't prove the existence of God." He went on to predict that replicating the mystical experience "would be a catastrophe for religion," distorting religious meaning.[33]

But we have never entertained the idea of proving the existence of God! Our goals are decidedly more modest. The only thing that neuroscientists can really determine is whether current neuroscience provides useful information about mystical states and experiences. Specifically, we wanted to know two things: whether brain activity during mystical consciousness is localized in the temporal lobe, as some have argued, and whether mystical contemplation produces brain states not associated with ordinary consciousness.

In any event, mystics themselves, far from justifying the popular idea that they want to make a mystery out of mystical consciousness, are often quite happy to engage in formal study of consciousness, provided it does not interfere with their vocation. For millennia, mystics have written lengthy and detailed treatises on states of consciousness. Mysticism researcher Evelyn Underhill quotes one nineteenth-century source as saying:

> Examine us as much as you like: our machinery, our veracity, our results. We cannot promise that you shall see what we have seen, for here each man must adventure for himself, but we defy you to stigmatize our experiences as impossible or invalid.[34]

The key recent development is the new neuroscientific tools for investigating the neural correlates to the subjectively experienced states.

An accusation we sometimes hear from the general public is that mystical contemplation is a mythical idea. The nuns are merely neurotics who are imagining things or even "faking it." A recent article in *The Economist* used that very expression and announced that we would find such an accusation "harder to rebut"[35] than other objections to our work.

Actually, we would not find that particular accusation hard to rebut at all. In a neuroscientific study, a person who is "faking it" should generate a lot of beta waves (typical of strenuous conscious activity) and not many theta[36] waves (typical of deep meditative states). It turns out that there are some things you just *can't* fake! Indeed, the very suggestion shows how little neuroscience is currently understood.

Another worry we sometimes heard was that some might try to commercialize mystical experiences, so to speak, perhaps by developing a pill for them. Well, if they did, it would hardly be new and wouldn't need to lean much on neuroscience. Throughout history, many cultures have developed "technologies" (drumming, sacred plants, fasting, meditation, etc.) that involve training in altered or nonordinary states of consciousness in order to interact with the spiritual world. Clearly, humans can make themselves more receptive to RSMEs by taking specific actions.

But it is never a simple matter. A significant alteration of the electro-chemical functioning of the brain is necessary for an RSME to take place and be consciously experienced. And even then, that is only half of the story. For an RSME to occur, the spiritual self living at the core of each individual must also be willing to dance, so to speak.

But of course our real problem wasn't the various objections; it was how to capture the mystical experience. Originally, we had naively hoped that the nuns might have such an experience in the lab, but Sister Diane merely laughed when it was suggested. "God can't be summoned at will," she replied. Indeed, she warned, "You can't search for it. The harder you search, the longer you will wait." Of course, in hindsight, we began to understand what she meant: the very demand for the experience becomes mental noise that must be overcome.

However, the human brain tends to use the same regions and pathways when people recall and relive an experience as when they first experienced it. Thus, when people are asked to recall a significant experience, we can find out which regions and pathways are most active.

> Shelley Winters, one of the world's great actors, has said that the actor must be willing to "act with your scars." Simply translated (which is not easy, because Shelley Winters is not a simple person), it means that when it is time for the actor to reveal those deepest, most frightening or painful experiences written by the author for the character he has created, the actor using our approach to the work has to find similar experiences in his own life, and be first willing, and then able to relive those experiences onstage as the "character."[37]
>
> – St. Louis's TheatrGROUP's
> method acting procedures

Our group had already studied this effect using fMRI in professional actors,[38] who have learned to use the neural circuits associated with their emotions as a technique, taught by acting coaches. Actors can recall an emotionally significant personal event while playing roles that require them to show a similar emotion. They are not being insincere, as is sometimes thought; they are expressing actual emotions in a fictional framework.

In our research, we compared the brain regions that were active when we asked actors to recall and reexperience sad or happy episodes in their own lives with those that were active when the actors watched film excerpts of emotional situations. In the same way, we decided we would ask the nuns to recall and relive, with their eyes closed, the most intense mystical experience ever felt in their lives as members of the Carmelite order.

Study 1: Brain Activity During a Mystical Experience

> Only something extraordinary could entice the Carmelite nuns of
> Montreal to break their vow of silence and venture out of the cloister.
> They have joined forces with science to look for a concrete sign from
> God—inside the human brain.[39]
> —*Ann McIlroy,* The Globe and Mail

In Study 1, we scanned the nuns with fMRI to determine which areas of the brain were active during a mystical experience. The main goal of this study was to test the hypothesis that there is a "God module" in the temporal lobes, as some researchers have proposed.[40]

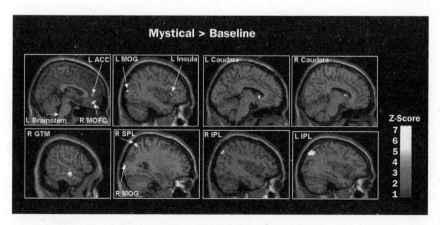

FMRI brain activation patterns of Carmelite nuns.

The fifteen nuns were scanned while they recalled and relived their most significant mystical experience (*mystical condition*) as well as their most intense state of union with another human (*control condition*) ever felt as members of the Carmelite order.[41] We also scanned the nuns during a *baseline condition,* a normal restful state, to measure brain activity during a normal state of consciousness. In all conditions eyes were closed.

Why bother with a control state, that is, a state that is not spiritual? The reason is that fMRI, which is related to the level of blood oxygenation in the brain, is not very sensitive with respect to the qualitative differences between various types of states and experiences. Indeed, as we have seen, some have argued that RSMEs are simply emotional experiences and nothing more. Distinguishing in a definitive way between two kinds of states and experiences would be useful. No, it won't tell us whether God exists, but it may help us determine whether people who have mystical experiences enter a state of altered consciousness that is mostly related to emotion. Or could it be something else?

Thus, we ask subjects to experience different states that involve cognitive processing or emotion, so we can be sure that we are identifying a significant pattern. In the same way, when neuroscientists study vision, they may ask their subjects to look at a dot for the control condition and a more complex geometrical pattern for the experimental condition. In other words, we wanted to be sure that we were distinguishing a specific mental state, rather than just any mental state that involves a lot of brain activity.

Study 2: The Neuroelectrical Correlates of Mystical Union

The same nuns participated in Study 2, and we used the same three experimental conditions (mystical, control, and baseline). But this time we recorded brain waves using QEEG. We asked the nuns to sit inside an isolation chamber, a small, dark, soundproof room—in other words, they were totally isolated both acoustically and electromagnetically (apart from an infrared camera that enables us to observe the subject continually). In this environment, a person can turn within without distractions. During the three conditions, we measured the QEEG electrical patterns, which reflect brain-wave patterns, on the surface of the scalp. These patterns can

Scale of Subjective Intensity

The scale used to assess the subjective intensity of the experience at the end of Study 1 and Study 2 was:

0 No experience of union with God
1 Very weak experience of union with God
2 Weak experience of union with God
3 Experience of union with God of a medium intensity
4 Strong experience of union with God
5 The most intense experience of God I have ever had in my life

be analyzed statistically, then translated into numbers and expressed later as color maps.

The Photo That Almost Ended the Project

The research proceeded as planned, with interesting results, but a media-related disaster nearly sank our project. Our studies have sometimes attracted publicity. Alas, it is usually the conventional "science versus religion" story that, intentionally or otherwise, plants the basic concepts of materialism in readers' minds. For example, the fact that mystical experiences and states may have identifiable neural correlates (which are the only aspect that neuroscience can actually study) has typically been interpreted by journalists as suggesting that the experiences are somehow a delusion. In itself, that is a confused idea, equivalent to assuming that if hitting a home run has identifiable neural correlates, the home run is a delusion. And of course, the results of our work are assumed to be a strike either for or against God.

On the whole, we didn't mind. We ourselves are interested in this area, so it stands to reason that others might be. However, in December 2003, an article in Canada's newspaper of record, *The Globe and Mail,* included a photo of the Carmelite prioress Sister Diane! The nuns, who were still a bit unsure about working with us, had specifically requested that there be as little publicity as possible, and certainly no photos that could identify them publicly. Traditional convents don't even have easily accessible mirrors. We are still not sure exactly how the photo got printed. We thought we had lost everything; the nuns would cease to trust us and would not agree to work with us again—and we would never get enough data to complete the studies.

The nuns have a good reason for strictly avoiding all types of personal publicity. The decision to become a cloistered nun or monk means, among other things, giving up any intention of influencing the world other than through the power of prayer and contemplation—or the power of suffering and martyrdom if necessary. Prayer and contemplation are viewed as helpful only if the nun has no desire to attract attention to herself. Thus the nuns support themselves and help others, but they restrict contact with the world outside the convent and guard their vocation jealously.

Fortunately, Vincent Paquette's admirable diplomacy persuaded the nuns to continue despite this lapse. Generally, when we demonstrate the techniques of our studies for the media now, we use stand-ins, not the actual nuns. For example, when the QEEG study was featured on Discovery Channel's *Daily Planet* and aired on Good Friday of 2004, a model stood in for one of our subjects.

Study 1: Findings

> I don't know how much time had passed. It is like a treasure, and
> intimacy. It is very, very personal. It was in the centre of my being, but
> even deeper. It was a feeling of fullness, fullness, fullness.[42]
>   —*Carmelite nun describing unio mystica*

The scanner room is certainly nothing like a retreat center; it looks more like something you would find at NASA. Despite that, the nuns managed to experience a mystical state during the mystical condition. Immediately at the end of the experiment, we asked the nuns to evaluate their own experiences. Not all studies do that, but we wanted to compare the objective and subjective perspectives. To put it another way, was the subject aware of experiencing something that correlated with the fMRI data?

In addition to asking the nuns to describe their experiences in their own words, we used Hood's Mysticism Scale to enable comparison with other research. We did make one adjustment: Hood's scale was not designed specifically for Christian mysticism, which means that not all questions may be applicable. Christian mystics typically see themselves as contacting a transpersonal entity rather than an impersonal entity, and they most often describe their experiences in terms of feeling greatly loved. So we used the fifteen questions that appeared most compatible with a Christian interpretation of the mystical experience.

The main items from Hood's Mysticism Scale associated with the nuns' experiences were:

I have had an experience which I knew to be sacred.

I have had an experience in which something greater than myself seemed to absorb me.

I have experienced profound joy.

During the qualitative interviews conducted at the end of the experiment, the nuns said that they had felt the presence of God and his unconditional and infinite love as well as plenitude and peace. Importantly, all of them reported that, from a first-person perspective, the experiences lived during the mystical condition differed from those used to self-induce a mystical state. They also reported the presence of visual and motor imagery during both the mystical and control conditions. In addition, the subjects experienced a feeling of unconditional love during the control condition. These observations are not, strictly speaking, part of Hood's scale, but we reported them because of their consistency.

Sample Items from Hood's Mysticism Scale

I have had an experience which was sacred.

I have had an experience during which something greater than myself seemed to absorb me.

I have had an experience during which I did not have anymore the sense of time and space.

I have had an experience which cannot be expressed with words.

I have had an experience during which I felt that everything in this world is part of the same whole.

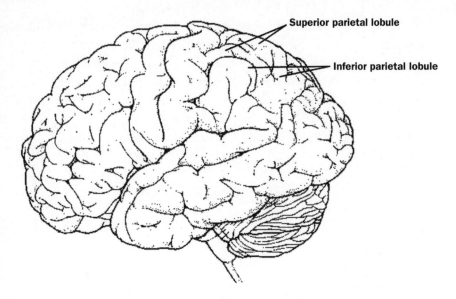

Sagittal representation of the inferior parietal lobule and superior parietal lobule, two areas of the parietal cortex.

From a neural perspective, the key finding from Study 1 was that many brain regions, not just the temporal lobes, are involved in mystical experiences. These include the inferior parietal lobule, visual cortex, caudate nucleus, and left brain stem as well as many other areas.

Our findings demonstrate that there is no single "God spot" in the brain located in the temporal lobes. Rather our objective and subjective data suggest that RSMEs are complex and multidimensional and mediated by a number of brain regions normally implicated in perception, cognition, emotion, body representation, and self-consciousness.

Study 2: Findings

In Study 2, we also asked the nuns to rate the intensity of their subjective experiences with the self-report scale ranging from 0 ("No experience of union") to 5 ("Most intense experience of union ever felt") and used the items from Hood's Mysticism Scale that are best adapted to traditional Christian mysticism. The main items from Hood's Mysticism Scale associated with the nuns' experiences in Study 2 were:

I have had an experience which I knew to be sacred.

I have had an experience in which something greater than myself seemed to absorb me.

I have experienced profound joy.

The View from Neuroscience

We found significant loci of activation in the mystical condition, relative to the baseline condition, in the inferior parietal lobule (IPL; Brodmann area—BA—7, 40), the visual cortex (BA 18, 19), and the caudate nucleus. Other significant loci of activation were seen in the right medial orbitofrontal cortex (MOFC; BA 11), right middle temporal cortex (MTC; BA 21), right superior parietal lobule (SPL; BA 7), left brain stem, left insula (BA 13), and left anterior cingulate cortex (ACC; BA 32). In addition, we found significantly more activation, in the mystical condition compared to the baseline condition, in the right MOFC (BA 11), right medial prefrontal cortex (MPFC; BA 10), right MTC (BA 21), right ACC (BA 32), left IPL (BA 40), and left SPL (BA 7).

We hypothesized that the right MTC activation was related to the subjective impression of contacting a spiritual reality. We also posited that the loci of activation detected in the caudate nucleus, right MOFC (BA 11), left MPFC (BA 10), left ACC (BA 32), left insula (BA 13), and left brain stem reflected changes in the various aspects (cognitive, physiological, feeling) related to the emotional state of the subjects.[43] As for the activations in the visual cortex, we proposed that they were related to visual imagery. Last, with regard to the loci of activation noted in the parietal cortex, given that the right SPL is also involved in the spatial perception of self,[44] we submitted that the activation of this parietal region (BA 7) during the mystical condition might reflect a modification of the body schema associated with the impression that something greater than the subjects seemed to absorb them. Moreover, there is evidence that the left IPL is part of a neural system implicated in the processing of visuospatial representation of bodies.[45] Therefore, the left IPL activation in the mystical state was perhaps related to an alteration of the body schema. However, the IPL plays an important role in motor imagery.[46] It is thus possible that the activations in the right (BA 40) and left (BA 7) IPL were related to the motor imagery experienced during the mystical condition.

I have had an experience which cannot be expressed with words.

I have had an experience during which I felt that everything in this world is part of the same whole.

I have had an experience which is impossible to communicate.

As in Study 1, several nuns mentioned that during the mystical condition, they felt the presence of God, his unconditional and infinite love, and plenitude and peace. They also felt a surrendering to God.

Our experimental strategy had worked beautifully. At the beginning of the mystical condition, the nuns had attempted to remember and relive a mystical experience (self-induction). This led to the experience of a mystical state that was subjectively different from the self-induction procedure. Several nuns reached deep mystical states while we measured what was going on electrically in their brains. For instance, Sister Nicole reported, in a dreamy, contented voice, that she was hearing Pachelbel's "Canon." The *unio mystica* she recalled achieving as a child and the mystical state she experienced during the QEEG experiment became blurred in her mind. Leaving the soundproof chamber where the experiment was conducted, she remarked, "I have never felt so loved."

The results of the experiment clearly indicate that the life of silent prayer and contemplation allowed the Carmelite nuns to reach deep mystical states simply by intensely recalling and reliving a previous mystical experience. This was something they had not expected to happen before they participated in the project.

Conclusions from the Studies

We learned two valuable things from our studies. The results of the two studies, taken together (QEEG and fMRI), dispose of the notion that there is a God spot in the temporal lobes of the brain that can somehow "explain" RSMEs. The results of our fMRI and QEEG studies suggest that RSMEs are neurally instantiated by different brain regions involved in a variety of functions, such as self-consciousness, emotion, body representation, visual and motor imagery, and spiritual perception. This conclusion correlates well with subjects' descriptions of RSMEs as complex and multidimensional.

The View from Neuroscience

As for the QEEG data, there was significantly more theta activity (theta waves range from 4 to 7 Hz) in the mystical condition, relative to the baseline condition, in the insula (BA 13), the right inferior parietal lobule (IPL; BA 40) and superior parietal lobule (SPL; BA 7), and the right inferior (BA 20) and middle (BA 20) temporal cortices. Moreover, there was significantly more theta activity in the mystical condition, compared to the control condition, in the anterior cingulate cortex (ACC; BA 24) and medial prefrontal cortex (MPFC; BA 9, 10).

As the abstract of our published study in *Neuroscience Letters* (2006) puts it:

> The main goal of this functional magnetic resonance imaging (fMRI) study was to identify the neural correlates of a mystical experience. The brain activity of Carmelite nuns was measured while they were subjectively in a state of union with God. This state was associated with significant loci of activation in the right medial orbitofrontal cortex, right middle temporal cortex, right inferior and superior parietal lobules, right caudate, left medial prefrontal cortex, left anterior cingulated cortex, left inferior parietal lobule, left insula, left caudate, and left brain stem. Other loci of activation were seen in the extra-striate visual cortex. These results suggest that mystical experiences are mediated by several brain regions and systems.[47]

Second, when the nuns were recalling autobiographical memories, the brain activity was different from that of the mystical state. So we know for certain that the mystical state is something other than an emotional state. The abundance of theta activity during the mystical condition clearly demonstrated a marked alteration of consciousness in the nuns. It is noteworthy that previous QEEG studies have shown increased theta activity in the frontal cortex during a type of Zen meditation called Su-soku,[48] and a blissful state in meditation (Sahaja Yoga meditation).[49]

The nuns told us in self-report scales and qualitative interviews conducted at the end of our experiments that the mystical states that they experienced during fMRI scanning and QEEG recording were different in quality from their recollections of their original mystical experiences (when they were asked, at the beginning of the experiment, to try to self-induce a mystical state). In other words, we had succeeded in measuring the brain activity of the nuns while they went on to an actual mystical state.

Do our findings prove that mystics contact a power outside themselves? No, because there is no way to prove or disprove that from one side only. If you volunteered as a subject at our lab, our studies could not show that you were remembering a conversation with a traffic officer, your high-school heart throb, or a dying relative, if you did not tell us that and we had no data on how you usually react in those kinds of situations.

What we *can* do, however, is determine the patterns that are consistent with certain types of experiences. Thus we can rule out some explanations, because, for example, a complex pattern is not consistent with a simple explanation. To the extent that spiritual experiences are experiences in which we contact the reality of our universe, we should expect them to be complex. We can certainly say that the patterns of serious mystics definitely are.

Science and Spirituality

From my own point of view, I can hope that this long sad story will come to an end at some time in the future and that this progression of priests and ministers and rabbis and ulamas and imams and bonzes and bodhisattvas will come to an end, that we'll see no more of them. I hope that this is something to which science can contribute and if it is, then I think it may be the most important contribution that we can make.[50]
—*Nobel Prize–winning physicist Steven Weinberg*

I am unable to see how the fact of the moral consciousness, and, in particular, the fact of the opposition between "is" and "ought," between desire and duty, can be explained in terms of purely natural causation. . . . [They] can be explained only on the assumption that, in addition to the natural, there is also a non-natural order of the universe which is immanent in and on occasion intrudes actively into the natural.[51]
—*C. E. M. Joad,* The Recovery of Belief

My husband, a laser physicist, tells me that scientists who study particle physics are more likely to become religious. Scientists are notoriously hard to convince of anything. Yet, when these skeptical scientists see the perfect, natural order of the world they decide nano and up, that this world was planned. The marvelous design before them becomes the miracle they need to become convinced.[52]

—*Software developer Tamar Sofer*

There is no need to choose between science and spirituality. But there is certainly a need, as there always has been, to choose between materialism and spirituality.

Science cannot prove or disprove the existence of God, nor can it adjudicate controversies between religions on doctrines. But it can rule out inadequate theories of RSMEs concocted by materialists.

The evidence presented in this book has shown that RSMEs are not the outcome of particular genes or neural disorders, nor can they be created merely by the use of a technology (although many cultures attempt to *assist* them using various methods or technologies). It also shows that the "hard problem" of consciousness is simply not resolvable in a materialist frame of reference.

But that hard problem ceases to be a problem once we understand the universe itself as a product of consciousness. We might expect living beings to evolve toward consciousness if consciousness underlies the universe. Consciousness is an irreducible quality. The study of consciousness in the twenty-first century promises to be an exciting endeavor. But it will be stymied if the only purpose is to reduce consciousness to something it is not or to demonstrate that it is an illusion.

We have also seen that the human brain cannot be understood apart from the mind that it instantiates. Indeed, understanding the relationship correctly gives us valuable neuroscientific tools for successfully treating psychological disorders such as OCD and phobias, some of which have proven intractable in the past. Similarly, we need a better understanding of phenomena connected with death such as NDEs. For example, van Lommel's work showed that a disproportionate number of NDE experiencers do not survive the recovery room. In other words, either NDEs are a reliable predictor of higher mortality or the patient's likelihood of survival is reduced by a currently ineffectual response to them. It would certainly be useful to know which explanation is more likely because, as high-tech medicine increasingly penetrates societies around the globe, a greater proportion of patients can be brought back from clinical death.

However we understand these phenomena, we need to understand them better.

As we have seen, people who have RSMEs, far from being out of touch, are typically mentally and physically healthy. RSMEs are normal experiences that are positively associated with physical and mental health, because they express a natural spiritual function of the human being. Although one can never prove it from one side only, the data are consistent with an experience in which the experiencers contact a spiritual reality outside of their own minds.

With regard to researching the many issues this book presents, a key question is, what do we mean by the term "scientific"? If, by "scientific," we mean "only those findings that uphold a materialist worldview," our understanding of the human brain will be forever truncated. However, if by "scientific," we mean "using the methods and standards of science," then the studies of the neural correlates of meditative and contemplative states are scientific. Specifically, neuroscience can contribute useful information to a discussion of these states. And to the extent that RSMEs are normally associated with better physical and mental health, there is a public benefit in sponsoring neuroscientific research that sheds more light on them. Is the real purpose of science to help us understand the world we live in or to provide support for a specific, narrow view of that world? The choice is ours.

The Carmelites: From Mt. Carmel to the Present Day

Now summon the people from all over Israel to meet me on Mount Carmel.[53]

—The prophet Elijah

It is easier to understand the Carmelites' mystical vocation if we look briefly at how the order started, struggled, reformed, and survived, despite considerable opposition. A mystical vocation is not a recipe for boredom, as we shall see.

The Original Carmelites

The ancient Carmelite order, which originated in Palestine, is named for Mt. Carmel, a low mountain range, of which a promontory near the city of

Haifa in Israel rises steeply 185 meters out of the Mediterranean Sea. Carmel has been a religious site for millennia, a place where prophets (Hebrew *nabis*) "experienced God in an unusual or immediate way."[54] On Mt. Carmel, the biblical prophet Elijah confronted the prophets of the fertility god Baal, probably in the ninth century B.C.E.[55] Elijah's successor Elisha and his other followers, the "sons of the prophets," lived there, as did early Christian monks, centuries later, praying in its caves.

Legend traces the Carmelite order back to Elijah himself, but the order that exists today began to take shape around 1150 C.E. when European pilgrims and Crusaders, aware of Mt. Carmel's history, settled there to lead a solitary life of prayer. They considered themselves latter-day sons of the prophets; their prophetic vocation was modeled on the recorded lives of Elijah and of Jesus's mother, Mary. The Carmelites considered Mary the ideal figure to make the prophetic vocation, which was sometimes associated with violence and fanaticism, a fully Christian one.

The solitary life of the order did not mean a refusal to ever engage with society. Rather, Carmelites were to emerge from contemplation and prayer to teach, warn, or help, as Elijah or Mary would do. These early prophets sensed that shaping their own lives through contemplation and prayer was essential to providing real insight for others, and that the force of events themselves brought the right moment to speak or act. There was no need to go out and seek it.

The Carmelite order for men was confirmed in the Catholic Church in 1226, with a rule that has been called a "rule of mysticism," aimed at continual prayer, silence, asceticism, and simplicity of life. The Carmelites gradually migrated from Palestine to Europe because of increasing hostility from Muslims who wanted to rid the area of Europeans during and after the Crusades. They became known in Europe as the Whitefriars, on account of their white woolen mantles. They had some difficulty adjusting to a more urban society, and their strict rule was changed in 1247 to permit higher education. Teresa of Avila (1515–82), the best-known Carmelite, later cautioned, "Those who walk in the way of prayer have need of learning, and the more spiritual they are, the greater their need." But, as historian Peter-Thomas Rohrbach notes, in general their work was

> individual and inspirational, rather than organized and institutional. We notice a definite pattern to avoid an involvement with an organized school or hospital or parochial arrangement, despite a few isolated cases. The prophetic tradition demanded a freer and less

institutional approach to human problems—the prophet emerging from his solitude to preach the instant and necessary message, to give aid and comfort where and when it was needed.[56]

Carmelite Women's Orders

In the medieval period, there were established women's religious orders, but many women, known as *beguines,* also attempted to live a contemplative life informally and independently of the church, either by themselves or in groups. The Carmelite fathers encouraged these women to adopt the Carmelite tradition, which allowed for independence within a disciplined contemplative life.

Orders of Carmelite nuns (second orders[57]) were formally established by the mid-fifteenth century, though not without struggle. Frances d'Amboise, for example, a young widow of noble family, wanted to enter a Carmelite convent in 1459, but her family forbade her because a second marriage would benefit them financially. For three years Frances held off suitors. Then one day at Mass, just as the priest was distributing Communion, she got up and loudly recited a public vow of perpetual chastity, at which point her family's hopes of finding her a wealthy husband vanished. They relented and allowed her to establish and enter a Carmelite convent.

Orders for lay people (third orders) were also founded in the mid-fifteenth century. One of the Carmelites' trademark garments since the mid-thirteenth century has been the brown scapular, which symbolizes the special protection of Mary.[58] This tradition of piety later became a means of introducing many millions of lay Catholic Christians to the Carmelite tradition of spirituality.

Loss of the Original Vision

The order fell on hard times in the fourteenth and fifteenth centuries, as did many other religious orders. One factor was the bubonic plague, beginning about 1349, which killed about one-third of the population of Europe. In the aftermath, the religious orders took in many young boys, hoping that they would somehow develop a religious vocation. These boys professed their final vows as teenagers. Many, of course, were unsuited to the contemplative life, and they responded by slowly relaxing the rule of the order. In 1435, the Carmelite rule was formally relaxed. After the vow of poverty was relaxed, class divisions followed, leading to strife and disaffection. For some, the Carmelite habit amounted to nothing more than a literal cover for fashionable idleness—they were wearing street clothes underneath.

One of the most famous of these street orphans–turned–Carmelite monks was the renowned artist Fra Filippo Lippi (1406?–1469). Lippi was known both for a groundbreaking naturalist style of painting—and a scandalous lifestyle. His lifestyle was common enough among artists of the period; the scandal was that he was a professed Carmelite. The English poet Robert Browning (1812–89) wrote about him:

> You should not take a fellow eight years old
> And make him swear never to kiss the girls.[59]

At least one Carmelite, Thomas Connecte (d. 1433), sometimes called the "Carmelite Savonarola," reacted to the decline in an opposite way. Departing from the tradition of the order's ancient and fruitful prophetic stance, he elicited a huge public uproar about sexual vice, real and imagined, which eventually resulted in his execution. Connecte's unfortunate career underlines the importance that mature contemplative traditions place on reform of the self before any attempt is made to address the problems of others.

Stormy Controversies over Reform

Many women with no special attraction to or capacity for a contemplative life also idled in convents. In 1550 in Avila, Spain, it was a point of pride for local families to put a daughter in the overflowing local convent, as reformer Teresa of Avila discovered. Similarly, in Italy, the famous Galileo (1564–1642) put his two illegitimate daughters in a Poor Clares convent, where they were professed as very young teenagers. The elder, Suor Marie-Celeste, adapted well and went on to assist her father with his work, but the younger, Suor Arcangela, was very unhappy as a nun.[60]

As a result, Teresa and John of the Cross found that restoring the Carmelites' original "Elijahan" tradition was exceedingly difficult and dangerous. Most people who donated to convents' charitable works wanted the convents to house landless men and unmarriageable women. Contemplation and spirituality were low priorities at best in those days. In 1573, a recently widowed Spanish princess arrived at one of Teresa's reformed convents, accompanied by a grand retinue of courtiers and servants. She proceeded to insist that ancient monastic practices that interfered with her social life be changed. When the prioress (head nun) pointed out that the princess's social life would be more conveniently conducted in high society than in a convent, the great lady departed in a huff. She then harassed the nuns until Teresa was forced to relocate them in another district.

Remarkably, however, Teresa and John succeeded, by both example and persuasion, in restoring the mystical contemplative tradition to the order. Since then, the Carmelite tradition has spread to North America and eastern Asia, and today there are thousands of Carmelites worldwide. They are a major spiritual influence in the Christian tradition, with such distinguished members in the modern era as Thérèse of Lisieux and Edith Stein.

Teresa of Avila (1515–82)

Be assured that the more progress you make in loving your neighbor, the greater will be your love for God. His Majesty loves us so much that he repays us for loving our neighbor by increasing our love for him in a thousand ways. I cannot doubt this.[61]
—Teresa of Avila

Teresa, born in Spain into a prosperous family, showed an early interest in spirituality. When she was seven, she persuaded her eleven-year-old brother to run away with her to a Muslim community, hoping to be killed because she "wanted to see God." (The two children were found by an uncle on the Salamanca road and brought home.[62]) Vivacious and popular, she liked romance novels and disliked giving up the excitement the world offered. But she was inspired by an eighty-year-old nun at her convent school and attracted by the inner life that many nuns enjoyed. Her father opposed her wishes, thinking it more appropriate that his attractive, outgoing, nineteen-year-old daughter marry. So she "secretly" presented herself as a candidate at the local convent, and the ensuing publicity forced her father's consent.

Teresa did not find unreformed convent life challenging. She spent over eighteen years in a pleasant spinsterish environment, chatting with townspeople about trivialities, offering advice, and worrying about her health. Yet, outside her convent's walls, Europe was rent by theological controversies and sometimes outright warfare during the Protestant

Reformation (1517–30) and the Catholic Counter-Reformation (1545–63). She sensed that she was missing her calling. At thirty-eight, she suddenly began to experience a radical change, which included a number of mystical experiences. She found herself echoing Augustine's heartfelt cry from the fourth century, "When? Tomorrow, tomorrow? Why not today?" She decided to found convents based on the original Carmelite rule of life that encouraged contemplation.

The lively Teresa no longer had to choose between excitement and the convent. Once she committed herself to the reform[63] of the Carmelite order, she got plenty of both. Despite the fact that Spain was a devout— indeed, militantly—Catholic country, Teresa and her associates had a very difficult time founding reformed convents. In 1571, Teresa was ordered by a church authority to act as prioress of a convent in her home town of Avila, and when she arrived:

> the provincial attempted to lead her into the choir to install her in office, but he found the entrance blocked by an angry, hostile group of nuns. He marched to another entrance, and was met by another group of formidable nuns who shouted at them to leave their convent. From somewhere inside the choir a small group of nuns who approved of the appointment started to chant the *Te Deum* in thanksgiving, but their voices were drowned out by the yells and catcalls from the others.[64]

Eventually, the police were summoned to maintain order. The nuns' behavior sounds puzzling today, but we must keep in mind that many women in Teresa's day entered convents to solve an economic or social problem in a respectable way. Such women would hardly wish to radically change a comfortable lifestyle merely because someone else had had a mystical experience.

And yet Teresa's reform group was also correct in insisting that the Carmelites' raison d'être was a prophetic vocation that looked back through millennia to the prophet Elijah. Thus, the conflict was intractable in principle. But more ominously, Philip II of Spain was usually at odds with the Pope in an age when few distinguished clearly between politics and religion. As a result, religious issues of the day became highly politicized. Teresa was denounced from the pulpits in her hometown, decried by a high-ranking bishop as "a restless gadabout, a disobedient and contumacious woman," and threatened with the Inquisition.

Teresa laughed at, ignored, or circumvented these problems. She was a woman of vast good sense who loved laughter and fun. A Carmelite historian recounts that, when introduced to a group of pious do-gooders, she confided, "They were saints in their own opinion, but when I got to know them better they frightened me more than all the sinners I had ever met."[65] She pioneered the use of the small prayer group, which is used worldwide in the Christian tradition today, in which people with different life experiences assist each other in developing spirituality. Her own group consisted of a married man, a lay widow, two priests, and herself.

Teresa founded a number of reformed Carmelite convents and monasteries that exist to this day. She also took the time to write several spiritual classics, including *The Interior Castle.* And, as historian Peter-Thomas Rohrbach has said, she "has the unique distinction of being the only woman in the history of the Church ever to reform an order of men."[66]

John of the Cross (1542–91)

Shepherds, you who go
up through the sheepfolds to the hill,
if by chance you see
him I love most,
tell him I am sick, I suffer and I die.[67]

—John of the Cross,
on his imprisonment at Toledo

John was born in poverty. His father had been disinherited on account of an imprudent marriage for love—and then died young. John, a small, quiet man, helped out in a local hospital, often distracting the patients from their pain by composing and singing songs. He was early attracted to the contemplative life, but he had to become a Carmelite in secret because benefactors hoped that the talented boy would choose a more worldly vocation. He was quickly drawn into Teresa's reform. As a priest who was an astute psychologist, he served as spiritual director for many uncertain young people who felt drawn to a meditative life. Psychiatrist Gerald May writes:

Teresa's psychological insights compare favorably with those of Freud and his twentieth-century followers. John's descriptions of attachment brilliantly enhance modern addiction theory. Their imagery has a universal quality that speaks to the hearts of today's spiritual seekers.[68]

But John paid a high price for his insights and his devotion. In December 1577, he was kidnapped, handcuffed, and secretly imprisoned in a monastery at Toledo. Despite attempted bribes and threats, he refused to renounce the reform. As a result, he was ritually beaten three nights a week for months. Teresa tried her best to rescue him, but without success. No one seemed to know exactly where he was being held.[69] One outcome of his misery and despair was that he began to have profound mystical experiences, which he expressed in some of the finest poetry ever composed in Spanish.[70]

Finally, in August 1578, John seized the opportunity to make a daring escape. Vaulting the wall, he fled to a convent of reformed nuns. When his former captors stormed the nuns' convent to look for him, the prioress declared ambiguously, "It would be a miracle if you were to see any friar here." No such miracle occurred; she had hidden John too cleverly.

In 1580, the reformed convents were given separate jurisdiction, which helped resolve the conflict that had made John's life so difficult. His works, such as *Spiritual Canticle, Dark Night of the Soul,* and *Ascent of Mount Carmel,* have continued to guide spiritual seekers in the Christian tradition for centuries, though most of his letters of spiritual guidance were destroyed by their recipients for fear of repercussions.

The Carmelite Martyrs of Compiègne

What the future holds in store, what fate awaits us, I do not know. I expect from heaven, in its bounty, only those modest blessings that the rich and mighty of this world look down upon and hold in scorn: good will to all living things, endless patience and tender conciliation.[71]

—A prioress comforting younger nuns
during the Reign of Terror

During the Reign of Terror (1792–94) of the French Revolution, many religious were persecuted. After the fourteen Carmelite nuns and two servants at the convent at Compiègne were imprisoned in 1793, they did not try to escape. They offered their lives daily for the peace of France.

Convicted of crimes against the state, they were sentenced to death. Because their Carmelite habits had been taken away, they quickly put together makeshift ones from salvaged clothes. In the shadow of the guillotine, on July 17, 1794, in what is now the Place de la Nation, they knelt and chanted a hymn, renewed aloud their baptismal and religious vows, and went calmly to their deaths. The usually raucous crowd was completely silent.

The Carmelite martyrs have been commemorated in many works, including an opera, *Dialogues of the Carmelites,* by Francis Poulenc and Emmet Lavery.[72] But the memorial that would matter to them was the end of the Reign of Terror about ten days later.

Edith Stein (1891–1941)

Those who seek the truth seek God, whether they realize it or not.[73]
—Carmelite philosopher Edith Stein

Edith Stein, a clever Jewish girl born in Breslau, Germany, was attracted to existentialism and considered herself an atheist. However, one day she stayed up all night reading the biography of Carmelite mystic Teresa of Avila. On finishing it, she declared, "There, that is truth!" She became a Catholic Christian the following year. Her devoted—and devoutly Jewish—

mother did not, of course, see truth quite as her daughter did, which was one of many painful dilemmas that marked Stein's life. Stein both wrote and taught at a teacher-training college; she could not work at a university because of a prevailing prejudice against women philosophers. However, she was highly esteemed as a model for Catholic laywomen of her day.

A much deeper shadow fell across her life when Hitler forbade Jews to teach.[74] She was offered the safety of a chair at a South American university, but she sensed that she ought to suffer with others of Jewish ancestry. In 1933, she entered the Carmel (Carmelite convent) of Cologne, renaming herself Teresa Benedicta of the Cross, a name that not only recognized Teresa of Avila but expressed the new Teresa's foreboding about her own future. At the Carmel, she continued to write books and to monitor the increasing terrorism against Jews. When Hitler's Final Solution loomed in 1938, her presence became a danger to the other sisters, so on New Year's Eve she was taken secretly to the Carmel at Echt in Holland.

After Holland was overrun by Nazis, plans were made to smuggle Stein to neutral Switzerland. But in July 1942, the Dutch Catholic Church issued a pastoral letter, read from all pulpits, condemning the persecution of the Jews. The Nazis responded by arresting all Jewish converts in Holland, including Teresa Benedicta and her sister Rosa (who had joined her at the Carmel in Echt). They were promptly scheduled for the extermination camps. Teresa had anticipated that, and she readied herself. One witness, a Jewish businessman, recalled:

> Sister Benedicta stood out from among those brought to the prison camp because of her great calmness and recollection. The cries, distress and confused state of the new arrivals was indescribable. Sister Benedicta went among the women as an angel of mercy, calming and helping them. Many of the mothers were on the verge of madness, succumbing to a black and brooding melancholia. They neglected their children and could only weep in dumb despair. Sister Benedicta took care of the little children, washing them and combing their hair, and bringing them food and looking after their other basic needs.[75]

Stein was gassed at Auschwitz in 1942, along with her sister. Had she lived in happier and safer times, she might have encouraged women's involvement in politics, a cause that had always been dear to her heart. She once wrote, "The nation ... doesn't simply need what we have. It needs what we are."[76]

Carmelite Doctors of the Church

Three Carmelite mystics, Teresa of Avila (1970), John of the Cross (1926), and Thérèse of Lisieux (1997), have all received the title "Doctor of the Church" from the Catholic Church. The title, so far given to only thirty-three people in the last two millennia, means that the person's life and teaching demonstrate both eminent learning and a high degree of spiritual sanctity, and that therefore all Christians can benefit from their teachings. (The title does not imply that their teachings are free of error or infallible or that they have always lived in a perfect way.)

Teresa and Thérèse are two of only three women to be declared Doctors of the church. The third is the Dominican mystic Catherine of Siena (1347–80, declared a Doctor in 1970). Despite her humble background, Catherine corrected the dignitaries of the violent Italian society of her day with impunity. For example, she told Pope Urban VI to control his harsh and violent temper, lest he undermine her efforts at conflict resolution— and got away with it.

> You know that you do ill, but like a sick and passionate woman, you let yourself be guided by your passions.[77]
>
> —Catherine's message to the queen of Naples, suspected of murdering her husband

The fact that all three women doctors were mystics underlines a paradox of many mystics' lives. On the one hand, they live an ascetic life, according to an ancient rule, avoiding worldly power or publicity. None of these three women would have been permitted a formal role in the hierarchy of the Catholic Church, for example. On the other hand, mystics often experience considerable intellectual and social freedom, which leads to significant achievements.

TEN

Did God Create the Brain or Does the Brain Create God?

The most beautiful emotion we can experience is the mystical. It is the power of all true art and science. He to whom this emotion is a stranger, who can no longer wonder and stand rapt in awe, is as good as dead.[1]
—*Physicist Albert Einstein*

As we have seen throughout this book, materialist neuroscientists and philosophers hold that mind, consciousness, and self are by-products of the brain's electrical and chemical processes, and that RSMEs are "nothing but" brain states or delusions created by neural activity. Accordingly these scientists and philosophers believe that there is no spiritual source for RSMEs, that is, they think that the human brain creates these experiences and, in so doing, creates God. As this book has been a refutation of their views from a number of angles, it is only fair that I now set out my own view.

We have already seen that RSMEs and their neural correlates do not constitute a direct proof of the existence of God and the spiritual world. It is unlikely that anything can constitute such a proof to a person who is determined to deny their existence. However, demonstrating that specific brain states are associated with RSMEs does not show that such experiences are "nothing but" brain states. And the fact that RSMEs have neural substrates does not mean that they are merely illusions. Thoughts and emotions are also associated with specific brain regions and circuits, but only radical materialists would say that they are illusions merely because they are neurally grounded.

Materialist neuroscience cannot reduce mind, consciousness, self, and RSMEs to "mere neurobiology." I think that the evidence supports the view that individuals who have RSMEs do in fact contact an objectively real "force" that exists outside themselves.

> It is very likely, indeed almost certain, that these older reports [of mystical experiences], phrased in terms of supernatural revelation, were, in fact, perfectly natural, human peak experiences of the kind that can easily be examined today.[2]
>
> —*Psychologist Abraham Maslow*

The Spiritual Nature of Humans

The transcendental impulse to connect with God and the spiritual world represents one of the most basic and powerful forces in *Homo sapiens sapiens.* For that reason, RSMEs point to a fundamental dimension of human existence. These experiences are at the heart of the world's great religions. Not surprisingly, RSMEs are commonly reported across all cultures.[3] For instance, a 1990 Gallup poll[4] assessing the incidence of RSMEs in the American adult population revealed that more than half (54 percent) of the persons polled answered yes to the following question: *Have you ever been aware of, or influenced by, a presence or a power—whether you call it God or not—which is different from your everyday self?* RSMEs can have life-changing effects and lead to a marked psychospiritual transformation. In line with this, the U.S. General Social Survey of 1998 found that 39 percent of those polled have had a RSME that had changed their lives.[5]

This high incidence of RSMEs in the American adult population indicates that such experiences should be considered normal rather than pathological. This is an important point, given that, historically, psychiatry has attempted to pathologize RSMEs.[6] One of the main contributors to this state of affairs was Sigmund Freud, who claimed that the experiences of mystics could be reduced to a "regression to primary narcissism."[7] Standing firmly against this conception, Abraham Maslow—one of the founders of transpersonal psychology, the branch of psychology that recognizes that spiritual/mystical experiences provide important insights about the nature of reality and can be studied scientifically—hypothesized that RSMEs are a sign of mental health. This hypothesis is supported empirically by the results of studies showing that people reporting RSMEs score lower on psychopathology measures and higher on psychological well-being scales than people not reporting such experiences.[8]

The psychospiritual transformation that often follows RSMEs can involve changes in thoughts, emotions, attitudes, core beliefs about self and the world, and behaviors. Maslow's work and that of other pioneers such as James and Hardy has shown that RSMEs are commonly associated with a transcendence of the personal identity and an enhanced sense of connection to and unity with others and the world.[9] This process of self-transcendence awakens one to one's transcendental or spiritual self.

It is noteworthy that similar changes are frequently seen in NDErs following their NDEs.[10] Thus, spiritual values of love and compassion for oneself, others, and nature and acquiring knowledge about the divine often become much more important after NDEs, whereas such values as wealth, status, and material possessions become much less important.

In the Christian tradition, two well-known examples of people profoundly transformed by an RSME are the apostle Paul and Francis of Assisi. Paul was a violent persecutor who targeted the early Christian church in Palestine and Syria and participated in at least one death by stoning. Yet, following his life-changing vision on the Damascus road, in which he was knocked to the ground and struck blind by a light (Acts 9:1–9), Paul spent the rest of his life serving the Christian community he had persecuted (Gal. 1:12). As for Francis of Assisi, when he was content with life as a young nobleman, no one loved pleasure as he did. Not at all interested in piety, Francis was described as handsome, joyful, gallant, and self-indulgent. During an illness, when he was about twenty, he had a vision of a huge hall hung with armor marked with the cross. He heard a voice telling him, "These are for you and your soldiers." After this vision, Francis abandoned pleasure for a simple life of silent prayer and serving the poor. He became one of the most loved saints of all time, venerated for his concern for the poor and for nature. He was especially noted for his empathy with the sufferings of animals.[11]

The error of evolutionary psychology, which has been critiqued in this book, is not its underpinnings in the fact of evolution, but rather its attempt to ground spiritual experience in the qualities that animal nature requires in order to survive. Such accounts provide no explanation for the most significant evidence regarding spirituality and are unlikely ever to do so.

The Brain Mediates but Does Not Produce RSMEs

There is no scientific evidence showing that delusions or hallucinations produced by a dysfunctional brain can induce the kind of long-term positive changes and psychospiritual transformation that often follow RSMEs. In fact, delusions and hallucinations usually constitute negative experiences from a subjective perspective.

Materialist neuroscientists have not succeeded in providing a satisfactory neurobiological theory of how mind, consciousness, self, and RSMEs arise from the interaction between various brain regions, neural circuits, and neurotransmitters. In my view, this enterprise is doomed to failure. Why? Because of the immense epistemological gap between the psychological realm (*psyche*) and the physical realm (*physis*). Mapping the brain activity underlying the discovery of Gödel's Incompleteness Theorem would reveal little with respect to its mathematical content. By virtue of this cardinal difference *psyche* cannot be reduced to *physis*. Nevertheless, *psyche* and *physis* represent complementary aspects of the same underlying principle; neither can be entirely discounted in favor of the other.

As already noted, the findings from studies of NDErs and, in particular the case of Pam Reynolds,[12] suggest that mind and consciousness can continue when clinical criteria of death have been reached and the brain no longer functions. These findings also indicate that RSMEs can occur when the brain is not functioning. Such findings lead me to posit that the transformative power of RSMEs arises from an encounter with an objectively real spiritual force that exists independently from the individuals who have the experience.

This conclusion is compatible with William James's hypothesis that the brain does not generate but transmits and expresses mental processes/events.[13] From this perspective, the brain can be compared with a television receiver that translates electromagnetic waves (which exist apart from the TV receiver) into picture and sound. Along similar lines, Henri Bergson[14] and Aldous Huxley[15] have proposed that our brains do not produce mind and consciousness, but rather act as reducing valves, allowing us the experience of only a narrow portion of perceivable reality. This outlook implies that the brain normally limits our experience of the spiritual world. In keeping with this view, the results of our neuroimaging studies conducted with Carmelite nuns suggest that neuroelectric, neurochemical, and neurometabolic changes are necessary for an RSME to take place.

A Nonmaterialist View

In this last section of this final chapter, I want to present, very briefly, key elements of a nonmaterialist view of mind, consciousness, self, and RSMEs. This personal view—which strongly rejects the extreme version of the materialist doctrine that humans are biological automatons ("meat puppets") controlled by their genes and neurons—is based not only on the findings of various scientific disciplines (some of which are presented in this book), but also on a series of mystical experiences that I have had since my childhood. Some of these experiences have included states that psychiatrist Richard Maurice Bucke has called "Cosmic Consciousness."[16]

One of these experiences occurred twenty years ago while I was lying in bed. I was very weak at the time because I was suffering from a particularly severe form of what is now called chronic fatigue syndrome. The experience began with a sensation of heat and tingling in the spine and the chest areas. Suddenly, I merged with the infinitely loving Cosmic Intelligence (or Ultimate Reality) and became united with everything in the cosmos. This unitary state of being, which transcends the subject/object duality, was timeless and accompanied by intense bliss and ecstasy. In this state, I experienced the basic interconnectedness of all things in the cosmos, this infinite ocean of life. I also realized that everything arises from and is part of this Cosmic Intelligence. This experience transformed me psychologically and spiritually, and gave me the strength necessary to successfully recover from my disease.

According to the nonmaterialist view, the death of the brain does not mean the annihilation of the person, that is, the eradication of mind, consciousness, and self. Individual minds and selves arise from and are linked together by a divine Ground of Being (or primordial matrix). That is the spaceless, timeless, and infinite Spirit, which is the ever-present source of the cosmic order, the matrix of the whole universe, including both *physis* (material nature) and *psyche* (spiritual nature). Mind and consciousness represent a fundamental and irreducible property of the Ground of Being. Not only does the subjective experience of the phenomenal world exist within mind and consciousness, but mind, consciousness, and self profoundly affect the physical world.

Normally, individual selves are not aware of this Ground of Being. However, under certain circumstances, usually involving altered states of consciousness, individual selves can become aware of and even united with the Ground of Being, which underlies both the physical and psychological realms and constitutes the ultimate foundation of the self. Such mystical states implicate the direct intuitive experience of the "organic" unity and interconnectedness of everything in the universe. It is this fundamental unity and interconnectedness that allows the human mind to causally affect physical reality and permits psi interaction between humans and with physical or biological systems. With regard to this issue, it is interesting to note that quantum physicists increasingly recognize the mental nature of the universe.[17]

> The concepts which now prove to be fundamental to our understanding of nature ... seem to my mind to be structures of pure thought.... The universe begins to look more like a great thought than a great machine.[18]
> —*Physicist James Jeans (1877–1946)*

A New Scientific Frame of Reference

If we are to make significant breakthroughs with regard to our understanding of human mind and consciousness as well as the development of the spiritual potential of humanity, we need a new scientific frame of reference. Such a frame will recognize that dogmatic materialist scientism is not synonymous with science. A scientific frame of reference must bring together the inner and the outer, the subjective and the objective, the first-person perspective and the third-person perspective. Mystical experience from various spiritual traditions indicates that the nature of mind, consciousness, and reality as well as the meaning of life can be apprehended through an intuitive, unitive, and experiential form of knowing. A scientific frame of reference must address the evidence for that. Such a framework would greatly stimulate the scientific investigation of the neural, physiological, psychological, and social conditions favoring the occurrence of RSMEs as well as the effects of RSMEs and spiritual practices on health and psychological and social functioning.

There is a trend in human evolution toward spiritualization of consciousness. The proposed new scientific frame of reference may accelerate our understanding of this process of spiritualization and significantly contribute to the emergence of a planetary type of consciousness.[19] The development of this type of consciousness is absolutely essential if humanity is to successfully solve the global crises that confront us (e.g., destruction of the biosphere, extremes of poverty and wealth, injustice and inequality, wars, nuclear arms, clashing political interests, opposing religious beliefs, etc.) and wisely create a future that benefits all humans and all forms of life on planet earth.

Notes

CHAPTER ONE: TOWARD A SPIRITUAL NEUROSCIENCE

1. This philosophical approach to nature is called "materialism," "naturalism," or "metaphysical naturalism." In this book, the term "materialism" is usually preferred, but some quoted sources use the term "naturalism."

2. "Natural selection, the blind, unconscious, automatic process which Darwin discovered, and which we now know is the explanation for the existence and apparently purposeful form of all life, has no purpose in mind. It has no mind and no mind's eye. It does not plan for the future. It has no vision, no foresight, no sight at all. If it can be said to play the role of the watchmaker in nature, it is the blind watchmaker" (*The Blind Watchmaker* [New York: Norton, 1996; first published 1986], p. 5).

3. Michael Shermer, "The Woodstock of Evolution," *Scientific American,* June 27, 2005, http://www.sciam.com/print_version.cfm?articleID=00020722–64FD–12BC-A0E483414B7FFE87. Among the attendees, Shermer lists William Calvin, Daniel Dennett, Niles Eldredge, Douglas Futuyma, Peter and Rosemary Grant, Antonio Lazcano, Lynn Margulis, William Provine, William Schopf, Frank Sulloway, and Timothy White.

4. Ricki Lewis, "Individuality, Evolution, and Dancing," *The Scientist,* June 13, 2005, http://media.the-scientist.com/blog/display/2/65/. Lewis describes herself as "embedded with the biologists on San Cristobal."

5. A clade is a group of life forms with similar organs, most likely derived from a common ancestor.

6. Lewis, "Individuality, Evolution, and Dancing." Examining claims about origins generally in any detail is well beyond the scope of this book, which focuses on the spiritual nature of humans. However, currently there is much controversy about how evolution occurs. For example, Lewis notes, "The level at which natural selection acts remains an unresolved issue." If, after 150 years, the *level* at which natural selection acts remains an unresolved issue, there is clearly room for new approaches to the topic of evolution. The same may be said about the origin of the cell, about which cell biologist Franklin Harold writes, we have only "a variety of wishful speculations" (*The Way of the Cell* [Oxford: Oxford University Press, 2001]).

7. In an interview with Alan Alda in Scientific American Frontiers, transcript online at www.pbs.org/saf/1103/features/dennett.htm.

8. Andrew Brown, "The Semantic Engineer," *Guardian Unlimited,* April 17, 2004.

9. See, for example, the Center for Naturalism, www.naturalism.org, which explicitly denies the existence of free will.

10. Phillip E. Johnson, *Darwin on Trial* (Downer's Grove, IL: InterVarsity Press, 1993), p. 169.
11. Quoted at BrainyQuote, www.brainyquote.com.
12. From an undated interview at the *Edge*, "A Biological Understanding of Human Nature," http://www.edge.org/3rd_culture/pinker_blank/pinker_blank_print.html. Accessed via http://news.bbc.co.uk/2/hi/technology/3280251.stm.
13. Daniel C. Dennett, *Brainchildren: Essays on Designing Minds* (Cambridge: MIT Press, 1998), p. 346. See also Daniel Dennett, "An Overview of My Work in Philosophy," http://ase.tufts.edu/cogstud/papers/Chinaoverview.htm (accessed January 17, 2007).
14. Dennett, *Brainchildren,* chap. 25.
15. Dennett has attempted, in his recent book, *Freedom Evolves* (New York: Viking Press, 2003), to construct an account of free will based on Darwinian evolution, but he is not generally thought to have succeeded. Fellow Darwinist David P. Barash writes, in an otherwise gushing review, "I'm not convinced that Dennett's distinction between 'determined' and 'inevitable' is as significant as he so triumphantly maintains," which pretty much cuts the heart out of Dennett's thesis ("Dennett and the Darwinizing of Free Will," *Human Nature Review* 3 [2003]: 222). Damningly, Roger William Gilman implies in *Logos* ("Daniel Dennett's Choice," *Logos* 3.2 [Spring 2004]) that Dennett's notion of free will compares to the generally held idea of free will in the same way that certain types of "lite" weight-loss foods compare to regular food. About those "lite" products, the best that can be said is that they may legally be sold as food.
16. Tom Wolfe, "Sorry, but Your Soul Just Died," Athenaeum Reading Room, 1996, http://evans-experientialism.freewebspace.com/wolfe.htm.
17. Wolfe, "Sorry, but Your Soul Just Died."
18. That statement, of course, makes the underlying assumption that no aspect of religious experience can be subjected to the evidence-gathering methods of science. Today, a number of scientists study various religious phenomena.
19. Jerry Adler, "Special Report: Spirituality 2005," *Newsweek,* September 5, 2005, pp. 48–49.
20. Adler, "Special Report," p. 49.
21. Uwe Siemon-Netto, "Atheism Worldwide in Decline," *Insight on the News,* August 29, 2005.
22. This figure is cited by Ronald Aronson in "Faith No More?" in Alister McGrath's *The Twilight of Atheism: The Rise and Fall of Disbelief in the Modern World* (New York: Doubleday, 2005), reviewed in *Bookforum,* October/November 2005. We may want to keep in mind that most of these people were living in official atheist states that were intolerant of religion; their true views cannot likely be recovered now.
23. Flew's story can be found in *Philosophia Christi,* http://www.biola.edu/antonyflew/.
24. Edward J. Larson and Larry Witham, "Leading Scientists Still Reject God," *Nature* 394 (1998): 313.
25. Research fellow Paul Pettitt, of Keble College, Oxford, notes that Neanderthal burial practices are probably very old. See Paul Pettitt, "When Burial Begins," *British Archaeology* 66 (August 2002). Indeed, the very idea of burial implies both an idea of the self and a consciousness of death. For the Neanderthal practice of burying the dead in the fetal position, see *The Interdisciplinary Encyclopedia of Religion and Science,* "Man, Origin and Nature."
26. Pettitt, "When Burial Begins."
27. Most spiritual traditions do not see God as a father; Christianity is unique among the major religions in doing so. As for personal survival, many traditions either do not emphasize it strongly (Judaism) or discourage concern with self altogether because a focus on self is thought to hinder spiritual enlightenment (Buddhism).
28. This is the definition in the entry for "evolutionary psychology" given in *Wikipedia,* http://en.wikipedia.org/wiki/Evolutionary_psychology (accessed August 24, 2005).
29. Dawkins, *Blind Watchmaker,* p. 316.
30. Mark Buchanan, "Charity Begins at *Homo sapiens,*" *New Scientist,* March 12, 2005.
31. Buchanan, "Charity Begins at *Homo sapiens.*"
32. Mark Steyn, "Trust Politicians to Do Nothing Useful," *Opinion Telegraph,* August 9, 2005.

33. Faithnet, sponsored by Stephen Richards, head of religious studies at a British grammar school; http://www.faithnet.org.uk/AS%20Subjects/Ethics/evolutionarypsychology.htm (accessed January 11, 2007).

34. Cathy Giulli, "Why I Gave a Stranger a Kidney," *National Post,* September 17, 2005. The stranger was a forty-six-year-old Montreal man with two children. He had advertised for help on a Web site.

35. An interesting article, "The Samaritan Paradox," by Ernst Fehr and Suzanne-Viola Renninger in *Scientific American Mind* (2004), pp. 16–21, summarizes such theories and offers a critique.

36. See, for example, the book of essays slamming evolutionary psychology *Alas, Poor Darwin: Arguments Against Evolutionary Psychology,* edited by Hilary Rose and Steven Rose (London: Random House, Vintage, 2001).

37. Jerry A. Coyne, "The Fairy Tales of Evolutionary Psychology," *New Republic,* March 4, 2000, a review of *A Natural History of Rape: Biological Bases of Sexual Coercion,* by Randy Thornhill and Craig T. Palmer (Cambridge, MA: MIT Press, 2000). Dr. Coyne teaches in the Department of Ecology and Evolution at the University of Chicago. He was complaining about a book that offered an explanation of rape as an evolutionary advantage for men.

38. Evelyn Underhill, *Mysticism: A Study in the Nature and Development of Man's Spiritual Consciousness* (New York: New American Library/Meridian, 1974; originally published in 1911), pp. 16–17.

39. Fehr and Renninger, "The Samaritan Paradox," p. 21.

40. George Meredith, "The Woods of Westermain," lines 74–78 (1883).

SIDEBAR

    41. Chris Stephen and Allan Hall, "Stalin's Half-man, Half-ape Super-Warriors," *The Scotsman,* December 20, 2005.

    42. Richard Dawkins, "Gaps in the Mind," in Paola Cavalieri and Peter Singer, eds., *The Great Ape Project* (London: Fourth Estate, 1993).

43. The genus *Homo* includes modern humans (*Homo sapiens*) and the now extinct Neanderthals (*Homo neanderthalensis*). Two species of chimpanzee comprise the genus *Pan,* the common chimpanzee (*Pan troglodytes*) and the bonobo (*Pan paniscus*). The study "Implications of Natural Selection in Shaping 99.4% Nonsynonymous DNA Identity Between Humans and Chimpanzees: Enlarging Genus *Homo,*" by Derek E. Wildman, Monica Uddin, Guozhen Liu, Lawrence I. Grossman, and Morris Goodman, which appeared in the *Proceedings of the National Academy of Sciences* (100 [June 2003]: 7181–88), argued that "We humans appear as only slightly remodeled chimpanzee-like apes," citing a figure of 99.4 percent for genetic closeness, using the authors' own rules of measurement. The political motive is undisguised: "Moving chimps into the human genus might help us to realize our very great likeness, and therefore treasure more and treat humanely our closest relative," study co-author Morris Goodman told *National Geographic News* (May 20, 2003). Nonetheless, he argued, the study gives "an objective view" of the human being. So far, the reclassification scheme has not caught on.

SIDEBAR

    44. Stephen Jay Gould, *Ever Since Darwin: Reflections in Natural History* (1978; repr., Penguin: London, 1991), p. 55.

    45. David P. Barash, "When Man Mated Monkey," *Los Angeles Times,* July 17, 2006.

    46. Denyse O'Leary, "Science Fiction Star Mixes in Mystery," an interview with Rob Sawyer, *Mystery Review* (Winter 1999).

47. Carl Sagan, *The Dragons of Eden: Speculations on the Nature of Human Intelligence* (New York: Random House, 1977), p. 126.

48. Jonathan Marks, *What It Means to Be 98% Chimpanzee: Apes, People, and Their Genes* (Berkeley and Los Angeles: University of California Press, 2002), p. 197.

49. In a recent comprehensive comparison of the genetic differences between humans and chimpanzees, genomic analysts unexpectedly found hundreds of genes that showed a pattern of sequence change in human ancestors in the sense of smell, digestion, long-bone growth, hairiness, and hearing. See Andrew G. Clark, Stephen Glanowski, Rasmus Nielsen, Paul D. Thomas, Anish Kejariwal, Melissa A. Todd et al., "Inferring Non-Neutral Evolution from Human-Chimp-Mouse Orthologous Gene Trios," *Science,* December 12, 2003. A given estimate can choose to include or exclude information like this, depending on how it is taken.

50. Robert Sussman and Paul Garber, "Rethinking the Role of Affiliation and Aggression in Primate Groups," a presentation at the annual meeting of the American Association for the Advancement of Science (AAAS), 2002.

51. Colin Woodward, "Clever Canines: Did Domestication Make Dogs Smarter?" *Chronicle of Higher Education,* http://chronicle.com/free/v51/i32/32a01201.htm (accessed April 15, 2005).

52. Marks, *What It Means to Be 98% Chimpanzee,* p. 182.

53. Marks, *What It Means to Be 98% Chimpanzee,* p. 184.

54. Andrew Newberg, Eugene D'Aquili, and Vince Rause, *Why God Won't Go Away: Brain Science and the Biology of Belief* (New York: Ballantine, 2001), p. 65.

55. Marks, *What It Means to Be 98% Chimpanzee,* p. 192.

56. Frans B. M. De Waal, "We're All Machiavellians," Chronicle Review, *Chronicle of Higher Education,* September 23, 2005.

57. Quoted in *Hansard Nova Scotia,* December 8, 2005.

58. Elaine Morgan, *The Aquatic Ape: A Theory of Human Evolution* (1982; repr., London: Souvenir Press, 1989), pp. 17–18. The aquatic ape theory advanced by Morgan seems to have been first suggested by Alister Hardy.

59. For more predictions from artificial intelligence guru Ray Kurzweil, see *The Age of Spiritual Machines* (New York: Penguin, 1999).

60. Douglas Adams, *Hitchhiker's Guide to the Galaxy* (London: Macmillan, 2002), p. 152. First published in 1979. The question was eventually answered at the end of Adams's *The Restaurant at the End of the Universe* (London: Macmillan, 1980), p. 197.

61. A philosopher defending artificial intelligence may wish to argue that a computer could come up with concepts of mind and spirit that are too advanced for humans to understand. But if there is no way to assess the meaningfulness of the computer's concepts, they cannot really count as concepts. Douglas Adams's portrayal of an arithmetically challenged computer in *Hitchhiker's Guide* hints at this problem.

62. Robert J. Sawyer, *The Terminal Experiment* (New York: HarperCollins, 1995), p. 4.

63. John R. Searle, *Mind: A Brief Introduction* (Oxford: Oxford University Press, 2004), pp. 69–70.

64. See also William A. Dembski, "Are We Spiritual Machines?" *First Things* (October 1999).

65. See "How Stuff Works," http://computer.howstuffworks.com/chess1.htm for an explanation.

66. Sagan, *Dragons of Eden,* p. 221.

67. Robert Plummer, "Humanity Counts in Chess Battle," *BBC News Online,* (November 18, 2003), http://news.bbc.co.uk/2/hi/technology/3280251.stm (accessed January 11, 2007).

68. Learn more about the enigmatic Kasparov at *Wikipedia,* http://en.wikipedia.org/wiki/Garry_Kasparov, and about Deep Junior at *Wired,* http://www.wired.com/news/culture/0,1284,57345,00.html (accessed January 11, 2007).

69. Timothy McGrew, "The Simulation of Expertise: Deeper Blue and the Riddle of Cognition," *Origins and Design* 19.1 (1998).

70. McGrew notes that computer programs tend to be short-sighted, which is to say that grandmasters who use them program in a "greedy" tendency to jump at an advantage, and grandmasters who do not use them have learned to take advantage of the fact that the program itself cannot forecast a later disadvantage.

71. Kenneth Silber, "Searching for Bobby Fischer's Platonic Form," *Tech Central Station,* April 6, 2004.

72. Quoted in Neal Lao, "Falling Prey to Machines: Can Sentient Machines Evolve," Eurekalert! February 11, 2003, University of Michigan College of Engineering, http://www.eurekalert.org/pub_releases/2003-02/uomc-fpt021103.php#.

73. Searle, *Mind,* p. 74.

74. Robert J. Sawyer, a well-known Canadian science fiction writer, suggests in a Nebula Award–winning book that just such a being brought the universe into existence. See Robert J. Sawyer, *The Calculating God* (New York: Tor Books, 2000).

75. First published in Russell's *A Free Man's Worship* in 1903.

76. See Karl Popper and John C. Eccles, *The Self and Its Brain* (Oxford: Routledge, 1984), p. 97.

77. Gonzalez was not named in the statement, but the primary organizer, associate professor of religious studies Hector Avalos, admitted that he was indeed the target. Avalos was assisted by professors Jim Colbert and Michael Clough (Kate Strickler, "Intelligent Design Debate Lingers," *Iowa State Daily,* September 1, 2005, http://www.iowastatedaily.com/media/storage/paper818/news/2005/09/01/News/Intelligent.Design.Debate.Lingers-1105333.shtml?norewrite2007011 12013&sourcedomain=www.iowastatedaily.com). Avalos stated that he was concerned that Iowa State would be seen as an "intelligent design center." No evidence has surfaced that the university is seen as an intelligent design center as a result of the fact that Gonzalez teaches there.

78. See Guillermo Gonzalez, "Habitable Zones in the Universe," *Origins of Life and Evolution of Biospheres,* September 1, 2005. Hundreds of planets have been discovered orbiting stars other than our sun; hence the recent interest in habitability. For a lucid book-length discussion of planetary requirements for life, see Michael J. Denton, *Nature's Destiny: How the Laws of Biology Reveal Purpose in the Universe* (New York: Free Press, 1998).

79. Guillermo Gonzalez and Jay W. Richards, *The Privileged Planet: How Our Place in the Cosmos Is Designed for Discovery* (Washington, DC: Regnery, 2004). Gonzalez and his coauthor, philosopher Jay Richards, also appeared in a film of the same name, shown (controversially) at the Smithsonian in Washington in June 2005. See Denyse O'Leary, "Design Film Sparks Angst," *Christianity Today,* August 2005. Contrary to a widespread belief that resulted from an error in a New York Times story, neither the film nor the book addresses biological evolution. Also, contrary to other reports, both authors accept the standard age for the universe, approximately 13 billion years.

80. Quoted in Reid Forgrave, "Life: A Universal Debate," *Des Moines Register,* August 31, 2005.

81. Forgrave, "Life."

82. It is significant that Avalos is faculty adviser to the ISU Atheist and Agnostic Society, but Gonzalez is adviser to Truth Bucket, a Christian student organization (Strickler, "Intelligent Design Debate Lingers").

83. Edward Willett, "Robert J. Sawyer Calculates God," 2001, http://www.edwardwillett.com/Arts%20Columns/calculatinggod.htm (posted September 22, 2004). Sawyer's book on this theme is *The Calculating God.* Generally, the large number of apparent coincidences that favor the existence of life on earth are called the "anthropic coincidences."

84. Paul Davies, "The Synthetic Path," in John Brockman, ed., *The Third Culture* (New York: Simon & Schuster, Touchstone, 1996), p. 308. See, particularly, an interview with him at the Edge, http://www.edge.org/documents/ThirdCulture/za-Ch.18.html.

85. For a full-length argument for the existence of innumerable other universes, see Max Tegmark, "Parallel Universes," *Scientific American,* May 2003. The article makes explicit that a key reason for accepting the existence of many other universes is the extraordinary fine-tuning of the universe we live in.

86. Cosmologist Lee Smolin argues for something like this in "A Theory of the Whole Universe," in Brockman, ed., *Third Culture,* p. 294. He counts on Darwinian evolution to sort out the winners from the losers. The mere existence of other universes would not, of course, establish Russell's

point. What if they all operate on the same laws as our own? Or different laws, but all are successful? Only a junk heap of failed universes would provide evidence that ours is accidentally successful.

87. Wolfe, "Sorry, but Your Soul Just Died."

SIDEBAR

88. "About" at William Dembski, Denyse O'Leary, Barry Arrington et al., Uncommon Descent, http://uncommondescent.com/about.

89. Interview with George Neumayr, "Mummy Wrap," *The American Spectator,* January 10, 2005; http://www.spectator.org/dsp_article.asp?art_id=7601. Wolfe commented further, "Just think about the theory of the Big Bang or this ridiculous theory about where the first cell came from. Now they say it probably came from outer space when an asteroid hit the earth and a few of these things bounced out. It is because of all this silly stuff that Darwinism is going to go down in flames." Wolfe's take on the war of ideas should not be ignored. He has, after all, given us such defining phrases as "the right stuff," "radical chic," "the Me Decade," and "good ol' boy."

90. Many elite scientists favor Russell's view over Gonzalez's, but that is not evidence.

91. An article on lying, "Natural-Born Liars," by David Livingstone Smith (*Scientific American Mind,* 2005, pp. 16–23), compares human lying to the fact that certain orchids resemble and smell like female wasps, thus causing amorous male wasps to pollinate them. Smith makes clear that he thinks that similar processes govern the behavior of life forms that have a mind and those that do not.

92. John Eccles, *Evolution of the Brain: Creation of the Self* (London: Routledge, 1989), p. 241.

93. Some philosophers of mind argue that we need a new language to reflect the fact that we do not really make choices or decisions, because current language reinforces the popular illusion that we do. This is discussed in Chapter Five.

94. Lucretius, *De rerum natura (On the Nature of the Universe),* quoted in Shimon Malin, *Nature Loves to Hide: Quantum Physics and the Nature of Reality, a Western Perspective* (Oxford: Oxford University Press, 2001), p. 13.

95. Quoted in Malin, *Nature Loves to Hide,* pp. 13–14.

96. "Quantum" means something like "packet." The quantum is a packet, like the 50-watt setting on the bulb. To get more light, you must get the next packet, which is 100 watts. Another way of thinking about this is to consider how eggs are sold in the supermarket. You can get a carton of a half dozen or a dozen, but you cannot buy seven or eleven eggs.

97. Timothy Ferris, *The Whole Shebang: A State-of-the-Universe(s) Report* (New York: Simon & Schuster, Touchstone, 1997), p. 97.

98. Paul A. M. Dirac, "The Development of Quantum Mechanics," paper presented at a conference held April 14, 1972, in Rome at the Accademia Nazionale dei Lincei (1974).

99. The effect is named after Zeno, a Stoic philosopher, who argued that a continuously observed arrow should never land. He may have been wrong about the arrow (it was Zeno's paradox, after all), but quantum particles proved him right in the end.

100. See J. M. Schwartz, H. Stapp, and M. Beauregard, "Quantum Theory in Neuroscience and Psychology: A Neurophysical Model of Mind/Brain Interaction," *Philosophical Transactions of the Royal Society B: Biological Sciences* 360 (2005): 1309–27.

101. See, for example, J. Lévesque et al., "Neural Circuitry Underlying Voluntary Suppression of Sadness," *Biological Psychiatry* 53.6 (March 15, 2003): 502–10, where sadness was voluntarily suppressed; also V. Paquette et al., "'Change the Mind and You Change the Brain': Effects of Cognitive-Behavioral Therapy on the Neural Correlates of Spider Phobia," *Neuroimage* 18.2 (February 2003): 401–9, where spider phobia was voluntarily overcome; and M. Pelletier et al., "Separate Neural Circuits for Primary Emotions? Brain Activity During Self-Induced Sadness and Happiness in Professional Actors," *Neuroreport* 14.8 (June 11, 2003):1111–16, where pro-

fessional actors were shown to separate stage emotions from personal ones. This material is addressed in more detail in later chapters.

102. For a detailed discussion of this research, see Jeffrey M. Schwartz and Sharon Begley, *The Mind and the Brain: Neuroplasticity and the Power of Mental Force* (New York: HarperCollins, Regan Books, 2003).

103. Schwartz, Stapp, and Beauregard, "Quantum Theory in Neuroscience and Psychology."

104. As noted, the physicist causes the particle to fail to decay simply by continuing to measure it. In other experiments, physicists have caused electrons to alter their state in order to match other electrons with which they could not have been in contact. These are examples of nonmechanical causation.

105. William James faced a definitional problem of this type and commented, "With states that can only by courtesy be called religious we need have nothing to do, our only profitable business being with what nobody can possibly feel tempted to call anything else." He chose to look at exaggerated phenomena in order to focus on the specific areas he wished to study. See William James, *The Varieties of Religious Experience* (1902; New York: Simon & Schuster, Touchstone, 1997), p. 30.

106. This book will not address any phenomena that can be considered attempts at magic. James argues (*Varieties of Religious Experience,* p. 24) that magic can just as easily be called primitive science as primitive religion. It might even better be considered primitive technology; magic aims at control of the natural world. RSMEs pursue understanding or enlightenment; the experiencer is not directly seeking benefits from or control over the material world.

CHAPTER TWO: IS THERE A GOD PROGRAM?

1. Dean Hamer, *The God Gene: How Faith Is Hardwired into Our Genes* (New York: Doubleday, 2004), p. 49.

2. "Humans on Display at London's Zoo," *CBS News,* August 26, 2005. Most stories repeated essentially the same information, picked up from Associated Press.

3. "Humans on Display at London's Zoo."

4. Edward O. Wilson, *On Human Nature* (Cambridge, MA: Harvard University Press, 1978), chap. 1.

5. Matthew Alper, *The "God" Part of the Brain: A Scientific Interpretation of Human Spirituality and God* (New York: Rogue, 2001), p. 67.

6. "Excellent reading" is Wilson's back-cover endorsement; Mark Waldman, senior editor of the *Transpersonal Review,* praises the Socratic technique.

7. Alper, *"God" Part of the Brain,* p. 1.

8. Alper, *"God" Part of the Brain,* p. 8.

9. Alper, *"God" Part of the Brain,* p. 56.

10. Alper, *"God" Part of the Brain,* p. 102.

11. Alper, *"God" Part of the Brain,* p. 140.

12. Alper, *"God" Part of the Brain,* p. 134, footnote.

13. Pascal Boyer, *Religion Explained: The Evolutionary Origins of Religious Thought* (New York: Basic Books, 2001), p. 4.

14. In the twentieth century, some Melanesian peoples of the South Pacific came to believe that Western manufactured goods (cargo) had been created by ancestral spirits for their benefit, and that white races had unfairly gained control of them. For more on cargo cults, see Vanuatu Travel Guide http://www.southpacific.org/text/finding_vanuatu.html: "Prince Philip was regarded as a god by participants in the cult."

15. In Chapter One we looked briefly at early human burial practices that reflect such a view.

16. James George Frazer, *The Golden Bough,* ed. Mary Douglas, abridg. Sabine McCormack (London: Macmillan, 1978), p. 86.

17. Frazer, *Golden Bough,* p. 94. For a modern account of such beliefs, see *First People,* "A Cherokee Legend," http://www.firstpeople.us/FP-Html-Legends/TheFour-footedTribes-Cherokee.html. Generally, in traditional cultures even trees were often thought to have spirits. The wrath of the gods dogged the impious person who cut down a tree without first propitiating its spirit.

18. *First People,* "A Cherokee Legend."

19. Michael Joseph Gross, "Hard-wired for God," *Salon,* February 1, 2001.

20. Alper, *"God" Part of the Brain,* p. 106.

21. Alper, *"God" Part of the Brain,* p. 11.

22. Hamer, *God Gene,* p. 8.

23. Jeffrey Kluger, Jeff Chu, Broward Liston, Maggie Sieger, and Daniel Williams, "Is God in Our Genes?" *Time,* October 25, 2004. The article's teaser reads, "A provocative study asks whether religion is a product of evolution. Inside a quest for the roots of faith."

24. Quoted in Kluger et al., "Is God in Our Genes?"

25. Kluger et al., "Is God in Our Genes?"

26. Kluger et al., "Is God in Our Genes?"

27. Hamer recounts this story in *God Gene,* p. 197.

28. Hamer, *God Gene,* p. 18.

29. Quoted in Kluger et al., "Is God in Our Genes?"

30. Quoted in Kluger et al., "Is God in Our Genes?"

SIDEBAR

    31. *Beliefnet* provides a list of twelve such questions at http://www.beliefnet.com/section/quiz/index.asp?sectionID=&surveyID=37.

32. Hamer, *God Gene,* p. 38.

33. Hamer, *God Gene,* p. 49.

34. See, for example, "Obesity Gene Pinpointed," *BBC News* (August 12, 2001), http://news.bbc.co.uk/2/hi/health/1484659.stm (accessed January 12, 2007). Below the headline, we learn that "the majority of people in Europe carry the gene—so it is only one piece in the jigsaw of reasons why obesity develops." Although up to two-thirds of children may inherit the gene variant, many fewer are obese. Again, the *BBC News* site apprises us (November 3, 2003) that some researchers have found a gene that may be responsible for obesity in one of ten seriously overweight people, but "Lead researcher Professor Philippe Froguel said obesity was a complex problem, which could not be entirely explained by one factor alone." One would think that the increase in sedentary lifestyles and high-fat diets should be factored in.

35. Journalist Wendy McElroy tracked the media progress of the infidelity gene at *Fox News* (November 30, 2004), http://www.foxnews.com/story/0,2933,140074,00.html (accessed January 12, 2007). Notably, epidemiologist Tim Spector, author of *Your Genes Unzipped: How Your Genetic Inheritance Shapes Your Life* (2003), who suggests based on his twin studies that there might be such a gene, had not even published his study of the subject before the media melted down.

36. See Dean Hamer, *The Science of Desire: The Gay Gene and the Biology of Behavior* (New York: Simon & Schuster, 1994). Science writer John Horgan recounts the rise and fall of the gay gene in "Do Our Genes Influence Behavior?" *Chronicle of Higher Education,* November 26, 2004. For example, Canadian researchers G. Rice et al. found no increase in the likelihood of male homosexuality linked to genetic region Xq28 in a paper in *Science* (284, 5414 [April 23, 1999]: 571).

37. Hilary Rose, "Spot the Infidelity Gene," *Guardian Unlimited,* December 1, 2004.

38. In "Churches Attack God Gene Claim by Scientist" (*The Scotsman,* November 15, 2004), Shan Ross quotes Donald Bruce, the Church of Scotland's society, religion, and technology project director as saying: "We were both on the advisory board at the conference and I asked him if he thought the book's title was irresponsible. Dr. Hamer agreed the words 'God gene' as well as the

book's title were misleading." See also Bill Broadway, "Do We Have a Propensity for Religious Belief?" *Washington Post,* December 4, 2004. Carl Zimmer points out in "Faith-Boosting Genes: A Search for the Genetic Basis of Spirituality," his review of Hamer's book in *Scientific American* (September 27, 2004), that Hamer begins disowning his title by p. 77.

39. Chet Raymo, "The Genetics of Belief," *Notre Dame Magazine,* Spring 2005.

40. Zimmer, "Faith-Boosting Genes."

41. Horgan makes the case in "Do Our Genes Influence Behavior?" that science writers know that stories promoting genetic determinism are popular with editors and that therefore they are implicitly encouraged to produce them.

42. Dorothy Nelkin, "Less Selfish Than Sacred? Genes and the Religious Impulse in Evolutionary Psychology," in Hilary Rose and Steven Rose, eds., *Alas, Poor Darwin: Arguments Against Evolutionary Psychology* (London: Random House, Vintage, 2001), p. 18.

43. Hamer, *God Gene,* p. 77.

44. See, for example, Lea Winerman, "A Second Look at Twin Studies," *APA Online* 35, no. 4 (April 2004), http://www.apa.org/monitor/apr04/second.html (accessed January 12, 2007), where Winerman lists cautions regarding twin research, including the following: "Twin researchers ... assume that fraternal and identical twins raised in the same homes experience equally similar environments. But some research suggests that parents, teachers, peers and others may treat identical twins more similarly than fraternal twins." Although child-raising experts discourage this approach to identicals, popular culture encourages it.

45. Hamer, *God Gene,* pp. 54–55.

46. A poll taken in early August 2005 for *Newsweek* and *Beliefnet* found that 64 percent of Americans follow a religion and 57 percent consider spirituality "a very important part" of daily life.

47. Natalie Angier, "Separated by Birth?" *New York Times,* February 8, 1998. Angier also notes that many identical twins separated at birth who participate in separated-at-birth studies have "met periodically throughout their lives," which raises a question about how much of the influence is really genetic.

48. Barbara J. King, "Spirituality Explained? Reflections on Dean Hamer's *The God Gene, Bookslut,* June 2005.

49. Laura Sheahen, "The Brain Chemistry of the Buddha," an interview with Dean Hamer, *Beliefnet,* http://www.beliefnet.com/story/154/story_15451_1.html (accessed January 12, 2007).

50. Carl Zimmer, "The God Gene Meme," *The Loom,* October 21, 2004.

51. C. S. Lewis, *The Abolition of Man* (Glasgow: Collins, 1978), p. 48.

52. In African American novelist Toni Morrison's novel *The Bluest Eye,* a girl prays for blue eyes in order to seem more attractive in a racist environment. However, unrelated cultural stereotypes associate blue eyes with emotional coldness.

CHAPTER THREE: DOES THE GOD MODULE EVEN EXIST?

1. V. S. Ramachandran, Reith Lectures, Lecture 1, 2003; available online at http://www.bbc.co.uk/radio4/reith2003/.

2. Jonah Goldberg, "Giving Thanks—and Not Just for Evolutionary Reasons," *Jewish World Review,* November 23, 2005.

3. Mark Salzman, *Lying Awake* (New York: Knopf, 2000), p. 120.

4. Salzman, *Lying Awake,* p. 153.

5. Liz Tucker, "God on the Brain," *BBC News,* March 20, 2003.

6. See, for example, Steve Connor, "'God Spot' Is Found in Brain," *Los Angeles Times,* October 29, 1997; Robert Lee Hotz, "Brain Region May Be Linked to Religion," *Los Angeles Times,* October 29, 1997; Bob Holmes, "In Search of God," *New Scientist,* April 21, 2001; Tucker, "God on the Brain."

7. This statement appears in Tucker, "God on the Brain." The article, taken as a whole, is a classic in the genre described here. Tucker states, unblinking, "We will never know for sure whether religious figures in the past definitely did have the disorder [TLE], but scientists now believe the

condition provides a powerful insight into revealing how religious experience may impact on the brain." Now, *either* the religious figures in the past are irrelevant or the uncertainty about them impairs the TLE hypothesis. Tucker appears not to notice this problem and goes on to say, "They believe what happens inside the minds of temporal lobe epileptic patients may just be an extreme case of what goes on inside all of our minds." In the context, this statement is nearly meaningless, and it is followed up by, "For everyone, whether they have the condition or not, it now appears the temporal lobes are key in experiencing religious and spiritual belief." But nothing in the article warrants such a decisive statement about the role of the temporal lobes as opposed to other brain areas. Articles such as this give the public a grossly misleading impression about the state of neuroscientific evidence for religious experience. Critical readers may begin to suspect that neuroscience is, by its very nature, as tendentious as the media accounts—which hardly helps the cause of research.

8. Jeffrey L. Saver and John Rabin, "The Neural Substrates of Religious Experience," *Journal of Neuropsychiatry and Clinical Neurosciences* 9 (1997): 498–510.

9. Saver and Rabin, "Neural Substrates of Religious Experience," p. 507. "The limbic-marker hypothesis provides an entirely different explanation for the ineffability of religious experience. The perceptual and cognitive contents of numinous experience are seen as similar to those of ordinary experience, except that they are tagged by the limbic system as of profound importance.... Consequently, descriptions of the contents of the numinous experience resemble descriptions of the contents of ordinary experience, and the distinctive feelings appended to them cannot be captured fully in words."

10. Quoted in Holmes, "In Search of God."

11. Saver and Rabin, "Neural Substrates of Religious Experience."

12. Saver and Rabin, "Neural Substrates of Religious Experience," pp. 501–2.

13. See the program summary at http://www.bbc.co.uk/science/horizon/2003/godonbrain.shtml.

14. There are, of course, various understandings of RSMEs, but the Christian mystical tradition, which is extensively documented, is the tradition followed by my primary research subjects, Carmelite nuns in Quebec. This book focuses mainly on the Christian tradition.

15. After W. T. Stace, *Mysticism and Philosophy* (Los Angeles: Tarcher, 1960).

16. One possible reason may be that a diagnosis of epilepsy can result not only in treatment, but in social restrictions (driving) or career limitations (ineligibility for employment). Epileptics who have not attracted attention may be ambivalent about self-reporting.

17. Richard Restak, "Complex Partial Seizures Present Diagnostic Challenge," *Psychiatric Times* 12, no. 9 (September 1995) offers classifications of typical hallucinations, none of which are exotic.

18. Jenna Martin, "Progression in Temporal Lobe Epilepsy: An Interview with Dr. Bruce Hermann," www.epilepsy.com (accessed November 9, 2005). See also E. Johnson, J. E. Jones, M. Seidenberg, and B. P. Hermann, "The Relative Impact of Anxiety, Depression, and Clinical Seizure Features on Health-Related Quality of Life in Epilepsy," *Epilepsia* 45 (2004): 544–50.

19. Saver and Rabin, "Neural Substrates of Religious Experience," p. 504.

20. Saver and Rabin, "Neural Substrates of Religious Experience," p. 504.

21. J. Hughes, "The Idiosyncratic Aspects of the Epilepsy of Fyodor Dostoevsky," *Epilepsy & Behavior* 7 (2005): 531. Hughes's endorsement is particularly noteworthy because he is generally (and justifiably) a skeptic of claims regarding epilepsy as a common affliction of famous people. But see his comment on Vincent van Gogh below.

22. Saver and Rabin ("Neural Substrates of Religious Experience, p. 504") say that D. M. Bear and P. Fedio ("Quantitative Analysis of Interictal Behavior in Temporal Lobe Epilepsy," *Archives of Neurology* 34 [1977]: 454–67) report such a finding, but the following fail to confirm it: L. J. Willmore, K. M. Mailman, and B. Fennell, "Effect of Chronic Seizures on Religiosity," *Transactions of the American Neurological Association* 105 (1980): 85–87; T. Ensky, A. Wilson, R. Petty, et al., "The Interictal Personality Traits of Temporal Lobe Epileptics: Religious Belief and Its Association with Reported Mystical Experiences," in *Advances in Epileptology*, ed. R. Porter (New York, Raven, 1984), pp. 545–49; D. M. Tucker, R. A. Nevelly, and P. J. Walker, "Hyper-

religiosity in Temporal Lobe Epilepsy: Redefining the Relationship," *Journal of Nervous and Mental Disorders* 175 (1987): 181–84.

23. John R. Hughes, "A Reappraisal of the Possible Seizures of Vincent van Gogh," *Epilepsy & Behavior* 6 (2005): 504–10. Van Gogh drank heavily and often went without food for long periods; under these conditions, blackouts unrelated to seizures could have occurred.

24. D. F. Benson, "The Geschwind Syndrome," *Advances in Neurology* 55 (1991): 411–21.

25. From Hughes, "A Reappraisal": "Benson and Hermann have spelled out the majority opinion of epileptologists today that there are only 'a subset of patients with epilepsy in general and TLE in particular who present with features of the Geschwind syndrome.' I think that Vincent van Gogh is likely the best example of the Geschwind syndrome that can be found. However, the syndrome has been described as a part of TLE, and if there is no clear TLE, then the syndrome is an orphan without a parent condition." It is also worth noting that advice manuals directed at patients living with epilepsy do not usually suggest that religious delusions are to be expected.

26. See Sallie Baxendale, "Epilepsy at the Movies: Possession to Presidential Assassination," *Lancet Neurology* 2, no. 12 (December 2003): 764–70; see also "Memories Aren't Made of This: Amnesia at the Movies," *British Medical Journal* 329 (2004): 1480–83. Her quoted comment is from *Lancet*'s Science Blog for November 2003.

27. John R. Hughes, "Did All Those Famous People Really Have Epilepsy?" *Epilepsy & Behavior* 6 (2005): 115–39. In this study, Hughes looks at forty-three famous individuals who are widely claimed to have had epilepsy and concludes that none definitely did. See also John R. Hughes, "Alexander of Macedon, the Greatest Warrior of All Times: Did He Have Seizures?" *Epilepsy & Behavior* 5 (2004): 765–67; "Dictator Perpetuus: Julius Caesar—Did He Have Seizures? If So, What Was the Etiology?" *Epilepsy & Behavior* 5 (2004): 756–64; "Emperor Napoleon Bonaparte: Did He Have Seizures? Psychogenic or Epileptic or Both?" *Epilepsy & Behavior* 4 (2003): 793–96; "The Idiosyncratic Aspects of the Epilepsy of Fyodor Dostoevsky," *Epilepsy & Behavior* 7 (2005): 531–38; and "A Reappraisal of the Possible Seizures of Vincent van Gogh," *Epilepsy & Behavior* 6 (2005): 504–10. Hughes offers that, although it is difficult to reach into the past to diagnose historical figures, symptoms such as pain (not associated with epilepsy), long duration of seizure (unlikely with epilepsy), and failure to lose consciousness during a severe attack all point to nonepileptic disorders.

28. Judith Peacock, *Epilepsy* (Mankato, MN: Capstone, 2000).

29. Peacock, *Epilepsy*.

30. Claims in patient literature should be treated with caution. See, for example, "Alexander of Macedon, the Greatest Warrior of All Times," where Hughes firmly states, "Alexander the Great did *not* have epilepsy and his name should be removed from the list of famous individuals who have had seizures." Apparently, Alexander only had seizures following a dose of medication—in other words, iatrogenic illness.

31. Epilepsy Ontario provides useful information on distinguishing between psychogenic and epileptic attacks at its Web site, http://www.epilepsyontario.org/client/EO/EOWeb.nsf/web/Psychogenic+Seizures (accessed January 12, 2007).

32. For a useful discussion of nonepileptic attack disorder (NEAD), formerly called pseudoseizures, see Alice Hanscomb and Liz Hughes, *Epilepsy* (London: Ward Lock, 1995), pp. 24–25.

33. Hanscomb and Hughes, *Epilepsy*, pp. 24–25.

34. Saver and Rabin, "Neural Substrates of Religious Experience." These figures are of particular interest because both Paul and Joan of Arc have had a major cultural influence on the Christian tradition. Both Teresa and Thérèse were Carmelite mystics, as are the subjects of our studies, described in Chapter Nine.

35. Paul's personal name was Saul, but, as a Roman citizen, he also took a Latin name (Paul) that was a close phonetic equivalent, according to the custom of the day (see Acts 13:9).

36. The entire story is recounted in Acts 9:1–31. For Saul's previous career, see Acts 8:1.

37. *The Catholic Encyclopedia* (http://www.newadvent.org/cathen/11567b.htm [accessed January 12, 2007]) suggests doubt, remorse, fear, ophthalmia, fatigue, fever, and excitable nervous temperament as historically proposed causes.

38. "To keep me from becoming conceited because of these surpassingly great revelations, there was given me a thorn in my flesh, a messenger of Satan, to torment me. Three times I pleaded with the Lord to take it away from me. But he said to me, 'My grace is sufficient for you, for my power is made perfect in weakness'" (2 Cor. 12:7–9, NIV).

39. See 2 Cor. 12:2. Paul's claim to have been "caught up to the third heaven" can be interpreted in the light of Jewish mysticism of his day, according to philosopher Eliezer Segal. The third heaven was held to be a resting place for accomplished mystics (*Jewish Star,* November 13–16, 1989, pp. 4–5).

40. Saver and Rabin, "Neural Substrates of Religious Experience," p. 501.

41. Verena Jucher-Berger, "'The Thorn in the Flesh'/'Der Pfahl im Fleisch': Considerations About 2 Corinthians 12:7–10 in Context with 12:1–13," in *The Rhetorical Analysis of Scripture: Essays from the 1995 London Conference* (pp. 386–97).

42. John M. Mulder, "The Thorn in the Flesh," sermon preached at Calvary Episcopal Church, Memphis Tennessee, February 28, 2002.

43. Hughes, "Did All Those Famous People Really Have Epilepsy?" A life-threatening condition called *status epilepticus* results in continual seizures, ending in death if untreated. Joan is most unlikely to have remained in such a condition for hours.

44. Dr. Bruce Hermann, in Martin, "Progression in Temporal Lobe Epilepsy," noted that poorly controlled TLE, present in 20–25 percent of patients seen at his center, shows a deterioration in cognitive performance over time. In Joan's day, no effective treatment was available.

45. Saver and Rabin, "Neural Substrates of Religious Experience," p. 500.

46. Hughes, "The Idiosyncratic Aspects of the Epilepsy of Fyodor Dostoevsky." A passage from *The Idiot* by Russian novelist Dostoevsky (who suffered epilepsy) is sometimes cited (e.g., in Saver and Rabin, "Neural Substrates of Religious Experience," p. 503, and in Orrin Devinsky, "Religious Experiences and Epilepsy," *Epilepsy & Behavior* 4 [2003]: 76): "I have really touched God. He came into me myself; yes, God exists, I cried, and I don't remember anything else," without critical evaluation of the fact that Dostoevsky undoubtedly chose his character's words for effect, rather than for clinical accuracy. In this article, Hughes offers some useful observations from the literature.

47. Hughes provides an explanation: "Pleasant auras, like ecstasy, are … very rare because the essence of a seizure state with hypersynchronous high amplitudes is usually associated with an unpleasant affective tone" (see "The Idiosyncratic Aspects of the Epilepsy of Fyodor Dostoevsky").

48. Bjørn Åsheim Hansen and Eylert Brodtkorb, "Partial Epilepsy with 'Ecstatic' Seizures," *Epilepsy & Behavior* 4 (2003): 667–73. This study examined eleven patients who actually experienced pleasant symptoms associated with seizures, eight of whom wished to experience them again and five of whom could initiate them voluntarily. Although the authors identify that five patients described a "religious/spiritual" experience, it is not clear how they arrived at that conclusion from the descriptions of the cases.

49. Saver and Rabin, "Neural Substrates of Religious Experience," p. 503.

50. Devinsky, "Religious Experiences and Epilepsy," pp. 76–77.

51. They cite Spratling, who reported a religious aura in 4 percent of patients with epilepsy in 1904, which is not a large proportion.

52. Kenneth Dewhurst and A. W. Beard, "Sudden Religious Conversions in Temporal Lobe Epilepsy," *Epilepsy & Behavior* 4 (2003): 78.

53. The six cases who had conversion/deconversion experiences are taken from the twenty-six patients "with religiosity" out of a total of sixty-nine. It's not clear what "with religiosity" means (Dewhurst and Beard, "Sudden Religious Conversions in Temporal Lobe Epilepsy," p. 79). In

the acknowledgments, Professor Sir Denis Hill and Dr. Eliot Slater are thanked "for permission to publish the case histories of patients under their care" (p. 86).

54. Saver and Rabin, "Neural Substrates of Religious Experience," p. 507, citing T. Lynch, M. Sano, K. S. Marder, et al., "Clinical Characteristics of a Family with Chromosome 17-Linked Disinhibition-Dementia-Parkinsonism-Amyuonophy Complex," *Neurology* 44 (1994): 1875–84. Even if the researchers have stumbled on a valid link, the situation is somewhat unusual and cannot be extrapolated to behavior in the population at large, past or present.

55. Saver and Rabin, "Neural Substrates of Religious Experience," p. 499.

56. Devinsky, "Religious Experiences and Epilepsy," p. 77.

57. Quoted in Ian Sample, "Tests of Faith," *Guardian,* February 24, 2005; V. S. Ramachandran and Sandra Blakeslee, *Phantoms in the Brain: Probing the Mysteries of the Human Mind* (New York: Morrow, 1998), p. 179.

58. For a discussion of split-brain experiments, see Jay Ingram, *Theater of the Mind: Raising the Curtain on Consciousness* (Toronto: HarperCollins, 2005), pp. 206–15, 221–23. For an account of how brains are reorganized after such splits, see Jeffrey M. Schwartz and Sharon Begley, *The Mind and the Brain: Neuroplasticity and the Power of Mental Force* (New York: HarperCollins, Regan Books, 2003), pp. 98–103.

59. Quoted in Ramachandran and Blakeslee, *Phantoms in the Brain,* p. xxi (epigraph).

60. V. S. Ramachandran, Reith Lectures, 2003; http://www.bbc.co.uk/radio4/reith2003/.

61. Claims recorded in Connor, "'God Spot' Is Found in Brain." The last item is Connor's paraphrase.

62. Quoted in Hotz, "Brain Region May Be Linked to Religion."

63. Quoted in Ian Sample, "Tests of Faith." See also Ramachandran and Blakeslee, *Phantoms in the Brain,* pp. 182–83.

64. This is a classic *attribution* hypothesis. An important strand of current neuroscience argues that our thoughts are actually the random workings of our neurons, but we invent reasons and attribute them to meaningless data because we have evolved as creatures who were naturally selected for such behavior. This idea is addressed in Chapter Five.

65. Ramachandran and Blakeslee, *Phantoms in the Brain,* p. 183.

66. Ramachandran and Blakeslee, *Phantoms in the Brain,* p. 186. Later, he told the BBC, "These patients are more prone to religious belief." The program summary makes it sound as though Ramachandran is saying that TLE patients are in general more prone to religious belief. In fact, he is probably alluding only to the fact that he had asked specialists to recruit patients known to be religious (from a sample of unknown size). See Tucker, "God on the Brain."

67. Ramachandran and Blakeslee, *Phantoms in the Brain,* p. 186.

68. Ramachandran and Blakeslee, *Phantoms in the Brain,* p. 186.

69. Nonetheless, the media acclaim continued. For example, Ramachandran's finding was heralded by *BBC News* as "the very first piece of clinical evidence revealing that the body's response to religious symbols was definitely linked to the temporal lobes of the brain." See Tucker, "God on the Brain."

70. Sample, "Tests of Faith."

71. M. Beauregard and V. Paquette, "Neural Correlates of a Mystical Experience in Carmelite Nuns," *Neuroscience Letters* 405 (2006): 186–90.

72. Salzman, *Lying Awake,* p. 169.

73. Indeed, a strong argument can be made that the dilemma in the novel is, in certain ways, an allegorical account of the novelist's own struggle to write a very difficult book. Salzman, an agnostic, wrestled with his key character, a contemplative religious, for six years. As Carol Lloyd comments in *Salon* (January 10, 2001), the "other story" of the book is about "the tortured novelist who endures hell until he experiences a transcendent empathy with his own protagonist." But Salzman's empathy is with a vision of the spiritual life as an essentially irrational pursuit. Again, Lloyd: "He wasn't so different from his main character after all—his faith in writing

was every bit as illusive and irrational (and almost as sacrificial) as his character's burning faith in God."

74. Erik K. St. Louis, review of *Lying Awake* in *Medscape General Medicine*, March 12, 2002.

75. The ability to communicate with a large popular audience comprises a large number of analyzable skills acquired both consciously and unconsciously, usually over a long period of time. It seems implausible that Sr. John's ability to write effective devotional materials would simply disappear if her temporal-lobe tumor was removed without extensive damage because the tumor cannot have been the source of the skills.

CHAPTER FOUR: THE STRANGE CASE OF THE GOD HELMET

1. Robert Hercz, "The God Helmet," *Saturday Night*, October 2002, p. 41.

2. Bob Holmes, "In Search of God," *New Scientist*, April 21, 2001.

3. Raj Persaud, "Test Aims to Link Holy Visions with Brain Disorder," *London Daily Telegraph*, March 24, 2003.

4. Quoted in Persaud, "Test Aims to Link Holy Visions with Brain Disorder."

5. The BBC transcript renders "god" in lower case, as do some British science magazines. "God on the Brain" was broadcast April 17, 2003, on BBC Two; program summary: http://www.bbc.co.uk/science/horizon/2003/godonbrain.shtml.

6. The apparent slight incoherence is due to the fact that this is a transcript of a tape, not an edited version.

7. See, for example, Jeremy Licht, "A Push to Map the Mystical," *Baltimore Sun*, August 18, 2003. Neurotheology need not, of course, have that intent or that effect, but if materialist reductionism is the starting point, then neurotheology's only purpose would be to accumulate evidence for materialism.

8. Jeffrey Kluger et al., "Is God in Our Genes?" *Time*, October 25, 2004.

9. Hercz, "God Helmet," p. 43. Persinger has also written an article for *Skeptic* magazine (December 2002) arguing, based on experiments with rats, that accounts of Jesus's resurrection can best be explained by his theory of temporal-lobe sensitivity and the ingestion of drugs. Of this, Canadian science journalist Jay Ingram says, "I have to admit that at one point I wondered if the article was a clever parody of the rational scientist's need to explain absolutely everything, no matter how baroque the explanation." But, he concludes, apparently not ("Did Jesus Suffer from Epilepsy? Scientist Theorizes over Resurrection," *The Hamilton Spectator*, April 11, 2003).

10. Kluger et al., "Is God in Our Genes?"

11. In a 2002 paper, Persinger and colleague F. Healey said: "We have not attempted to refute or to support the absolute existence of gods, spirits, or other transient phenomena that appear to be prominent features of people's beliefs about themselves before and after death.... However, we have shown that the experience of these phenomena, often attributed to spiritual sources, can be elicited by stimulating the brain with specific weak complex magnetic fields. These fields contain energies well within the range expected to be produced within the brain during these specific states. Religious beliefs, in large part reinforced by personal experiences of sensed presences, are a persistent and powerful variable in large-scale killings of groups who endorse the belief in one kind of god by other groups who define themselves by a belief in a different god" ("Experimental Facilitation of the Sensed Presence: Possible Intercalation between the Hemispheres Induced by Complex Magnetic Fields," *Journal of Nervous and Mental Diseases* 190 [2002]: 533–41).

12. As quoted in the transcript for "God on the Brain," BBC (April 17, 2003), http://www.bbc.co.uk/science/horizon/2003/godonbraintrans.shtml.

13. Patchen Barss, "O Me of Little Faith," *Saturday Night*, October 2005.

14. Quoted in Hercz, "God Helmet," p. 42.

15. Hercz, "God Helmet," p. 40.

16. Ian Cotton, *The Hallelujah Revolution: The Rise of the New Christians* (London: Prometheus, 1996), p. 187.

17. Persinger's hypothesis of the "sensed presence" should not be confused with the work of J. Allan Cheyne, as in, for example, "The Ominous Numinous: Sensed Presence and 'Other' Hallucinations," *Journal of Consciousness Studies* 8, nos. 5–7 (2001). In that paper, Cheyne discusses a fear of attack by a shadowy entity that is specific to sleep paralysis (an intermediate state between waking and sleeping). Of Persinger's work, Cheyne says: "Even the sensed presence has been viewed as a right-hemisphere analogue of the left-hemisphere sense of self (Persinger, 1993). Considerations raised here point to a more sinister and primordial other of concern to us at the most fundamental biological roots of our being" (p. 16).

18. Persinger and Healey, "Experimental Facilitation of the Sensed Presence," p. 533.

19. Michael Persinger, "Religious and Mystical Experiences as Artifacts of Temporal Lobe Function: A General Hypothesis," *Perceptual and Motor Skills* 57 (1983): 1255–62.

20. "God on the Brain," BBC. In "Experimental Simulation of the God Experience: Implications for Religious Beliefs and the Future of the Human Species" (in *Neurotheology*, ed. R. Joseph [Berkeley and Los Angeles: University of California Press, 2002], pp. 267–84), Persinger claims that clinical records of individuals who were diagnosed as complex partial epileptics with a focus in the right limbic or temporal lobe abound. Chapter Three demonstrates that this is not a view that is supported empirically (it is neuromythology).

21. Persinger himself originally called the helmet "the Octopus," but it was quickly renamed "the God helmet" by the media.

22. Persinger and Healey, "Experimental Facilitation of the Sensed Presence."

23. Persinger and Healey, "Experimental Facilitation of the Sensed Presence," p. 537. The experimenters did not question the subjects about the nature of the sensed presence (p. 538). This is an unfortunate omission, because it would be useful to know whether subjects believed that the sensed presence was actually another individual who had been concealed from them until they were blindfolded and the chamber was darkened. Such a finding might point away from a spiritual experience, as usually defined.

24. Did the latter group report an unusual experience simply because they had been selected for the experiment? If so, this is the familiar placebo effect (the subject thinks that a treatment is being received and experiences its anticipated effects). For more on the placebo effect, see Chapter Six. This implies that the study is not double-blind. Persinger himself argues that a quantum mechanical effect accounts for the experience of the sensed presence in the sham-field group: "Effectively, the result may have been a Heisenberg variant whereby the measurement can influence and may even add to the resultant phenomena" (p. 539). As Pehr Granqvist's team's findings demonstrate, a more probable interpretation of Persinger 2002 is the placebo effect or suggestion.

25. Persinger and Healey, "Experimental Facilitation of the Sensed Presence," p. 541.

26. Jack Hitt, "This Is Your Brain on God," *Wired,* November 1999.

27. Hercz, "God Helmet." The journalists were not part of the 2002 published study; that study recruited among psychology students at Laurentian only.

28. Cotton, *Hallelujah Revolution,* p. 194.

29. Cotton, *Hallelujah Revolution,* p. 197.

30. Hercz, "God Helmet."

31. Jay Ingram, "Aliens and the Sudbury Connection," *Toronto Star,* January 14, 1996.

32. Hitt, "This Is Your Brain on God." Hitt felt like a failure. He defends Persinger stoutly, however: "I mean, who among all the churchgoers and alien fiends will let some distant egghead with a souped-up motorcycle helmet spoil their fun? It goes without saying that the human capacity to rationalize around Persinger's theory is far greater than all the replicated studies science could produce." Hitt assumes that Persinger's findings had been or soon would be replicated.

33. Susan Blackmore, "Alien Abduction," *New Scientist,* November 19, 1994, pp. 29–31; http://www.susanblackmore.co.uk/journalism/ns94.html (accessed January 12, 2007).

34. Hitt, "This Is Your Brain on God."

35. Hercz, "God Helmet."

36. The BBC's "God on the Brain—Questions and Answers" file helpfully explains: "So that there is no risk of 'suggestion,' the only information that the subjects are given is that they are going in for an experiment. Neither the subject nor the experimenter carrying out the test has any idea of the purpose of the experiment. In addition to this, the experiment is also run with the field off and on. This procedure Dr. Persinger claims will induce an experience in over 80% of subjects" (BBC Two, April 17, 2003; http://www.bbc.co.uk/science/horizon/2003/godonbrainqa.shtml). Persinger has stated: "The reinforcement for volunteering for the experiment was a 2% bonus mark for the final grade in a first-year psychology course. These volunteers were told that the experiment involved relaxation, but were not told about the types of phenomena that may be experienced" (p. 534).

37. Jerome Burnes of the *Times of London* explains that Persinger "designed and built Room C002B, otherwise known as the 'Heaven and Hell' chamber, back in the mid-eighties, in which over 1,000 subjects have now been induced to experience ghostly presences" ("Ghosts in a Machine," *[London] Times,* Body & Soul, March 5, 2005). Ian Cotton notes that Persinger's lab was referred to locally as "The Dungeon" (*Hallelujah Revolution,* p. 185).

38. Hitt, "This Is Your Brain on God."

39. Holmes, "In Search of God." Similarly, Jerome Burnes reports: "People saw a wide variety of phenomena. What others have experienced in Room C002B depended on their cultural or religious beliefs. Some saw Jesus, the Virgin Mary, Muhammad, or the Sky Spirit. Others, with more than a passing faith in UFOs, tell of something that sounds more like a standard alien-abduction story" ("Ghosts in a Machine").

40. Scientists are not immune to suggestibility. A famous example occurred in the seventeenth century, when Van Leeuwenhoek (who invented the microscope), having discovered spermatozoa in 1678, proposed in 1683 that pregnancy results when sperm impregnate an ovum (egg). Many scientists assumed that sperm or eggs must already contain tiny babies (preformation), which enlarged in the womb. As a result, some biologists (such as Andry, Dalenpatius, and Gautier) believed that they could see tiny complete humans inside sperm cells under their early microscopes.

41. Hercz, "God Helmet."

42. Hercz, "God Helmet."

43. The familiar science decision-making tool called Occam's razor (try the simplest explanation first) seems to have been ignored here. For example, instead of saying that Dawkins lacks temporal-lobe sensitivity (a concept for which there is no significant literature), one might venture that he scores low on suggestibility. There is a large body of research on suggestibility.

44. In the published study (2002), Persinger and Healey argue that the amygdaloid-hippocampal formation would be a primary candidate for the neural substrate for the sensed presence. But without neuroimaging data, they cannot know if the magnetic fields employed in their experiments really have the intended effect on the neuroelectrical activity generated within the amygdala and hippocampus (which are part of the mesial portion of the temporal lobes).

45. BBC *Horizon,* "God on the Brain," March 2003. The narrator was filling in time while waiting for Richard Dawkins to have a spiritual experience while wearing the God helmet.

46. Ingram, "Aliens and the Sudbury Connection."

47. Hercz, "God Helmet."

48. Burnes, "Ghosts in a Machine."

SIDEBAR

49. John Horgan, "The Myth of Mind Control: Will Anyone Ever Decode the Human Brain?" *Discover* 25, no. 10 (October 2004).

50. E. Halgren et al., "Mental Phenomena Evoked by Electrical Stimulation of the Human Hippocampal Formation and Amygdala," *Brain* 101.1 (1978): 83–117.

51. Hercz, "God Helmet," p. 44.

SIDEBAR
    52. Horgan, "Myth of Mind Control."

53. Hercz, "God Helmet."
54. "Persinger was quoted recently in *Time*" magazine as saying that "'God is an artefact of the brain,' while Murphy, interviewed for this article, was keen to emphasise that his aim was to 'enhance spirituality, not to replace it'" (Burnes, "Ghosts in a Machine").
55. Murphy explains in "The Structure and Function of Near-Death Experiences: An Algorithmic Reincarnation Hypothesis Based on Natural Selection": "A simple, first statement about rebirth is that: *Information which enables individuals to adapt is conserved at death, and passed on to other individuals still undergoing prenatal development elsewhere.* To say that anything more than information is reborn would involve making assumptions for which there is no evidence. Unless this information is somehow adaptive, it is unlikely that any evolutionary mechanism would have favored its conservation" (Spirituality and the Brain, http://www.shaktitechnology.com/rebirth.htm ([accessed January 12, 2007]).
56. See Todd Murphy, "The Structure and Function of Near-Death Experiences: An Algorithmic Reincarnation Hypothesis." This lay-directed article is based on a peer-reviewed piece in the *Journal of Near-Death Studies* 20 no. 2 (December 2001), 101–118.
57. Brent Raynes, "Interview with Todd Murphy," *Alternate Perceptions* #78, April 2004; http://www.mysterious-america.net/interviewwithtod.html (accessed January 12, 2007). Most scientists would call this procedure "cherry-picking"—picking only the desired results rather than analyzing the entire series.
58. Information is from *Skeptical Investigations'* "Who's Who of Media Skeptics," http://www.skepticalinvestigations.org/whosewho/index.htm (accessed January 12, 2007).
59. Richard W. Flory, "Promoting a Secular Standard: Secularization and Modern Journalism, 1870–1930," in Christian Smith, ed., *The Secular Revolution: Power, Interests, and Conflict in the Secularization of American Public Life* (Berkeley and Los Angeles: University of California Press, 2003), p. 413.
60. Flory, "Promoting a Secular Standard," p. 427.

SIDEBAR
    61. Evelyn Underhill, *Mysticism: A Study in the Nature and Development of Man's Spiritual Consciousness* (New York: New American Library / Meridian, 1974). See particularly pp. 71, 48, 81. The nature of mysticism is discussed in more detail in Chapter Seven.
    62. Genuine mystical experiences are rare, so words or images that describe them are not in general use (Underhill, *Mysticism,* p. 79). Some experiences may, of course, be indescribable in any event.
    63. *The Cloud of Unknowing* (2nd ed., London: John M. Watkins, 1922), chap. 6.
    64. Underhill, *Mysticism,* p. 81.

65. Hercz, "God Helmet," p. 45.
66. Roxanne Khamsi, "Electrical Brainstorms Busted as Source of Ghosts," *Nature News,* December 9, 2004, http://www.nature.com.
67. Khamsi, "Electrical Brainstorms Busted as Source of Ghosts."
68. Granqvist told *Nature* that the level of spiritual experiences was "quite high overall," though not higher than Persinger's control groups (Khamsi, "Electrical Brainstorms Busted as Source of Ghosts"). However, it's worth noting that half of Granqvist's study participants were theology students, so perhaps spiritual experiences should not have been a surprise.
69. "In spite of high power for detecting differences between groups at a small effect size level, there were no significant differences between experimental and control group participants on any of the dependent variables" (Pehr Granqvist et al., "Sensed presence and mystical experiences are

predicted by suggestibility, not by the application of transcranial weak complex magnetic fields," *Neuroscience Letters,* doi:10.1016/j.neulet.2004.10.057 (2004).

70. Granqvist et al., "Sensed presence," p. 2.
71. Khamsi, "Electrical Brainstorms Busted as Source of Ghosts." Granqvist et al. comment: "Highly suggestible individuals may not have been affected by the application of the magnetic fields but may simply have been more prone to pick up on and respond to the experimenter's potentially differential treatments across groups. Presupposing even subtly differential treatments, this does not seem unlikely considering the nature of the suggestibility trait in connection with the vagueness and wide scope of experiences covered in the EXIT form" ("Sensed presence"). Persinger's inventory scales have not been independently verified, unlike Hood's and Tellagen's scales.
72. Persinger and Healey, "Experimental Facilitation of the Sensed Presence," p. 535.
73. Even if students did not know what Persinger's team was interested in, simply typing "Michael Persinger" into the Google search window provided key information.
74. "An additional methodological problem with the studies cited is that they consistently used an outcome measure (the EXIT scale), constructed inductively and with unknown reliability and construct validity. Many of the experiences listed on the scale are rather vague ('tingling sensations,' 'felt odd'), and their relations to the paranormal and mystical experiences, to which the findings are generalized, remain disputable. Thus it is important to investigate if the findings can be reproduced with measures with well-documented reliability and validity, such as Hood's Mysticism scale" (Granqvist et al., "Sensed presence," p. 2).
75. Granqvist et al., "Sensed presence."
76. See, for example, "God and the Gap: A Challenge to the Idea That Religious Experiences Can Be Stimulated Artificially," *The Economist,* December 16, 2004; and Julia C. Keller, "Swedish Scientists Can't Replicate Religious Experience in Lab," *Science & Theology News,* February 1, 2005.
77. Keller, "Swedish Scientists Can't Replicate Religious Experience in Lab."
78. Jay Ingram, "Close Encounters of the Magnetic Kind," *Toronto Star,* December 26, 2004. The e-mail exchange between Persinger's team and Granqvist's team that followed the announcement of Granqvist's findings (http://laurentian.ca/neurosci/_news/emailj.htm, accessed January 11, 2006) does not provide much hope that the two teams could easily cooperate.
79. Quoted in Khamsi, "Electrical Brainstorms Busted as Source of Ghosts." Granqvist's concerns as quoted here are focused on the psychology students who were the subjects in Persinger's published, peer-reviewed studies. Obviously, science journalists who test the God helmet in pursuit of a story are at high risk for the effects of suggestion.
80. Granqvist, "Sensed presence," p. 5.
81. "God and the Gap."
82. Ingram, "Close Encounters of the Magnetic Kind."
83. Keller, "Swedish Scientists Can't Replicate Religious Experience in Lab."
84. A Brocken specter is one's own shadow projected onto a bank of mist or fog, visible when the sun shines low on the horizon. The specter owes its name to Brocken Mountain of the Harz range in Germany. In context, Lewis writes: "The Brocken spectre 'looked to every man like his first love' because she was a cheat. But God will look to every soul like its first love because he is its first love. Your place in heaven will seem to be made for you and you alone" ("The House with Many Mansions"; C. S. Lewis, *The Problem of Pain* [New York: Simon and Schuster Touchstone, 1996] p. 132). Although Lewis was not himself a mystic, he understood the mystics' desire to break free of the products of psychological suggestion in order to understand a reality at the heart of human spirituality.
85. Khamsi, "Electrical Brainstorms Busted as Source of Ghosts."
86. Given that many regions of the brain mediate RSMEs, as will be demonstrated in Chapter Nine, the materialist hope was a nonstarter to begin with.
87. Quoted in John Leo, "Aphorisms 2006," www.townhall.com, December 26, 2005.

CHAPTER FIVE: ARE MIND AND BRAIN IDENTICAL?

1. Greg Peterson, "God on the Brain: The Neurobiology of Faith," *Christian Century,* January 27, l999; a review of James B. Ashbrook and Carol Rausch Albright, *The Humanizing Brain: Where Religion and Neuroscience Meet* (Cleveland, OH: Pilgrim, 1999).

2. B. Alan Wallace, *The Taboo of Subjectivity: Toward a New Science of Consciousness* (Oxford: Oxford University Press, 2000), p. 136.

3. Project on the Decade of the Brain, July 17, 1990.

4. William J. Bennett, "Neuroscience and the Human Spirit," *National Review,* December 31, 1998.

5. John Horgan, "The Myth of Mind Control: Will Anyone Ever Decode the Human Brain?" *Discover* 25, no. 10 (October 2004).

6. Peterson, "God on the Brain."

7. Jeffrey M. Schwartz and Sharon Begley in *The Mind and the Brain: Neuroplasticity and the Power of Mental Force* (New York: HarperCollins, Regan Books, 2003) provide a useful discussion of this point, especially on pp. 15–16, 96–131.

8. Schwartz and Begley, *Mind and the Brain,* pp. 184–87.

9. Jean-Pierre Changeux, *Neuronal Man: The Biology of Mind,* trans. Laurence Garey (New York: Oxford University Press, 1985), p. 282. In the same passage, Changeux notes that "axons and dendrites preserve a remarkable capacity to regenerate even in the adult," but he does not appear to have the high hopes for a practical outcome that blossomed in later decades, as the extent of neuroplasticity became more widely recognized.

10. Quoted in Kathleen Yount, "The Adaptive Brain," *UAB Publications,* Summer 2003. This article, which won the Robert G. Fenley award for basic science writing (2004), provides a good (and relatively nontendentious) discussion of some implications of neuroplasticity for medical treatment.

11. Michael D. Lemonick, "Glimpses of the Mind," *Time,* July 17, 1995.

12. Lemonick, "Glimpses of the Mind."

13. Schwartz and Begley, *Mind and the Brain,* p. 365.

14. Although concepts such as consciousness, mind, and self can be distinguished, they overlap. In this book, distinctions will be made when they assist in explanation.

15. Mind, as understood here, is an interrelated variety of mental functions such as attention, perception, thought, reason, memory, and emotion. Mind is not a substance (an entity), but rather a collection of mental processes and events.

16. Amy Butler Greenfield, *A Perfect Red: Empire, Espionage, and the Quest for the Color of Desire* (New York: HarperCollins, 2005).

17. Diane Ackerman, "To Dye For," *Washington Post,* July 24, 2005, BW08; a review of Greenfield, *A Perfect Red.*

18. Francis Crick, *The Astonishing Hypothesis: The Scientific Search for the Soul* (New York: Simon & Schuster, Touchstone, 1995), p. 258. It is interesting that Crick refers to the "limitations of quantum mechanics." What quantum mechanics actually does is seriously limit the applicability of the classical physics that underlies Crick's view.

19. V. S. Ramachandran, Reith Lectures, Lecture 5, 2003; http://www.bbc.co.uk/radio4/reith2003/.

20. Quoted in B. Alan Wallace, *The Taboo of Subjectivity: Toward a New Science of Consciousness* (Oxford: Oxford University Press, 2000), p. 139.

SIDEBAR

21. Quoted in Schwartz and Begley, *Mind and the Brain,* pp. 39–40.

22. Daniel C. Dennett, *Breaking the Spell: Religion as a Natural Phenomenon* (New York: Viking, 2006), p. 107.

23. "The identity theory of mind" in *Stanford Encyclopedia of Philosophy,* http://plato.stanford.edu/entries/min-identity (accessed January 12, 2007).

24. As he elaborated it in his Nobel address (December 8, 1981): "The events of inner experience, as emergent properties of brain processes, become themselves explanatory causal constructs in their own right, interacting at their own level with their own laws and dynamics."

25. John Eccles and Daniel N. Robinson, *The Wonder of Being Human: Our Brain and Our Mind* (New York: Free Press, 1984), p. 43.

26. Helen Phillips, "The Ten Biggest Mysteries of Life." *New Scientist,* September 4–10, 2004.

27. Quoted in Dean Radin, *The Conscious Universe: The Scientific Truth of Psychic Phenomena* (San Francisco: HarperSanFrancisco, 1997), p. 265.

28. Eccles and Robinson, *Wonder of Being Human,* p. 37.

29. Quoted in Phillips, "Ten Biggest Mysteries of Life."

30. Space considerations prevent addressing consciousness in animals. It should be noted, however, that consciousness is not *sentience*—the capacity to feel. Animals with brains are generally sentient, but it does not necessarily follow that all vertebrates, for example, experience a type of consciousness that integrates their sensations into a sense of self that is stable over time.

31. Wallace, *Taboo of Subjectivity,* p. 3.

32. Wallace, *Taboo of Subjectivity,* p. 136 (emphasis in the original).

33. B. F. Skinner, *Beyond Freedom and Dignity* (New York: Knopf, 1971), p. 198.

34. Ray Kurzweil, *The Age of Spiritual Machines* (New York: Penguin, 1999), p. 63.

35. Gerald M. Edelman and Giulio Tononi, *A Universe of Consciousness: How Matter Becomes Imagination* (New York: Basic Books, 2000), p. 6. Edelman argues that consciousness arises through the communication within and between the thalamocortical system and the limbic brain-stem system. But his theory does not really explain how the interaction of the electrical activity of billions of neurons (which are nonconscious material elements) found in these brain systems produces consciousness or a unified conscious experience. It is difficult to see how his belief can be empirically tested.

36. Edelman and Tononi, *A Universe of Consciousness,* p. xi.

37. Lemonick, "Glimpses of the Mind."

38. Crick, *Astonishing Hypothesis,* p. 262.

39. Peterson, "God on the Brain."

SIDEBAR

40. Steven Pinker, *How the Mind Works* (New York: Norton, 1997), p. 83.

41. Mark Halpern, "The Trouble with the Turing Test," *New Atlantis,* Winter 2006, http://www.thenewatlantis.com/archive/11/halpern.htm (accessed January 12, 2007), pp. 9, 42–63.

42. Albert Bandura, "Social Cognitive Theory: An Agentic Perspective," *Annual Review of Psychology* 52 (2001): 1–26.

43. Quoted at Neuroscience for Kids, http://faculty.washington.edu/chudler/quotes.html.

44. Halpern, "Trouble with the Turing Test," pp. 5, 13, 62–63.

45. Radin, *Conscious Universe,* p. 259.

46. Pinker, *How the Mind Works,* p. 558.

47. Quoted in Edelman and Tononi, *Universe of Consciousness,* p. 4.

48. Crick, *Astonishing Hypothesis,* p. 3.

49. In response to the World Question Center 2006 question, "What is your dangerous idea?" http://www.edge.org/3rd_culture/ramachandran06/ramachandran06_index.html (accessed January 12, 2007). In the context, he was responding to Crick's "pack of neurons" comment, among others.

50. Changeux, *Neuronal Man,* p. 169.

51. Lemonick, "Glimpses of the Mind."

52. See, for example, Wallace, *Taboo of Subjectivity,* pp. 85–87.

53. Ramachandran, Reith Lectures, Lecture 5.

54. David Livingstone Smith, "Natural-Born Liars," *Scientific American Mind* 16, no. 2 (2005): 16–23.

55. See J. M. Schwartz, H. Stapp, and M. Beauregard, "Quantum Theory in Neuroscience and Psychology: A Neurophysical Model of Mind/Brain Interaction" (*Philosophical Transactions of the Royal Society B: Biological Sciences* 360 [2005]: 1309–27), for a model of free will that avoids this problem, based in quantum mechanics.

56. Daniel C. Dennett, *Kinds of Minds: Toward an Understanding of Consciousness* (New York: Basic Books, 1996), p. 55.

57. Tom Clark, "Denying the Big God *and* the Little God: The Next Step for Atheists," subtitled "An Open Letter to the Atheist Community," Center for Naturalism, http://www.naturalism. org/atheism.htm (accessed January 17, 2006).

58. Pinker, *How the Mind Works,* p. 55.

59. Pinker, *How the Mind Works,* p. 55.

60. George Grant, *Lament for a Nation: The Defeat of Canadian Nationalism* (Don Mills: Oxford University Press Canada, 1970), p. 56.

61. Clark, "Denying the Big God *and* the Little God." Board members of the center include Susan Blackmore and Daniel Dennett.

62. In response to the World Question Center 2006 question, "What is your dangerous idea?"

63. C. S. Lewis, *The Abolition of Man* (London: Collins, 1978), p. 40. Lewis's book is a brief but brilliant defense of objective moral order, in which he addresses the impossibility of shared ethical values when the spiritual nature of the human is denied.

64. Psychologist Daniel Wegner, in *The Illusion of Conscious Will* (Cambridge, MA: MIT Press, 2002), makes a slightly more sophisticated case that, even though we have no free will, we should be held responsible for our actions in order that we can be manipulated to behave better. But such an account fails to provide an ethical justification for the manipulation.

65. Quoted in Eccles and Robinson, *Wonder of Being Human,* p. 36.

66. Peter Watson, "Not Written in Stone," *New Scientist,* August 29, 2005.

67. Harold J. Morowitz, "Rediscovering the Mind," in Douglas R. Hofstadter and Daniel C. Dennett, *The Mind's I: Fantasies and Reflections on Self and Soul* (New York: Basic Books, 2000), p. 35.

68. Crick, *Astonishing Hypothesis,* p. 7.

69. Eccles and Robinson, *Wonder of Being Human,* p. 47.

70. Morowitz, "Rediscovering the Mind," p. 41.

71. Wallace, *Taboo of Subjectivity,* p. 81.

72. Edelman and Tononi, *A Universe of Consciousness,* p. 81.

73. On pp. 80–81 of *A Universe of Consciousness,* Edelman and Tononi do use the term "spiritualism" to refer to Alfred Russel Wallace's interests in nineteenth-century spiritualism, but that is not clearly the meaning of the term as used here.

74. Eric Harth, *The Creative Loop: How the Brain Makes a Mind* (Reading, MA: Addison-Wesley, 1993), p. 102.

75. Edelman and Tononi, *A Universe of Consciousness,* pp. 220–21.

76. Edelman and Tononi, *A Universe of Consciousness,* p. 221.

77. Pinker, *How the Mind Works,* p. 305.

78. Wallace, *Taboo of Subjectivity,* p. 82. Quantum physics offers a model of how mental states and brain might interact without simply reducing mental processes to neural processes (Schwartz, Stapp, and Beauregard, "Quantum Theory in Neuroscience and Psychology").

79. Wallace, *Taboo of Subjectivity,* p. 81.

80. Morowitz, "Rediscovering the Mind," p. 34.

CHAPTER SIX: TOWARD A NONMATERIALIST SCIENCE OF MIND

1. Quoted in Harold J. Morowitz, "Rediscovering the Mind," in Douglas R. Hofstadter and Daniel C. Dennett, *The Mind's I: Fantasies and Reflections on Self and Soul* (New York: Basic Books, 2000), p. 35; from Carl Sagan, *The Dragons of Eden* (New York: Random House, 1977).

2. John Eccles and Daniel N. Robinson, *The Wonder of Being Human: Our Brain and Our Mind* (New York: Free Press, 1984), p. 36.

3. Daniel Dennett, in Samuel Guttenplan, ed., *A Companion to the Philosophy of Mind* (Oxford: Blackwell, 1994), p. 237.

4. Jeffrey M. Schwartz and Sharon Begley, *The Mind and the Brain: Neuroplasticity and the Power of Mental Force* (New York: HarperCollins, Regan Books, 2003), pp. 54–55.

5. Schwartz and Begley, *The Mind and the Brain,* pp. 17–18.

6. Schwartz and Begley, *The Mind and the Brain,* pp. 57–58.

7. Schwartz and Begley, *The Mind and the Brain,* p. 71.

8. OCD is not restricted to humans. It occurs in domestic cats. See, for example, Diane Frank's paper, "Obsessive-Compulsive Disorder in Felines," given at the World Small Animal Veterinary Association World Congress in Vancouver (2001). It is not known whether cats have any mental associations with their obsessive-compulsive behavior rituals, but they can react quite aggressively to attempts to prevent the rituals.

9. Schwartz and Begley, *Mind and the Brain,* p. 77.

10. Schwartz and Begley, *Mind and the Brain,* p. 82.

11. Schwartz and Begley, *Mind and the Brain,* p. 83.

12. Schwartz and Begley, *Mind and the Brain,* pp. 88–90.

13. Schwartz and Begley, *Mind and the Brain,* p. 90.

14. Miranda Devine, "Muslim Cleric: Women Incite Men's Lust with 'Satanic Dress,'" *The Sun-Herald* (Australia), April 24, 2005. Some sources press the connection between doubts about men's self-control and current extremist Islamic sects. However, such beliefs have been widespread in Europe as well as Asia; they have lasted longer in the Middle East but are not the invention of any one religion.

15. Tom W. Clark, "Maximizing Liberty: Retribution, Responsibility, and the Mentor State," Center for Naturalism, http://www.naturalism.org/maximizing_liberty.htm (accessed January 13, 2007).

16. M. Beauregard, J. Lévesque, and P. Bourgouin, "Neural Correlates of Conscious Self-regulation of Emotion," *Journal of Neuroscience* 21 (2001): RC165 (1–6).

17. Beauregard, Lévesque, and Bourgouin, "Neural Correlates of Conscious Self-regulation of Emotion."

SIDEBAR

18. Beauregard, Lévesque, and Bourgouin, "Neural Correlates of Conscious Self-regulation of Emotion."

19. Not that you would know this from the Center for Naturalism's comments on "Materialism and Morality," criticizing both psychologist Steven Pinker, for being concerned about the possible moral consequences of disbelief in free will, and also former New York Mayor Ed Koch, for hoping that a brutal rapist would soon be brought to justice.

20. Depression Guide, http://www.depression-guide.com/depression-quotes.htm (accessed January 16, 2007).

21. Quoted at Quote Garden, http://www.quotegarden.com/psychology.htm (accessed January 13, 2007).

22. These figures are from "Frequently Asked Questions About Suicide," sponsored by the National Institute of Mental Health, http://www.nimh.nih.gov/suicideprevention/suicidefaq.cfm (accessed January 13, 2007).

Much higher figures for suicide are quoted in some media reports because they express the percentage of persons who died by suicide during a follow-up of fatalities *within a few years of treatment.* However, most persons treated for depression do not die from any cause within the next few years.

23. J. Lévesque et al., "Neural Circuitry Underlying Voluntary Suppression of Sadness," *Biological Psychiatry* 53 (2003): 502–10.

24. Some have wondered why our research team has studied sexual arousal in men and sadness in women. When recruiting volunteer subjects from the general population for a neuroscientific study, it is relatively easier to get men to admit to sexual arousal and women to admit to sadness.

25. No control group was used in this study or in the previously noted study on male sexual arousal because data from persons who had seen no films at all would not provide useful information in the context.

SIDEBAR

26. J. Lévesque et al., "Neural Circuitry Underlying Voluntary Suppression of Sadness."

27. J. Lévesque et al., "Neural Circuitry Underlying Voluntary Suppression of Sadness."

28. J. Lévesque et al., "Neural Basis of Emotional Self-Regulation in Childhood," *Neuroscience* 129 (2004): 361–69.

29. Hazel Curry, "Spiders Are Not Out to Get You," *Daily Telegraph,* February 22, 2000. The accounts of British women's spider-phobic (arachnophobic) behavior are taken from a *Telegraph* account of a session in which spiderphobes described their fears and strategies as part of a desensitization program.

30. Folklore is inconsistent on the significance of spiders, presenting the hapless arthropod sometimes as good luck and sometimes as bad. Most likely, personal experience triggers the phobia, and the folklore is recruited, if at all, in support of an existing fear.

31. V. Paquette et al., "Change the Mind and You Change the Brain: Effects of Cognitive-Behavioral Therapy on the Neural Correlates of Spider Phobia," *Neuroimage* 18.2 (February 2003): 401–9.

32. J. M. Gorman et al., "Neuroanatomical Hypothesis of Panic Disorder," revised, *American Journal of Psychiatry* 157 (2000): 493–505; M. M. Antony and R. P. Swinson, "Specific Phobia," in M. M. Antony and R. P. Swinson, eds., *Phobic Disorders and Panic in Adults: A Guide to Assessment and Treatment* (Washington, DC: American Psychological Association, 2000), pp. 79–104.

33. See, for example, A. L. Brody et al., "Regional Brain Metabolic Changes in Patients with Major Depression Treated with Either Paroxetine or Interpersonal Therapy: Preliminary Findings," *Archives of General Psychiatry* 58, (2001): 631–40.

34. See, for example, J. M. Schwartz et al., "Systematic Changes in Cerebral Glucose Metabolic Rate After Successful Behavior Modification Treatment of Obsessive-Compulsive Disorder," *Archives of General Psychiatry* 53 (1996): 109–13.

35. All studies reported here featured voluntary, informed consent from subjects recruited through advertisement and were approved by the university's research ethics committee.

36. Tom Wolfe, "Sorry, but Your Soul Just Died," Athenaeum Reading Room, 1996, http://evans-experientialism.freewebspace.com/wolfe.htm.

SIDEBAR

37. Paquette et al., "Change the Mind and You Change the Brain."

38. Dean Radin, *The Conscious Universe: The Scientific Truth of Psychic Phenomena* (San Francisco: HarperSanFrancisco, 1997), p. 258.

39. Quoted in Brian Reid, "The Nocebo Effect: Placebo's Evil Twin," *Washington Post,* April 30, 2002.

40. Thomas J. Moore, "No Prescription for Happiness: Could It Be That Antidepressants Do Little More Than Placebos?" *Boston Globe,* October 17, 1999.

41. Herbert Benson and Marg Stark, *Timeless Medicine: The Power and Biology of Belief* (New York: Scribner, 1996), p. 109.

42. Gary Greenberg, "Is It Prozac or Placebo?" *Mother Jones,* November/December 2003.

43. Greenberg gives this figure in "Is It Prozac or Placebo?" Similar figures are found elsewhere.

44. Michael Brooks, "Anomalies: 13 Things That Don't Make Sense," *New Scientist,* March 19–25, 2005.

45. F. Benedetti, L. Colloca, E. Torre, et al. "Placebo-Responsive Parkinson Patients Show Decreased Activity in Single Neurons of Subthalamic Nucleus," *Nature Neuroscience* 7 (2004): 587–88.

46. R. de la Fuente-Fernández et al., "Expectation and Dopamine Release: Mechanism of the Placebo Effect in Parkinson's Disease," *Science* 293 (August 10, 2001): 1164–66. They write: "Our observations indicate that the placebo effect in PD is mediated by an increase in the synaptic levels of dopamine in the striatum. Expectation-related dopamine release might be a common phenomenon in any medical condition susceptible to the placebo effect. PD patients receiving an active drug in the context of a placebo-controlled study benefit from the active drug being tested as well as from the placebo effect."

47. Tor D. Wager, James K. Rilling, Edward E. Smith, Alex Sokolik, Kenneth L. Casey, Richard J. Davidson, Stephen M. Kosslyn, Robert M. Rose, Jonathan D. Cohen, "Placebo-Induced Changes in fMRI in the Anticipation and Experience of Pain," *Science* 303, no. 5661 (February 20, 2004): 1162–67. They write: "In two functional magnetic resonance imaging (fMRI) experiments, we found that placebo analgesia was related to decreased brain activity in pain-sensitive brain regions, including the thalamus, insula, and anterior cingulate cortex, and was associated with increased activity during anticipation of pain in the prefrontal cortex, providing evidence that placebos alter the experience of pain."

SIDEBAR

48. W. Grant Thompson, *The Placebo Effect and Health: Combining Science and Compassionate Care* (Amherst, MA: Prometheus, 2005), p. 42.

49. P. Petrovic, T. R. Dietrich, P. Fransson, J. Andersson, K Carlsson, and M. Ingvar, "Placebo in Emotional Processing–Induced Expectations of Anxiety Relief Activate a Generalized Modulatory Network," *Neuron* 46 (2005): 957–69. From the study findings: "Behaviorally, there was a strong decrease in the subjective rating of unpleasantness for the placebo conditions as compared to control conditions. For the placebo responders, the activity in extrastriate visual areas was significantly reduced in the placebo condition relative to the blocker condition for the unpleasant pictures. A correlation was found between the degree of change in unpleasantness rating due to placebo treatment and the suppression of placebo-dependent activity in the visual areas and amygdala/para-amygdaloid complex. Activation of the right lateral orbitofrontal cortex (lObfc), rostral anterior cingulate cortex (rACC), and ventrolateral prefrontal cortex (vlPFC) was also detected in placebo responders during the placebo response." Since a similar network has previously been shown to be activated in placebo analgesia, Petrovic and her colleagues (2005) concluded that modulatory processes in placebo are not specific for placebo analgesia, but are rather a part of the mechanisms generally implicated in emotional self-regulation, including instances of cognitive modulation of pain.

50. Barbara Lantin, "Healing Can Be All in the Mind," *Daily Telegraph,* October 25, 2002. See also Margaret Talbot, "The Placebo Prescription," *New York Times Magazine,* January 9, 2000.

51. C. McRae et al., "Effects of Perceived Treatment on Quality of Life and Medical Outcomes in a Double-Blind Placebo Surgery Trial," *Archives of General Psychiatry* 61 (2004): 412–20.

52. Herbert Benson and Marg Stark, *Timeless Medicine: The Power and Biology of Belief* (New York, Scribner, 1996), pp. 228–29.

53. R. Temple, "Implications of Effects in Placebo Groups," *Journal of the National Cancer Institute* 95, no. 1, 2–3 (January 1, 2003).

54. Lauran Neergaard, "The Placebo Effect May Be Good Medicine" *Pittsburgh Post Gazette,* November 30, 2005.

55. A paraphrase of material from the Mayo Clinic, "Placebo Effect: Harnessing Your Mind's Power to Heal," December 30, 2003.

56. Thompson, *Placebo Effect and Health,* p. 46. Some researchers have argued that the Hawthorne effect did not really occur at the Hawthorne plant. But practitioners tend to concur with Thompson that the effect really *does* occur in placebo-controlled studies, whether or not it occurred at Hawthorne.

57. Quoted in Reid, "Nocebo Effect."

58. This original meaning of *placebo* and its association with infant soothers is mute testimony to the fact that, in general, materialist medicine did not expect much from the placebo effect. The much more recent term, *nocebo* ("I will *harm*"), which first appeared in 1961, comes nearer the truth.

59. Reid, "Nocebo Effect."

60. See Benson and Stark, *Timeless Medicine,* pp. 40–43.

61. Susan McCarthy, "Spin Doctoring," *Salon,* July 15, 1999.

62. For a discussion of historical incidents, see Benson and Stark, *Timeless Medicine,* pp. 40–43.

63. For an excellent overview of the placebo/nocebo effect, see Thompson, *Placebo Effect and Health.*

64. See, for example, Thompson, *Placebo Effect and Health,* pp. 227–28.

65. Thompson, *Placebo Effect and Health,* p. 45.

66. Quoted in Thompson, *Placebo Effect and Health,* p. 49; originally from S. Wolf, "The Pharmacology of Placebos," *Pharmacological Reviews* 11 (1959): 689–74.

67. Thompson, *Placebo Effect and Health,* pp. 45–46.

68. For example, at the online (unidirectional) skeptic's dictionary, *Skepdic* (www.skepdic.com), a longish entry attempts to determine whether the placebo effect is psychological or physical, apparently on the assumption that it cannot be both (accessed February 18, 2006).

69. A. Hróbjartsson and P. Götzsche, "Is the Placebo Powerless? An Analysis of Clinical Trials Comparing Placebo with No Treatment," *New England Journal of Medicine* 344, no. 21 (May 24, 2001).

70. Alun Anderson, in response to the World Question Center 2006 question, "What is your dangerous idea?" http://www.edge.org/q2006/q06_6.html#23andersona (accessed January 13, 2007).

71. Jon-Kar Zubieta put it this way at a Society for Neuroscience meeting on the placebo effect in Washington, DC, on November 15, 2005: "These findings can have a tremendous impact on medicine as well as help us understand how the brain manipulates itself."

72. Lantin, "Healing Can Be All in the Mind."

73. Martin O'Malley, *Doctors* (Toronto: Macmillan, 1983), p. 2.

74. Thompson provides a useful discussion of this point (*Placebo Effect and Health,* p. 213).

75. McCarthy, "Spin Doctoring."

76. In both Africa and Asia it is common for educated urbanites to keep a foot in both camps by going to traditional as well as modern practitioners, citing the fact that traditional treatments help, while admitting that the doctrines underlying them are outdated.

77. Charles Sherrington, *Man on his Nature* (1940).

78. E. Perreau-Linck, M. Beauregard, P. Gravel, J. P. Soucy, M. Diksic, G. K. Essick, and C. Benkelfat, "Serotonin Metabolism During Self-Induced Sadness and Happiness in Professional Actors," paper presented at the Society for Neuroscience 34th Annual Meeting, October 23–27, 2004, San Diego, CA.

79. See M. Pelletier et al., "Separate Neural Circuits for Primary Emotions? Brain Activity During Self-Induced Sadness and Happiness in Professional Actors," *NeuroReport* 14 (2003): 1111–16.

80. See the discussion of altruism in Chapter One. Genuine altruism means that the individual helps others without thought of reward, and even at risk or cost, because such actions are perceived as morally right. This type of choice should not be confused with altruism studies in animals in which an individual helps its own genetic kin, forgoes a current benefit in order to claim a later one, or helps in order to gain higher status. In human affairs, these choices are not considered altruism.

81. B. Alan Wallace, *The Taboo of Subjectivity: Toward a New Science of Consciousness* (Oxford: Oxford University Press, 2000), p. 5.

82. Pim van Lommel, "About the Continuity of Our Consciousness," in *Brain Death and Disorders of Consciousness,* ed. Calixto Machado and D. Alan Shewmon (New York: Kluwer Academic / Plenum, 2004), p. 115.

83. From her own recollection on her Web site, http://www.geocities.com/pamreynoldsus/ (accessed March 9, 2006).

84. A large excerpt from Reynolds's account of her NDE is available at http://thegroundoffaith. orcon.net.nz/pam.html (accessed March 9, 2006).

85. Van Lommel, "About the Continuity of Our Consciousness," pp. 115–32.

86. Other accounts of perceiving a verifiable fact while in a state of apparent unconsciousness near death are recounted in K. Ring and M. Lawrence, "Further Evidence for Veridical Perception During Near-Death Experiences," *Journal of Near-Death Studies* 11.4 (1993): 223–29. For example, a nurse at Hartford Hospital states that she worked with a patient who described an NDE in which she saw a red shoe on the roof of the hospital during her OBE, which a janitor then retrieved. Kenneth Ring describes three such cases, involving shoes, shoelaces, and a yellow smock, and also tells a story from a Seattle social worker who also retrieved a shoe outside on a window ledge that was identified by a patient during an NDE.

87. See, for example, Robert S. Bobrow, "Paranormal Phenomena in the Medical Literature: Sufficient Smoke to Warrant a Search for Fire" (*Medical Hypotheses* 60.6 [2003]: 864–68), where anomalous cases are referenced.

88. Thomas Kuhn, *The Structure of Scientific Revolutions,* 2d ed. (Chicago: University of Chicago Press, 1970), pp. 17–18.

89. A Gallup survey in the United States in the early 1980s revealed that NDEs have been reported in about 4 percent of people who have been close to death. G. Gallup, *Adventures in Immortality: A Look Beyond the Threshold of Death* (New York: McGraw-Hill, 1982).

90. The use of the term "prospective" does not mean that he knew that specific individuals were going to have heart attacks, but that he intended to interview a group of presenting patients in the near future, while memories might be fresh.

91. Van Lommel, "About the Continuity of Our Consciousness," p. 121.

92. Van Lommel, "About the Continuity of Our Consciousness," pp. 120–23.

93. Van Lommel, "About the Continuity of Our Consciousness," p. 121.

94. Philosopher Sam Harris, doubts this, protesting, "I know my soul speaks English, because that is the language that comes out of me whenever I speak or write" (*The End of Faith: Religion, Terror, and the Future of Reason* [New York: Norton, 2004], pp. 278–79). The ability to produce language is universal among humans; English is a limited, local example of the tendency. Harris's soul might possibly draw from a larger well.

95. Kenneth Ring and Sharon Cooper, *Near Death and Out of Body Experiences in the Blind* (Palo Alto, CA: William James Center, 1999). Ring and Cooper interviewed thirty-one blind and sight-impaired persons who had NDEs and OBEs and found that most of them reported "visual" experiences, some in detail. In-depth case studies are presented and carefully analyzed to evaluate these claims, including verification from outside observers in some cases. Ring and Cooper contend that some form of vision without physical senses, which they call "mindsight," appears to have occurred during these experiences. Kenneth Ring is professor emeritus of psy-

chology at the University of Connecticut and co-founder and past president of the International Association for Near-Death Studies.

96. There is some controversy in the literature on impaired sight as to whether blind persons see in dreams. An obvious difficulty is that only the dreamer experiences a dream. A blind dreamer may "see" his beloved guide dog, and a sighted dreamer may "see" the same dog. But neither dreamer sees the actual dog. The advantage that the sighted may have over the blind in dreams needs careful delineation.

97. Developed by NDE researcher Bruce Greyson, the scale scores the depth of an experience based on graded responses to sixteen questions for a total score of 32. A minimum score of 7 generally qualifies as an NDE.

98. Michael Sabom, *Light and Death: One Doctor's Fascinating Account of Near-Death Experiences* (Grand Rapids, MI: Zondervan, 1998), pp. 32–34.

99. The religious mix for the whole group was 70 percent Protestant, 14 percent Catholic, 6 percent Jewish, 4 percent other faiths, and 5 percent of no religious affiliation. One person (not an NDEr) was an atheist. This is not an unusual statistical mix in the southern United States, where Catholics are a smaller demographic group and professed atheism is rare.

100. Sabom, *Light and Death,* p. 170.

101. Sabom, *Light and Death,* pp. 165–73. See also Bruce Greyson and Nancy Bush, "Distressing Near-Death Experiences," *Psychiatry,* 55.1 (February 1992): 95–110. Distressing experiences included loss of control, sense of nothingness, and nightmares come true.

102. Sabom notes, "Psychiatrists have studied this effect on suicide attempters and have postulated that during an NDE one feels a 'sense of cosmic unity' that causes the person to deemphasize 'worldly goals and begin to view his or her individual losses and failures as irrelevant from a transpersonal perspective'" (*Light and Death,* p. 211), thus obviating suicide attempts.

103. A. J. Ayer, "What I Saw When I Was Dead," *National Review,* October 14, 1988, pp. 38–40, quoted in Sabom, *Light and Death,* p. 209.

104. William Cash, "Did Atheist Philosopher See God When He 'Died'?" *National Post,* March 3, 2001.

105. Quoted in Sabom, *Light and Death,* p. 174.

106. Neal Grossman, "Who's Afraid of Life After Death?" *Journal of Near-Death Studies* 21.1 (Fall 2002): 21.

107. Van Lommel, "About the Continuity of Our Consciousness," p. 118.

108. Sabom lists the results from this questionnaire in the Table 4 appendix, p. 227, in *Light and Death.* The questionnaire was developed by NDE researcher Kenneth Ring to evaluate the effect of an NDE on subsequent life beliefs.

109. Sabom, *Light and Death,* pp. 96–97.

110. In response to the World Question Center 2006 question, "What is your dangerous idea?" ("The history of science is replete with discoveries that were considered socially, morally, or emotionally dangerous in their time; the Copernican and Darwinian revolutions are the most obvious"); http://www.edge.org/q2006/q06_12.html#23bloom (accessed January 13, 2007). January 1, 2006 *Edge* Question—a collection of mostly materialist essays.

111. O. Blanke, S. Ortigue, T. Landis, and M. Seeck, "Stimulating Illusory Own-Body Perceptions: The Part of the Brain That Can Induce Out-of-Body Experiences Has Been Located," *Nature* 419 (2002): 269–70.

112. Van Lommel, "About the Continuity of Our Consciousness," p. 119.

113. Jay Ingram, *Theatre of the Mind: Raising the Curtain on Consciousness* (Toronto: HarperCollins, 2005), pp. 56–57.

114. Susan Blackmore, *The Meme Machine* (Oxford: Oxford University Press, 1999), p. 181.

115. Jeffrey L. Saver and John Rabin, "The Neural Substrates of Religious Experience," *Journal of Neuropsychiatry and Clinical Neurosciences* 9 (1997): 498–510.

116. Saver and Rabin, "Neural Substrates of Religious Experience," p. 505.

117. From a conservative evangelical Christian megasite sponsored by Eden Communications, Christian Answers, http://www.christiananswers.net/q-eden/rfsm-nde.html (accessed March 9, 2006).

118. Grossman, "Who's Afraid of Life After Death?" p. 14.

119. Van Lommel, "About the Continuity of Our Consciousness," p. 115.

120. Grossman, "Who's Afraid of Life After Death?" p. 21.

121. Sabom, *Light and Death,* p. 66.

122. Van Lommel, "About the Continuity of Our Consciousness," p. 118.

123. Grossman, "Who's Afraid of Life After Death?" p. 8.

124. Grossman, "Who's Afraid of Life After Death?"

125. A. M. Turing, excerpt from "Computing Machinery and Intelligence," *Mind* 59, no. 236 (1950), reprinted in Hofstadter and Dennett, *Mind's I,* p. 66.

126. Hofstadter and Dennett, *Mind's I,* p. 68. Hofstadter and Dennett (p. 67) begin by reassuring their readers that the situation is not as bad as Turing thinks; the majority of physicists and psychologists doubt the existence of extrasensory perception in any form.

127. Radin, *Conscious Universe,* p. 2.

128. John McCrone, "Power of the Paranormal: Why It Won't Surrender to Science," *New Scientist,* March 13–19, 2004.

129. McCrone, "Power of the Paranormal," p. 37.

130. McCrone, "Power of the Paranormal."

131. Radin, *Conscious Universe,* p. 2.

132. Harris, *End of Faith,* p. 41.

133. Harris, *End of Faith,* p. 41.

134. Quoted in Radin, *Conscious Universe.* The preceding information regarding the mainstreaming of the study of psi effects is from Radin, pp. 3–5.

135. From material supplied by the James Randi Foundation at its Web site, http://www.randi.org/library/coldreading/index.html (accessed January 13, 2007).

136. Radin, *Conscious Universe,* p. 207.

137. "Self-Proclaimed 'Police Psychics' Can't Find Bodies, but They've Found the Spotlight," Center for Inquiry, July 1, 2005; http://www.centerforinquiry.net/newsrooms/070105.html (accessed January 13, 2007).

138. Carl Sagan, *The Demon-Haunted World: Science as a Candle in the Dark* (New York: Ballantine, 1996), p. 224.

139. Radin, *Conscious Universe,* p. 84.

140. Radin, *Conscious Universe,* p. 88.

141. Radin, *Conscious Universe,* p. 88.

142. Radin, *Conscious Universe,* pp. 138–45.

143. Radin, *Conscious Universe,* pp. 138–45.

144. Jiří Wackermann et al., "Correlations Between Brain Electrical Activities of Two Spatially Separated Human Subjects," *Neuroscience Letters* 336 (2003): 60–64. They state: "Six channels electroencephalogram (EEG) were recorded simultaneously from pairs of separated human subjects in two acoustically and electromagnetically shielded rooms. While brain electric responses to visual pattern-reversal stimuli were elicited in one subject, the other subject relaxed without stimulation. EEGs of both subjects were averaged at times of stimulus onset, effective voltage of the averaged signals was computed within a running window, and expressed as ratio (Q) to the effective voltage of averaged EEG signal from non-stimulation periods. These ratios in non-stimulated subjects at the latency of the maximum response in stimulated subjects were analysed. Significant departures of Q ratios from reference distributions, based on baseline EEG in non-stimulation periods, were found in most non-stimulated subjects. The results indicate that correlations between brain activities of two separated subjects may occur, although no biophysical mechanism is known."

145. Quoted in Radin, *Conscious Universe,* p. 207.

146. Ursula Goodenough, guest on "Healing Powers," PBS, May 20, 1996, broadcast.

147. Radin, *Conscious Universe,* p. 209.

148. Quoted in Radin, *Conscious Universe,* p. 213. He made the comment in "Chance," *Scientific American,* October 1965, pp. 44–54.

149. On April 27, 1900, Lord Kelvin gave a lecture to the Royal Institution of Great Britain, "Nineteenth-Century Clouds over the Dynamical Theory of Heat and Light," in which he adverted to these two clouds.

150. Radin, *Conscious Universe,* pp. 206–7.

151. Radin, *Conscious Universe,* pp. 250–51.

152. Radin, *Conscious Universe,* p. 287. The whole discussion (chap. 16) is illuminating.

153. Behaviorism postulated that a given stimulus resulted in a given response, and that no intervening mental state should be treated as significant. In humans, that account is clearly inaccurate. Pain, for example, is not simply the observed behavior of a subject in pain, but includes the subject's consciousness of pain which, as we have seen, can be greatly influenced by the placebo or nocebo effect. The *Stanford Encyclopedia of Philosophy* online provides a useful entry on this problem, http://plato.stanford.edu/entries/behaviorism/ (accessed January 13, 2007).

154. Radin, *Conscious Universe,* p. 263.

155. Harald Wallach and Stefan Schmidt, "Repairing Plato's Life Boat with Ockham's Razor: The Important Function of Research in Anomalies for Consciousness Studies," *Journal of Consciousness Studies* 12, no. 2 (2005): 52–70.

156. Radin, *Conscious Universe,* p. 295.

157. Why is it called Plato's Lifeboat? The Platonic school of astronomy argued that a scientific theory must accommodate all the data ("saving the appearances"); thus, a simplicity that ignores persistent counterexamples will not suffice in the long run. There is a limit to the usefulness of razors. See Wallach and Schmidt, "Repairing Plato's Life Boat with Ockham's Razor," pp. 54–55.

158. Wallach and Schmidt, "Repairing Plato's Life Boat with Ockham's Razor," p. 62.

159. Wallach and Schmidt might not have considered rescuing this effect (sometimes called the poltergeist effect) except for the curious case of theoretical physicist Wolfgang von Pauli (1900–1958), who predicted the neutrino, but apparently caused experiments to go wrong just by being in the lab. Radin notes George Gamow's witness to the locally disastrous "Pauli effect": "Apparatus would fall, break, shatter or burn when he merely walked into a laboratory" (Radin, *Conscious Universe,* p. 131). The cautious Otto Stern (1888–1969) apparently forbade Pauli to come into his laboratory on that account. Wallach and Schmidt note, "He himself took his so called 'Pauli-Effect' very seriously (Pietschmann, 1995; Enz, 1995). Pauli himself felt that these macro-PK effects were probably due to his inner psychological conflicts. Through the realization of his personality problems and their solution Pauli developed a strong conviction that physics would only be complete if it took into consideration consciousness as a part of reality (Meier, 1992; von Meyenn, 1996; Pauli, 1954). Therefore he stated the necessity of accounting for mentality in a physical theory (Pauli, 1952). It seems to us, therefore, that the occasional possibility of macro-PK should at least also find a place in Plato's Life Boat" (p. 63).

SIDEBAR

160. Dr. Kolb was speaking at the University of Toronto, September 23, 2005.

161. Members of elite science organizations, such as the National Academy of Sciences, may differ very much from the general public polled by statistics organizations.

162. E. Goode, *Paranormal Beliefs* (Prospect Heights, IL: Waveland, 2000), p. 2.

163. According to the Gallup organization, the beliefs include extrasensory perception (ESP), haunted houses, ghosts, mental telepathy, clairvoyance, astrology, communicating with the dead, witches, reincarnation, and channeling—in short, a risky mélange of assumptions about reality.

164. J. M. Schwartz, H. Stapp, and M. Beauregard, "Quantum Theory in Neuroscience and Psychology: A Neurophysical Model of Mind/Brain Interaction," *Philosophical Transactions of the Royal Society B: Biological Sciences* 360 (2005): 1309–27.

165. Schwartz and Begley, *Mind and the Brain,* p. 364.

166. See Chapter One for the controversies that enveloped astronomer Guillermo Gonzalez and taxonomist Richard Sternberg in 2005.

CHAPTER SEVEN: WHO HAS MYSTICAL EXPERIENCES AND WHAT TRIGGERS THEM?

1. William James, *The Varieties of Religious Experience* (New York: Random House, 1902), p. 80.

2. James, *Varieties of Religious Experience,* p. 281.

3. Evelyn Underhill, *Mysticism: A Study in the Nature and Development of Man's Spiritual Consciousness* (New York: New American Library / Meridian, 1974), p. xiv.

4. Richard Conn Henry, "The Mental Universe," *Nature* 436, no. 29 (July 7, 2005). Henry is a professor in the Henry A. Rowland Department of Physics and Astronomy at Johns Hopkins University.

5. W. T. Stace, *The Teachings of the Mystics* (New York: Macmillan, 1960), pp. 10–11. Specifically, he said, "Sometimes anything is called 'mystical' which is misty, foggy, vague, or sloppy. It is absurd that 'mysticism' should be associated with what is 'misty' because of the similar sound of the words. And there is nothing misty, foggy, vague, or sloppy about mysticism."

6. Stace, *Teachings of the Mystics,* p. 14. Stanford's online encyclopedia of philosophy gives the following definition: "A (purportedly) super sense-perceptual or sub sense-perceptual unitive experience granting acquaintance of realities or states of affairs that are of a kind not accessible by way of sense-perception, somatosensory modalities, or standard introspection." Jerome Gellman, "Mysticism," *Stanford Encyclopedia of Philosophy,* ed. Edward N. Zalta, spring 2005 ed., http://plato.stanford.edu/ archives/spr2005/entries/mysticism/.

7. Dean Radin, *The Conscious Universe: The Scientific Truth of Psychic Phenomena* (San Francisco: HarperSanFrancisco, 1997), p. 19.

8. Allan Smith, Psi Taste, http://www.issc-taste.org/arc/dbo.cgi?set=expom&id=00004&ss=1 (accessed January 13, 2007). This experience was written up in some detail in A. Smith and C. Tart, "Cosmic Consciousness Experience and Psychedelic Experiences: A First Person Comparison," *Journal of Consciousness Studies,* 5, no. 1 (1998): 97–107. In referring to Cosmic Consciousness, Smith follows the interpretation of early Canadian psychiatrist R. M. Bucke (*Cosmic Consciousness* [New Hyde Park, NY: University Books, 1961; originally published 1901], p. 8). Psi Taste provides an archive of a number of scientists' experiences of a great variety of states of altered consciousness.

9. Underhill, *Mysticism,* p. 83.

10. Underhill, *Mysticism,* p. 81.

11. Underhill, *Mysticism,* p. 46.

12. B. Alan Wallace, *The Taboo of Subjectivity: Toward a New Science of Consciousness* (Oxford: Oxford University Press, 2000), p. 6.

13. Wallace, *Taboo of Subjectivity,* pp. 103–18.

14. James, *Varieties of Religious Experience,* p. 283.

15. James is always conscious of materialism, but maintains his position nonetheless. He writes: "The current of thought in academic circles runs against me, and I feel like a man who must set his back against an open door quickly if he does not wish to see it closed and locked. In spite of its being so shocking to the reigning intellectual tastes, I believe that a candid consideration of piecemeal supernaturalism and a complete discussion of all its metaphysical bearings will show it to be the hypothesis by which the largest number of legitimate requirements are met" (p. 387). For a man of his time, who did not know how the battle would go, that was brave.

16. "Western" mystics are influenced by the Christian, Jewish, Sufi (and probably other) Muslim traditions, and by Platonism and neo-Platonism. Generally, they assume a divine author of or law-giving power behind the universe.

17. This, readers will recall, is similar to one of the problems raised with Persinger's research (Chapter Four). Persinger had developed a set of measurement tools that did not correspond to the ones generally used.

SIDEBAR

18. James, *Varieties of Religious Experience,* pp. 281–83. These are only brief quotations from a much fuller and very useful discussion. James's *Varieties* can be downloaded at Project Gutenberg, http://onlinebooks.library.upenn.edu/webbin/gutbook/lookup?num=621 (accessed January 13, 2007).

19. James's claim regarding transiency has been questioned. Some mystics have experienced mystical states that lasted for days. See Gellman, "Mysticism."

20. Underhill, *Mysticism,* p. 81.

21. *Emile Durkheim on Morality and Society,* ed. Robert N. Bellah, Heritage of Sociology Series (Chicago: University of Chicago Press, 1973), p. 51.

22. For an explanation of why this view does not account for the evidence, see Rodney Stark, "Why Gods Should Matter in Social Science," *Chronicle Review,* June 6, 2003. There is no consistent relationship between the performance of ritual and the spiritual or moral aspects of a religious tradition.

SIDEBAR

23. Stace, *Teachings of the Mystics,* pp. 20–21. Stace notes, "Not only in Christianity and Hinduism but everywhere else we find that the essence of this experience is that it is an undifferentiated unity, though each culture and each religion interprets this undifferentiated unity in terms of its own creeds and dogmas."

24. One can argue that these religious proclamations aim at social stability by restoring a better social order, but contemporary officeholders seldom agree.

25. Peter Berger, *The Desecularization of the World* (Grand Rapids, MI: Eerdmans, 1999), p. 2.

26. Berger, *Desecularization of the World,* p. 4. Berger depicts a typical secular intellectual from Western Europe visiting the faculty club at the University of Texas: "He may think he is back home. But then picture him trying to drive through the traffic jam on Sunday morning in downtown Austin—or, heaven help him, turning on his car radio! What happens then is a severe jolt of what anthropologists call culture shock" (p. 11).

27. S. Arzy et al., "Why Revelations Have Occurred on Mountains? Linking Mystical Experiences and Cognitive Neuroscience," *Medical Hypotheses* 65 (2005): 841–45.

28. James, *Varieties of Religious Experience,* p. 51. James received this account from a collection made by a Professor Flournoy and translated it from the original French.

29. Quoted in James, *Varieties of Religious Experience,* p. 309.

30. Underhill, *Mysticism,* p. 80.

31. Rudolf Otto, *The Idea of the Holy,* trans. John W. Harvey (London: Oxford University Press, 1971), pp. 23–24. Otto does not deprecate all theological controversy, but rather controversy based on word choices for experiences that, although authentic, defy effective description.

32. 1 Cor. 2:9, NIV. Paul admitted to a mystical bent (see Chapter Three).

33. For useful discussions of description by negation, see Otto, *Idea of the Holy,* pp. 29, 34–35, or James, *Varieties of Religious Experience,* pp. 308–9.

34. James, *Varieties of Religious Experience,* p. 308.

35. Gellman, "Mysticism."

36. John of the Cross, "En Una Noche Escura." Quoted in Evelyn Underhill, *Mysticism* (New York: New American Library, 1974), p. 371.

37. Anne McIlroy, "Hard-Wired for God," *Globe and Mail,* December 6, 2003.

38. Some Buddhist writings sound like familiar Western genres, such as the hellfire sermon. This example is from the monk Bodhidharma, who brought Buddhism from India to China in 540 B.C.E.: "When delusions are absent, the mind is the land of buddhas. When delusions are present, the mind is hell.... You go from one hell to the next." From http://www.zaadz.com/quotes/topics/buddhism (accessed March 31, 2006).

39. Underhill, *Mysticism,* pp. 370–71.

40. Stace, *Teachings of the Mystics,* p. 15. Gellman agrees, noting: "Care should be taken not to confuse mystical experience with 'religious experience.' The latter refers to any experience having content or significance appropriate to a religious context or that has a 'religious' flavor. This would include much of mystical experience, but also religious visions and auditions, nonmystical Zen experiences, and various religious feelings, such as religious awe and sublimity" ("Mysticism").

41. Barna Research, "Born Again Christians," in "Defining Evangelicalism," Institute for the Study of American Evangelicals, 2003; http://www.wheaton.edu/isae/defining_evangelicalism.html (accessed January 13, 2007).

42. Adapted from Larry Eskridge, "Defining Evangelicalism," a report provided by the Institute for the Study of American Evangelicals, 1995, revised 2006; http://www.wheaton.edu/isae/defining_evangelicalism.html.

43. Quoted in Gellman, "Mysticism" (Russell, 1935, 188).

SIDEBAR

44. Adapted from Eskridge, "Defining Evangelicalism."

45. Some argue that children and uneducated adults are more likely to experience these "veridical" visions. If so, they may be related to a less developed faculty for abstraction.

46. Quoted in Underhill, *Mysticism,* p. 280.

47. Quoted in Underhill, *Mysticism,* p. 281.

48. Stace, *Teachings of the Mystics,* p. 12.

49. Underhill, *Mysticism,* p. 224.

50. Gellman lists "hypersuggestibility, severe deprivation, severe sexual frustration, intense fear of death, infantile regression, pronounced maladjustment, and mental illness as well as non-pathological conditions, including the inordinate influence of a religious psychological 'set' (see Davis, 1989, chap. 8, and Wulff, 2000)" ("Mysticism").

51. See, for example, Fales, 1996a, 1996b, as noted by Gellman in "Mysticism."

52. Gellman, "Mysticism."

53. Underhill, *Mysticism,* p. 60.

54. Gerald M. Edelman and Giulio Tononi, *A Universe of Consciousness: How Matter Becomes Imagination* (New York: Basic Books, 2000), p. 191.

55. Deborah Solomon, "The Nonbeliever," an interview with Daniel Dennett, New York Times, January 22, 2006.

56. Alister Hardy, "Natural History Old and New," an inaugural address, University of Aberdeen, 1942 (reprinted from *Fishing News*).

57. Alister Hardy, *The Spiritual Nature of Man* (Oxford: Clarendon, 1979), p. 21.

58. Hardy, *Spiritual Nature of Man,* p. 1. Some of these experiences may have involved mystical consciousness.

59. Hardy, *Spiritual Nature of Man,* p. 91.

60. Hardy, *Spiritual Nature of Man,* pp. 83– 84.

61. Hardy, *Spiritual Nature of Man,* p. 123.

62. Hardy, *Spiritual Nature of Man,* p. 28.

63. Hardy, *Spiritual Nature of Man,* pp. 131–32.
64. Hardy, *Spiritual Nature of Man,* p. 2.
65. See Hardy, *Spiritual Nature of Man,* pp. 126ff. The quoted expression is the original, written by Michael Weisskopf of the *Washington Post* (February 1, 1993), though it sometimes appears in the form echoed by Michael Kinsley, also of the *Post* (July 3, 2005), as "poor, undereducated and easily led."

SIDEBAR

66. Stephen Fraser, "Newly Released Letters Tell of Jesus Calling Mother Teresa 'My Little Wife,'" *Scotland on Sunday,* December 8, 2002.

67. Hardy, *Spiritual Nature of Man,* pp. 30, 127.
68. James McClenon, "Mysticism," *Encyclopedia of Religion and Society,* ed. William H. Swatos, Jr., Hartford Institute for Religion Research, Altamira Press, http://hirr.hartsem.edu/ency/Mysticism.htm (accessed April 5, 2006).
69. Hardy, *Spiritual Nature of Man,* pp. 104–8.
70. Hardy, *Spiritual Nature of Man,* p. 106.
71. Hardy, *Spiritual Nature of Man,* p. 141.
72. See, for example, Hardy's discussion of God as a loving parent (*Spiritual Nature of Man,* p. 135), where he argues that humans resemble juvenile chimpanzees and thus seek parental love. One difficulty with his thesis is that a strong emphasis on God as a *personal and loving* parent (whether Father or Mother), as opposed to an impersonal All-Father or Earth Mother, was not widespread in known antiquity. The teachings of Jesus, who called God *abba* ("Daddy"), were highly controversial when first introduced around 30 C.E.
73. Steve Waldman, "On Belief: The Pearly Gates Are Wide Open," Beliefnet, http://www.beliefnet.com/story/173/story_17348_1.html (accessed April 4, 2006).
74. Underhill, *Mysticism,* p. 96
75. Quoted in Underhill, *Mysticism,* p. 85.
76. Subhuti was one of Gautama's ten major disciples.
77. It is sometimes difficult to disentangle mystical experiences from attempts at magic in early cultures, but they are separable. An excellent introduction to magical thinking is James George Frazer's *The Golden Bough* (1890), of which the 1922 edition is online and searchable at www.bartleby.com. Frazer's technologically primitive subjects urgently want material benefits for themselves and material evils for enemies. Their magical thinking bears no relation to the classic stance of the mystic: "Though he slay me, yet will I love him" (Job 13:15) or "I fell at his feet as one dead" (Rev. 1:17), entirely detached from material self-interest and seeking only to know ultimate reality, whatever the cost.
78. Underhill, *Mysticism,* pp. 42, 370–71.
79. Aldous Huxley, *The Perennial Philosophy* (New York: Harper and Brothers, 1945), p. 134.
80. Gellman ("Mysticism") notes that William Wainwright proposed four modes of mystical extrovertive experience and two of introvertive ones: *mystic extrovertive experiences:* "a sense of the unity of nature, of nature as a living presence, a sense that everything transpiring in nature is in an eternal present, and the Buddhist unconstructed experience"; *mystic introvertive experiences:* "pure empty consciousness, and theistic experience marked by an awareness of an object in 'mutual love'" (Wainwright, 1981, chap. 1). He also adds that R. C. Zaehner (1961) classified mystic consciousness into three types, a sense of union with all of nature, a sense of union with the universe that transcended space and time, and a sense of union with a divine presence.
81. Gellman notes that Stace has been rebuked for "simplifying or distorting mystical reports" noting that Moore (1973) summarizes such instances: "For example, Pike criticizes the Stace-Smart position because in Christian mysticism union with God is divided into discernable phases, which find no basis in Christian theology. These phases, therefore, plausibly reflect experience and not forced interpretation (Pike, 1992, Chapter 5)" ("Mysticism").

82. For an interesting discussion, see Gellman, "Mysticism."

83. Francis Galton, *National Review* 23 (1894): 755.

84. Edward O. Wilson, *Sociobiology,* abridged ed. (Cambridge, MA: Harvard University Press, 1980), p. 286.

85. Underhill, *Mysticism,* p. 17.

86. Underhill, *Mysticism,* p. 55.

87. James, *Varieties of Religious Experience,* pp. 70–71.

88. James, *Varieties of Religious Experience,* p. 370. See the whole discussion, pp. 368–72.

89. The process by which philosophers arrived at this point is meticulously described by Australian philosopher David Stove in *Darwinian Fairytales* (Aldershot, UK: Avebury, 1995).

90. Edward O. Wilson, "Intelligent Evolution: The Consequences of Charles Darwin's 'One Long Argument,'" *Harvard Magazine,* November–December 2005, p. 30.

91. Michael Shermer, "Unweaving the Heart: Science Only Adds to Our Appreciation for Poetic Beauty and Experience of Emotional Depth," *Scientific American,* October 2005.

92. J. R. Minke, "Psyching Out Evolutionary Psychology: Interview with David J. Buller," *Scientific American,* July 4, 2005.

93. Links to articles available in 2005 advancing these claims are provided at http://www.arn.org/ blogs/index.php/2/2006/04/03/lstrongglemgdarwinian_fairy_tales_l_emg__9.

94. *Neurotheology* is defined thus at http://www.answers.com/neurothology (accessed 10/5/2005). The same entry identifies Persinger's God helmet work (see Chapter Four) as "an instant sensation" and "a landmark study."

95. Indeed, evolutionary psychology has popularized a tense in English, the "would have had" of prehistoric conjecture, as in "The men of the Pleistocene *would have had* to kill their stepchildren in order to …" History for which we have evidence is written in the simple past tense.

96. The French government provides a virtual tour at http://www.culture.gouv.fr/culture/arcnat/lascaux/en/.

97. The Museum of Natural History, Vienna, http://www.nhm-wien.ac.at/nhm/Prehist/Collection/ Objekte_PA_01_E.html.

98. Deborah Solomon, "The Nonbeliever," an interview with Daniel Dennett, *New York Times,* January 22, 2006.

99. Casper Soeling and Eckert Voland, "Toward an Evolutionary Psychology of Religiosity," *Neuroendocrinology Letters: Human Ethology & Evolutionary Psychology* 23, suppl. 4 (December 2002), from the abstract.

100. Steve Paulson, "Religious Belief Itself Is an Adaptation," an interview with E. O. Wilson, *Salon,* March 21, 2006.

101. E. O. Wilson, *Consilience: The Unity of Knowledge* (New York: Random House, 1998), p. 288.

102. Wilson, *Consilience,* p. 291.

103. Paulson, "Religious Belief Itself Is an Adaptation."

104. Soeling and Voland, "Toward an Evolutionary Psychology of Religiosity."

105. David Sloan Wilson, *Darwin's Cathedral: Evolution, Religion, and the Nature of Society* (Chicago: University of Chicago Press, 2002), p. 228.

106. Wilson, *Darwin's Cathedral,* p. 228. Actually, many messed-up atheist historians have been drawn to the life of Jesus, but typically they gain more insight than they provide.

107. Wilson, *Darwin's Cathedral,* p. 228.

108. Wilson, *Darwin's Cathedral,* p. 230.

109. Thomas Kuhn, *The Structure of Scientific Revolutions,* 2d ed. (Chicago: University of Chicago Press, 1970), p. 68.

110. Leon Wieseltier, "The God Genome," *New Republic,* February 19, 2006, a review of Daniel C. Dennett's *Breaking the Spell: Religion as a Natural Phenomenon* (New York: Viking, 2006).

111. Pascal Boyer, *Religion Explained: The Evolutionary Origins of Religious Thought* (New York: Basic Books, 2001), p. 329.

112. Boyer, *Religion Explained,* p. 4.

113. Boyer, *Religion Explained,* p. 328.
114. Pascal Boyer, "Why Is Religion Natural?" *Skeptical Inquirer,* March 2004.
115. This point is made by W. G. Runciman, in "Are We Hardwired for God?" a review of Boyer's *Religion Explained, Guardian Unlimited,* February 7, 2002.
116. Keith E. Stanovich, *The Robot's Rebellion: Finding Meaning in the Age of Darwin* (Chicago: University of Chicago Press, 2004); pp. 4–11 can be read online at http://www.press.uchicago.edu/Misc/Chicago/770893.html (accessed January 13, 2007).
117. Jerry Fodor, "The Selfish Gene Pool," *Times Literary Supplement,* July 27, 2005, a review of David J. Buller, *Adapting Minds* (Cambridge, MA: MIT Press, 2005).
118. Mary Midgley, quoted in Alister McGrath, *Dawkins's God: Genes, Memes, and the Meaning of Life* (Oxford: Blackwell, 2005), p. 41.
119. Steven Pinker, "Yes, Genes Can Be Selfish," *Times,* March 4, 2006, http://www.timesonline.co.uk/article/0,,23114-2066881,00.html (accessed January 13, 2007).
120. See Chapter Five.
121. Fodor, "The Selfish Gene Pool."
122. Fodor, "The Selfish Gene Pool."
123. Stove, *Darwinian Fairytales,* p. 27. The late David Stove, an agnostic who accepted evolution and was most certainly *not* trying to promote a religion, offers a closely reasoned critique of selfish-gene theory, from the standpoint of human nature, as historically known. (*Note:* The huge increase in human population in recent decades derives mainly from increasing life expectancies, not increasing birthrates.)
124. Richard Dawkins, *The Selfish Gene* (New York: Oxford University Press, 1989), p. 193.
125. Susan Blackmore, "The Forget-Meme-Not Theory," *Times Higher Education Supplement,* February 26, 1999. The term *meme* was coined by Dawkins in 1976 by analogy to *phoneme,* a unit of spoken language, via *mimeme,* a theoretical unit of imitation.
126. William L. Benzon, "Colorless Green Homunculi," *Human Nature Review* 2 (October 17, 2002): 454–62, a review of Robert Aunger, *The Electric Meme: A New Theory of How We Think* (New York: Free Press, 2002).
127. Susan Blackmore, "The Power of Memes," *Scientific American* 283, no. 4 (October 2000): 52–61.
128. Blackmore, "The Power of Memes."
129. Dawkins famously referred to religions as "viruses of the mind" (*Free Inquiry,* Summer 1993, pp. 34–41).
130. Alister McGrath has noted that Dawkins in *The Selfish Gene* defined memes in such a way as to make them equivalent not to genes, but to phenotypes, the actual body plans produced by genes. However, Dawkins changed his description of memes between *The Selfish Gene* (1976) and the less widely read *The Extended Phenotype* (1982). But most popular discussion assumes either the "selfish gene" model or the viral one, or else does not clearly distinguish between them.
131. Dawkins, *Selfish Gene,* p. 214–15.
132. Blackmore, "The Forget-Meme-Not Theory."
133. Susan Blackmore, *The Meme Machine* (Oxford: Oxford University Press, 1999), p. 192.
134. Blackmore, *Meme Machine,* p. 203.
135. Dawkins, *A Devil's Chaplain* (New York: Houghton Mifflin, 2003), p. 145, quoted in McGrath, p. 124.
136. McGrath, *Dawkins's God,* p. 124.
137. A handy test is to read any given text that discusses "memes" and substitute the word "ideas." Note whether loss of information results.
138. McGrath, *Dawkins's God,* p. 128.
139. Jiří Wackermann et al., "Correlations Between Brain Electrical Activities of Two Spatially Separated Human Subjects," *Neuroscience Letters* 336 (2003): 60–64.
140. McGrath, *Dawkins's God,* p. 137.

141. Robert C. Aunger, ed., *Darwinizing Culture: The Status of Memetics as a Science* (Oxford: Oxford University Press, 2001).

142. Aunger, ed., *Darwinizing Culture;* chap. 1 is available as a .pdf at http://www.cus.cam.ac.uk/~rva20/Darwin1.pdf (accessed January 13, 2007).

143. Susan Blackmore, "Can Memes Get off the Leash?" in Aunger, ed., *Darwinizing Culture,* chap. 2.

144. Blackmore, "Can Memes Get off the Leash?"

145. McGrath, *Dawkins's God,* p. 135.

146. Richard Brodie, *Virus of the Mind: The New Science of the Meme* (Seattle: Integral Press, 1996), p. 15.

147. Aunger, ed., *Darwinizing Culture,* from chap. 1, .pdf at http://www.cus.cam.ac.uk/~rva20/Darwin1.pdf (accessed January 13, 2007).

148. Benzon, "Colorless Green Homunculi."

149. Joseph Giovannoli, *The Biology of Belief: How Our Biology Biases Our Beliefs and Perceptions* (New York: Rosetta, 2000).

150. Howard Bloom, *The Lucifer Principle* (New York: Atlantic Monthly Press, 1997), p. 98.

151. Brodie, *Virus of the Mind,* p. 13.

152. Brodie, *Virus of the Mind,* p. 14.

153. Brodie, *Virus of the Mind,* pp. 187–88.

154. Brodie, *Virus of the Mind,* p. 191.

155. Sharon Begley, "Evolutionary Psych May Not Help Explain Our Behavior After All," *Wall Street Journal,* April 29, 2005. Begley is commenting on Buller's *Adapting Minds.*

156. Hilary Rose, in "Colonising the Social Sciences?" in Hilary Rose and Steven Rose, eds., *Alas, Poor Darwin: Arguments Against Evolutionary Psychology* (London: Random House, Vintage, 2001), notes that abusers are usually not "stepparents" as such but live-in mates who have never desired or accepted responsibility for any children, their own or others', a fact identified more often by crime-beat reporters than by evolutionary psychologists. She writes, "It is embarrassing to have to praise the journalists' account of family and sexual relationships as more precise than that of the psychologists" (p. 122). She also observes that in racist societies, natural fathers ignore genetic children of the "subjugated" race, which hardly supports the view that there is either a genetic or a neural program for recognizing and rewarding one's own children.

157. Buller, *Adapting Minds.*

158. Minke, "Psyching Out Evolutionary Psychology." See also Mike Holderness, "We're Not the Flintstones," *New Scientist,* April 16, 2005, a review of Buller, *Adapting Minds.*

159. Stove sets out his argument in *Darwinian Fairytales.*

160. David J. Buller, "Evolutionary Psychology: The Emperor's New Paradigm," *Trends in Cognitive Science* 9.6 (June 2005): 277–83.

161. Adam Kirsch, "If Men Are from Mars, What's God?" *New York Sun,* February 8, 2006.

162. Roger Scruton, "Dawkins Is Wrong About God," *Spectator,* January 12, 2006.

163. The German original, *Das Heilige,* appeared in 1917; the English translation by John W. Harvey, *The Idea of the Holy,* in 1923. Quotations are taken from a 1971 reissue (London: Oxford University Press).

164. Otto, *Idea of the Holy,* pp. 6, 15.

165. The Spirit (Kermode) Bear is a variety of black bear found in western Canada that has a white coat and is thus visible from a distance. It has, of course, been the focus of considerable lore and legend as well as passionate conservation efforts.

166. Otto, *Idea of the Holy,* p. 35; italics in original.

167. Otto thought (*Idea of the Holy,* p. 33) that the numinous might have originated in attempts at magic, but gradually become detached from them, as pursuit of a growing awareness of the numinous became a goal for its own sake. His view is consistent with the fact that traditional shamans have typically practiced both mysticism and magic, but developed religions later separated them (and often strictly forbade magic).

168. Otto, *Idea of the Holy,* pp. 26–27, 35.

169. Otto, *Idea of the Holy,* p. 55.

170. An excellent fair-minded source for the Toronto Airport Blessing is James Beverley, *Holy Laughter and the Toronto Blessing: An Investigative Report* (Grand Rapids, MI: Zondervan, 1995).

CHAPTER EIGHT: DO RELIGIOUS, SPIRITUAL, OR MYSTICAL EXPERIENCES
CHANGE LIVES?

1. Alister McGrath, *Dawkins's God: Genes, Memes, and the Meaning of Life* (Oxford: Blackwell, 2005), p. 136.

2. Deborah Solomon's "The Nonbeliever," an interview with Daniel Dennett (*New York Times,* January 22, 2006), certainly fits this category. From it, we learn such Dennett pearls as: "Churches make a great show about the creed, but they don't really care. A lot of the evangelicals don't really care what you believe as long as you say the right thing and do the right thing and put a lot of money in the collection box." Far from asking Dennett to substantiate such large claims, Solomon merely replies, "I take it you are not a churchgoer." Similar puffs extrude from George Johnson, "Getting a Rational Grip on Religion," *Scientific American,* December 26, 2005; and Tim Adams, "Darwin's Defender," *Guardian,* March 12, 2006.

3. Adam Kirsch, "If Men Are from Mars, What's God?" *New York Sun,* February 8, 2006.

4. Leon Wieseltier, "The God Genome," *New Republic,* February 19, 2006, a review of Daniel C. Dennett, *Breaking the Spell: Religion as a Natural Phenomenon* (New York: Viking, 2006).

5. Roger Scruton, "Dawkins Is Wrong About God," *Spectator,* January 12, 2006, commenting on Dawkins's Channel 4 TV series *The Root of All Evil?*

6. Madeleine Bunting. "No Wonder Atheists Are Angry: They Seem Ready to Believe Anything," *Guardian,* January 7, 2006, a review of *The Root of All Evil?* (UK TV Channel 4).

7. David P. Barash, "Dennett and the Darwinizing of Free Will," *Human Nature Review* 3 (2003): 222–25, a review of Daniel C. Dennett, *Freedom Evolves* (New York: Viking, 2003).

8. Kirsch, "If Men Are from Mars."

9. Herbert Benson and Marg Stark, *Timeless Medicine: The Power and Biology of Belief* (New York: Scribner, 1996), p. 121.

10. Darwinian fitness means leaving fertile descendants. Religiously devout communities usually succeed at that, but so do other organized and peaceful communities such as nonreligious kibbutzes—and, as we have seen, RSMEs are rarely embraced for that purpose.

11. Benson and Stark, *Timeless Medicine,* p. 17.

12. Benson and Stark, *Timeless Medicine,* p. 21.

13. Benson and Stark, *Timeless Medicine,* p. 30.

14. Benson and Stark, *Timeless Medicine,* p. 45.

15. Benson and Stark, *Timeless Medicine,* pp. 116–17.

16. Benson and Stark, *Timeless Medicine,* p. 45.

17. Benson and Stark, *Timeless Medicine,* pp. 99–100.

18. See, for example, the opposition to the decision to ask the Dalai Lama to address a recent neuroscience meeting, discussed at the beginning of Chapter Nine.

19. The relationship between mental stress and high blood pressure (hypertension) is still uncertain. What's no longer controversial is the idea that stress could, *in principle,* be a factor.

20. L. Hawkley and J. Cacioppo, "Loneliness Is a Unique Predictor of Age-Related Differences in Systolic Blood Pressure," *Psychology and Aging* 21.1 (March 2006): 152–64. The study was funded in part by the Templeton Foundation.

21. William Harms, "Loneliness Linked to High Blood Pressure in Aging Adults," *Science Daily,* March 28, 2006. NIA was also a source of funds for the Hawkley and Cacioppo study.

22. Shankar Vedantam, "Drugs Cure Depression in Half of Patients: Doctors Have Mixed Reactions to Study Findings," *Washington Post,* March 23, 2006. A federal advisory panel noted that, despite the very high level of patient care provided in a tax-funded study (the largest of its kind), Celexa, Wellbutrin, Zoloft, and Effexor helped only about half of patients. They "work in very

different ways yet had roughly equal effectiveness when it came to treating depression. This suggests that the underlying brain mechanisms of depression are far more complicated than simple notions of a single chemical imbalance."

23. Benson and Stark, *Timeless Medicine*, p. 152.

24. Benson and Stark, *Timeless Medicine*, p. 172.

25. Jeff Levin and Harold G. Koenig, eds., *Faith, Medicine, and Science: A Festschrift in Honor of Dr. David B. Larson* (New York: Haworth, 2005), pp. 15–16.

26. In Levin and Koenig, eds., *Faith, Medicine, and Science*, p. 219.

27. In Levin and Koenig, eds., *Faith, Medicine, and Science*, p. 19.

28. In Levin and Koenig, eds., *Faith, Medicine, and Science*, p. 82.

29. Michael Sabom, *Light and Death: One Doctor's Fascinating Account of Near-Death Experiences* (Grand Rapids, MI: Zondervan, 1998), p. 82.

30. Levin and Koenig, eds., *Faith, Medicine, and Science*, pp. 16, 140.

31. Levin and Koenig, eds., *Faith, Medicine, and Science*, p. 16.

32. Levin and Koenig, eds., *Faith, Medicine, and Science*, pp. 142–43.

33. Levin and Koenig, eds., *Faith, Medicine, and Science*, p. 20.

34. Levin and Koenig, eds., *Faith, Medicine, and Science*, p. 85.

35. Sabom, *Light and Death*, pp. 81–82.

36. H. M. Helm et al., "Does Private Religious Activity Prolong Survival: A Six-Year Follow-Up Study of 3,851 Older Adults," *Journals of Gerontology*, Series A, Biological and Medical Sciences 55 (2000): M400–405. This advantage of RSMEs cannot result from evolution by natural selection (Darwinian evolution), as evolutionary psychologists might wish to argue, because the age group represented is *too old* for reproduction to provide a selection factor. If the advantage relates to evolution, it points to non-Darwinian factors that have not so far been adequately addressed.

37. K. I. Pargament et al., "Religious Struggle as a Predictor of Mortality Among Medically Ill Elderly Patients," *Archives of Internal Medicine* 161 (August 13/27, 2001): 1881–85.

38. Sabom, *Light and Death*, p. 126.

39. G. McCord, Valerie J. Gilchrist, Steven D. Grossman, Bridget D. King, Kenelm F. McCormick, Allison M. Oprandi et al., "Discussing Spirituality with Patients: A Rational and Ethical Approach," *Annals of Family Medicine* 2 (2004): 256–361.

40. Farr A. Curlin, John D. Lantos, Chad J. Roach, Sarah A. Sellergren, Marshall H. Chin, "Religious Characteristics of U.S. Physicians," *Journal of General Intern Medicine* 20 (2005): 629–34.

41. Amy L. Ai, Christopher Peterson, Willard L. Rodgers, and Terrence N. Tice, "Faith Factors and Internal Health Locus of Control in Patients Prior to Open-heart Surgery," *Journal of Health Psychology* 10.5 (2005): 669–76. The study warns against using the question of internal vs. external locus of control as equivalent to good vs. poor coping styles; the subject may accurately recognize the amount of control that he or she actually has over events surrounding major surgery. See also Miranda Hitti, "Religious Beliefs May Lessen Post-Op Stress," *WebMD* (Fox News), August 10, 2006, http://www.foxnews.com/story/0,2933,207881,00.html an account of Ai and her colleagues' work presented at the American Psychological Association's 2006 convention.

42. Michael Conlon, "Study Fails to Show Healing Power of Prayer," *Reuters,* March 30, 2006.

43. Oliver Burkeman, "If You Want to Get Better—Don't Say a Little Prayer," *Guardian,* April 1, 2006.

44. M. Krucoff, S. Crater, and L. Kerry, "From Efficacy to Safety Concerns: A Step Forward or a Step Back for Clinical Research and Intercessory Prayer? The Study of Therapeutic Effects of Intercessory Prayer," *American Heart Journal* 151.4 (April 2006): 763.

45. Quoted in Gregory M. Lamb, "Study Highlights Difficulty of Isolating Effect of Prayer on Patients," *Christian Science Monitor,* April 3, 2006.

46. H. Benson et al., "Study of the Therapeutic Effects of Intercessory Prayer (STEP) in Cardiac Bypass Patients: A Multicenter Randomized Trial of Uncertainty and Certainty of Receiving Intercessory Prayer," *American Heart Journal* 151.4 (April 2006): 934–42.

47. William S. Harris et al., "A Randomized, Controlled Trial of the Effects of Remote, Intercessory Prayer on Outcomes in Patients Admitted to the Coronary Care Unit," *Archives of Internal Medicine* 159 (1999): 2273–78. The conclusion was: "Remote, intercessory prayer was associated with lower CCU course scores. This result suggests that prayer may be an effective adjunct to standard medical care."

48. D. A. Matthews, S. M. Marlowe, and F. S. MacNutt, "Effects of Intercessory Prayer on Patients with Rheumatoid Arthritis," *Southern Medical Journal* 93.12 (December 2000): 1177–86. "Patients receiving in-person intercessory prayer showed significant overall improvement during 1-year follow-up. No additional effects from supplemental, distant intercessory prayer were found. Conclusions: In-person intercessory prayer may be a useful adjunct to standard medical care for certain patients with rheumatoid arthritis. Supplemental, distant intercessory prayer offers no additional benefits."

49. Lamb, "Study Highlights Difficulty."

50. Benson et al., "STEP in Cardiac Bypass Patients," p. 934. "In the 2 groups uncertain about receiving intercessory prayer, complications occurred in 52 percent (315/604) of patients who received intercessory prayer versus 51 percent (304/597) of those who did not (relative risk 1.02, 95 percent CI 0.92–1.15). Complications occurred in 59 percent (352/601) of patients certain of receiving intercessory prayer compared with the 52 percent (315/604) of those uncertain of receiving intercessory prayer (relative risk 1.14, 95 percent CI 1.02–1.28). Major events and 30-day mortality were similar across the 3 groups."

51. Krucoff et al., "From Efficacy to Safety Concerns," p. 763.

52. Krucoff et al., "From Efficacy to Safety Concerns."

53. Krucoff et al., "From Efficacy to Safety Concerns."

54. Krucoff et al., "From Efficacy to Safety Concerns."

55. This is a difficult problem. Most patients enrolled in a study assume that they are in the experiment group, not the control group, even if their chances are 50-50 or less. That factor helps to power the placebo effect.

56. Lamb, "Study Highlights Difficulty."

57. Quoted in Lamb, "Study Highlights Difficulty."

58. Krucoff et al, "From Efficacy to Safety Concerns."

59. Richard Sloan, professor of behavioral medicine at Columbia University, quoted in Burkeman, "If You Want to Get Better."

60. Gary P. Posner, "God in the CCU? A Critique of the San Francisco Hospital Study on Intercessory Prayer and Healing," *Free Inquiry,* Spring 1990.

61. R. C. Byrd, "Positive Therapeutic Effects of Intercessory Prayer in a Coronary Care Unit Population," *Southern Medical Journal* 81.7 (July 1988): 826–29.

62. Alister Hardy, *The Spiritual Nature of Man* (Oxford: Clarendon, 1979), p. 56. This RSME experiencer seems to have critiqued her ordinary stream of thoughts from a consciousness that includes it, but is clearly *not* identical with it.

63. "Love That Never Runs Out," unsigned editorial in *The Christian Science Monitor,* December 9, 2005.

64. Edward O. Wilson, *Sociobiology,* abridged ed. (Cambridge, MA: Harvard University Press, 1980), p. 288.

65. Pat Wingert and Martha Brant, "Reading Your Baby's Mind," *Newsweek,* August 15, 2005. They go on to note: "Researchers played for infants tapes of other babies crying. As predicted, that was enough to start the tears flowing. But when researchers played babies recordings of their own cries, they rarely began crying themselves." They quote Martin Hoffman, psychology professor at New York University: "There is some rudimentary empathy in place, right from

birth. The intensity of the emotion tends to fade over time. Babies older than 6 months no longer cry but grimace at the discomfort of others. By 13 to 15 months, babies tend to take matters into their own hands. They'll try to comfort a crying playmate. What I find most charming is when, even if the two mothers are present, they'll bring their own mother over to help."

66. Mary Katharine Ham, "Two Girls, One Strength," Townhall, May 3, 2006.

67. Roy Hattersley, "Faith Does Breed Charity: We Atheists Have to Accept That Most Believers Are Better Human Beings," *Guardian,* September 12, 2005.

68. Hardy, *Spiritual Nature of Man,* pp. 98–103.

69. Hardy, *Spiritual Nature of Man,* p. 101.

70. Arthur C. Brooks, "Religious Faith and Charitable Giving," *Policy Review* 121 (October/November 2003).

71. Stan Guthrie, "The Evangelical Scandal," an interview with Ron Sider, *Christianity Today,* April 2005.

72. Gregory S. Paul, "Cross-National Correlations of Quantifiable Societal Health with Popular Religiosity and Secularism in the Prosperous Democracies: A First Look," *Journal of Religion and Society* 7 (2005).

73. Ruth Gledhill, "Societies Worse Off 'When They Have God on Their Side,'" *Times,* September 27, 2005.

74. George H. Gallup, Jr., "Dogma Bites Man: On the New and Biased Research Linking Faith and Social Ills," *Touchstone,* December 2005, p. 61.

75. Gallup, "Dogma Bites Man," pp. 62–63.

76. Chip Berlet, "Religion and Politics in the United States: Nuances You Should Know," *Public Eye Magazine,* Summer 2003. See also Edith Blumhofer, "The New Evangelicals," *Wall Street Journal,* February 18, 2005.

77. Of course, they understand such an experience in Christian terms, which means accepting the morality of the New Testament as a guide for life and stressing the importance of Christ's sacrifice on the cross. See Berlet, "Religion and Politics in the United States." Catholic charismatics hold similar views.

78. Harald Wallach and K. Helmut Reich, "Science and Spirituality: Towards Understanding and Overcoming a Taboo," *Zygon* 40, no. 2 (June 2005): 424.

79. Unattributed, "A Catholic Worker Response to Welfare Reform," posted March 1997, http://www.catholicworker.org/winona/welfare.htm, quoting from Dorothy Day, *Loaves and Fishes,* p. 210.

80. Quoted at *Wikipedia* Wikiquote.

81. The Christian mystic Catherine of Genoa (1447–1510) was manager and treasurer of the large Hospital of Genoa.

82. Evelyn Underhill, *Mysticism: A Study in the Nature and Development of Man's Spiritual Consciousness* (New York: New American Library / Meridian, 1974), p. 436.

83. From a letter written by Thomas Merton to Jim Forest dated February 21, 1966. The full text of this letter is published in *The Hidden Ground of Love: Letters of Thomas Merton,* ed. William Shannon (New York: Farrar, Straus and Giroux, 1985), excerpt reproduced in *Catalyst* 19, no. 2 (March–April, 1996): 8.

84. David Glenn, "Religious Belief Is Found to Be Less Lacking Among Social Scientists," *Chronicle of Higher Education,* August 15, 2005.

85. These results are in stark contrast to public opinion poll findings. Where identical questions are not asked, a direct comparison with the general public is not possible but, for example, polls generally show that over 90 percent of Americans believe in God in some sense and 59 percent of Americans say that they pray daily, according to the 2004 General Social Survey available from the Association of Religion Data Archives (ARDA).

86. Craig Lambert, "The Marketplace of Perceptions," *Harvard Magazine,* March–April 2006.

SIDEBAR
    87. Salim Mansur, "A Bedouin State of Mind," *Western Standard,* August 14, 2006.

CHAPTER NINE: THE CARMELITE STUDIES: A NEW DIRECTION?
1. Benedict Carey, "Scientists Bridle at Lecture Plan for Dalai Lama," *New York Times,* October 19, 2005.
2. Carey, "Scientists Bridle."
3. Quoted in Jon Hamilton, "The Links Between the Dalai Lama and Neuroscience," National Public Radio, November 11, 2005.
4. See B. Alan Wallace, *The Taboo of Subjectivity: Toward a New Science of Consciousness* (Oxford: Oxford University Press, 2000), pp. 103ff.
5. David Adam, "Plan for Dalai Lama Lecture Angers Neuroscientists," *Guardian,* July 27, 2005.
6. The petition, "Against Dalai Lama's Lecture at SfN 2005," addressed to Dr. Carol Barnes, the president of the Society for Neuroscience (SfN), was available for signature between August 8 and August 10, 2005, at www.petitiononline.com/sfn2005/. Although the petition garnered 1,007 signatures, some signatories used the Comments space to advertise contrary views. So the number of protesters does not actually add up to 1,007.
7. Unattributed editorial, "Science and Religion in Harmony," *Nature* 436 (August 18, 2005): 889. The protesters would not likely be satisfied with *Nature's* proposed solution because, among other complaints, they protested the fact that they were expected to sit out the lecture and then write their questions/comments on cards that would be collected and brought to the podium by ushers. They described the practice as a "restriction of free discussion."
8. Britt Peterson, "Despite Controversy, Dalai Lama Preaches Harmony," *Science and Theology News,* December 13, 2005.
9. Antoine Lutz et al., "Long-term Meditators Self-Induce High-Amplitude Gamma Synchrony During Mental Practice," *Proceedings of the National Academy of Sciences USA* 101, no. 46 (November 16, 2004): 16369–73.
10. Carey, "Scientists Bridle."
11. Adam, "Plan for Dalai Lama Lecture."
12. There may have been an entanglement with politics too. Peterson ("Despite Controversy, Dalai Lama Preaches Harmony") quotes John Ackerley, president of the International Campaign for Tibet, which helped sponsor the Dalai Lama's visit, as saying that the petition was a potential "litmus test" for scientists who depend on Beijing for funds and protection.
13. Dalai Lama, preface to Joe Fisher, *The Case for Reincarnation* (London: Souvenir, 2001).
14. *Catechism of the Catholic Church, Popular and Definitive Edition* (New York: 2003), item 1013, p. 231. This catechism was supervised by Benedict XVI when he was Joseph, Cardinal Ratzinger.
15. John H. Hannigan, cellular neurobiologist, letter to *Neuroscience Quarterly,* Fall 2005.
16. Andrew Newberg, Eugene D'Aquili, and Vince Rause, *Why God Won't Go Away: Brain Science and the Biology of Belief* (New York: Ballantine Books, 2001), pp. 145–46, 113.
17. A. Newberg et al., "The Measurement of Regional Cerebral Blood Flow During the Complex Cognitive Task of Meditation: A Preliminary SPECT Study," *Psychiatry Research: Neuroimaging* 106 (2001): 113–22.
18. A. Newberg et al., "Cerebral Blood Flow During Meditative Prayer: Preliminary Findings and Methodological Issues," *Perceptual and Motor Skills* 97 (2003): 625–30.
19. Newberg offers: "Gene and I began, as all scientists do, with the fundamental assumption that all that is really real is material. We regarded the brain as a biological machine composed of matter and created by evolution to perceive and interact with the physical world. After years of research, however, our understanding of various key brain structures and the way information is channeled along neural pathways led us to hypothesize that the brain possesses a neurological mechanism for self-transcendence" (*Why God Won't Go Away,* pp. 145–46).

20. Newberg et al., *Why God Won't Go Away,* p. 111.
21. Newberg et al., *Why God Won't Go Away,* p. 174.
22. Anne McIlroy, "Hardwired for God," *Globe and Mail,* December 6, 2003.
23. Evelyn Underhill, *Mysticism: A Study in the Nature and Development of Man's Spiritual Consciousness* (New York: New American Library / Meridian, 1974), p. 447.
24. Mystical experiences that occur between the ages of twenty and forty have often led to significant social outcomes, such as the founding of the great religious orders or religions. This has led some to propose a materialist explanation for these experiences as an accident of young adult biochemistry. But the age range of *historically significant* mystical experiences probably reflects mainly the relative freedom of a vigorous young adult to act in a way that impacts others. Children and seniors who have such experiences may be unable to act on them in ways that would impact a whole society. Thus, the distribution of the experiences is probably broader than their public impact.
25. W. T. Stace, *The Teachings of the Mystics* (New York: Macmillan, 1960).
26. Dean Hamer, among others, has popularized a definition of self-transcendence based on the work of psychiatrist Robert Cloninger (see Dean Hamer, *The God Gene: How Faith Is Hardwired into Our Genes* [New York: Doubleday, 2004], p. 18). Hamer, following Cloninger, identifies "three distinct but related components of spirituality: self-forgetfulness, transpersonal identification, and mysticism" (p. 23). This definition is incomplete. Major components that it does not address include compassion, unconditional love, and long-term positive changes in attitude and behavior.
27. We specifically wanted to identify brain areas that are active during spiritual experiences. Various lines of evidence have demonstrated that *entheogens*—psychedelic drugs used in a spiritual context (e.g., LSD-25, mescaline, psilocybin)—can lead to genuine states of unitive consciousness (Grof, 1998). Indeed, psychedelic experiences frequently parallel the various dimensions characterizing religious numinous and mystical experiences (e.g., depersonalization, euphoria, awareness of a larger intelligence or presence; Strassman, 1995). Thus, mescaline has been used to promote religious experiences in the Native American church, and psilocybin has been shown to provoke mystical experiences during Protestant church services (Doblin, 1991). Moreover, in a series of 206 observed hallucinogen-ingestion sessions (mainly of LSD-25 and mescaline), 58 percent of subjects reported having encountered religious figures (Masters and Houston, 1966). Entheogens involve an agonistic effect on serotonin (5-HT) receptors in the brain (Glennon, 1990). Current views in psychopharmacology attribute the psychedelic properties of entheogens with serotonergic agonist activity, particularly at 5-HT1a, 5-HT1c, and 5-HT2 receptors. These serotonergic receptors are widely distributed in basal ganglia, neocortex, and temporolimbic structures (Strassman, 1995; Joyce et al., 1993). Interestingly, the drug MDMA (3,4-methylenedioxymetamphetamine), which is often associated with "unconditional love" and a profound state of empathy for self and other in the most general terms—a state of empathy where the feeling is that the self, the other, and the world are basically "good" (Eisner, 1989)—acts mainly by temporarily increasing the synaptic concentration of the neurotransmitter serotonin (5-HT) in the brain. All together, these findings strongly suggest that, from a neurochemical perspective, 5-HT may be crucially involved in RSMEs. For discussions of these issues, see in particular R. Doblin, "Pahnke's 'Good Friday Experiment': A Long-term Follow-up and Methodological Critique," *Journal of Transpersonal Psychology* 23 (1991): 1–28; B. Eisner, *Ecstasy: The MDMA Story* (Berkeley, CA: Ronin, 1989); R. A. Glennon, "Do Classical Hallucinogens Act as 5-Ht2 Agonists or Antagonists?" *Neuropsychopharmacology* 3 (1990): 509–17; S. Grof, *The Cosmic Game: Explorations of the Frontiers of Human Consciousness* (Monaco: Du Rocher, 1998); J. N. Joyce, A. Share, N. Lexow, et al., "Serotonin Uptake Sites and Serotonin Receptors Are Altered in the Limbic System of Schizophrenics," *Neuropsychopharmacology* 8 (1993): 315–36; R. E. L. Masters and J. Houston, *The Varieties of Psychedelic Experience* (New York: Holt, Rinehart, and Winston, 1966); and R. J. Strassman, "Hallucinogenic Drugs in Psychiatric Research and Treatment," *Journal of Nervous and Mental Disorders* 183 (1995): 127–38.

28. In the first few years after its founding in 1983, the center did few studies on humans. It mostly tested visual systems in animals such as cats, rats, and raccoons. (Raccoons are of special interest because one-third of the cells in the cortex are associated with their sensitive, handlike front paws.) Currently, the center also does research on humans, for example, on the way in which brain plasticity enables blind people to use brain areas normally used for eyesight for other purposes. CERNEC currently supports the work of over thirty researchers, including myself, through grants from the Natural Sciences and Engineering Research Council of Canada (NSERC), Canadian Health Research Institutes (CIHR), Fonds de Recherche en Santé du Québec (FRSQ), and private donors.

29. Quoted in Hannah Ward and Jennifer Wild, eds., *Doubleday Christian Quotation Collection* (New York: Doubleday, 1997), p. 224.

30. "'Mystical Union': A Small Band of Pioneers Is Exploring the Neurology of Religious Experience," *Economist*, March 4, 2004.

31. From a letter of March 1578 to Maria de San Jose Salazar, the prioress in Seville. That said, Teresa wrote her own spiritual autobiography, at the direction of a confessor.

32. For example, with the grant received from the Metanexus Institute and John Templeton Foundation, we were expected to conduct a third study, a PET (positron emission tomography) study, on the nuns, in this case at the Brain Imaging Center of the Montreal Neurological Institute (MNI, the famous institute created by Wilder Penfield in the 1920s). The goal of the study was to measure serotonin (5-HT) synthesis capacity during the same conditions (baseline, control condition, mystical condition). The project was blocked by the PET Working Committee. We were given to understand that some committee members reacted violently to our submission. They thought that mystical states *could not* be studied scientifically (and they probably did not want the MNI to be associated with what they consider pseudoscience). We ended up using the money for another project in which we examine brain activity (with fMRI and QEEG) in NDErs who have been spiritually transformed by their NDEs.

33. Jennifer Woods, "Study Asks Whether Chemicals and Communion Are One," *Science and Theology News*, October 11, 2004.

34. Coventry Patmore, quoted in Underhill, *Mysticism*, pp. 24–25.

35. "Mystical Union," *Economist*.

36. This slow brain-wave pattern (theta waves) is not unique to the Christian tradition; it has been found in Hindu yogis and Buddhist monks, so it appears to be a characteristic of mysticism generally.

37. TheatrGROUP, a St. Louis, Missouri theater company, provides some insight into how actors teach themselves to do this at http://www.theatrgroup.com/methodM/ (accessed January 17, 2007).

38. M. Pelletier et al., "Separate Neural Circuits for Primary Emotions? Brain Activity During Self-Induced Sadness and Happiness in Professional Actors," Neuroreport 14.8 (June 11, 2003): 1111–16.

39. McIlroy, "Hardwired for God."

40. We had also intended to use PET (positron emission tomography) to measure the levels of the mood regulator serotonin, but could not get access to the needed equipment.

41. The week before the experiment, we asked the fifteen nuns who participated to practice remembering and reliving their most significant mystical experience and their most intense state of union with another human ever felt in their lives while they were members of the Carmelite order.

42. McIlroy, "Hardwired for God."

SIDEBAR

43. For a discussion of the role of these brain regions in emotion, see M. Beauregard, P. Lévesque, and V. Paquette, "Neural Basis of Conscious and Voluntary Self-Regulation of Emotion," in *Consciousness, Emotional Self-Regulation and the Brain*, ed. M. Beauregard (Amsterdam: John Benjamins, 2004), pp. 163–94.

44. S. F. Neggers et al., "Interactions Between Ego- and Allocentric Neuronal Representations of Space," *Neuroimage* (2006).

45. O. Felician et al., "Pointing to Body Parts: A Double Dissociation Study," *Neuropsychologia* 41 (2003): 1307–16.

46. J. Decety, "Do Imagined and Executed Actions Share the Same Neural Substrate?" *Brain Research: Cognitive Brain Research* 3 (1996): 87–93.

47. M. Beauregard and V. Paquette, "Neural Correlates of a Mystical Experience in Carmelite Nuns," *Neuroscience Letters* 405 (2006): 186–90.

48. Y. Kubota et al., "Frontal Midline Theta Rhythm Is Correlated with Cardiac Autonomic Activities During the Performance of an Attention Demanding Meditation Procedure," *Brain Research: Cognitive Brain Research* 11.2 (April 2001): 281–87; T. Takahashi et al., "Changes in EEG and Autonomic Nervous Activity During Meditation and Their Association with Personality Traits," *International Journal of Psychophysiology* 55.2 (February 2005): 199–207.

49. L. I. Aftanas et al., "Affective Picture Processing: Event-Related Synchronization Within Individually Defined Human Theta Band Is Modulated by Valence Dimension," *Neuroscience Letters* 303 (2001): 115–18.

50. Steven Weinberg, "Free People from Superstition," *Freethought Today,* April 2000.

51. C. E. M. Joad (1891–1953), *The Recovery of Belief* (London: Faber and Faber, 1952), http://cqod.gospelcom.net/cqod9904.htm (accessed January 13, 2007).

52. Tamar Sofer, "Seeing Miracles," *Aish,* April 30, 2006.

SIDEBAR

53. 1 Kings 18:19. The ancient Israelites had begun to abandon monotheistic religion in favour of a popular fertility cult introduced by new rulers. Elijah was demanding a confrontation with the priests of the cult.

54. Except where indicated, the information on the Carmelite order has been taken from Peter-Thomas Rohrbach, *Journey to Carith: The Story of the Carmelite Order* (Garden City, NY: Doubleday, 1966). For Elijah and the Old Testament prophetic tradition, see p. 23ff. For Mary, see p. 46ff. The Magnificat, Mary's only long recorded quotation in Luke 2, certainly demonstrates the prophetic stance.

55. See 1 Kings 18:17–40. For Elijah's career, see 1 Kings 17–19; 2 Kings 1–2.

56. Rohrbach, *Journey to Carith,* p. 66.

57. Numbers such as "second" and "third" reflect the chronological order of foundation, not of importance.

58. Originally, the scapular was simply a garment that a monk or nun wore to protect the habit (approved dress of a religious order) from dirt, but the garment acquired a religious significance in its own right for the Carmelites. A smaller, modified version is made available to laypeople who promise to carry out certain spiritual traditions.

59. Robert Browning, "Fra Lippo Lippi," ll. 224–25, in E. K. Brown and J. O. Bailey, eds., *Victorian Poetry,* 2d ed. (New York: Ronald Press, 1962), p. 207.

60. Dava Sobel, *Galileo's Daughter* (Toronto: Viking, 1999). Sobel explains that because the girls were born out of wedlock, they were unlikely to marry well (pp. 4–5).

61. Teresa of Avila, *The Interior Castle,* trans. Mirabai Starr (New York: Riverhead, 2003), p. 140.

62. Rohrbach, *Journey to Carith,* p. 138. Details of Teresa's life and of the Carmelite order are generally from the account provided by Rohrbach, a Carmelite historian.

63. The reform group was called the "Discalced" Carmelites. Literally the term means "barefoot." However, the nuns and monks did not actually go barefoot; Teresa's nuns wore cheap sandals and otherwise avoided excess.

64. Rohrbach, *Journey to Carith,* p. 176.

65. Rohrbach, *Journey to Carith,* p. 146.

66. Rohrbach, *Journey to Carith,* p. 137.

67. John of the Cross, *Spiritual Canticle,* quoted in Wilfrid McGreal, *John of the Cross* (London: HarperCollins, 1996), p. 35.

68. Gerald G. May, *The Dark Night of the Soul* (San Francisco: HarperSanFrancisco, 2004), p. 38.

69. John's imprisonment has been described as a hostage taking. He had not committed an offense, and his captors had no obvious right to imprison him. He was one of many victims of the conflict between the pope and Philip II over jurisdiction of religious matters in Spain.

70. McGreal, *John of the Cross,* p. 19.

71. Francis Poulenc, *Dialogues of the Carmelites* (English version), Ricordi's Collection of Opera Librettos (New York: Ricordi, 1957), p. 36.

72. Based on a play by Georges Bernanos, it was first performed at La Scala in Milan in 1957. It was originally based on a novel by Gertrude von Le Fort based on *Relation by Mother Marie of the Incarnation of God.*

73. Steven Payne, "Edith Stein: A Fragmented Life," *America,* October 10, 1998.

74. Hitler's anti-Semitism was racist, not religious. He had little use for Christianity, and no inclination to protect Jewish converts.

75. Rohrbach, *Journey to Carith,* p. 357.

76. Laura Garcia, "Edith Stein—Convert, Nun, Martyr," *Crisis* 15, no. 6 (June 1997): 32–35.

77. Catherine of Siena, *Letters of St. Catherine of Siena,* ed. Vida D. Scudder, (London, New York: J.M. Dent and E.P. Dutton, 1905) http://www.domcentral.org/trad/cathletters.htm (accessed January 13, 2007), p. 278.

CHAPTER TEN: DID GOD CREATE THE BRAIN OR DOES THE BRAIN CREATE GOD?

1. Albert Einstein, "The World as I See it," 1931. The essay was originally published in *Forum and Century,* vol. 84, pp. 193–194, the thirteenth in the Forum series Living Philosophies.

2. Abraham H. Maslow, *Religions, Values, and Peak Experiences* (New York: Arana, 1970), p. 20.

3. D. Hay, *Religious Experience Today: Studying the Facts* (London: Mowbray, 1990); A. Hardy, *The Biology of God* (New York: Taplinger, 1990); R. Wuthnow, "Peak Experiences: Some Empirical Tests," *Journal of Humanistic Psychology* 18.3 (1978): 59–75.

4. Gallup Poll–American Institute of Public Opinion, 1990.

5. General Social Survey (Chicago: National Opinion Research Center, 1998).

6. D. Lukoff, F. Lu, and R. Turner, "Toward a More Culturally Sensitive DSM-IV: Psychoreligious and Psychospiritual Problems," *J Nerv Ment Dis.* 180 no. 11 (1992 Nov): 673–82.

7. Sigmund Freud, *Civilization and Its Discontents* (New York: Norton, 1961).

8. B. Spilka et al., *The Psychology of Religion: An Empirical Approach,* 3d ed. (New York: Guilford, 2003).

9. Abraham Maslow, *Religious Aspects of Peak-Experiences* (New York: Harper & Row, 1970).

10. M. Morse and P. Perry, *Transformed by the Light* (New York: Ballantine, 1992); P. van Lommel et al., "Near-Death Experience in Survivors of Cardiac Arrest: A Prospective Study in the Netherlands," *Lancet* 358 (2001): 2039–45; S. Parnia and P. Fenwick, "Near-Death Experiences in Cardiac Arrest: Visions of a Dying Brain or Visions of a New Science of Consciousness," *Resuscitation* 52 (2002): 5–11.

11. Mysticism often results in an unusual degree of empathy with animals. Underhill notes that Francis is said to have persuaded the villagers of Gubbio to feed a lone wolf that was ravaging their flocks. Brushing aside warnings, he spoke kindly but firmly to the wolf, which submitted to him. The wolf thereafter lived in an abandoned hut on the edge of the village as a semi-tame animal, fed by the villagers until its death a few years later from natural causes. This story is

often dismissed as legend, but it is worth considering that the wolf is a pack animal that will submit to a stronger personality that undertakes to provide food for it and defend it, in return for unquestioning obedience. See Evelyn Underhill, *Mysticism: A Study in the Nature and Development of Man's Spiritual Consciousness* (New York: New American Library / Meridian, 1974), p. 260ff.

12. Michael Sabom, *Light and Death: One Doctor's Fascinating Account of Near-Death Experiences* (Grand Rapids, MI: Zondervan, 1998).

13. William James, "Human Immortality: Two Supposed Objections to the Doctrine," in G. Murphy and R. O. Ballou, eds., *William James on Psychical Research* (New York: Viking, 1960), pp. 279–308; original delivered as a lecture (1898).

14. Henri Bergson, presidential address, *Proceedings of the Society for Psychical Research* 27 (1914): 157–75.

15. Aldous Huxley, *The Doors of Perception* (New York: Harper & Row, 1954).

16. R. M. Bucke, *Cosmic Consciousness: A Study in the Evolution of the Human Mind* (New Hyde Park, NY: University Books, 1961; originally published 1901).

17. Richard Conn Henry, "The Mental Universe," *Nature* 436, no. 29 (July 7, 2005).

18. Quoted in Dean Radin, *The Conscious Universe: The Scientific Truth of Psychic Phenomena* (San Francisco: HarperSanFrancisco, 1997), p. 264.

19. This global form of consciousness, which entails the realization that all species are interconnected, is planet-centered. It transcends egotism, nationalism, cultural and religious intolerance, and disrespect for the environment.

Glossary

adaptive trait: A trait that promotes survival and the ability to produce fertile offspring.

amygdala: Located just behind the hypothalamus, which mediates emotions, especially those related to safety or well-being. It is sometimes called the *amygdalas* because it comprises two almond-shaped masses of neurons.

anterior cingulate cortex (ACC): A sort of collar that surrounds the corpus callosum, which links the right and left hemispheres of the brain; it plays a role in decision making.

autonomic nervous system: The portion of the nervous system that controls automatic activities such as heart rate, breathing, and the activities of glands, functions that occur whether one is conscious of them or not.

basal ganglia: A region at the base of the brain that consists of three large clusters of neurons that play a role in directing habitual activities.

Brodmann areas: Areas of the brain mapped by cellular structure.

caudate nucleus: One of the basal ganglia, a tail-like structure that plays a role in voluntary movement and emotion.

cerebellum: A region of the brain that plays a pivotal role in the integration of sensory perception and motor output.

cingulate gyrus: A layer of neurons above the main connection between the brain's two hemispheres (the *corpus callosum*) that coordinates pleasant sights and smells with pleasant memories. The cingulate gyrus also participates in the emotional reaction to pain and in the regulation of emotion.

clade: A group of life forms with similar organs, most likely derived from a common ancestor.

clinical death: The state in which vital signs have ceased: the heart is in ventricular fibrillation, there is a total lack of electrical activity on the cortex of the brain (flat EEG), and brain-stem activity is abolished (loss of the corneal reflex, fixed and dilated pupils, and loss of the gag reflex); cardiopulmonary resuscitation (CPR) can revive the patient within a window of about ten minutes; after that, brain damage makes revival unlikely.

constructivism: The view that culture and assumptions shape mystical experience to such a degree that there is no one underlying reality.

contemplation: The practice of intentionally concentrating consciousness on one object or idea, sometimes called meditation, recollection, or interior silence; distractions are simply noted and dismissed in the hope of encountering hidden levels of consciousness.

corpus callosum: A white matter structure in the brain that connects the left and right cerebral hemispheres.

cortex (cerebrum): The largest and uppermost portion of the human brain, divided into four lobes, frontal, parietal (upper side), occipital (back), and temporal (lower side, over the ears).

dark night of the soul: Term coined by John of the Cross to describe the sense of abandonment mystics sometimes feel when contemplation does not produce mystic consciousness; often associated with a residual unwillingness to give up a false sense of self.

dopamine: A neurotransmitter involved in movement, cognition, motivation, and pleasure.

double-blind experiment: An experiment in which neither the experimenter nor the subject can influence the results by knowing either (1) what the study is about or (2) whether the subject is a member of the experimental group (where significant things should happen) or the control group (an apparently identical situation where nothing significant should happen); it is difficult to achieve in psychological experimentation on humans because humans are adept at picking up cues, often unconscious ones; when achieved, it is highly valued as a "gold standard" in research.

down-regulate: To observe something in a dispassionate, nonevaluative, and nonjudgmental manner.

dualism: A philosophy that accepts the coexistence of fundamentally different entities (e.g., matter and mind).

electrodermal response (EDR): A measure of skin conductivity from the fingers and/or palms, a nonvoluntary physiological reaction the subject may or may not be aware of or able to assign a reason for.

evolutionary psychology: The branch of psychology that maintains that human brains, including any component that involves religion or spirituality, comprise adaptations or psychological mechanisms that have evolved by natural selection to benefit the survival and reproduction of the human organism.

exobiology: The study of whether life forms have existed or now exist on Mars or planets orbiting stars other than the sun (extrasolar planets); such life forms are considered possible in principle but have not so far been found.

fMRI: *See* functional magnetic resonance imaging.

functional magnetic resonance imaging (fMRI): A technique that produces images of brain changes by means of radio waves within a strong magnetic field.

Geschwind syndrome: A tendency toward religiosity that, according to some clinicians, is associated with temporal-lobe epilepsy.

gyrus: A fold of the brain.

Heisenberg uncertainty (indeterminacy) principle: The principle that subatomic particles do not occupy definite positions in space or time; we can find out where they are only as a series of probabilities about where they might be (we must decide what we want to know).

hippocampus: Cerebral structure belonging to the limbic system and located inside the temporal lobe. The hippocampus, which resembles a seahorse, is involved in memory and spatial navigation.

hypothalamus: Below the thalamus, a sort of central thermostat that regulates body functions such as blood pressure and breathing, and also governs the intensity of emotional behavior. The hypothalamus also controls the pituitary gland, the gland that regulates growth and metabolism.

insula: Region of the lower part of the cerebral cortex that is implicated in the representation of bodily states that color conscious experiences.

interpersonal viscosity: A tendency to cling to others in a way that may damage relationships.

lateral prefrontal cortex (LPFC): An area of the front part of the brain, toward the side of the head, that plays a role in assessing alternatives.

limbic system: A system, including the hypothalamus, the hippocampus, and the amygdala, that surrounds and underlies the thalamus; it plays a key role in our emotional experiences and in the ability to form memories.

materialism: The philosophy that matter is all that exists and everything has a material cause.

meditation: *See* contemplation.

meme: A hypothetical unit of thought that replicates itself in brains, an idea pioneered by Richard Dawkins.

metacognitive: Pertaining to thinking about thinking, or monitoring one's own thoughts.

metaphysical naturalism. *See* naturalism.

mind-matter interaction: The capacity of mind to influence material objects such as random number generators (RNGs).

monism: A philosophy that assumes that everything that exists is fundamentally of only one substance (e.g., matter).

monistic mysticism: The mystical experience of sensing that the created universe revolves around a center from which everything issues.

motor cortex: The part of the cerebral cortex implicated in the planning, control, and execution of motor functions.

MRI scan: *See* functional magnetic resonance imaging.

mystical union (*unio mystica*): Mystical union with God or the Absolute in love.

mysticism: The experience of certain, mystical contact with a higher truth or a greater power underlying the universe, usually interpreted in the context of a religious tradition.

naturalism: The philosophy that nature is all that exists and everything has a natural cause.

neurotheology: An approach to RSMEs that seeks a neurological and evolutionary basis for spiritual experiences.

neurotransmitters: Chemicals in the brain that relay and modulate electrical signals between nerve cells (neurons).

nigrostriatal dopamine system: Neural pathway that connects the substantia nigra with the striatum, playing a role in movement.

nocebo effect: The harmful health effect created by a sick person's belief and expectation that a powerful source of harm has been contacted or administered; medical practices may unintentionally create nocebo effects.

Occam's (or Ockham's) razor: A scientific principle that, of two adequate explanations, the simpler should be preferred.

occipital cortex: The portion of the brain that processes visual information.

orbital frontal cortex (OFC): The part of the front of the brain just above and behind the eyes that plays a role in detecting errors.

pantheistic mysticism: The mystical experience of sensing that the entire external world is the ultimate power and that the experiencer is part of that power.

parahippocampal cortex: Brain region inside the temporal lobe associated with orienting oneself in familiar surroundings.

parapsychology: As a scientific discipline, the study of psi effects, usually psychokinesis and telepathy.

perennialism, perennial philosophy: The view that mystics of all traditions perceive the divine ground of the universe that underlies consciousness, but may interpret it differently.

PET, PET scan: *See* positron emission tomography.

placebo effect: The significant healing effect created by a sick person's belief and expectation that a powerful remedy has been applied when the improvement cannot have been the physical result of the remedy.

Plato's Lifeboat: Principle acknowledging phenomena for which there is at least some good evidence, but whose relationship to the total picture is unclear.

positron emission tomography (PET): The imaging of brain activity using the emissions from decaying radioactive isotopes.

prefrontal cortex (PFC): The cortical regions of the frontal lobe of the brain, known to be associated with complex behavior, including cognition, personality, and appropriate social behavior.

psi effect: Telepathic and psychokinetic phenomena generally.

putamen: A portion of the basal ganglia which, together with the caudate nucleus, forms the striatum. This structure is involved in reinforcement learning and emotion.

quantitative electroencephalography (QEEG): The measurement and analysis (expressed as a color map) of electrical patterns at the surface of the scalp that reflect brain-wave patterns.

scientism: The view that only the methods of natural sciences such as physics and chemistry provide real knowledge.

selfish genes: Richard Dawkins's hypothesis that human behavior is driven by the apparent (though not actual) agency of genes in getting passed on.

single photon emission computed tomography (SPECT): A technique for mapping blood flow and metabolism after the injection of radioactive substances that can be used to study brain changes after a psychological challenge.

striatum: The largest part of the basal ganglia, which includes the caudate, putamen, and globus pallidus.

substantia nigra: The portion of the brain that produces dopamine.

suggestion/suggestability: The increased probability that we will experience an effect if our surroundings encourage us to anticipate it.

sympathetic nervous system: The portion of the autonomic nervous system that activates when stress or danger is perceived; it helps to regulate pulse and blood pressure, dilates pupils, and changes muscle tone.

telekinesis: The ability of mind to move matter; scientific study focuses on micropsychokinesis, the ability to influence randomly generated events.

teleologically oriented: Purposeful rather than random.

telepathy: The communication of two minds by currently unknown means; scientific study focuses on sensory deprivation experiments in which the subject must guess which of four mental images another subject experienced at the same time.

temporoparietal region: The part of the brain located at the intersection of the temporal and parietal cortices.

theistic mysticism: The mystical experience of sensing the presence of the highest power in the universe or a power from beyond the universe.

third chimpanzee: Humans if classified with the two species of chimpanzee currently recognized, the common chimpanzee (*Pan troglodytes*) and the smaller bonobo (*Pan paniscus*).

ventrolateral prefrontal cortex (VLPFC): A lower part of the side of the prefrontal cortex that is involved in the integration of viscero-sensory information with emotional signals.

Bibliography

Aftanas, L. I., A. A. Varlamov, S. V. Pavlov, V. P. Makhnev, and N. V. Reva. "Affective Picture Processing: Event-Related Synchronization Within Individually Defined Human Theta Band Is Modulated by Valence Dimension." *Neuroscience Letters* 303 (2001): 115–18.

Alper, Matthew. *The "God" Part of the Brain: A Scientific Interpretation of Human Spirituality and God*. New York: Rogue, 2001.

Antony, M. M., and R. P. Swinson. "Specific Phobia." In M. M. Antony and R. P. Swinson, eds., *Phobic Disorders and Panic in Adults: A Guide to Assessment and Treatment*. Washington, DC: American Psychological Association, 2000, pp. 79–104.

Arzy, S., M. Idel, T. Landis, and O. Blanke. "Why Have Revelations Occurred on Mountains? Linking Mystical Experiences and Cognitive Neuroscience." *Medical Hypotheses* 65 (2005): 841–45.

Aunger, Robert C., ed. *Darwinizing Culture: The Status of Memetics as a Science*. Oxford: Oxford Univ. Press, 2001.

Bandura, A. "Social Cognitive Theory: An Agentic Perspective." *Annual Review of Psychology* 52 (2001): 1–26.

Beauregard, M., J. Lévesque, and P. Bourgouin. "Neural Correlates of Conscious Self-regulation of Emotion." *Journal of Neuroscience* 21 (2001): RC165 (1–6).

Beauregard, M., J. Lévesque, and V. Paquette. "Neural Basis of Conscious and Voluntary Self-Regulation of Emotion." In M. Beauregard, ed., *Consciousness, Emotional Self-Regulation and the Brain*. Amsterdam: John Benjamins, 2004, pp. 163–94.

Beauregard, M., and V. Paquette. "Neural Correlates of a Mystical Experience in Carmelite Nuns." *Neuroscience Letters* 405 (2006): 186–90.

Beauregard, M., V. Paquette, M. Pouliot, and J. Lévesque. "The Neurobiology of the Mystical Experience: A Quantitative EEG Study." Society for Neuroscience 34th Annual Meeting, October 23–27, 2004. San Diego, CA.

Bell, J. S. *Speakable and Unspeakable in Quantum Mechanics.* Cambridge: Cambridge Univ. Press, 2004.

Benson H., J. A. Dusek, J. B. Sherwood, P. Lam, C. F. Bethea, W. Carpenter, S. Levitsky, P. C. Hill, D. W. Clem, Jr., M. K. Jain, D. Drumel, S. L. Kopecky, P. S. Mueller, D. Marek, S. Rollins, and P. L. Hibberd. "Study of the Therapeutic Effects of Intercessory Prayer (STEP) in Cardiac Bypass Patients: A Multicenter Randomized Trial of Uncertainty and Certainty of Receiving Intercessory Prayer." *American Heart Journal* 151.4 (April 2006): 934–42.

Benson, Herbert, and Marg Stark. *Timeless Medicine: The Power and Biology of Belief.* New York, Scribner, 1996.

Berdyaev, Nicolas, "Freedom from Fear." *Times of India,* February 8, 2007.

Berger, Peter. *The Desecularization of the World.* Grand Rapids, MI: Eerdmans, 1999.

Bibby, Reginald. *The Poverty and Potential of Religion in Canada.* Toronto: Irwin, 1987.

Blackmore, Susan. *The Meme Machine.* Oxford: Oxford Univ. Press, 1999.

Blanke, O., S. Ortigue, T. Landis, and M. Seeck. "Stimulating Illusory Own-Body Perceptions: The Part of the Brain That Can Induce Out-Of-Body Experiences Has Been Located." *Nature* 419 (2002): 269–70.

Bloom, Howard. *The Lucifer Principle: A Scientific Expedition into the Forces of History.* New York: Atlantic Monthly Press, 1995.

Blum, Deborah. *Sex on the Brain: The Biological Differences Between Men and Women.* New York: Viking, Penguin, 1997.

Bobrow, Robert S. "Paranormal Phenomena in the Medical Literature: Sufficient Smoke to Warrant a Search for Fire." *Medical Hypotheses* 60.6 (2003): 864–68.

Boswell, James. *Life of Johnson.* Edited by R. W. Chapman and J. D. Fleeman. Unabridged edition. Oxford: Oxford Univ. Press, 1998, p. 929.

Boyer, Pascal. *Religion Explained: The Evolutionary Origins of Religious Thought.* New York: Basic Books, 2001.

Brodie, Richard. *Virus of the Mind: The New Science of the Meme.* Seattle: Integral Press, 1996.

Brody, A. L., S. Saxena, P. Stoessel, L. A. Gillies, L. A. Fairbanks, S. Alborzian, M. E. Phelps, S. C. Huang, H. M. Wu, M. L. Ho, M. K. Ho, S. C. Au, K. Maidment, and L. R. Baxter, Jr. "Regional Brain Metabolic Changes in Patients with Major Depression Treated with Either Paroxetine or Interpersonal Therapy: Preliminary Findings." *Archives of General Psychiatry* 58 (2001): 631–40.

Brown, Geoffrey. *Minds, Brains and Machines.* New York: St. Martin's Press, 1989.

Buchanan, Mark. "Charity Begins at Homo sapiens." *New Scientist,* March 12, 2005.

Bucke, R. M. *Cosmic Consciousness: A Study in the Evolution of the Human Mind.* New Hyde Park, NY: Univ. Books, 1961. Originally published in 1901.

Buller, D. J. "Evolutionary Psychology: The Emperor's New Paradigm." *Trends in Cognitive Science* 9.6 (June 2005): 277–83.

Byrd, R. C. "Positive Therapeutic Effects of Intercessory Prayer in a Coronary Care Unit Population." *Southern Medical Journal* 81.7 (July 1988): 826–29.

Cairns-Smith, A. G. *Seven Clues to the Origin of Life.* Cambridge: Cambridge Univ. Press, 1985.

Changeux, Jean-Pierre. *Neuronal Man: The Biology of Mind.* Translated by Laurence Garey. New York: Oxford Univ. Press, 1985.

Cheyne, J. A. "The Ominous Numinous: Sensed Presence and 'Other' Hallucinations." *Journal of Consciousness Studies* 8, nos. 5–7 (2001).

Churchland, Patricia Smith. *Brain-Wise: Studies in Neurophilosophy.* Cambridge, MA: MIT Press, 2002.

Cotton, Ian. *The Hallelujah Revolution: The Rise of the New Christians.* London: Prometheus, 1996.

Crick, Francis. *The Astonishing Hypothesis: The Scientific Search for the Soul.* New York: Simon & Schuster, Touchstone, 1995.

Dawkins, Richard. *The Selfish Gene.* New York: Oxford Univ. Press, 1989.

De la Fuente-Fernández, R., Thomas J. Ruth, Vesna Rossi, Michael Schulzer, Donald B. Calne, and A. J. Stoessl. "Expectant and Dopamine Release: Mechanism of the Placebo Effect in Parkinson's Disease." *Science* 293 (August 10, 2001): 1164–66.

Decety, J. "Do Imagined and Executed Actions Share the Same Neural Substrate?" *Brain Research: Cognitive Brain Research* 3 (1996): 87–93.

Dembski, William A. *No Free Lunch: Why Specified Complexity Cannot Be Purchased Without Intelligence.* Lanham, MD: Rowman & Littlefield, 2002.

Dennett, Daniel C. *Kinds of Minds: Toward an Understanding of Consciousness.* New York: Basic Books, 1996.

Denton, Michael J. *Nature's Destiny: How the Laws of Biology Reveal Purpose in the Universe.* New York: Free Press, 1998.

D'Espagnat, Bernard. *Reality and the Physicist: Knowledge, Duration and the Quantum World.* Cambridge: Cambridge Univ. Press, 1989. Originally published in French as *Une incertaine réalité.*

Devinsky, O. "Religious Experiences and Epilepsy." *Epilepsy & Behavior* 4 (2003): 76–77.

Dewhurst, K., and A. W. Beard. "Sudden Religious Conversions in Temporal Lobe Epilepsy." *Epilepsy & Behavior* 4 (2003).

Eccles, Sir John, and Daniel N. Robinson. *The Wonder of Being Human: Our Brain and Our Mind.* New York: Free Press, 1984.

Edelman, Gerald M., and Giulio Tononi. *A Universe of Consciousness: How Matter Becomes Imagination.* New York: Basic Books, 2000.

Felician, O., M. Ceccaldi, M. Didic, C. Thinus-Blanc, and M. Poncet. "Pointing to Body Parts: A Double Dissociation Study." *Neuropsychologia* 41 (2003): 1307–16.

Felten, David L., and Ralph F. Józefowicz. *Netter's Atlas of Human Neuroscience.* Teterboro, NJ: Icon Learning Systems, 2003.

Ferris, Timothy. *A State-of-the-Universe(s) Report.* New York: Simon & Schuster, Touchstone, 1997.

Flory, Richard W. "Promoting a Secular Standard: Secularization and Modern Journalism, 1870–1930." In Christian Smith, ed., *The Secular Revolution: Power, Interests, and Conflict in the Secularization of American Public Life.* Berkeley and Los Angeles: Univ. of California Press, 2003.

Frazer, James George. *The Golden Bough.* Edited by Mary Douglas. Abridged by Sabine McCormack. London: Macmillan, 1978.

Gellman, Jerome. "Mysticism." In the *Stanford Encyclopedia of Philosophy.* Edited by Edward N. Zalta. Spring 2005. http://plato.stanford.edu/archives/spr2005/entries/mysticism/.

Giovannoli, Joseph. *The Biology of Belief: How Our Biology Biases our Beliefs and Perceptions.* New York: Rosetta, 2000.

Gonzalez, Guillermo, and Jay W. Richards. *Privileged Planet: How Our Place in the Cosmos Is Designed for Discovery.* Washington, DC: Regnery, 2004.

Gorman, J. M., J. M. Kent, G. M. Sullivan, and J. D. Kaplan. "Neuroanatomical Hypothesis of Panic Disorder, Revised." *American Journal of Psychiatry* 157 (2000): 493–505.

Granqvist, Pehr, Mats Fredrikson, Dan Larhammar, Marcus Larsson, and Sven Valind. "Sensed presence and mystical experiences are predicted by suggestibility, not by the application of transcranial weak complex magnetic fields." *Neuroscience Letters,* doi:10.1016/j.neulet.2004.10.057 (2004).

Grant, George. *Lament for a Nation: The Defeat of Canadian Nationalism.* Don Mills: Oxford Univ. Press Canada, 1970.

Greyson, Bruce, and Nancy E. Bush. "Distressing Near-Death Experiences." *Psychiatry* 55.1 (February 1992): 95–110.

Gross, Francis L., Jr., with Toni L. Gross. *The Making of a Mystic: Seasons in the Life of Teresa of Avila.* Albany: State Univ. of New York Press, 1993.

Grossman, N. "Who's Afraid of Life After Death?" *Journal of Near-Death Studies* 21.1 (Fall 2002).

Halgren E., R. D. Walter, D. G. Cherlow, and P. H. Crandall. "Mental Phenomena Evoked by Electrical Stimulation of the Human Hippocampal Formation and Amygdala." *Brain* 101.1 (1978): 83–117.

Hamer, Dean. *The God Gene: How Faith Is Hardwired into Our Genes.* New York: Doubleday, 2004.

Hanscomb, Alice, and Liz Hughes. *Epilepsy.* London: Ward Lock, 1995.

Hansen, B. A., and E. Brodtkorb. "Partial Epilepsy with 'Ecstatic' Seizures." *Epilepsy & Behavior* 4 (2003): 667–73.

Hardy, Alister. *The Spiritual Nature of Man.* Oxford: Clarendon, 1979.

Harris, Sam. *The End of Faith: Religion, Terror, and the Future of Reason.* New York: Norton, 2004.

Harris, William S., Manohar Gowda, Jerry W. Kolb, Christopher P. Strychaz, James L. Hacek, Philip G. Jones, Alan Forker, James H. O'Keefe, and Ben D. McCallister. "A Randomized, Controlled Trial of the Effects of Remote, Intercessory Prayer on Outcomes in Patients Admitted to the Coronary Care Unit." *Archives of Internal Medicine* 159 (1999): 2273–78.

Harth, Erich. *The Creative Loop: How the Brain Makes a Mind.* Reading, MA: Addison-Wesley, 1993.

Hawking, Stephen. *The Illustrated A Brief History of Time.* Rev. ed. New York: Bantam, 1996.

Hawkley, L., and J. Cacioppo. "Loneliness Is a Unique Predictor of Age-Related Differences in Systolic Blood Pressure." *Psychology and Aging* 21.1 (March 2006): 152–64.

Helm H. M., J. C. Hays, E. P. Flint, H. G. Koenig, and D. G. Blazer. "Does Private Religious Activity Prolong Survival: A Six-Year Follow-Up Study of 3,851 Older Adults." *Journals of Gerontology.* Series A, Biological and Medical Sciences. 55 (2000): M400–405.

Hobson, J. Allan. *The Chemistry of Conscious States: How the Brain Changes Its Mind.* Boston: Little, Brown, 1994.

Hofstadter, Douglas R., and Daniel C. Dennett. *The Mind's I: Fantasies and Reflections on Self and Soul.* New York: Basic Books, 2000.

Hooper, Judith, and Dick Teresi. *The 3-Pound Universe.* New York: Macmillan, 1986.

Horgan, John. *The Undiscovered Mind: How the Human Brain Defies Replication, Medication, and Explanation.* New York: Free Press, 1999.

Hróbjartsson, A., and P. Götzsche. "Is the Placebo Powerless? An Analysis of Clinical Trials Comparing Placebo with No Treatment." *New England Journal of Medicine* 344, no. 21 (May 24, 2001).

Hughes, J. R. "Emperor Napoleon Bonaparte: Did He Have Seizures? Psychogenic or Epileptic or Both?" *Epilepsy & Behavior* 4 (2003): 793–96.

———. "Dictator Perpetuus: Julius Caesar—Did He Have Seizures? If So, What Was the Etiology?" *Epilepsy & Behavior* 5 (2004): 756–64.

———. "Alexander of Macedon, the Greatest Warrior of All Times: Did He Have Seizures?" *Epilepsy & Behavior* 5 (2004): 765–67.

———. "Did All Those Famous People Really Have Epilepsy?" *Epilepsy & Behavior* 6 (2005): 115–39.

———. "A Reappraisal of the Possible Seizures of Vincent van Gogh." *Epilepsy & Behavior* 6 (2005): 504–10.

———. "The Idiosyncratic Aspects of the Epilepsy of Fyodor Dostoevsky." *Epilepsy & Behavior* 7 (2005): 531.

Huxley, Aldous. *The Perennial Philosophy.* New York: Harper and Brothers, 1945.

———. *The Doors of Perception.* New York: Harper & Row, 1954.

Ingram, Jay. *Theatre of the Mind: Raising the Curtain on Consciousness.* Toronto: HarperCollins, 2005.

Isaacson, Walter. "In Search of the Real Bill Gates." *Time,* January 5, 1997.

James, William. *The Varieties of Religious Experience.* New York: Random House, 1902.

Jeans, J. *The Mysterious Universe.* London: AMS Press, 1933.

Johnson, Phillip E. *Darwin on Trial.* Downer's Grove, IL: InterVarsity Press, 1993.

Kimura, Doreen. *Sex and Cognition.* Cambridge, MA: MIT Press, 2000.

Kubota, Y., W. Sato, M. Toichi, T. Murai, T. Okada, A. Hayashi, and A. Sengoku. "Frontal Midline Theta Rhythm Is Correlated with Cardiac Autonomic Activities During the Performance of an Attention Demanding Meditation Procedure." *Brain Research: Cognitive Brain Research* 11.2 (2001): 281–87.

Kuhn, Thomas. *The Structure of Scientific Revolutions.* 2nd ed. Chicago: Univ. of Chicago Press, 1970.

Larson, Edward J., and Larry Witham. "Leading Scientists Still Reject God." *Nature* 394 (1998): 313.

Lévesque, J., F. Eugène, Y. Joanette, V. Paquette, M. Boualem, G. Beaudoin, J-M. Leroux, P. Bourgouin, and M. Beauregard. "Neural Circuitry Underlying Voluntary Suppression of Sadness." *Biological Psychiatry* 53 (2003): 502–10.

Lévesque, J., Y. Joanette, B. Mensour, G. Beaudoin, J-M. Leroux, P. Bourgouin, and M. Beauregard. "Neural Basis of Emotional Self-Regulation in Childhood." *Neuroscience* 129 (2004): 361–69.

Levin, Jeff, and Harold G. Koenig, eds. *Faith, Medicine, and Science: A Festschrift in Honor of Dr. David B. Larson.* New York: Haworth, 2005.

Lewis, C. S. *The Abolition of Man.* London: Collins, 1978.

Lewis, C. S. *The Four Loves.* Glasgow: William Collins Sons & Co., [1960] 1979, p. 67.

Lewis, C. S. *The Problem of Pain.* New York: Simon and Schuster Touchstone, 1996.

Lusting, Abigail, Robert J. Richards, and Michael Ruse. *Darwinian Heresies.* Cambridge, MA: Cambridge Univ. Press, 2004.

Lutz Antoine, Lawrence L. Greischar, Nancy B. Rawlings, Matthieu Ricard, and Richard J. Davidson. "Long-Term Meditators Self-Induce High-Amplitude Gamma Synchrony during Mental Practice." *Proceedings of the National Academy of Sciences USA* 101, no. 46 (November 16, 2004): 16369–73.

Malin, Shimon. *Nature Loves to Hide: Quantum Physics and the Nature of Reality, a Western Perspective.* Oxford: Oxford Univ. Press, 2001.

Marks, Jonathan, *What It Means to Be 98 Percent Chimpanzee: Apes, People, and Their Genes.* Berkeley and Los Angeles: Univ. of California Press, 2002.

Maslow, Abraham. *Religious Aspects of Peak-Experiences.* New York: Harper & Row, 1970.

May, Gerald G. *The Dark Night of the Soul.* San Francisco: HarperSanFrancisco, 2004.

McGrath, Alister. *Dawkins's God: Genes, Memes, and the Meaning of Life*. Oxford: Blackwell, 2005.

McGreal, Wilfrid. *John of the Cross*. London: HarperCollins, 1996.

McRae, C., E. Cherin, T. G. Yamazaki, G. Diem, A. H. Vo, D. Russell, J. H. Ellgring et al. "Effects of Perceived Treatment on Quality of Life and Medical Outcomes in a Double-Blind Placebo Surgery Trial." *Archives of General Psychiatry* 61 (2004): 412–20.

Merton, Robert K. "Science and the Social Order." *Philosophy of Science* 5 no. 3 (July 1938): 321–337.

Midgeley, Mary. *The Myths We Live By*. London: Routledge, 2003.

Minsky, Marvin. *Society of Mind*. New York: Simon & Schuster, 1988, p. 306.

Mitcham, Carl, and Alois Huning, eds. *Philosophy and Technology II: Information Technology and Computers in Theory and Practice*. Vol. 2, Selected Proceedings of an International Conference held in New York, September 3–7, 1983, and organized by the Philosopyy & Technology Studies Center of the Polytechnic Institute of New York in conjunction with the Society for Philosophy and Technology. New York: Springer, 1986, p. 169.

Morse M., and P. Perry. *Transformed by the Light*. New York: Ballantine, 1992.

Neggers, S. F., R. H. Van der Lubbe, N. F. Ramsey, and A. Postma. "Interactions Between Ego- and Allocentric Neuronal Representations of Space." *Neuroimage* (2006).

Newberg, A., A. Alai, M. Baime, M. Pourdehnad, J. Santana, and E. G. D'Aquili. "The Measurement of Regional Cerebral Blood Flow During the Complex Cognitive Task of Meditation: A Preliminary SPECT Study." *Psychiatry Research: Neuroimaging* 106 (2001): 113–22.

Newberg, A., M. Pourdehnad, A. Alavi, and E. G. D'Aquili. "Cerebral Blood Flow During Meditative Prayer: Preliminary Findings and Methodological Issues." *Perceptual and Motor Skills* 97 (2003): 625–30.

Newberg, Andrew, Eugene D'Aquili, and Vince Rause. *Why God Won't Go Away: Brain Science and the Biology of Belief*. New York: Ballantine, 2001.

O'Leary, Denyse. *By Design or by Chance? The Growing Controversy on the Origins of Life in the Universe*. Minneapolis: Augsburg, 2004.

Ornstein, Robert. *The Evolution of Consciousness: The Origins of the Way We Think*. New York: Simon & Schuster, 1991.

———. *The Right Mind: Making Sense of the Hemispheres*. New York: Harcourt, Brace, 1997.

Otto, Rudolf. *The Idea of the Holy*. Translated by John W. Harvey. London: Oxford Univ. Press, 1971.

Paquette V., J. Lévesque, B. Mensour, J-M. Leroux, G. Beaudoin, P. Bourgouin, and M. Beauregard. "Change the Mind and You Change the Brain: Effects of Cognitive-Behavioral Therapy on the Neural Correlates of Spider Phobia." *Neuroimage* 18.2 (February 2003): 401–9.

Pargament, Kenneth I., H. G. Koenig, N. Tarakeshwar, J. Hahn. "Religious Struggle as a Predictor of Mortality Among Medically Ill Elderly Patients." *Archives of Internal Medicine* 161 (August 13/27, 2001): 1881–85.

Parnia, S., and P. Fenwick. "Near-Death Experiences in Cardiac Arrest: Visions of a Dying Brain or Visions of a New Science of Consciousness." *Resuscitation* 52 (2002): 5–11.

Peacock, Judith. *Epilepsy.* Mankato, MN: Capstone, 2000.

Pelletier M., A. Bouthillier, J. Levesque, S. Carrier, C. Breault, V. Paquette, B. Mensour, J-M. Leroux, G. Beaudoin, P. Bourgouin, and M. Beauregard. "Separate Neural Circuits for Primary Emotions? Brain Activity During Self-Induced Sadness and Happiness in Professional Actors." *Neuroreport* 14.8 (June 11, 2003): 1111–16.

Penfield, Wilder. *Second Thoughts: Science, the Arts, and the Spirit.* Toronto: McClelland and Stewart, 1970.

Persinger, M. "Religious and Mystical Experiences as Artifacts of Temporal-Lobe Function: A General Hypothesis." *Perceptual and Motor Skills* 57 (1983): 1255–62.

Persinger, M. A., and F. Healey. "Experimental Facilitation of the Sensed Presence: Possible Intercalation between the Hemispheres Induced by Complex Magnetic Fields." *Journal of Nervous and Mental Diseases* 190 (2002): 533–41.

Pettitt, Paul. "When Burial Begins." *British Archaeology* 66 (August 2002).

Pinker, Steven. *How the Mind Works.* New York: Norton, 1997.

Radin, Dean. *The Conscious Universe: The Scientific Truth of Psychic Phenomena.* San Francisco: HarperSanFrancisco, 2007.

Ramachandran, V. S., and Sandra Blakeslee. *Phantoms in the Brain: Probing the Mysteries of the Human Mind.* New York: Morrow, 1998.

Ratzsch, Del. *The Battle of Beginnings: Why Neither Side Is Winning the Creation-Evolution Debate.* Downers Grove, IL: InterVarsity Press, 1996.

Restak, Richard. *The Brain Has a Mind of Its Own: Insights from a Practicing Neurologist.* New York: Harmony, 1991.

Ring, K., and M. Lawrence. "Further Evidence for Veridical Perception During Near-Death Experiences." *Journal of Near-Death Studies* 11.4 (1993): 223–29.

Ring, Kenneth, and Sharon Cooper. *Near Death and Out of Body Experiences in the Blind.* Palo Alto, CA: William James Center, 1999.

Rohrbach, Peter-Thomas. *Journey to Carith: The Story of the Carmelite Order.* Garden City, NY: Doubleday, 1966.

Rose, Hilary, and Steven Rose. *Alas, Poor Darwin: Arguments Against Evolutionary Psychology.* London: Random House, Vintage, 2001.

Ruse, Michael. *The Evolution Wars: A Guide to the Debates.* Santa Barbara, CA: ABC-CLIO, 2000.

Russell, Bertrand. "Quotes on Determinism," The Society of Natural Science, http://www.determinism.com/quotes.shtml (accessed May 27, 2007).

Sabom, Michael. *Light and Death: One Doctor's Fascinating Account of Near-Death Experiences.* Grand Rapids, MI: Zondervan, 1998.

Sagan, Carl. *The Dragons of Eden: Speculations on the Nature of Human Intelligence.* New York: Random House, 1977.

———. *The Demon-Haunted World: Science as a Candle in the Dark.* New York: Ballantine, 1996.

Salzman, Mark. *Lying Awake.* New York: Knopf, 2000.

Saver, J. L., and John Rabin. "The Neural Substrates of Religious Experience." *Journal of Neuropsychiatry and Clinical Neurosciences* 9 (1997): 498–510.

Sawyer, Robert J. *The Terminal Experiment.* New York: HarperCollins, 1995.

Schwartz, J. M., H. Stapp, and M. Beauregard. "Quantum Theory in Neuroscience and Psychology: A Neurophysical Model of Mind/Brain Interaction." *Philosophical Transactions of the Royal Society B: Biological Sciences* 360 (2005): 1309–27.

Schwartz J. M., P. W. Stoessel, L. R. Baxter, Jr., K. M. Martin, and M. E. Phelps. "Systematic Changes in Cerebral Glucose Metabolic Rate After Successful Behavior Modification Treatment of Obsessive-Compulsive Disorder." *Archives of General Psychiatry* 53 (1996): 109–13.

Schwartz, Jeffrey M., and Sharon Begley. *The Mind and the Brain: Neuroplasticity and the Power of Mental Force.* New York: HarperCollins, Regan Books, 2003.

Searle, John R. *Mind: A Brief Introduction.* Oxford: Oxford Univ. Press, 2004.

Smith, A., and C. Tart. "Cosmic Consciousness Experience and Psychedelic Experiences: A First-Person Comparison." *Journal of Consciousness Studies* 5, no. 1 (1998): 97–107.

Soeling, Casper, and Eckert Voland. "Toward an Evolutionary Psychology of Religiosity." *Neuroendocrinology Letters, Human Ethology & Evolutionary Psychology* 23, suppl. 4 (December 2002).

Spiegel, Herbert, and David Spiegel. *Trance and Treatment: Clinical Use of Hypnosis.* New York: Basic Books, 1978.

Spilka, B., B. Hunsberger, R. Gorsuch, and R. W. Hood, Jr. *The Psychology of Religion: An Empirical Approach.* 3rd ed. New York: Guilford, 2003.

Stace, W. T. *The Teachings of the Mystics.* New York: Macmillan, 1960.

Stove, David. *Darwinian Fairytales.* Aldershot, UK: Avebury, 1995.

Takahashi, T., T. Murata, T. Hamada, M. Omori, H. Kosaka, M. Kikuchi, H. Yoshida, and Y. Wada. "Changes in EEG and Autonomic Nervous Activity During Meditation and Their Association with Personality Traits." *International Journal of Psychophysiology* 55.2 (February 2005): 199–207.

Temple, R. "Implications of Effects in Placebo Groups." *Journal of the National Cancer Institute* 95, nos. 1, 2–3 (January 1, 2003).

Teresa of Avila. *The Interior Castle.* Translated by Mirabai Starr. New York: Riverhead, 2003.

Tierney, Patrick. *Darkness in El Dorado: How Scientists and Journalists Devastated the Amazon.* New York: Norton, 2000.

Underhill, Evelyn. *Mysticism: A Study in the Nature and Development of Man's Spiritual Consciousness.* New York: New American Library / Meridian, 1974.

Van Lommel, P. "About the Continuity of Our Consciousness." In *Brain Death and Disorders of Consciousness.* Edited by Calixto Machado and D. Alan Shewmon. New York: Kluwer Academic / Plenum, 2004.

Van Lommel P., R. van Wees, V. Meyers, and I. Elfferich. "Near-Death Experience in Survivors of Cardiac Arrest: A Prospective Study in the Netherlands." *Lancet* 358 (2001): 2039–45.

Vercors [Jean Bruller]. *You Shall Know Them.* Translated by Rita Barisse from the original *Les Animaux Dénaturés.* Toronto: McClelland & Stewart, 1953.

Wackermann, Jiří, Christian Seiter, Holger Keibel, and Harald Wallach. "Correlations between Brain Electrical Activities of Two Spatially Separated Human Subjects." *Neuroscience Letters* 336 (2003): 60–64.

Wager, Tor D., James K. Rilling, Edward E. Smith, Alex Sokolik, Kenneth L. Casey, Richard J. Davidson, Stephen M. Kosslyn, Robert M. Rose, and Jonathan D. Cohen. "Placebo-Induced Changes in fMRI in the Anticipation and Experience of Pain." *Science* 303, no. 5661 (February 20, 2004): 1162–67.

Wallace, B. Alan. *The Taboo of Subjectivity: Toward a New Science of Consciousness.* Oxford: Oxford Univ. Press, 2000.

Wallach, Harald, and Stefan Schmidt. "Repairing Plato's Life Boat with Ockham's Razor: The Important Function of Research in Anomalies for Consciousness Studies." *Journal of Consciousness Studies* 12, no. 2 (2005): 52–70.

Wildman, Derek E., Monica Uddin, Guozhen Liu, Lawrence I. Grossman, and Morris Goodman. "Implications of Natural Selection in Shaping 99.4% Nonsynonymous DNA Identity Between Humans and Chimpanzees: Enlarging Genus *Homo.*" *Proceedings of the National Academy of Sciences* 100 (2003): 7181–88.

Wilson, David Sloan. *Darwin's Cathedral: Evolution, Religion, and the Nature of Society.* Chicago: Univ. of Chicago Press, 2002.

Wilson, Edward O. *Sociobiology.* Abridged ed. Cambridge, MA: Harvard Univ. Press, 1980.

———. *Consilience: The Unity of Knowledge.* New York: Random House, 1998.

INDEX